Quivering Families

Quivering Families

*The Quiverfull Movement and
Evangelical Theology of the Family*

EMILY HUNTER MCGOWIN

FORTRESS PRESS
MINNEAPOLIS

QUIVERING FAMILIES
The Quiverfull Movement and Evangelical Theology of the Family

Copyright © 2018 Fortress Press. All rights reserved. Except for brief quotations in critical articles or reviews, no part of this book may be reproduced in any manner without prior written permission from the publisher. Email copyright@1517.media or write to Permissions, Fortress Press, PO Box 1209, Minneapolis, MN 55440-1209.

Cover image: *Enveloped* by Kiana Mosley
Cover design: Rob Dewey

Print ISBN: 978-1-5064-2760-7
eBook ISBN: 978-1-5064-4660-8

The paper used in this publication meets the minimum requirements of American National Standard for Information Sciences — Permanence of Paper for Printed Library Materials, ANSI Z329.48-1984.

Manufactured in the U.S.A.

Contents

Acknowledgments — vii

Introduction — ix

1. Conceiving Quiverfull: The Movement in Historical and Cultural Perspective — 1
2. Stories from the Full Quiver — 55
3. Motherhood in the Full Quiver — 87
4. Children and Childhood in the Full Quiver — 125
5. The Family in the Full Quiver — 169

Conclusion — 223

Bibliography — 235

Index — 253

Acknowledgments

As with any book, this volume would not exist without the influence and assistance of many others. I begin by offering my deepest gratitude to my doctoral advisor, Vincent Miller, for his patient and careful guidance on the dissertation that gave rise to this book. I am a better scholar and writer because of his mentorship. Thank you seems woefully insufficient.

I am also grateful for a number of others who contributed much by way of advice and constructive criticism throughout the research and writing process. Jana Bennett has been an important friend and ally from my first visit to the University of Dayton. I first encountered Quiverfull while serving as her graduate assistant. Sandra Yocum had a crucial hand in steering me toward deeper, more complex analysis through ethnographic methods. Bill Trollinger has supported and cheered on this project from the beginning and offered me assistance in countless ways. I met Mary McClintock Fulkerson at a conference in 2012 and our conversation helped to convince me that Quiverfull was a subject in need of exploration. From the start, she has been a generous and thoughtful interlocutor. Sue Trollinger oversaw my first summer research fellowship and has been a trusted friend since that time. Heather MacLachlan helped me get my bearings in the discipline of ethnography, graciously allowing me to sit in on her classes and pepper her with questions along the way. I am also thankful for the periodic input of Sr. Laura Leming, James Bielo, and Margaret Bendroth.

The dissertation that led to *Quivering Families* was funded by the Graduate School at the University of Dayton. I completed early research with the help of two Graduate Student Summer Fellowships

(2012, 2014) and my final year of writing was funded with a Dissertation Year Fellowship (2014–2015).

Doctoral research is an often-grueling experience, but my time at UD was made enjoyable through the friendship of my colleagues. Thank you to Katherine Schmidt, Scott McDaniel, Jason Hentschel, and Adam Sheridan for their friendship and critical conversations about my research.

I am thankful to Michael Gibson at Fortress Press for believing in this project and helping make it stronger. Also, I owe special thanks to my project editor, Allyce Amidon, for her attention to detail.

When I was an undergraduate, Boyd Luter apprenticed me in the work of research, writing, and scholarly presentations. I would never have gotten to this point without his determined and warmhearted mentorship. For their encouragement and support throughout my career, I also want to acknowledge Glenn Kreider, Fred Smith, David Garland, Todd Still, and Roger Olson.

Of course, this book wouldn't exist without the generous assistance of my informants, who gave their time and energy to share their hearts and homes with a veritable stranger. I cannot thank them enough for their transparency with me as a researcher and charity for me as a human being. Whatever differences we have, I find their genuine love for God and their families inspiring. I am blessed to have known them.

There are no adequate words to thank my long-suffering friends, Gabby, Regina, Melissa, Kristi, and Katherine, who have supported and encouraged me every step of the way. I am forever grateful for their friendship.

Finally, I thank my family: my late grandfather, Hugh Hunter; my mom, Wendy Hunter; and my children, William, Emmelia, and Althea, who continually humble me with their love and devotion. Most of all, I thank my husband, Ronnie, who sacrificed in major ways for my doctoral studies and this book. Ronnie is an exemplar of faithfulness: faithfulness to his marriage, faithfulness to his children, and faithfulness to his calling. I am a better mother, scholar, and human being because of him. This book is dedicated to him and to our continued life together.

Introduction

When I tell people I am writing a book about the Quiverfull movement, many immediately assume I mean the Duggar family. The Duggars do not call themselves "Quiverfull," yet they are, for better or worse, the public face of Quiverfull in America. Millions have watched their TLC reality show, *19 Kids and Counting*, in voyeuristic fascination over the past several years. With a firm commitment to male headship, a willingness to bear nineteen children (so far), and educate all of those children at home, the Duggars have lived out in front of the cameras the Quiverfull ideal. I have heard more than one mother call the Duggars "Quiverfull royalty." But, as a "royal family" with a reality show, the Duggars are about as representative of Quiverfull families as *The Real Housewives of New Jersey* are representative of housewives. There are similarities, of course, but they only go so far.

The reaction of scholars and theologians to my research tends to be very different. When I explain that Quiverfull refers to evangelical Christian families that practice patriarchy, prolific childbearing, and homeschooling, often words like "fundamentalist," "lunatic," or "brainwashed" get thrown around. The women of the movement in particular are often accused of being uneducated, insane, and even masochistic. One scholar questioned the legitimacy of trying to make this kind of religious practice intelligible. "They're just crazy," he said dismissively. "They really are just crazy."

But that's not all there is to say. Human beings are infinitely complex creatures, especially when it comes to their religious practice. Surely theologians and scholars of American religion can do better than the simplistic conclusion, "They're just crazy."

Provoking both fascination and revulsion, the lived religion of the

Quiverfull movement is the subject of *Quivering Families*. In this book I seek to make the Quiverfull movement understandable to outsiders and explore what there is to learn from their way of embodying the family in contemporary America. Before going any further, however, some introduction is in order. What is Quiverfull exactly? And why am I writing about them? And what could they possibly have to say to those interested in theology?

ALL SCHOLARSHIP IS AUTOBIOGRAPHICAL

All scholarship is autobiographical and this is no less true for me. I came across the Quiverfull movement in the early days of my doctoral studies. Their particular instantiation of the family caught my attention for a number of reasons. As someone with a background in American evangelicalism, I was struck by the seriousness with which Quiverfull women take their commitment to stay-at-home motherhood. This is, of course, a common theme in evangelical culture: motherhood is a woman's highest calling and women are often enjoined to forgo careers to devote everything to it. But it seemed to me that Quiverfull mothers devote themselves to this ideal with unparalleled zeal. These women not only stay at home with their children full time but also have a lot of them—and then homeschool all of them. This is not to mention the men, who sign on to support a homeschooling mother and a large number of children on a single income. The Quiverfull movement appeared to be an embodiment of all of the evangelical ideals about the family taken to their most logical and enthusiastic conclusion.

I was also eager to know what Quiverfull families look like on the ground. It is one thing to write about the joys of homeschooling, receiving every child as a gift, and the God-ordained purpose of the family, but it is quite another to live those ideals, day in and day out, within the confines of the private family home. Moreover, I suspected that there is quite a bit of difference between the way spokespersons of the movement describe their work and the way Quiverfull mothers experience it in real life. For instance, what would average Quiverfull mothers have to say about pastor Doug Phillips's sermonizing about the "glories of motherhood"? And how would they respond to Nancy Campbell's insistence that the home is their "battle station" in the culture wars? The appearance of widespread cultural agreement is often just that—an appearance. I wondered what Quiverfull culture would look like when its families were examined more closely.

I was also intrigued by the number of women who, when telling the story of their "conversion" to the Quiverfull way of life, spoke of their own mind changing first and then their husband's. It was by and large the *women* who led the way into Quiverfull—a counterintuitive trend for such a stridently patriarchal movement. My curiosity was piqued: Is this patriarchal movement really a mother-led, mother-powered phenomenon? If so, what does that say about their patriarchal ideology? And why exactly would women sign on to such a grueling embodiment of Christian motherhood and family in the first place? I have enough respect for the intelligence and agency of women to reject simplistic notions that Quiverfull mothers are simply "brainwashed" or "just don't know any better." No, these are intelligent, thoughtful women who have knowingly signed on to a vigorous practice of motherhood. I wanted to know if women really were leading the way and, if so, why.

I began researching the lived experience of Quiverfull mothers in more depth, starting with Kathryn Joyce's important book, *Quiverfull: Inside the Christian Patriarchy Movement* (Beacon, 2009). What stood out to me from Joyce's work was that Quiverfull mothers claimed that the work they performed as wives, mothers, and home educators was not only their highest calling as women but also the way by which they fulfill their Christian mission in the world. This reinforced my instinct that these women and their mothering work should be taken seriously as a form of evangelical lived religion in America. Quiverfull women are seeking to be a witness to the truth of the gospel and a transformative force for change in American society. They are just doing it in a way that most scholars do not recognize: by submitting to their husbands, having babies, and homeschooling their children.

My research revealed a dearth of academic work on the Quiverfull movement, with nothing yet written on Quiverfull mothers in particular. In addition, the lived religion of Quiverfull seemed like a project well suited for the use of ethnographic methods (more about that below), something in which I had developed an interest since reading Mary McClintock Fulkerson's *Places of Redemption: Theology for a Worldly Church* (Oxford, 2010). And so, my foray into the Quiverfull movement began.

This personal narrative is meant not only to tell the reader how this book began but also to establish from the start that I do not pretend to approach the topic of the Quiverfull movement from a place of detached objectivity. I am a mother of three who has experience with the demands of pregnancy, nursing, and childrearing—all of which were at their most intense while I was completing my doctoral studies—and I cannot feign an unbiased point of view on these subjects. My thoughts on marriage, children, and family were inevitably formed in the crucible of that experience.

I am also a Christian theologian with an approach to theology shaped within the American evangelical context. Though US evangelicalism is no longer a comfortable fit, evangelicals remain my primary theological interlocutors. This means my research has been conducted with certain evangelical sensibilities, including a concern for the use and interpretation of scripture and an interest in the experiential aspects of women's lived religion. While some may see my roots in American evangelicalism as a drawback, I found my evangelical background served me well as I sought to listen closely to Quiverfull families and understand their way of life in a nuanced and sympathetic way.

In addition, I have spent the past few years working out a place for myself within the Anglican tradition. My move into a sacramental, liturgical, and more tradition-oriented context has affected the way I evaluate Quiverfull theologically and biblically. Arguably the most important influence on my work has been a new appreciation for the doctrine of the incarnation. Because of the theological centrality of the incarnation, I am compelled to assert that there is truth and goodness to be found even in ideologically problematic locations. It is precisely in the concrete stuff of daily life, with all of its tensions and difficulties, where I expect the transcendent to be manifested. Moreover, my theology of grace leads me to pay attention to the forms of life that Christians find compelling and through which they sincerely seek to follow Christ. There is grace to be found in these locations. To affirm that the Quiverfull way of life is graced, however, requires the simultaneous affirmation that it is no doubt imperfectly graced—perhaps acutely so. Still, I contend that Quiverfull families, in all of their imperfect complexity, can provide a site for fruitful reflection on the Christian family today.

Also, I am a theologian with deep convictions about the essentially egalitarian nature of the Christian vision for male-female relationships. Due to these convictions, I am troubled by the patriarchy of

Quiverfull discourse and its implications for women and their children. My critique of Quiverfull is broader than the matter of gender roles, but I cannot deny that my egalitarian sensibilities influence my perspective on the movement as a whole. I will make some claims about the surprising way women's agency works within the lived religion of Quiverfull families, but I want to be clear from the start that I have no desire to "baptize" the Quiverfull family discourse and declare Quiverfull mothers "anonymous feminists." Still, I am convinced by the work of Mary McClintock Fulkerson and R. Marie Griffiths, among others, that women's agency, even within the most patriarchal contexts, can be exercised in unexpected ways.[1] I will elucidate some of those ways in the following chapters even as I cannot deny my fundamental unease with the gender ideology of the movement as a whole.

Finally, I write as a white, middle-class woman and US citizen—an identity that comes with certain privileges, as well as blind spots. Though I have tried to write with a degree of self-awareness, I am certain that both my privilege and blind spots will be visible in the following chapters. There is no doubt more to say about the Quiverfull movement, especially those whose subject positions are located outside the presumed Quiverfull norm: white, American, and middle to lower class. I hope my work inspires others who are better suited to take up those critiques.

WHAT IS QUIVERFULL?

What is the Quiverfull movement exactly? The term *Quiverfull*, used both by outsiders and insiders, comes from the language of Psalm 127:3–5: "Children are a heritage from the Lord, offspring a reward from him. Like arrows in the hands of a warrior are children born in one's youth. Blessed is the man whose quiver is full of them. They will not be put to shame when they contend with their opponents

---

1. Mary McClintock Fulkerson, *Changing the Subject: Women's Discourses and Feminist Theology* (Minneapolis: Fortress Press, 1994); R. Marie Griffiths, *God's Daughters: Evangelical Women and the Power of Submission* (Berkeley: University of California Press, 1997). See also Elizabeth Brusco, *The Reformation of Machismo: Evangelical Conversion and Gender in Colombia* (Austin: University of Texas Press, 1995); Brenda Brasher, *Godly Women: Fundamentalism and Female Power* (New Brunswick, NJ: Rutgers University Press, 1997); and Christel Manning, *God Gave Us the Right: Conservative Catholic, Evangelical Protestant, and Orthodox Jewish Women Grapple with Feminism* (New Brunswick, NJ: Rutgers University Press, 1999).

in court."[2] This psalm is referenced in Mary Pride's early book *The Way Home: Beyond Feminism, Back to Reality*, but Rick and Jan Hess popularized it in their book *A Full Quiver: Family Planning and the Lordship of Christ*, which was published in 1990.[3] The Hesses argue strongly for viewing children as an unqualified blessing and childrearing the primary work of the Christian marriage. Though *A Full Quiver* has been out of print for some time, their book seems to have been the catalyst for the widespread use of the term *Quiverfull* for those who eschew family planning. Those who adopted the Hesses' perspective began to describe themselves as Quiverfull (i.e., "We are a Quiverfull family"). This led to the creation of a website devoted to the subject, Quiverfull.com, which also offered the *Quiverfull Digest*, an email newsletter available by subscription.[4] Quiverfull.com came online in 1995, which suggests that within five years of the publication of *A Full Quiver*, the term had become popularized and adopted by many families to describe their way of life—enough families, at least, to support a website and monthly newsletter. The internet also allowed for its popularization through the proliferation of merchandise using the Quiverfull moniker.[5] Members of the media picked up the term, too, as reports began to surface on Quiverfull practice.[6] By the time Kathryn Joyce published her book *Quiverfull: Inside the Christian Patriarchy Movement*, in 2009, the word had been in use for about ten years.

What do people mean by *Quiverfull*? Joyce and other outsiders who write about Quiverfull families typically have in mind conservative Christians that have intentionally large families and believe

---

2. Unless otherwise noted, I use the New International Version (NIV 2011) of the Bible.

3. Rick Hess and Jan Hess, *A Full Quiver: Family Planning and the Lordship of Christ* (Brentwood, TN: Wolgemuth & Hyatt, 1990).

4. It seems that Quiverfull.com has not been updated since 2011, which calls into question the usefulness of the website as a site of ongoing activity for Quiverfull families today. But, there is no doubt that it has been a location for networking and information sharing among Quiverfull families up until recently.

5. See, for example, the variety of things available at http://www.cafepress.com/quiver-full gifts, including bibs and hats imprinted with "Militant Fecundity" and tongue-in-cheek T-shirts that say, "Birth control is for sissies" or "Yes, they're all ours." Interestingly, Café Press groups other merchandise with their Quiverfull materials, including the categories *patriarch*, *antifeminism*, and *modesty*. This is indicative of the way that the beliefs and practices overlap among people who participate in Quiverfull discourse.

6. See, for example, the following articles: Newsweek Staff, "Making Babies the Quiverfull Way," *Newsweek*, November 12, 2006, http://tinyurl.com/ybqdbwlt; Kathryn Joyce, "Arrows for the War," *The Nation*, November 27, 2006, 11–18; Ted Gerstein and John Berman, "When Having Children Is a Religious Experience," January 3, 2007, http://tinyurl.com/y8yln7jw.

in some kind of "Christian patriarchy" (or "male headship"). Some also emphasize the long-term goal of transforming or Christianizing American culture through a major demographic shift.[7] When families call themselves Quiverfull, they are typically referring to their willingness to have as many children as possible (that is, as many children as God gives them). Such families may or may not assign to their reproduction the goal of cultural transformation, but all of them would eschew birth control. In all of these accounts of Quiverfull, the focus is primarily upon the practice of prolific childbirth—or, to be clearer, a constant openness and willingness to bear as many children as their married union produces. Thus, for insiders and outsiders, the term *Quiverfull* pinpoints both a practice (not using birth control and being open to many children) and a belief (children are an unqualified blessing—the more the better), which is often linked to Christian patriarchy.

The complicating factor in discussing the term *Quiverfull* is that in recent years the label has taken on distasteful stereotypes due to a number of public scandals. For this reason, many families today, despite affirming the practices and beliefs indicated above, reject the label *Quiverfull* due to its negative connotations. Deborah Olson, a Quiverfull mother we will meet later, wants to be careful about the designation: "I'm not part of anything purposefully. I'm very conscious about not following individuals. But that doesn't mean that if you were trying to do a sociology project that I'm not going to get grouped with other people like this. . . . But any group of people that you write about will have divisions within them."[8]

In this book I use the term *Quiverfull* to refer to families who participate in three practices: homeschooling, gender hierarchy, and pronatalism.[9] Homeschooling refers to the practice of educating one's children in one's home rather than in traditional brick and mortar schools. The mother in the private family home conducts the vast majority of Christian homeschooling and the practice is central to everyday life. Pronatalism is the academic term for the Quiverfull

---

7. See, for example, Libby Anne's distinction between Quiverfull and Christian patriarchy in "Christian Patriarchy/Quiverfull," *Love, Joy, Feminism*, http://tinyurl.com/p6fxhaw.

8. Stacy McDonald, a leading voice in the Quiverfull subculture, began to separate herself from the term long before the scandals involving Bill Gothard and Doug Phillips. On December 12, 2010, McDonald said the following on her blog: "Am I 'Quiverfull'? No, I think I'd rather be 'Jesus-Full,'" (http://tinyurl.com/ycr4vpyb).

9. For a helpful discussion of three contemporary accounts of practice that come to bear on the discussion of discourse, see Mary McClintock Fulkerson, "Practice," in *Handbook of Postmodern Biblical Interpretation*, ed. A. K. A. Adam (St. Louis: Chalice, 2000), 189-98.

desire to have many children. It doesn't simply mean someone who loves children or even wants to have a large family, but specifically refers to a family seeking to have as many children as possible. Gender hierarchy refers to their practice of male headship and belief in a gender-based hierarchical arrangement in the home, church, and world—one where men, in general, lead and women, in general, support and follow them. Each of these things—homeschooling, pronatalism, and gender hierarchy—entails certain beliefs, which emerge from particular biblical texts, but more importantly, they are lived out in daily life. Together, they make up the threefold discourse at the heart of the Quiverfull movement. If we can conceive of homeschooling, pronatalism, and gender hierarchy as circles in a Venn diagram, then it is at the center where the three circles converge that the Quiverfull discourse is located:

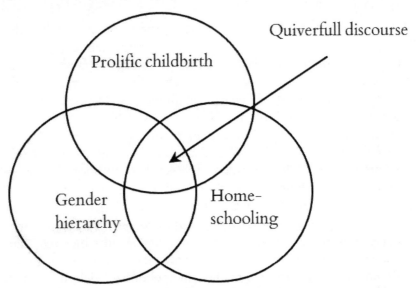

Participants in this discourse are also participants in a subculture of evangelicalism. Thus, individuals and families can be Quiverfull; and these individuals and families, by participating in certain cultural institutions, are participants in the Quiverfull subculture. Both the families and the subculture are identifiable as Quiverfull because of the presence of all three aspects of their discourse: homeschooling, gender hierarchy, and pronatalism. In this definition, I am expanding the scope of the term as it has been used to this point. Rather than see militant fecundity as the focal practice, I include homeschooling and gender hierarchy as well. Moreover, the three practices demarcated by the term *Quiverfull* may or may not include an orientation toward the goal of cultural transformation. And I use *Quiverfull* for teachers, leaders, authors, bloggers, and families at the grassroots level, regardless of whether they use it to describe themselves.[10]

The first element of the Quiverfull discourse is homeschooling. I argue in chapter 1 that the Quiverfull movement as it has come to be recognized today is a subgroup that developed over the past forty years within the broader networks of the Christian homeschooling movement.[11] While Joyce and other commentators focus almost exclusively on the patriarchal and pronatalist practices of Quiverfull families, it is important to see that homeschooling is just as central to their lived experience. For families on the ground, the practice of homeschooling is the primary structure within which their way of life is ordered. The production of a large family is not an end in itself. The couple's "militant fecundity"[12] is for the purpose of rearing godly Christian children who will carry on the faith and transform society in the decades and centuries to come, something pastor Voddie Baucham calls "multigenerational faithfulness." This phrase

---

10. Due to the negotiations taking place around the application of the term *Quiverfull*, it would, perhaps, be preferable to use another word. But, I have been unable to find a label that encompasses and properly names the combination of three practices outlined above. At this point, it has been almost twenty-five years since *A Full Quiver* was published, and the term is now part of the vernacular of American evangelicalism. Also, it continues to be used by journalists and bloggers. And, perhaps most importantly, it retains the symbolic link to Ps 127:4, which is key to the lives of the families under consideration in this project. Thus, I will retain the term *Quiverfull* as a shorthand for persons and families who participate in the three practices of homeschooling, gender hierarchy, and pronatalism, as well as the subculture they have produced, all the while cognizant of the fact that I will sometimes do so in the case of people who would personally eschew the label for various reasons.

11. Adult Quiverfull daughter Libby Anne, of *Love, Joy, Feminism*, confirms my interpretation of homeschooling's centrality to Quiverfull discourse: "Christian Patriarchy/Quiverfull is made up of a loosely connected group of organizations that promote extremely strict gender differences, submission to the family patriarch, and raising up armies of children for Christ. These organizations have gained a great deal of influence in the Christian segment of the homeschool movement, and evangelicals and fundamentalists who homeschool encounter Christian Patriarchy/Quiverfull, sometimes unwittingly, through homeschool literature, conferences, and leaders. This is how Christian Patriarchy/Quiverfull gains its new recruits." Her post clarifying the differences between evangelicals, fundamentalists, Christian homeschoolers, and what she calls "Christian Patriarchy/Quiverfull" is illuminating: http://tinyurl.com/y8n3jz44.

12. David Bentley Hart, "Freedom and Decency," *First Things*, June 2004, http://tinyurl.com/ya8vd4yc. One can find merchandise emblazoned with the words "Militant Fecundity" at the website Café Press. Virtually anything, including baby bibs, coffee mugs, and underwear, can be imprinted with a slogan showing one's commitment to prolific reproduction.

expresses the desire that all of their children continue in the Christian faith for multiple generations. While other homeschooling families might point to academic excellence or college readiness as the focus of homeschooling, Quiverfull families have as their primary goal the transmission of their Christian faith to the next generation.[13] And Christian homeschooling is the crucial means by which this training is carried out. Although curriculum and pedagogy vary considerably from family to family, the central practice is the same: the education of children is undertaken as the primary responsibility of parents and conducted within the home.[14] Thus, while there are many homeschooling families that are not Quiverfull, there is no such thing as a Quiverfull family that does not homeschool.

Gender hierarchy is also vital to the daily practice of Quiverfull families. In chapter 1, I say more about the roots of their gender ideology in evangelical history, but for now it will suffice to point out the link between homeschooling and gender hierarchy. Mitchell Stevens, in his groundbreaking work on the American homeschool movement, has observed that gender dualism—a rigid split between male and female roles or spheres—is ubiquitous and key to the Christian homeschooling movement.[15] "Ultimately," he says, "it is conservative Protestants' deep commitment to full-time motherhood that has

---

13. The concern for "multigenerational faithfulness" is another way of saying that their central concern is for the production of Christian children. This concern is rooted in studies over the past few decades that show a decreasing number of youth remaining in the church after they graduate from high school. Many such studies accuse secular state schools of being the primary problem. Based upon those concerns, Quiverfull families seek to do whatever it takes "to raise sons and daughters who walk with God," in Voddie Baucham's words. They devote themselves to a total lifestyle committed to biblical family values, trusting that if they do it "right," their children will remain Christian.

14. Libby Anne offers the following observation: "You can't be Quiverfull and not homeschool. Currently, Quiverfull exists as a segment of the homeschool movement. The whole point is to let God give you lots of children to train up for his glory, and if that's the point, why would you then send them off to the public schools to be indoctrinated into secular humanism? I mean, that's how they phrase it, anyway. If you tried to be Quiverfull and not homeschool, you would be shunned, questioned, or made to feel left out by every other Quiverfull family" (Libby Anne, blogger at *Love, Joy, Feminism*, email message to author, August 10, 2012).

15. Stevens distinguishes between two different kinds of homeschoolers: "inclusives" and "believers." Inclusives are homeschoolers from a variety of faith traditions and cultures who do not separate themselves for religious reasons. Believers are homeschoolers from conservative Christian backgrounds who tend to separate themselves from inclusives and form their own networks, co-ops, newsletters, and other organizations. Although the early homeschooling movement was inclusive in nature, "believers" now make up the majority of American homeschoolers. The story of this shift is told in Mitchell Stevens, *Kingdom of Children: Culture and Controversy in the Homeschooling Movement*, Princeton Studies in Cultural Sociology (Princeton: Princeton University Press, 2003), as well as Milton Gaither, *Homeschool: An American History*, 1st ed. (New York: Palgrave Macmillan, 2008).

made them such a ready audience for home education."¹⁶ One might even say that the conservative Protestant commitment to gender hierarchy (and the corresponding stay-at-home motherhood ideal) is the ideological fuel that powers Christian homeschooling.

Quiverfull families call their practice of gender hierarchy many different things, including *biblical patriarchy*, *Christian patriarchy*, and *male headship*. For the past few decades, many Quiverfull families have openly embraced the term *patriarchy* for its antifeminist valence.¹⁷ But recent years have seen a slow defection from the term because of its association with disgraced public figures who have been denounced as too extreme.¹⁸ In this book I do not employ the term *patriarchy* to characterize the gender dynamics of Quiverfull discourse. Instead, I use *gender hierarchy*, *gender dualism*, and *male headship*, depending on the subject under discussion. I do so in part to avoid the implication of a universal experience of patriarchy.¹⁹ Also, I wish to avoid becoming entangled in the internal debates of Quiverfull and homeschooling families regarding the right or wrong application of the term *patriarchy*. Gender hierarchy, as I am using it, refers to the biblically rooted belief in male headship (the language of which comes from Eph 5:23), which posits a general principle of male rule in all areas of life, due primarily to the order of creation (Genesis 2), which is understood to teach both gender-based roles and a dualism of gendered spheres. As we will see in chapter 1, this way of envi-

16. Stevens, *Kingdom of Children*, 187.

17. There was even a *Patriarch* magazine published by Philip Lancaster from 1993 to 2004. Their website described their mission as follows: "*Patriarch*'s mission is to bring about a return to patriarchy, leadership by strong, godly men in every sphere of life" (*Patriarch*, http://tinyurl.com/yafeft9j). Lancaster is a former associate of Doug Phillips who spoke at many Vision Forum events and homeschooling conferences around the country. He also authored the book *Family Man, Family Leader: Biblical Fatherhood as the Key to a Thriving Family* (San Antonio, TX: Vision Forum, 2003).

18. The scandals alluded to here will be discussed in more detail in chapter 5. Whether these denunciations are sincere or simply the result of a desire not to be associated with disgraced leaders remains to be seen. Prominent ex-Quiverfull and ex-homeschooling blogs call into question the denunciations of patriarchy now coming forth from leaders who have, in the past, certainly endorsed it. See, for example, the discussion at the website devoted to homeschooling graduates, Homeschoolers Anonymous: R. L. Stollar, "What 'Christian Patriarchy' Is Not," April 28, 2014, http://tinyurl.com/y8th82fx.

19. The term *patriarchy* has a long history within a variety of academic disciplines as a way of naming the hegemonic structure of masculine domination. But recently, some academics, especially those working in gender theory, have called into question the usefulness of the term, particularly when it implies, in Judith Butler's words, a "categorical or fictive universality of the structure of domination" in order to establish "women's common subjugated experience" (Judith Butler, *Gender Trouble: Feminism and the Subversion of Identity* [New York: Routledge, 1990], 5).

sioning the genders and their prescribed roles in the family has a long history in American evangelicalism. Within the Quiverfull discourse, though, the responsibility for education is added to women's primary responsibility for the care and nurture of children.[20]

Finally, along with homeschooling and gender hierarchy is the practice of pronatalism. *Pronatalism* names both the Quiverfull rejection of birth control and their desire to, in their words, have as many children as God chooses to give them. In practice, pronatalism has active and passive aspects. The choice not to do anything to prevent conception could be called *passive pronatalism*. Quiverfull wives reject the Pill, condoms, and other forms of birth control in order to leave control of their fertility to God. In this sense, pronatalism is about what a couple is *not* doing. On the other hand, the choice to have sex during the fertile times in a woman's cycle might be called *active pronatalism*.[21] The couple's choice for sexual intercourse when they know conception is likely moves beyond merely not preventing pregnancy to actively pursuing it. The active and passive aspects of Quiverfull pronatalism can vary depending on the couple and can fluctuate based upon a variety of circumstances in the family's life, including sickness and injury, financial instability, and more. No matter how the practice takes shape in the lives of Quiverfull couples, though, two convictions are constant: (1) the belief that God is in direct control of the conception of children; and (2) the belief that all children are an unqualified blessing or gift from God.[22]

---

20. One adult daughter of a Quiverfull family put it this way: "It is possible to be Quiverfull and yet not patriarchal, but from what I've seen that's very rare—very rare. Part of that is probably because Quiverfull sets itself up against feminism, and thus sort of actually invites patriarchy. But if you go through all of the Quiverfull organizations—Above Rubies, Vision Forum, etc.—every single one also endorses patriarchy. Every one. Joyfully, happily. A woman's place is at home having babies, submitting to her husband who in turn protects her and provides for her. It just all goes together" (Libby Anne, blogger at *Love, Joy, Feminism*, email message to author, August 8, 2012).

21. Tracking the fertile times in a woman's cycle and having intercourse based upon that cycle is often called Natural Family Planning (NFP) in Catholic circles. But even NFP is dismissed by the most ardent Quiverfull teachers as an attempt to usurp God's control over the womb.

22. Some, though not all, families have as the goal of their pronatalism the production of "arrows for the war" over American culture. Among many Quiverfull couples, the activist impulse inherent to evangelical Christianity works itself out in a transformative goal for their pronatalist practice. For these couples, it's not simply about having many children for their own sake, but also for the instigation of a massive demographic shift over the next few hundred years. See, for example, Kathryn Joyce, "The Quiverfull Conviction: Christian Mothers Breed Arrows for the War," *The Nation*, November 27, 2006, 11–18. The phrase "arrows for the war" originates with Nancy Campbell in her book, *Be Fruitful and Multiply: What the Bible Says about Having Children* (San Antonio, TX: Vision Forum Ministries, 2003), 79–90.

For most Quiverfull families, the pronatalist practice emerges alongside of their convictions about homeschooling and gender hierarchy. It becomes a bit of a chicken and egg dilemma to discern which, in fact, comes first. Mary Pride, an early proponent of homeschooling, has published many books to help homeschooling mothers, as well as a number of monthly magazines.[23] Pride also promotes pronatalism, encouraging her readers to surrender their bodies totally to God's will for procreation. Thus, women who consult Pride for homeschooling assistance also receive instruction in pronatalism—if they are not committed to it already. This is how mothers Renee Tanner and Deborah Olson first encountered the pronatalist discourse. Renee found in Pride's book *The Way Home* a vision of homemaking that included pronatalism and homeschooling. And Deborah, through a search for homeschooling materials, came across *Family Driven Faith* by Voddie Baucham, a book that presented openness to many children and homeschooling as incumbent upon all Christian wives. If children are blessings, the reasoning goes, and a couple's primary means of influencing the world for Christ, then the more children, the better.

Still, it's important to make clear that not all families who homeschool are pronatalist or patriarchal. And not all families who are patriarchal are also pronatalist or choose to homeschool. Many Christian families practice one or two of these things without being Quiverfull. I am using the term in this book to refer to the families in which all three practices occur at the same time. Again, if these three parts are circles in a Venn diagram, then it is at the center where the circles converge that the Quiverfull discourse is located. Moreover, not all Quiverfull families conceive of and participate in these practices in the same way. So, in the case of homeschooling, some Quiverfull families will be very concerned about college preparedness and emphasize high academic achievement to that end. Other Quiverfull families do not consider college a foregone conclusion for their children and will emphasize the formation of godly character and education in practical skills for adult life. In both of these cases,

---

23. See, for example, the following books by Mary Pride: *The Way Home: Beyond Feminism, Back to Reality* (Fenton, MO: Home Life Books, 1985); *All the Way Home: Power for Your Family to Be Its Best* (Wheaton, IL: Crossway, 1989); and *The Big Book of Home Learning*, 3 vols., 4th ed. (Chandler, AZ: Alpha Omega, 2000). Her magazine, *Practical Homeschooling* (formerly *HELP for Growing Families*), is in its twenty-second year.

homeschooling is a primary reference point for their cultural action, but families embody that commitment in different ways.

In the case of pronatalism, some Quiverfull families have never and will never seek to limit or space their children. They attain the Quiverfull ideal in practice, regardless of how they feel about their choice to do so. Other Quiverfull families, while believing that all children are gifts from God, will struggle to adhere to the strict no-limit ideal. They will utilize family planning methods at various times, but often feel guilt and shame because they are falling short of the ideal. Again, the pronatalist discourse is key to their way of life, but the families will interact with and exercise that discourse in different ways. Thus, while defining Quiverfull as a three-part discourse of homeschooling, pronatalism, and gender hierarchy, Quiverfull remains dialogic.[24] That is to say, Quiverfull is something that is always emerging and a matter of constant debate.[25]

QUIVERFULL AND EVANGELICALISM

It is also important to recognize that the Quiverfull movement is very much embedded in the evangelical culture in America. There

---

24. William Garriott and Kevin Lewis O'Neill have posited a "dialogic approach" to the anthropology of Christianity. This approach turns the focus toward the problems that Christians themselves encounter within Christianity. That is to say, Garriott and O'Neill encourage scholars to pay close attention to the way Christians debate Christian identity: "For as the numerous historical and ethnographic accounts of Christians and Christianity demonstrates, setting the terms for determining what and who counts as a Christian has been an incessant preoccupation of Christians and Christianity . . . since its inception." Thus Christian identity is *dialogic*: something that is constantly emerging through dialogue and debate—among elites and laypersons alike—over the correctness of particular teachings and practices (William Garriott and Kevin Lewis O'Neill, "Who Is a Christian? Toward a Dialogic Approach to the Anthropology of Christianity," *Anthropological Theory* 8, no. 4 [2008]: 381–98). I discovered Garriott and O'Neill's approach to this question while reading James Bielo's ethnography of an evangelical subculture: *Emerging Evangelicals: Faith, Modernity, and the Desire for Authenticity* (New York: New York University Press, 2011). Bielo draws on the dialogic concept in his account of emergent evangelicals. "Rather than focus on what makes them discrete," he says, "we focus on what continually enlivens them to be in dialogue with one another" (Bielo, *Emerging Evangelicals*, 202).

25. Many Quiverfull families have other discernible traits. They tend to read the Bible literally and propositionally. They tend to trade in nostalgia, particularly for the colonial and Victorian periods of American history. They often participate in homesteading practices designed to promote the family's independence, like making their own bread, sewing their own clothing, or canning their own goods. And, some look to their "full quiver" as the way to "take back" American culture for Christianity over the next few hundred years. But, these characteristics are variable and may not be present in all cases. So, for my purposes, the three basic requirements for qualifying as *Quiverfull* are homeschooling, pronatalism, and gender hierarchy.

would be no Quiverfull without American evangelicalism.[26] As I will explain in chapter 1, the Quiverfull movement emerged over the past forty years within the networks and organizations of the Christian homeschooling movement. Not all homeschoolers are Christians, but Christians are the most vocal and activist homeschoolers in the country. Homeschooling grew into a nationwide phenomenon in large part due to the activism of Christian families (mostly mothers) who created a plethora of local, state, and national organizations and networks for its promotion. Then, starting with teachers like Bill Gothard and Mary Pride and the families that adopted their approach, the threefold discourse of gender hierarchy, pronatalism, and homeschooling emerged in the 1980s as a discernible subculture. Today, enough time has passed that Quiverfull families can speak of first- and second-generation practitioners.

The necessary sociological research has yet to be done to accurately quantify the Quiverfull movement, but conservative estimates are that the number of adherents is in the tens of thousands, making Quiverfull a minority among Protestant evangelicals.[27] Most Quiverfull families operate on the margins of their church and community (unless the father happens to be a community or church leader). But, through the work of Kathryn Joyce and others, this minority has received significant attention from journalists and other interested observers in recent years. The popularity of the Duggars' reality show, not to mention the scandals surrounding their oldest son, Josh, has also contributed to the recognition of the Quiverfull movement. It might seem that the renown of Quiverfull in America is disproportionate to their small numbers. But we should not overlook their persuasive symbolic power among evangelicals. As Joyce says, "The movement is . . . significant for representing an ideal family structure that many conservatives reference as a counterexample when they condemn modern society. Not every family has to be Quiverfull in the sense of having eight children for the movement to make an impact."[28] Indeed, while Quiverfull families are a minority in evangelicalism, they remain an instantiation of what many evangelicals

---

26. Many outsiders characterize Quiverfull families as "fundamentalist," while others use the more neutral term "evangelical." I will employ evangelicalism and evangelical throughout. But, I am going to save my reasoning for this choice and the discussion of the relation between evangelicalism and fundamentalism for chapter 1.

27. This estimate comes from Joyce, "The Quiverfull Conviction," 11.

28. Kathryn Joyce, *Quiverfull: Inside the Christian Patriarchy Movement* (Boston: Beacon, 2009), 171.

say is the ideal family. Quiverfull women, in particular, embody what many believe is the ideal of Christian womanhood: stay-at-home moms, open to bearing many children, focused on discipleship, and submissive to their husbands. While conservative evangelicals are prone to criticize strongly those perceived as too "liberal," they are happy to support those who apply the Bible more stringently than they do. "Too conservative" isn't really a problem. As a result, some evangelical leaders are pointing to the Quiverfull way of life as an example worth emulating.[29] It is the deep symbolic resonance of the movement within the broader evangelical culture that, among other things, points us toward the need for understanding. Furthermore, the persuasiveness of the Quiverfull symbolism suggests that their practice of the family is a direction in which more conservative evangelicals are likely to move in the future.[30]

As a result, despite their relatively marginal status, *Quivering Families* claims that the Quiverfull movement is very much a part of evangelical and American culture. Quiverfull families are "one of us" in many ways. Not only are they very much a part of the evangelical story in America but, as an ideologically inflected subgroup of American evangelicalism, they are also inheritors of important American and evangelical tendencies. Certainly, the Quiverfull lived religion is distinct on the American religious landscape today, but they are not so distinct as to be unique. Most investigations of Quiverfull thus far have emphasized their distinctiveness from American culture, but this book will emphasize their resemblance (without losing sight of the

---

29. For example, R. Albert Mohler Jr., president of the Southern Baptist Theological Seminary, applauds the increasing number of evangelicals questioning the practice of birth control. In a 2014 *Religion News Service* op-ed, he said the following: "Our concern is to raise an alarm about the entire edifice of modern sexual morality and to acknowledge that millions of evangelicals have unwittingly aided and abetted that moral revolution by an unreflective and unfaithful embrace of the contraceptive revolution" (R. Albert Mohler Jr., "Al Mohler Responds: The Evangelical Unease over Contraception," *Washington Post*, January 8, 2014, http://tinyurl.com/yc389vvh). But, certainly not all evangelical leaders are happy to endorse Quiverfull practice. Wade Burleson, a notable Southern Baptist pastor, has been a vocal critic of Quiverfull theology and practice for some time. See, for example, Wade Burleson, "Exposing the Biblical Holes in Quiverfull Theology," *Istoria Ministries*, November 4, 2009, http://tinyurl.com/y7pw3d5q.

30. This is particularly true among evangelicals within the Reformed tradition. Reformed leaders are showing a public friendliness to the movement, and Reformed-oriented blogs have begun to publish material very much in line with Quiverfull teaching regarding contraception, children, and motherhood. I also conducted interviews with at least two Reformed subjects who, while not adopting the Quiverfull label, happily espouse Quiverfull ideology. All of this together suggests to me that a further rightward shift may be in progress among Reformed evangelicals, motivated at least in part by the persuasive symbolic power of the Quiverfull family as presented in their literature and media.

specific things that make them different). As it turns out, a careful look at the practice of Quiverfull families can teach us a lot about ourselves.

ETHNOGRAPHY IN THE STUDY OF QUIVERFULL

In the past few decades, there has been a proliferation of academic research on American evangelicalism across multiple academic disciplines. But this is the first book to address Quiverfull as a lived religion and the first to prioritize the voices of Quiverfull women. Key to both of these aims is the use of ethnography, a qualitative research method. Qualitative research methods seek to gather in-depth information about human beings and human behavior, particularly the *why* and *how* of such behavior.[31] For this reason, qualitative research tends to use smaller samples and usually the findings produced by the data collection are not generalized beyond the particular cases studied.[32] Qualitative research methods include questionnaires, focus groups, participant observation, interviews, and the analysis of archives and other written materials.[33]

Ethnography is a kind of qualitative research method. The word *ethnography*, derived from Greek, literally means "writing culture"—that is, the description of a people and their way of life. To be more precise, ethnography is "a process of attentive study of, and learning from, people—their words, practices, traditions, experiences, memories, insights—in particular times and places in order to understand how they make meaning."[34] Ethnography is distinguishable from other qualitative methods due to the fact that it is almost always conducted in "natural" settings (often referred to as "the field"), in which the everyday language and behavior of people is followed as it occurs. Thus, the analysis that ethnographers produce is necessarily

---

31. For more information, suitable for use by theologians, see John Swinton and Harriet Mowat, *Practical Theology and Qualitative Research* (London: SCM, 2006).
32. Even this point is debated, however. See, for example, Bent Flyvbjerg, "Five Misunderstandings About Case Study Research," *Qualitative Inquiry* 12, no. 2 (April 2006): 219–45. Flyvbjerg argues that qualitative research findings may be used, in some cases, both for hypothesis-testing and for generalizing principles beyond the specific cases studied.
33. Michael V. Angrosino, ed., *Doing Cultural Anthropology: Projects in Ethnographic Data Collection*, 2nd ed. (Long Grove, IL: Waveland, 2007).
34. Christian Scharen and Aana Marie Vigen, eds., *Ethnography as Christian Theology and Ethics* (London: Continuum, 2011), 16.

inductive because explanatory theories emerge from the experience as it is observed in real life.

While the practice of crafting descriptive accounts of people and places goes back to antiquity, ethnography as we know it today emerged from the discipline of cultural anthropology. Arguably the greatest insight of cultural anthropology has been the concept of culture itself: "the idea that people's behaviors, beliefs, interactions, and material productions were not random, but rather formed a 'complex whole' that was meaningful, logical, more or less consistent, and worthy of respect on its own terms."[35] Of course, this concept of culture requires scholarly tools for the careful collection and analysis of the many details composing the cultures of the world. Today, the investigation of culture is carried out through ethnographic methods in a variety of disciplines. Most important for my purposes, however, is its increasingly central role in the study of religion and religious communities, especially evangelical Christianity.

In addition to the increasing use of ethnography for the study of evangelicalism, the past few decades have also seen a swell of academic research in the experiences and agency of evangelical Protestant women.[36] Utilizing a variety of theoretical approaches as well as ethnographic research within evangelical and fundamentalist groups, scholars have revealed that the experience of women within patriarchal movements is by no means uniform and very often defies tidy explanation. Some feminist researchers have even claimed that the women in their studies find avenues of agency and liberation within explicitly patriarchal environments.[37]

Feminist theologians have also complicated the manner in which we discuss women's subjectivity and agency in conservative religious movements. Leading the way in this regard is Mary McClintock

---

35. Angrosino, *Doing Cultural Anthropology*, 2.

36. See, for example, Judith Stacey, *Brave New Families: Stories of Domestic Upheaval in Late Twentieth Century America* (New York: Basic Books, 1990); R. Marie Griffith, *God's Daughters: Evangelical Women and the Power of Submission* (Berkeley: University of California Press, 1997); Brenda Brasher, *Godly Women: Fundamentalism and Female Power* (New Brunswick, NJ: Rutgers University Press, 1998); Christel Manning, *God Gave Us the Right: Conservative Catholic, Evangelical Protestant, and Orthodox Jewish Women Grapple with Feminism* (New Brunswick, NJ: Rutgers University Press, 1999); and Julie Ingersoll, *Evangelical Christian Women: War Stories in the Gender Battle* (New York: New York University Press, 2003).

37. Those who draw these conclusions include Judith Stacey, *Brave New Families*; R. Marie Griffith, *God's Daughters*; and Brenda Brasher, *Godly Women*. More recent scholars like Julie Ingersoll want to challenge this thesis somewhat, but they do not deny the larger point: the experience of women within patriarchal movements is much more complicated than it at first appears.

Fulkerson, whose book *Changing the Subject: Women's Discourses and Feminist Theology* (1994) uses poststructuralist analysis to offer a way to discuss women's agency in non-essentializing ways and conceive of the subject *woman* as possessing multiple identities.[38] Fulkerson's research shows that even women who do not identify as feminists have faith practices that have their own "registers" of resistance to patriarchy. Her work has challenged theologians (particularly feminist and liberation theologians) to reconsider their representations of women's experience.

There is no doubt that women are the primary actors in the Quiverfull subculture. Quiverfull centers the bodies and work of women in a way that even complicates their patriarchal convictions. Women are the mothers, homemakers, and homeschoolers focused on birthing and nurturing "arrows" for the Christian "war" over American culture.[39] The testimony of Quiverfull teachers is that their women are the most important agents of change, contributing to the goal of Christian dominion in the decades and centuries to come. Thus, sustained focus on the women of Quiverfull is a valuable approach toward understanding the movement as a whole.

Ethnography is well suited for research on the women of Quiverfull because they are arguably the least visible within the movement. Women are believed to be divinely ordained to be submissive wives and mothers, while men are called to be the leaders in the home, church, and society. Women operate the majority of Quiverfull blogs, and there are multiple publications authored by women and directed to a female audience. But many of these works are explicitly or implicitly stated to be under the "headship" of the women's husbands, which calls into question the extent to which the material is representative of women's experience. Moreover, works intended to promote and reinforce Quiverfull teaching are unlikely to include challenges to prevailing ideas and practices. So, if researchers want to know the lived experience of Quiverfull mothers, a method of study is needed that will take their stories into account.

Ethnographic methods also help researchers deal with the reality that the Quiverfull movement is thoroughly decentralized. There is no officially recognized leader and no governing ecclesial body

---

38. Fulkerson, *Changing the Subject*.
39. This warfare language is especially prolific in the writing of Nancy Campbell, noted Quiverfull advocate and teacher, in her volume *Be Fruitful and Multiply*, as well as Rachel Giove Scott, *Birthing God's Mighty Warriors* (Maitland, FL: Xulon, 2004).

claiming Quiverfull as authorized practice. Quiverfull theology and practices are disseminated mostly by word of mouth, through books passed from person to person, blogs recommended by email or text message, social networking, and a variety of homeschooling publications and conferences. Furthermore, the daily life of the Quiverfull family necessarily operates in a way that is, for the most part, closed off from public access. While many Quiverfull families sustain their identity through online support groups and blogs, very often these sources are unavailable to researchers without going through a selective subscription process. It is insufficient, therefore, for a researcher to study only the notable teachers and authors of the movement. Though the texts produced by these thinkers are important—central as they are to the shaping of Quiverfull discourse—they cannot address the pertinent questions of the movement's practical coherence and consistency in the lives of women and families on the ground.

So, I begin my ethnographic research with the anthropological axiom that despite appearances to the contrary, Quiverfull is not a monolithic, thoroughly consistent whole, but an internally fractured entity with permeable boundaries. Researchers can anticipate that while Quiverfull adherents may hold to certain shared ideas and practices, they do not necessarily agree as to the exact meaning of the ideas to which they appeal, nor do their practices look the same in day-to-day life. The only way to shed light on the shades of difference within the Quiverfull movement is to employ methods that allow for comparison between Quiverfull literature and the experiences of Quiverfull families.

THE SCOPE OF MY ETHNOGRAPHIC RESEARCH

The ethnographic research that forms the basis for this book was gathered mostly through in-depth interviews with three Quiverfull mothers over the course of two years. I chose these women because of their enthusiasm about helping me and because they had social locations and personal stories quite different from one another. I met in person with Deborah Olson twice: once at a coffee shop and once in her home, where I spent the afternoon with her and her children. At the coffee shop, I took notes by hand. But in the home visit, I recorded our entire visit on a digital recorder, which I later transcribed. The rest of our interviews were conducted by phone with follow-up email correspondence for clarification. I met in person with Carley Miller once, recording our conversation on a digital recorder, which I later transcribed. The rest of our interviews were conducted by phone with follow-up email correspondence. Because of her location in the Southwest, all of my interviews with Renee Tanner were conducted by phone.

Although I closely followed the prepared questions for each interview, I also improvised questions depending on the subjects raised by my informants. My open-ended interviews addressed issues related to marriage and gender roles, sex and reproduction, motherhood and mothering, children and childrearing, the nuclear family, church and family religion, and American culture and politics.

I also interviewed a number of others in the course of my research, including two ministers of so-called family integrated churches (more about family integrated churches in chapter 1), one adult daughter of a Quiverfull family, and one mother of a large homeschooling family who does not consider herself Quiverfull. These conversations were helpful especially as I sought to clarify the boundaries and chief characteristics of Quiverfull, but I ended up not giving sustained attention to these informants.

In addition to interviews, my ethnographic research also included a broad survey of Quiverfull print materials and Quiverfull blogs and websites, all of which can be found in the bibliography and will be referenced throughout. I consulted these resources in correlation with the data culled through interviews. In some cases, I drew topics from the print and internet resources for use in interviews or used the printed rhetoric to question the on-the-ground discourse of my informants. In other cases, I drew topics from my interviews to bring to the print and internet resources or used the points raised in my interviews to question what was offered in print. For example, when the Doug Phillips scandal broke, I asked my informants for their reaction. I discovered that none of them would characterize Phillips as a compelling teacher, and all of them were suspicious of his strident patriarchy—even before his fall from grace. Despite the fact that Phillips has garnered public attention and is often seen as a chief Quiverfull representative, the mothers in my research did not identify with him. This is important because, more often than not, popular-level writing about Quiverfull draws exclusively on print and internet resources. My inquiries about Phillips show that print and internet resources may not be representative of Quiverfull families on the ground. The use of books, websites, and interviews complicates our picture of Quiverfull as a movement, giving researchers a more accurate sense of this still-emerging evangelical phenomenon.

As with any project, mine has some limitations. First, I have focused almost exclusively on the experience and perspective of Quiverfull mothers. There are a number of reasons for this. The mothers are most certainly at the center of the Quiverfull movement. Their bodies and prolific work in the home literally and figuratively give life to the movement. Not only that, but, by their own testimony, mothers are often the ones who lead their husbands into the Quiverfull discourse. Many Quiverfull testimonies are built around the careful, prayerful persuasion of husbands, who often must be convinced by their wives in a way that is appropriately submissive and deferential.[40] Moreover, by virtue of their myriad responsibilities, Quiverfull mothers often don't have the time or ability to talk about their lived religion in a public way. Put simply, I wanted to hear the voices of women who do not maintain a public persona.

In addition to the focus on mothers, this book is limited in the number of critical themes examined. For example, I wish the important matters of race and class could have played more of a role in this book. Neither came up in an overt way in my interviews or the print and internet materials I surveyed. The matter of race is important in some segments of the movement, especially those focused on American demographic trends. Because the Quiverfull discourse is a generally white and middle- to lower-class phenomenon, there is need for a study that brings the subjects of race and class to the forefront. But for this first foray into the movement, my primary interests lie elsewhere. Still, it is important to keep in mind that whiteness and white experience is the assumed norm among Quiverfull families, and most would be categorized as middle to lower class.

In addition to race and class, this book does not give much explicit attention to the subject of homeschooling. There are many homeschooling subjects worthy of consideration: the curriculum used by mothers, the way homeschooling mothers cooperate with one another, the way children with special needs are educated, and the long-term consequences for homeschooled children. Indeed, sustained inquiry into how Quiverfull children are educated would add

---

40. The woman-led nature of Quiverfull is especially evident in the testimonies found in Natalie Klejwa, *Three Decades of Fertility: Ten Ordinary Women Surrender to the Creator and Embrace Life* (Saint Paul, MN: Visionary Womanhood, 2013).

to the growing body of research on Christian home education in America.[41] But, no book can do it all.

In the end, the ethnographic data offered in this book cannot be understood as representative of all Quiverfull families. This is particularly true of the three mothers that serve as my main focus. This sample size—if it can even be called a sample size—is too small. Also, simply by virtue of their willingness to talk to me, it is possible that these mothers are qualitatively different from other Quiverfull mothers. They may have more outgoing personalities or they may be less world-averse than their peers. Also, these women come from a limited portion of the United States, which certainly influences their theology and practice. Still, the research I have conducted is representative enough for a project of this kind. I am not offering an ethnography of the Quiverfull movement per se. But, I have brought together historical, ethnographic, and theological methods and applied them to the Quiverfull instantiation of the family. I present these findings convinced that what I'm offering is valuable for understanding the Quiverfull movement, as well as American evangelicalism as a whole.

ETHNOGRAPHY AND THEOLOGICAL STUDIES

In terms of how ethnography and theology are employed together, there are two major approaches in the field of theological studies. Some theologians use ethnography to describe and then reflect on the expression of faith in a given time and place. This is theological reflection *on* ethnography. Other theologians argue that the contextualized faith of a particular people actually has something constructive to say for the work of Christian theology today. This is theology *from* ethnography. Although there are times when I draw theological insights from ethnographic data, my work in this book is more accurately described as theological reflection on ethnography. I use ethnographic research to better understand the theology at work in particular locations (Quiverfull families). Then, I engage that

---

41. That research includes the following: Gaither, *Homeschool*; Stevens, *Kingdom of Children*; Robert Kunzman, *Write These Laws on Your Children: Inside the World of Conservative Christian Homeschooling* (Boston: Beacon, 2009); Joseph Murphy, *Homeschooling in America: Capturing and Assessing the Movement* (New York: Skyhorse, 2014); and Melissa Beth Sherfinski, "Blessed Under Pressure: Evangelical Mothers in the Homeschooling Movement" (PhD diss., University of Wisconsin-Madison, 2011).

theology in a critical way. Though this book suggests there are places where the contextualized faith of Quiverfull families has something constructive to say for the work of Christian theology today, I do not attempt to flesh out those constructive elements in a sustained way. I do, however, critique the Quiverfull movement and show how their religious practice exposes important weaknesses in evangelical theology.

How and on what basis is my theological critique employed? As a theologian formed in the evangelical tradition, I am intimately aware of the assets and deficits of evangelical theology and I recognize both in the Quiverfull movement. As a scholar of American Christianity, I recognize within Quiverfull a continuation of themes and tendencies that have been present in American evangelicalism from early on. In both of these ways, my subject position leads me to contextualize Quiverfull within evangelicalism and offer observations on its continuity and discontinuity with what I understand to be American evangelical norms.

In addition to my own concerns, however, critique can also arise from two central objectives within Quiverfull discourse itself: witness and transformation. Quiverfull practitioners want to bear *witness* to the truth and goodness of the gospel before the watching world. In their way of life, Quiverfull families seek to show their neighbors the fullness of life that Christ offers his followers. Being a witness in this way depends on faithfulness. The family's job is to be faithful to their calling regardless of the results. They may not convince anyone in their lifetime to adopt their way of life, but their calling is to be faithful nonetheless. Lacking any obvious sign that their work is accomplishing a higher purpose, Quiverfull mothers often attest that they are seeking only to be a good witness—to be faithful in their own context to God's word, regardless of the perceived results. So, one way to evaluate Quiverfull practice is to consider to what extent their way of life offers Christian witness to the world.

Quiverfull practitioners also express a desire to *transform* American society and culture through their way of life. Quiverfull families seek to have a significant long-term impact on American society, both through the number of children they produce and the quality of children they produce. By having more children than their non-Christian neighbors, Quiverfull families expect Christians to outnumber non-Christians within a few hundred years. By having better-quality children—that is, better educated and more strongly committed to their religious tradition—they also expect to have a slow, Christianizing effect on American culture. This transformative objective is often heard among Quiverfull elites (the key teachers and writers of the movement), who cast the vision for Quiverfull laity. The objective of transformation might seem counterintuitive given the concern for faithful witness. As I said, being a witness is unrelated to efficacy—that is, what the witness accomplishes. Being a witness requires faithfulness only, regardless of the consequences. But the objective of cultural and social transformation is very much dependent upon the matter of efficacy. Therefore, another criterion for evaluating Quiverfull discourse is whether or not Quiverfull lived religion is capable of accomplishing the transformation they desire.

THE THESIS AND STRUCTURE OF THIS BOOK

Quivering Families covers a lot of terrain, but it advances one primary thesis: despite the apparent strangeness of their lived religion, the Quiverfull movement in America is both thoroughly evangelical and thoroughly American. What they offer in their family-focused vision for Christian life is far from countercultural, but part and parcel of the American culture they seek to stand against. That is to say, "they" are very much a part of "us." As such, the Quiverfull movement serves as an illuminating case study of the weaknesses and blind spots of evangelical and American cultural conceptions of the family.

To advance my thesis, I have arranged this book into six chapters. In chapter 1, I tell the story of Quiverfull as a historical and cultural phenomenon. First, I offer a narrative of American evangelicalism as it pertains to gender, the family, and education, from the Victorian period to the present day. Then, I provide an examination of the Quiverfull movement as both a discourse and a subculture of American evangelicalism. As a subculture, Quiverfull has elite and lay levels, both of which are important to giving the Quiverfull movement its theological and practical cohesion. Also, the Quiverfull movement, like evangelicalism in general, is characterized by constant conflict and debate. In chapter 1, I explore these dynamics in more detail.

In chapter 2, I present the findings of two years of ethnographic research with Quiverfull mothers. The mothers' stories offer outsiders a better sense of the variety within the Quiverfull subculture. Quiverfull mothers are not the monolithic automatons that some journalistic accounts have mistakenly suggested. The insight they provide into the way Quiverfull discourse works on the ground offers vital material for the theological reflection in the chapters that follow. And perhaps more than anything else, the stories of Renee Tanner, Carley Miller, and Deborah Olson reveal the contextual give-and-take that occurs even within the very prescribed notions of Christian faithfulness in Quiverfull discourse.

Drawing on the historical and cultural analysis of chapter 1, and the ethnographic data summarized in chapter 2, chapters 3, 4, and 5 address the key themes of mothers and motherhood, children and childhood, and the family. Each chapter will do two things simultaneously: explore the ethnographic data more deeply and reflect theologically on those findings. The discussions found in these central chapters will reveal in their own ways the extent to which Quiverfull practitioners are distinct from and similar to their American neighbors.

Finally, in chapter 6, I conclude by arguing that Quiverfull families are responding to the challenges facing the family in the contemporary American context with a distinctly evangelical and American solution. Quiverfull families, like many today, look to the reordering of the private sphere to resolve what are fundamentally systemic problems. In so doing, they amplify some of the persistent tensions of evangelical religion, especially with modern American individualism. That is to say, Quiverfull subculture represents an extreme instantiation of broader, mainstream tendencies. Thus, Quiverfull women and their families are a manifestation of the impasse always faced by American Christians in discussions of the family: an eclipse of the communal and public through a focus on the individual and private. Ultimately, Quiverfull women and their families make it clear that evangelicals lack the tools to fashion a constructive answer to the instability of the American family and must reach beyond the bounds of the private home and evangelicalism to do so.

A FINAL WORD

As I finish this introduction, one of my informants is giving birth. Though my primary posture in this book is that of a researcher, I can't help but be preoccupied with concern for her well-being. This pregnancy has been difficult and her health somewhat fragile. I am worried about her. I hope she and the baby will be all right. My distractedness is an important reminder that this kind of research cannot be conducted in a thoroughly detached way. Even though I have sought to maintain a degree of objectivity, I cannot deny this book engages my heart in a way that other projects do not. I suspect that this has much to do with our shared faith as Christians and our shared experience as mothers. Our lives are very different, but we also have much in common. I have come to care about the women whose lives are explored in the chapters that follow. I hope that the women I have been privileged to know will recognize themselves in these pages. And I hope they know that I am forever grateful for their transparency and friendship.

1.

Conceiving Quiverfull: The Movement in Historical and Cultural Perspective

I met homeschooling mother of six, Deborah Olson, at a Family-Driven Faith Conference featuring Pastor Voddie Baucham, which was hosted by a Baptist church in Cincinnati.[1] She was eager to meet someone who lived near them since they had traveled quite a distance. After a long conversation in the parking lot, I told Deborah about my research on Quiverfull families and asked whether she would be interested in participating. She agreed and gave me her contact information. Over the next two years, I conducted many interviews with Deborah, both in person and by phone.

Deborah and Dan Olson live in the suburbs of a mid-sized city in the Midwest.[2] Their area is predominantly white (90 percent) with a median per family income of around $47,000. The Olsons are white and both college educated. Dan works for city government and Deborah is a full-time stay-at-home, homeschooling mother of six children, ranging in age from two to eleven years. Though she planned to have a career in teaching, after Deborah gave birth to their first child she never went back to the classroom. She began homeschooling when her kids were old enough to start formal schooling. They

---

1. The conference was named for Baucham's book of the same title, *Family-Driven Faith: Doing What It Takes to Raise Sons and Daughters Who Walk with God* (Wheaton, IL: Crossway, 2011).
2. Throughout the book, I have changed the names and modified some biographical details of my informants to protect their anonymity.

have never attended a brick and mortar school. Both Deborah and Dan grew up in conservative Christian homes. They met in church, went to college together, and wed following graduation. Deborah had always wanted a large family, but it was only after they had difficulty conceiving their first child that they decided to forgo birth control entirely. Now they want as many children as God gives them, even though Deborah has had what she calls "difficult pregnancies."

If it were possible to speak of a typical Quiverfull family, Deborah and Dan would be good candidates for the designation. The necessary sociological research has yet to be done to tell us the number of Quiverfull families in America, let alone the specific details of their households. But, broadly speaking, Quiverfull families are white, lower or middle class, sustained financially by the male breadwinning husband, and a homemaking mother who has had some college education. Quiverfull families seem evenly distributed among suburban and rural areas, though most idealize the rural life.[3] The families I interviewed for this book were from the Midwest and Southwest, but internet searches for Quiverfull blogs yield results all over the United States, including Alaska. There is no way to know the average number of children for Quiverfull families, but the families I interviewed had between six and eleven children. All of the mothers said that they remain "open to more."

Deborah was skeptical that her way of life would be the subject of research. She said:

> I have to admit, it seems bizarre to me the notion that what I am doing with my life is a "movement." Literally, it makes me giggle and feel sad at the same time. Clearly our convictions for living our lives the way we do is because we believe it was God's intention from the very beginning and that hopefully it mimics in ways what early Christians would have been doing, minus a lot of current-day culture that is impossible to rid from our lives. For that, we depend on God's grace, and a lot of it![4]

Deborah's incredulity raises a number of questions. Is Quiverfull really a movement after all?[5] What makes a family "Quiverfull" any-

---

3. I have yet to find a Quiverfull family that lives in an urban environment. It's very likely that the commitment to living on one income and the proliferation of children make urban life cost prohibitive, not to mention practically complicated for Quiverfull families.

4. Deborah Olson, email message to author, September 21, 2013.

5. Sociologists of religion are often guilty of making much of small, marginal, and bizarre religious groups. Sociologist Grace Davie takes note of this tendency in her book *The Sociology of Religion: A Critical Agenda* (Los Angeles: Sage, 2013), 163.

way? Can you be Quiverfull without accepting the label? And for what reasons do these families practice the Quiverfull way of life? Deborah claims they do so simply because they are convinced it was "God's intention from the very beginning" and because "it mimics in ways what early Christians would have been doing." But, isn't there more to it than that?

The following chapter provides a detailed account of Quiverfull as a phenomenon in contemporary American evangelicalism using the tools of history and cultural studies. I start by offering an explanation of some key terms. Then, I provide a condensed narrative of evangelical history in the United States with a focus on three themes: gender roles (principally within the institution of marriage), the family, and education. This account will begin in the Victorian period and end in the early 1990s. Then, I examine Quiverfull as a cultural phenomenon through the lenses of discourse and subculture, sketching broadly some key aspects of the movement.[6]

KEY TERMS

Before beginning, I want to be clear about some terms that come up in this chapter and the chapters to follow. As explained in the introduction, I use the term *Quiverfull* to refer to families who participate in three interconnected practices: homeschooling, gender hierarchy, and pronatalism. Participants in this three-part discourse also participate in a subculture of evangelicalism, which we will discuss in more detail below. Thus, individuals and families can be Quiverfull; and these individuals and families, by participating in certain institu-

---

6. Kathryn Joyce, a feminist journalist, was the first to offer a consideration of Quiverfull families as a defined movement within American evangelicalism. She published *Quiverfull* with Beacon Press in 2009. Joyce's consideration of the Quiverfull movement was the first of its kind, targeting the gender and family ideology of Quiverfull leaders and tracing their connections to mainstream evangelicalism, multiple organizations and ministries, as well as public policy groups and political activists. Joyce's work was well received and positively reviewed outside of evangelicalism. It was also the source of a number of internet and print articles on the same topic. Other authors have included discussions of Quiverfull in their works, but none of these authors offer new information on the Quiverfull movement. Rather, they lean on Joyce to make their arguments. See, for example, Monica Duffy Toft, "Wombfare: The Religious and Political Dimensions of Fertility and Demographic Change," in *Political Demography*, ed. Jack A. Goldstone, Eric P. Kaufmann, Monica Duffy Toft (Boulder: Paradigm, 2012), 213–25; Eric Kaufmann, "A Full Quiver: Fertility and the Rise of American Fundamentalism," in *Shall the Religious Inherit the Earth? Demography and Politics in the Twenty-First Century* (London: Profile, 2010), 74–117; and Megan Taylor, "Quiverfull: Family Reformation and Intentional Community" (BA thesis, Texas Christian University, Fort Worth, 2012).

tions, are also participants in Quiverfull subculture. Moreover, I use the term *Quiverfull* for teachers, leaders, authors, bloggers, and families regardless of whether they use it to describe themselves.[7]

Kathryn Joyce's book *Quiverfull* employs the term *movement* in reference to Quiverfull. I don't know if she was the first to do so, but her book and the articles that followed spread the phrase *Quiverfull movement* into the American mainstream. *Quiverfull movement* has become a normal way of speaking of the evangelical families who choose to eschew family planning, homeschool their children, and practice male headship.[8] Despite its popularity, however, those who study social movements today would not recognize Quiverfull as a true movement, regardless of their theoretical approach.[9] Compared to classic social movements like the American Civil Rights Movement, Quiverfull is not a *movement* in the strict sense of the term. Instead, it is better to see it as part of a discernible subculture of American evangelicalism. Still, *Quiverfull movement* has become a common way of referring to Quiverfull families in the media. More importantly, the term *movement* articulates the way many Quiverfull proponents view their own cultural action. Even if sociologists are disinclined to call the work of Quiverfull families a movement, there is no doubt that many such families are seeking social and cultural change.[10] So, even though Quiverfull families do not constitute a movement in sociological terms, I use the term *movement* because it names the evangelical zeal for cultural transformation that is vital to Quiverfull subculture.

---

7. See n. 10 in the introduction for an explanation of my choice to retain the term *Quiverfull* despite the debate surrounding its use.

8. For more on the Christian homeschooling movement in America, see Mitchell Stevens, *Kingdom of Children: Culture and Controversy in the Homeschooling Movement* (Princeton: Princeton University Press, 2001); Milton Gaither, *Homeschool: An American History* (New York: Palgrave Macmillan, 2008); Joseph Murphy, *Homeschooling in America: Capturing and Assessing the Movement* (Thousand Oaks, CA: Corwin, 2012); and, in a more popular vein, Robert Kunzman, *Write These Laws on Your Children: Inside the World of Conservative Christian Homeschooling* (Boston: Beacon, 2009).

9. For a review of approaches and concepts, see Jeff Goodwin and James M. Jasper, *The Social Movements Reader: Cases and Concepts*, 2nd ed. (Malden, MA: Wiley-Blackwell, 2009). For a helpful introduction to each of the approaches, as well as a discussion of how religion requires a more prominent place in social movement theory, see Sharon Erickson Nepstad, *Convictions of the Soul: Religion, Culture, and Agency in the Central America Solidarity Movement* (Oxford: Oxford University Press, 2004), 3–29.

10. James Davison Hunter offers a critique of evangelical attempts at cultural transformation in his book *To Change the World: The Irony, Tragedy, and Possibility of Christianity in the Late Modern World* (Oxford: Oxford University Press, 2010).

Telling the story of evangelicals in America is complicated by the challenge of defining *evangelical* and *evangelicalism*.[11] Most draw on David Bebbington's longstanding approach, which locates the roots of evangelicalism in the pietist revivalist movements of Britain and North America. Bebbington holds out four key traits of evangelicals, often called a quadrilateral: (1) conversionism, or belief in conversion and changed lives; (2) biblicism, or belief in the truthfulness and trustworthiness of the Bible; (3) activism through evangelism and mission (proselytizing and service to those in need); and (4) crucicentrism, or the belief that Christ's death is central to the salvation of humankind. The difficulty with Bebbington's four characteristics is that they are primarily focused on beliefs and very broadly conceived. The quadrilateral identifies a vast swath of people and institutions, which may share some beliefs but otherwise have little else in common.[12]

In *Apostles of Reason*, Molly Worthen suggests the evangelical story is primarily about the crisis of authority, which has been shaped by three unresolved problems: (1) how to reconcile faith and reason; (2) how to know Jesus; and (3) how to act publicly on faith in a post-Christendom society. I would add to her list of unresolved tensions the matter raised by Margaret Bendroth in *Fundamentalism and Gender*: the impulse toward egalitarianism versus the impulse to gender hierarchy.[13] Worthen's focus on the questions or tensions with which evangelicals are engaged provides a more three-dimensional approach. What matters is not that all evangelicals believe the same things but that they are engaged with the same questions.[14] Thus evangelicalism functions as a culture produced through

---

11. Donald Dayton calls evangelicalism an "essentially contested concept" and suggests doing away with the term altogether: Donald W. Dayton, "Some Doubts about the Usefulness of the Category 'Evangelical,'" in *The Variety of American Evangelicalism*, ed. Donald W. Dayton and Robert K. Johnston (Knoxville: University of Tennessee Press, 1991), 245. For more on the problem of defining evangelicalism (and fundamentalism), see George Marsden, *Understanding Fundamentalism and Evangelicalism* (Grand Rapids: Eerdmans, 1990), 66–68, 100–101.

12. David Bebbington, *Evangelicalism in Modern Britain: A History from the 1730s to the 1980s* (London: Routledge, 1989), 1–17. See also Mark Noll, *The Rise of Evangelicalism*, A History of Evangelicalism Series (Downers Grove, IL: InterVarsity, 2003), 17–20.

13. Margaret Lamberts Bendroth, *Fundamentalism and Gender, 1875 to the Present* (New Haven: Yale University Press, 1993).

14. This method is similar to that of anthropologist James Bielo, who suggests evangelicalism is essentially dialogical, a culture constantly emerging through debate over teachings and practices. Like Worthen, Bielo focuses on "what continually enlivens [evangelicals] to be in dialogue with one another." See James Bielo, *Emerging Evangelicals: Faith, Modernity, and the Desire for Authenticity* (New York: New York University Press, 2011), 202. Bielo draws on the work of William Garriott and Kevin Lewis O'Neill, "Who Is a Christian? Toward a Dialogic Approach to the Anthropology of Christianity," *Anthropological Theory* 8, no. 4 (2008): 381–98.

the interactions of churches, societies, networks, publishing houses, music producers, books and periodicals, blogs and websites, practices and rituals, and more. Not all participants in evangelical culture agree on the question of gender, authority, or how to faithfully know and follow Christ, but all of them will be engaged with the dialogue.[15]

The relationship between evangelicals and American culture is complicated. Sociologists of religion have shown that evangelicals are thoroughly embedded in American culture even as they are in constant negotiation with it. Christian Smith's "subcultural identity" theory of religious strength identifies evangelicalism as a subculture at once "embattled and thriving." That is to say, evangelicalism has thrived in the United States because it "possesses and employs the cultural tools needed to create both clear distinction from and significant engagement and tension with" the rest of American culture, "short of becoming genuinely countercultural."[16] Indeed, this "embattled and thriving" status has been a hallmark of evangelical subculture throughout American history, particularly in the matters of marriage, family, and education. And the way these negotiations take place is not always predictable.[17]

GENDER, FAMILY, AND SCHOOLING IN AMERICAN EVANGELICALISM

I have suggested that Quiverfull discourse exists at the intersection of three central practices: homeschooling, gender hierarchy, and pronatalism. In order to contextualize Quiverfull, therefore, a narrative of

---

15. How does this understanding of evangelicalism differ from fundamentalism? Evangelicals and fundamentalists participate in many of the same arguments. Generally speaking, though, *fundamentalist* is a more narrow historical term referring to conservative Protestants who distinguished themselves in the late nineteenth century by rejecting modernist influences in the church and academy. The emphases and expressions of historic fundamentalism (e.g., biblical inerrancy, gender hierarchy, and moralism) have been very influential in American evangelicalism as a whole, such that distinguishing the two can be difficult. But, most evangelicals today eschew the *fundamentalist* label due to its negative connotations. I will speak of *evangelicals* and *evangelicalism* unless historic fundamentalists are in view.

16. Christian Smith, *American Evangelicalism: Embattled and Thriving* (Chicago: University of Chicago Press, 1998), 118–19.

17. New historians of evangelicalism seem to affirm this basic approach to framing the evangelical story. See, for example, Paul S. Boyer, "Back to the Future: Contemporary Evangelicalism in Perspective," in *American Evangelicals and the 1960s*, ed. Axel R. Schäfer (Madison: University of Wisconsin Press, 2013), and Axel R. Schäfer, *Countercultural Conservatives: American Evangelicalism from the Postwar Revival to the New Christian Right*, Studies in American Thought and Culture Series (Madison: University of Wisconsin Press, 2011).

evangelicalism is needed that takes into consideration the development of evangelical gender and family ideology as well as the story of evangelicals and schooling in the United States. Many historians and sociologists of religion have documented these narratives individually, but I want to bring these strands together. I begin in the Victorian period because most historians agree that American evangelicals are deeply beholden to Victorian notions of gender and domesticity in their contemporary discourse.[18] For the sake of clarity, I divide the following narrative into discrete time periods, but the reader should keep in mind that these are not rigid, disconnected units of time.

1820–1875: THE SELF-MADE MAN, THE TRUE WOMAN, AND THE VICTORIAN FAMILY

From the time of the Revolution through the Jacksonian era, American evangelicals went through significant transformation. The most important of these transformations was their demographic ascendancy.[19] During and after the period often called the Second Great Awakening (ca. 1790–1820), the "old guard" Calvinism that had reigned prior to and immediately after the American Revolution was marginalized in favor of revivalist-style worship and preaching, with an emphasis on human freedom and personal holiness.[20] Almost all American denominations saw an increase in adherents during this period, but it was the revivalist evangelicals that saw the most growth. Though by no means homogenous in their theology and practice, by 1860 the vast majority of American congregations were evangelical.[21]

As evangelicals increased in number, their relationship with the American culture became ever warmer. John Bartkowski argues that

---

18. In fact, Colleen McDannell claims that even the fairly recent development of homeschooling has roots in Victorian "domestic Christianity." She argues, "To understand fundamentalism's impact on both American society and religion, we must recognize that conservative fascination with the home is not merely a result of political choices. It is rooted in a long tradition of Protestant domestic Christianity, articulated by Victorian ministers, novelists, reformers, and theologians. As with their Victorian counterparts, contemporary Christians understand the creation of an alternative Christian culture as beginning in the home" (Colleen McDannell, "Creating the Christian Home: Home Schooling in Contemporary America," in *American Sacred Space*, ed. David Chidester and Edward T. Linenthal [Bloomington: Indiana University Press, 1995], 189).

19. Mark Noll, *America's God: From Jonathan Edwards to Abraham Lincoln* (Oxford: Oxford University Press, 2002), 166.

20. Gaither, *Homeschool*, 31.

21. Noll, *America's God*, 170–71.

as the philosophy of John Locke and other Enlightenment thinkers saturated the new republic's social imagination, the egalitarian impulses within revivalist evangelicalism underwent significant change.[22] The patriarchal structure of Locke's "dual spheres" and a delineated "chain of duties" between husbands and wives (as well as parents and children, masters and servants) took hold in evangelical families. A new commitment to "highly ordered family relations" took center stage as evangelicals began to view the well-ordered family as key to the health of the church and the nation.[23]

Evangelicals in the pre-Revolutionary period showed an egalitarian impulse with a broader sphere of activity for women,[24] but the mainstreaming of evangelical religion led to that impulse being tamed and brought more fully into alignment with American cultural ideals. The patriarchal family structure became the evangelical norm, and evangelicals became as concerned with exalting the family as they had been with winning souls.[25] Over time, two general poles emerged within evangelical gender ideology. On the one hand, evangelical biblicism produced a highly ordered gender hierarchy that places the husband as the head of the wife and the wife as his subordinate. On the other hand, evangelical emphasis on conversion and life transformation produced a flattening of hierarchy due to the idea of the "priesthood of all believers," each of whom is equally filled and gifted by the Holy Spirit.[26]

What did the gender hierarchy of post-Revolutionary evangelicals look like? A lot like that of the white American middle class. Evangelicals in the Victorian period imagined male and female ideals in terms of the so-called Self-Made Man and the True Woman, each of which

---

22. Stephanie Coontz, *The Way We Never Were: American Families and the Nostalgia Trap* (New York: Basic Books, 2000).

23. John P. Bartkowski, "Changing of the Gods: The Gender and Family Discourse of American Evangelicalism in Historical Perspective," *History of the Family* 3, no. 1 (1998): 95–116.

24. Susan Juster, *Disorderly Women: Sexual Politics and Evangelicalism in Revolutionary New England* (Ithaca, NY: Cornell University Press, 1994). The focus of these revivalist evangelicals upon the individual's direct relationship with God and their employment of ecstatic worship style resulted in ecclesial practices where women held governing positions and preached at church gatherings. See Catherine Brekus, *Strangers and Pilgrims: Female Preaching in America, 1740-1845* (Chapel Hill: University of North Carolina Press, 1998), 42; quoted by Noll, *America's God*, 178.

25. John P. Bartkowski, *Remaking the Godly Marriage: Gender Negotiations in Evangelical Families* (New Brunswick, NJ: Rutgers University Press, 2001), 20.

26. Similarly, Noll differentiates between formalist and antiformalist evangelicals, with the formalists being more committed to rationalism and order and the antiformalists being more revivalist and experientially oriented. As one might expect, the evangelical poles on gender tend to break down along formalist and antiformalist lines (Noll, *America's God*, 175–76, 178).

occupied a different sphere. The Self-Made Man occupied the cut-throat sphere of work and politics where he was freed from traditional obligations in order to pursue his own self-interest as an uninhibited actor in the competitive market.[27] The True Woman occupied the private sphere of hearth and home where she guarded Christian moral virtue through her affection, altruism, and dependence.[28] The True Woman's work was sharply demarcated from the Self-Made Man's as she presided over domestic labor in the home and, occasionally, religious charity outside of it.[29]

As historian Stephanie Coontz argues, the Self-Made Man and the True Woman were interdependent: "Self-reliance and independence worked for men because women took care of dependence and obligation. . . . [T]he liberal theory of human nature and political citizenship did not merely leave women out: it works precisely because it was applied exclusively to half the population. Emotion and compassion could be disregarded in the political and economic realms only if women were assigned these traits in the personal realm."[30] Moreover, Nancy Hewitt notes that Victorians used the well-crafted ideal of the True Woman "to stabilize gender relations in the midst of rapid economic, social, political, and technological change."[31] In short, the white middle-class men of the Jacksonian era entrusted their women[32] with the responsibility of maintaining traditional values of home and church so that they could embrace secularism and materialism in a rapidly changing society.[33]

27. Gaither, *Homeschool*, 34; Coontz, *The Way We Never Were*, 52.
28. Barbara Welter, "The Cult of True Womanhood, 1820-1860," *American Quarterly* 18, no. 2 (Summer 1966), 151–74. This essay was later reprinted in Welter, *Dimity Convictions: The American Woman in the Nineteenth Century* (Athens: Ohio University Press, 1976), 21–41.
29. Coontz, *The Way We Never Were*, 52–53. Welter's essay on "True Womanhood," drawing on Victorian women's magazines and religious literature, has shown that the True Woman was characterized by the four "cardinal virtues" of piety, purity, submissiveness, and domesticity (Barbara Welter, "The Cult of True Womanhood," 152).
30. Coontz, *The Way We Never Were*, 55.
31. Nancy A. Hewitt, "Religion, Reform, and Radicalism in the Antebellum Era," in *A Companion to American Women's History*, ed. Nancy A. Hewitt (Malden, MA: Blackwell, 2002), 117.
32. It was only the middle-class white women of the Victorian period who could be identified as *ladies* and, thereby, symbolize bourgeois American prosperity. Working women and women of color, who generally made up the lower classes, could not be *ladies* and fell short of the True Woman's high standards. Much more could be said about the dependence of the middle-class ideal upon the oppression of lower classes and minorities.
33. Welter, "Cult of True Womanhood," 151; Hewitt, "Religion, Reform, and Radicalism," 117. Gerda Lerner has shown that the relegation of the white middle-class woman to the home was the result of increasing wealth, urbanization, industrialization, and professionalization in American society from the colonial period to the 1830s. Indeed, with the social "progress" of American capitalism came the gradual shrinking of "woman's proper sphere." For more, see

Victorian gender dualism led to the idealization of the family and romanticization of love and nurturing as uniquely female qualities.[34] Together, the Self-Made Man and the True Woman made up an idealized family that was private, ordered around maternal affection and self-sacrifice, with children entrusted to their mothers for education and character formation.[35] True Women were the guardians of private virtue, the "effective teachers of the human race" and "God's own police" in the benevolent protection of Christian morals.[36] Fathers were important in terms of the idealized domestic hierarchy, but their increasing relegation to the public sphere undermined their moral authority in the home. Still, for father and mother, the venerated home was increasingly important, especially for evangelicals who looked to the well-ordered private sphere as the primary means of maintaining good, Christian society.

Victorian notions of gender and family were strengthened by the emerging American social imagination about children. Following the theological triumph of Arminian free will over Calvinist determinism in the Second Great Awakening,[37] children were less often conceived of as innately depraved sinners in need of discipline and more often seen as innocent gifts in need of nurturance and education. Within this new mindset, childhood for middle-class white families became a period of formative innocence entrusted to the altruistic mother for cultivation.[38]

In this convergence of evangelical and Victorian ideals of gender, family, and children, schooling quickly became a central concern. The mother's education was supposed to form children in Christian virtue and prepare them (mainly boys) for competition in the industrialized world. The goal for Victorian mothers was to use persuasion and good example to inculcate morality and intelligence in children.[39] Mothers were urged to make a school of the home, both figuratively and literally. For example, Catharine Beecher and Harriet

---

Gerda Lerner, "The Lady and the Mill Girl: Changes in the Status of Women in the Age of Jackson," in *The Majority Finds Its Past: Placing Women in History*, 2nd ed. (Chapel Hill: University of North Carolina Press, 2005), 12.

34. Coontz, *The Way We Never Were*, 55.
35. Gaither, *Homeschool*, 34.
36. Gaither, *Homeschool*, 34–35.
37. Nathan Hatch, *The Democratization of American Christianity* (New Haven: Yale University Press, 1990); also, Mark Noll, *A History of Christianity in the United States and Canada* (Grand Rapids: Eerdmans, 1992), 173–78.
38. Gaither, *Homeschool*, 30.
39. Gaither, *Homeschool*, 37.

Beecher Stowe explained in *The American Woman's Home* (1869), "a small church, a school-house, and a comfortable family dwelling may be all united in one building." The Beecher sisters provided an architectural plan showing a cost-effective way to integrate into one space the locations for worship, education, and domesticity. As Colleen McDannell notes, this spatial imagining of family life was a representation of the ideological construction of the family. The Christian family, presided over by the omni-competent, omni-benevolent wife and mother, would serve as "the grand ministry, as [it was] designed to be, in training our whole race for heaven."[40]

1875–1930: THE DEMISE OF VICTORIANISM, THE RISE OF FUNDAMENTALISM, AND THE ASCENT OF PUBLIC SCHOOLS

The evangelical and Victorian consensus on gender and the family began to dissolve by the end of the nineteenth century. Historians suggest three reasons for the change. First, major economic transformations, especially the shift from cottage industries to corporate capitalism, gradually undermined the Victorian ideal of the Self-Made Man. In the words of Betty DeBerg, "Manly work in one's own shop, office, vehicle, or factory gave way to employment in bureaucratized, sterile corporate offices. . . . When American business became big business, men's ability to play the 'economic warrior' was reduced . . . and men became mere bureaucratic cogs in large business organizations."[41]

These broader economic changes further eroded Victorian gender and family norms as "the incorporation of America" transformed the domestic realm.[42] Because men's work outside the home required

---

40. Catharine Beecher and Harriet Beecher Stowe, *The American Woman's Home: Or, Principles of Domestic Science* (New York: J. B. Ford, 1869), 455, quoted by McDannell, "Creating the Christian Home," 189.

41. Betty DeBerg, *Ungodly Women: Gender and the First Wave of American Fundamentalism* (Minneapolis: Fortress Press, 1990), 25. Mechanization also played an important role in the reimagining of man's role as breadwinner. As Alan Trachtenberg notes, "The process of continual refinement and rationalization of machinery, leading to twentieth-century automation, represented to industrial workers a steady erosion of their autonomy, their control, and their crafts." As the laborer was more and more conceived of as "an interchangeable part" and business was increasingly professionalized and incorporated, the Victorian masculine identity became more and more difficult to sustain. See Alan Trachtenberg, *The Incorporation of America: Culture and Society in the Gilded Age* (New York: Hill & Wang, 2007), 56–69.

42. I am borrowing this language from Trachtenberg, *The Incorporation of America*.

longer commutes and increased hours, husbands and fathers were spending less and less time in the home. The "absentee Victorian husband/father was fast becoming a patriarch in name only."[43] Because the husband/father was ever more alienated from the daily activities of the household, "as often as not women had more say in the decisions made about their children than did men. And with the responsibility for training and guidance of the young came much real and symbolic power."[44] Thus, even as many evangelicals held firmly to notions of male leadership and fatherly authority, the structure of their daily lives whittled away at the substance of these ideas until they were left with little more than patriarchal rhetoric.

Victorian and evangelical gender ideals also contained the seeds of their own demise. Eventually, the presumed superior piety of the True Woman justified her entrance into the public sphere as she sought to bring her innate Christian virtue to bear on society. Indeed, the perceived moral superiority of women and their widespread dissatisfaction with male abuse of power led directly to militant reform efforts, which were the immediate forerunners of the movement for women's rights.[45] Abolitionism was led and widely supported by women and, following the Civil War, women also spearheaded efforts to address temperance, child protection, and more. Women's political activism was rooted in Victorian gender norms, but it also subverted them by calling into question the limited parameters of feminine domesticity.[46]

As economic, social, and cultural changes seriously weakened Victorian gender and family norms, a faction of American evangelicals began to unite in common cause under the banner of fundamentalism. Although they first joined forces in reaction to the perceived threats of modernism—particularly the application of higher critical

---

43. Bartkowski, *Remaking the Godly Marriage*, 24.

44. DeBerg, *Ungodly Women*, 35.

45. Carroll Smith-Rosenberg, *Disorderly Conduct: Visions of Gender in Victorian America* (New York: Oxford University Press, 1985), 109–28. Smith-Rosenberg points out that the Moral Reform Society of New York preceded the Seneca Falls Convention by fourteen years: "Women advocates of moral reform were among the very first American women to challenge their completely passive, home-oriented image. . . . They began, in short, to create a broader, less constricted sense of female identity" (127).

46. Speaking of the Women's Christian Temperance Union, the most famous women's activist group of the period, DeBerg writes: "Through such organizations, women across the country, but particularly urban middle class women, burst into the public sphere with a reforming zeal rooted in evangelical religion and the cult of domesticity. These wives and mothers may not have been employed, but leave the house they did, and men no longer could claim the political world as their own" (DeBerg, *Ungodly Women*, 32).

methods to the Bible and the promotion of Darwinian evolution—gender ideology was central to the fundamentalist movement. Indeed, Margaret Bendroth has argued convincingly that the fundamentalism of the early twentieth century was, in large part, a reaction against Victorian notions of superior female piety and the resulting influx of women into activism beyond the home.

According to Bendroth, the reason for fundamentalism's inextricable entanglement with issues of gender and family is rooted in evangelical revivalism. Revivalism's Arminian emphasis on free will and Christian holiness led to a widespread concern for social reform, especially among evangelical women. Separate women's organizations on behalf of charity, missions, and temperance avoided male participation and control, thereby carving out a field of influence within the public sphere previously assigned to men alone. The result of this female empowerment, however, was that by the end of the nineteenth century "religion had become an area of female prerogative."[47] This coupled with a perceived disaffection from religion among middle-class men led to evangelical leaders identifying "masculine passivity" as "one of the burning questions of the hour."[48] Thus, the socioeconomic decline of the Self-Made Man and patriarchal family was paired with a decline in male religious participation, creating a situation where "masculinity seemed everywhere on the retreat."[49]

In response to the disruption of gender and family norms, fundamentalist leaders posited a "muscular Christianity" to remedy America's ailing middle-class white men. Rhetorically, the fundamentalist insistence on biblical inerrancy and rigid orthodoxy was gendered in virile, masculine terms, while liberal acceptance of modernism was gendered as a weak, effeminate alternative. Preachers portrayed men in God's service as dynamic, brave, and bold.[50] Masculine emphases combined with the intentional targeting of men in evangelistic crusades and conferences gave fundamentalism an increasingly

---

47. Bendroth, *Fundamentalism and Gender*, 16–17.
48. Bendroth, *Fundamentalism and Gender*, 17.
49. Bendroth, *Fundamentalism and Gender*, 17. It's important to point out that American evangelical leaders have considered "male passivity" a problem from early on. Women's historians have shown, however, that despite the ubiquity of this "feminization" narrative, women have been a dominant force within American Christianity from the start. See, for example, Ann Braude, "Women's History *Is* American Religious History," in *Retelling U.S. Religious History*, ed. Thomas A. Tweed (Berkeley: University of California Press, 1997), 87–107; and Catherine A. Brekus, "Searching for Women in Narratives of American Religious History," in *The Religious History of American Women: Reimagining the Past*, ed. Catherin A. Brekus (Chapel Hill: University of North Carolina Press, 2007), 1–34.
50. Brekus, "Searching for Women," 22.

male-oriented focus.⁵¹ Yet, fundamentalist influence was largely dependent upon the support of women, so leaders had to take care not to alienate their female base. Bendroth notes, "The popular appeal of early fundamentalism was shaped by two opposing forces: a desire to win the hearts of men, and the practical necessity of involving women."⁵²

Over time, the fundamentalist promotion of "muscular Christianity" led to an overt antifeminism in the 1920s. A literalist interpretation of scripture played a major role, relegating women to subordinate status due either to a foreordained divine plan (according to Calvinist interpreters) or divine punishment of women for their participation in the fall (according to dispensationalist interpreters).⁵³ Dispensationalists especially scorned activist women who put their efforts into social reform, arguing their "brazenness" was evidence of the evil "last days" and the nearness of Christ's return. Both dispensationalist and Calvinist branches of fundamentalism placed high value upon order, and they saw well-ordered families as the spiritual antidote for lax morality in the Roaring Twenties. Fundamentalists concentrated on the "woman question" with increasing urgency due to the rising social freedom of women, epitomized in the suffrage amendment and symbolized by the defiant "flapper."⁵⁴

Along with the demise of Victorian gender ideology and the rise of Protestant fundamentalism, 1875 to 1930 also saw a major shift in the practice of schooling. Throughout the Victorian period, the home had been considered the proper site of instruction, but by

---

51. This is not to say that women didn't continue to enjoy the freedoms and influence gained through suffrage, denominational work, and their women-only organizations. This trend continued even as fundamentalist leaders increasingly identified feminine religiosity as a problem and rhetorically aligned femininity with liberalism. Many male evangelists shared the stage with capable women, and evangelical women flocked to newly formed Bible schools such as the Moody Bible Institute with great enthusiasm. Still, fundamentalist leaders eschewed cooperation with women's auxiliaries and other such organizations, asserting that a truly faithful church would require no such assistance. See Bendroth, *Fundamentalism and Gender*, 25–30.

52. Bendroth, *Fundamentalism and Gender*, 30.

53. Dispensationalism is a highly structured system of Bible interpretation that divides biblical history into a number of successive divine administrations called *dispensations*. It emphasizes predictive prophecy of the end times and anticipates a miraculous "rapture" of the church from the earth prior to the Second Coming of Christ. The origins of Dispensationalism are in the Plymouth Brethren movement, the teachings of John Nelson Darby, and the bestselling Scofield Reference Bible. More recently, Tim LaHaye and Jerry Jenkins popularized the dispensational interpretation of the Book of Revelation through the *Left Behind* series, published by Tyndale House from 1995 to 2007. For more on Dispensationalism, see Paul Boyer, *When Time Shall Be No More: Prophecy Belief in Modern American Culture* (Cambridge, MA: Harvard University Press, 1992).

54. Bendroth, *Fundamentalism and Gender*, 51.

the 1930s, there was widespread consensus that children should be educated in schools. Protestant fundamentalists were very much a part of this emerging consensus. With Victorian gender and family ideals weakened and the Anglo-Saxon Protestant hegemony beginning to dissipate, most Americans sought to shore up the social order and enforce traditional morality with the help of the government.[55] The American government and conservative Christians shared a concern for protecting the "traditional American family" (i.e., the white, middle-class, Protestant family with a homemaking mother and breadwinning father) even as they embraced all of the changes of industrial capitalism.[56] The New Deal programs of the postwar period illustrate this approach: the "family wage" was offered to men and not to women, the Social Security Act guaranteed pensions for jobs typically fulfilled by male breadwinners, and home-ownership programs provided long-term loans only to two-parent (white) households. "Whereas past generations of Americans had to look to the family to keep the nation strong," Gaither says, "it was now up to the nation to save the family."[57]

When it came to the instruction of the young, fundamentalists began to look to schools to accomplish the intellectual and moral purposes once entrusted to the family. They supported the emerging consensus in early twentieth-century America that government-run schools were the best places for children to learn.[58] The number of children attending public schools rose dramatically from the time of the Civil War through the 1930s. High-school enrollment almost doubled every decade from 1890 to 1930. By 1935, 40 percent of all American young people were graduating from high school.[59] This major influx of enrollees forced school leaders into the difficult work of forming a school system that could manage the students in a cost-effective and theoretically judicious way. The goals of these increas-

---

55. Gaither, *Homeschool*, 62.

56. For instance, the declining birthrates and soaring divorce rates among white Americans scandalized President Theodore Roosevelt and his administration. Roosevelt famously called this state of affairs "Race Suicide" and shamed American women who shirked their duty to bear "native" children. Also, many social programs arose aimed at saving the family by offering training for rural family life, such as what was offered by Homemaker and 4-H Clubs, or encouraging the production of "Better Babies" and "Fitter Families" via the American Eugenics Society (Gaither, *Homeschool*, 62–63). For more about the cooperation of mainline Protestants with these efforts see Amy-Laura Hall, *Conceiving Parenthood: American Protestantism and the Spirit of Reproduction* (Grand Rapids: Eerdmans, 2007).

57. Gaither, *Homeschool*, 64.
58. Gaither, *Homeschool*, 64.
59. Gaither, *Homeschool*, 66.

ingly large and more structured public schools were overall efficiency and the production of civilized, capable American citizens. Gaither observes, "Even as the family was becoming more intimate and informal, the school was growing larger, more impersonal, and further removed than it had been from home life, taking on more and more of the functions parents had historically performed."[60]

All of the above changes contributed to a particular construction of the family among white middle-class evangelicals. Seeking to salvage the separate gender spheres of the Victorian period, they endorsed a vision of family life with a breadwinning, solitary, "soldier for Christ" father and a chaste, submissive, supportive mother.[61] Evangelical leaders eschewed the entrance of women into the workplace and advised godly women to look to motherhood as the site of their vocation. The naturally more virtuous Victorian wife faded away in favor of the natural spiritual leadership of the husband. The goal of the virtuous family was to produce "the disciplined, autonomous self, created in the bosom of the bourgeois family."[62] But, the family occupied an ever-shrinking sphere as work and education were separated from the home.[63]

1940S TO 1970S: NEO-EVANGELICALS, CULTURAL REVOLUTIONS, AND THE TRIUMPH OF PUBLIC SCHOOLS

Following the Second World War, some fundamentalists sought to transform both their public reputation and methods of engagement with the modern world. Christening themselves "neo-evangelicals," they pursued scholarly and cultural respectability in America and Europe, a contrasting posture to the hardline separatism of early fundamentalism.[64] But, at the very same time, a number of rapid changes

60. Gaither, *Homeschool*, 67.
61. Bendroth, *Fundamentalism and Gender*, 68–72.
62. Gaither, *Homeschool*, 72.
63. The domestic space, overseen by the Christian mother, was the site of instruction in religious morality and proper etiquette, but also, more and more, the site of conspicuous material consumption. Lizabeth Cohen devotes an entire book to the examination of this shift in *A Consumer's Republic: The Politics of Mass Consumption in Postwar America* (New York: Knopf, 2003).
64. Molly Worthen, *Apostles of Reason: The Crisis of Authority in American Evangelicalism* (Oxford: Oxford University Press, 2013), 75–96. During the postwar rapprochement with American culture, neo-evangelicals created a number of institutions intended to transcend the bitter interdenominational fighting that had taken place in the previous decades. *Christianity*

to American society exacerbated the fundamentalist anxieties about gender and family. More and more white, middle-class, two-parent families moved away from the cities and into the suburbs aided by federal grants and loan guarantees.[65] This white suburbanization coincided with the massive migration of African Americans from the south into the north (often called the Second Great Migration), which lasted from around 1940 to 1970. This migration resulted in the urbanization of the black population in America, such that by 1970 about 80 percent of African Americans were living in cities. Finally, the postwar period also saw extraordinary economic expansion. The middle class grew in affluence in an unprecedented way and consumption became the central function of the home.[66] White evangelicals negotiated with American culture regarding gender and family norms in the midst of these social and economic changes.

From 1945 to 1970, the broader cultural understanding of marriage continued to change. Even though many middle-class women made their way back to the home following the war, marriage and family were increasingly understood in individualistic, therapeutic terms. That is to say, the more traditional functions of marriage and family, such as raising children and long-term social stability, were eclipsed by ideals of personal fulfillment.[67] But an emphasis on personal fulfillment did not mesh well with evangelical concerns for hierarchy, order, and obedience to God's design.[68] Many in the neo-evangelical camp turned to a Reformed (or Calvinist) vision of a divine "order of creation" to support women's subordinate position in marriage and family with limited roles. In church and home, in particular, God ordained men to be the guardians of religion and morality. Therefore, women's leadership was unnecessary as their "dominion" was relegated to the domestic sphere by divine design.[69]

Fundamentalist mothers, unlike Victorian mothers, did not view their domestic vocation as a basis for social reform. Instead, women

---

Today, Fuller Seminary, and the National Association of Evangelicals (NAE) all were the result of the neo-evangelical entrepreneurial spirit.

65. Cohen, *A Consumer's Republic*, 194–256.
66. Cohen, *A Consumer's Republic*, 112–65.
67. Bendroth, *Fundamentalism and Gender*, 131.
68. Cohen, *A Consumer's Republic*, 131–32. And, in the end, feminist critiques of women's "traditional" roles would draw strength from the redefined notion of marriage in personal, self-fulfilling terms.
69. This basic argument from the created order for gender essentialism and feminine domesticity remains relatively unchanged among Reformed evangelicals to the present day. Bendroth, *Fundamentalism and Gender*, 111.

did battle with modernism "from the safety of their private, domestic sphere."[70] Homemaking was the purview of the truly good Christian woman because capable homemaking "freed men for higher service."[71] Mothers were expected to begin their children's religious instruction as soon as possible, occupying the "first line of defense" against worldly influences outside the home. Popular preachers and evangelists strongly emphasized male leadership in the home.[72] Though often physically absent, the fundamentalist father was an indirect caregiver who "[expressed] his love through discipline and sacrifice."[73]

Despite their insistence on separation from American culture, however, evangelicals interacting with the 1960s counterculture also went through their own kind of sexual revolution.[74] Though they maintained a conservative stance on gender roles and homosexuality, evangelicals "devote[d] more attention to sex than they ever had before," some even loosening their stances on birth control and masturbation.[75] A new emphasis on the pleasures of marital sex led to frank discussions of female sexual needs, something that had been taboo in previous generations. But the rhetoric of gender hierarchy continued, now packaged as the secret to a fulfilling Christian marriage. For instance, even though Marabel Morgan's book *The Total Woman* (1973) urged women to embrace their sexuality, she also advised that a woman becomes truly beautiful to her husband only when she "surrenders her life . . . reveres and worships him."[76]

At the same time, some in the early 1970s began reformulating evangelical religion in feminist terms. Drawing on alternative readings of scripture and longstanding egalitarian impulses within evangelicalism itself, so-called biblical feminists argued for gender

---

70. Bendroth, *Fundamentalism and Gender*, 97–116.
71. Bendroth, *Fundamentalism and Gender*, 108.
72. See, for example, the highly patriarchal rhetoric in John R. Rice, *The Home: Courtship, Marriage, and Children* (Murfreesboro, TN: Sword of the Lord, 1946); and *God in Your Family* (Murfreesboro, TN: Sword of the Lord, 1971).
73. Bendroth, *Fundamentalism and Gender*, 104.
74. Amy DeRogatis provides a detailed discussion of this evangelical sexual revolution through a close reading of evangelical marriage and sex manuals in *Saving Sex: Sexuality and Salvation in American Evangelicalism* (Oxford: Oxford University Press, 2015), 42–70.
75. Daniel Williams, "Sex and the Evangelicals: Gender Issues, the Sexual Revolution, and Abortion in the 1960s," in *American Evangelicals and the 1960s*, 101–4.
76. Marabel Morgan, *The Total Woman* (Old Tappan, NJ: Revell, 1973), 127; quoted by Williams, "Sex and the Evangelicals," 110.

equality in home, church, and society.[77] By the mid-1970s, a number of social and economic changes helped bolster their cause. Inflation, the increasing price of housing, and the stagnation of men's wages all made the employment of middle-class women more and more necessary to maintain a middle-class standard of living. Even though the majority of evangelicals did not join the biblical feminist bandwagon, a number of evangelical women writers and speakers rose to prominence promoting traditional gender and family norms, transforming evangelical culture in the long term. Christian magazines gave columns to women writers, Christian publishing houses published books directly marketed to women, and women's conferences and retreats became increasingly popular. Their messages of male headship and wifely submission were directly opposed to feminism and they glorified women's domestic duties as God's calling. While the feminist movement was making national news and biblical feminists were seeking to change evangelicalism, "conservative evangelical women posited an alternative model of female empowerment."[78]

Alongside shifts in marriage and gender ideology, public schooling was on the ascendancy in America. In 1930, just under half of children between fourteen and sixteen were in school. By 1950, over 77 percent of children ages fourteen to sixteen were in school. As schools grew in enrollment the school year lengthened dramatically and many schools were consolidated from local districts into larger, regional units. Textbooks, buildings, testing, professional organizations, and federal involvement further standardized and homogenized schools across the country. All the while, despite their concerns about worldliness, evangelicals more or less cooperated with the expanding system because they continued to perceive the government as on the side of "traditional values." Sixty million Americans were enrolled in some sort of school by 1970 and 80 percent of school-age Americans were graduating from high school, including evangelicals.[79]

By the 1970s, however, the liberal counterculture was beginning

---

77. Sally Gallagher, *Evangelical Identity and Gendered Family Life* (Piscataway, NJ: Rutgers University Press), 44–46, 49–50.

78. Daniel Williams summarizes the appeal of these messages: "Borrowing heavily from 'separate spheres' ideology of the Victorian era, the conservative evangelical women who emerged as leaders in their movement in the late 1960s and 1970s outlined a vision for women that placed them as the center of the social and moral order. Because evangelicals believed that the home was the foundation for a stable society, a social vision that highlighted women's roles as moral guardians of the home appeared to give them a tremendous degree of moral authority" (Williams, "Sex and the Evangelicals," 109).

79. Gaither, *Homeschool*, 85.

to call into question the efficacy of public schooling, and some conservative evangelicals began to express similar doubts. Homeschooling among evangelicals did not begin to gain traction until the late 1970s and early 1980s, but its roots lie in the counterculture of the 1960s, which reacted strongly against "the profound expansion and standardization" of public schools.[80] Thus, even as evangelicals were engaged in cultural debates with feminists about gender and the family, they were also experiencing some doubt about the influence of public schools. Certainly the homogenization of schooling practices was part of evangelical concerns, but just as or even more important was the national upheaval surrounding the racial integration of schools, especially in the South.[81] These two factors taken together help make sense of rising evangelical suspicion toward public schooling. In previous decades evangelicals perceived government schools as a conserving influence on the family, but in the 1970s this perception fell by the wayside.

1970S TO THE 1990S: COUNTERCULTURAL RIGHT AND CONSERVATIVE CHRISTIAN HOMESCHOOLING

In the 1970s and following, evangelicals were increasingly aware of the gradual displacement and marginalization of their values in the United States. This period produced an endless number of books and articles on the subject of gender, marriage, sex, family, and parenting, as evangelicals attempted to strengthen their discourse in the face of ceaseless social and economic pressure. Evangelical messages also proliferated through the work of TV and radio preachers and, later, internet websites, email newsletters, and blogs. Also, following on the heels of a number of events, especially Supreme Court rulings on prayer, Bible reading in schools, and abortion, evangelicals in this period created a variety of organizations intended to turn the tide of social change back in their favor. The most visible result of this activist push was the rise of the Christian Right, led by Jerry Falwell and his Moral Majority. Alongside the Christian Right was the

---

80. Gaither, *Homeschool*, 85.
81. For discussion of the perceived interference of the federal government into Christian schools, see Joseph Crespino, "Civil Rights and the Religious Right," in *Rightward Bound: Making America Conservative in the 1970s*, ed. Bruce J. Schulman and Julian E. Zelizer (Cambridge, MA: Harvard University Press, 2008), 90–105. Randall Balmer has also written about the religious Right and white opposition to racial integration of schools in "The Real Origins of the Religious Right," *Politico*, May 27, 2014, http://tinyurl.com/yaelocjb.

birth of the conservative Christian homeschooling movement, which provided a way for evangelicals to reclaim their children's education from "worldly" public schools and simultaneously structure the Christian home in harmony with their gender norms.[82]

While the increasing numbers of evangelical women in the workplace resulted in less strident condemnations of "working women," the basic hierarchical construction of gender roles remained as it had been since the turn of the century. Yet, the packaging and delivery of this vision was quite different than in times past. Evangelicals borrowed heavily from the therapeutic language of self-fulfillment offered by pop psychology and, by and large, women led the way in its proclamation. Elisabeth Elliot, Beverly LaHaye, and Marabel Morgan each published their own handbook on godly womanhood. They made arguments from the Bible, biology, psychology, and even business for the submission of wives to their male "heads." Male headship, they argued, is not only God's design but also the way to a successful and fulfilling life. While affirming the fundamental equality of men and women, these writers marked off the home as a private institution where equality is irrelevant. Differences between men and women were viewed as essential, unchangeable, and translatable into a divinely ordained plan for both. As the years passed, the language of hierarchy would eventually be replaced by the language of complementarity, interdependence, and servant leadership. But, even with the softening of patriarchal language, evangelical literature on womanhood today retains a basic hierarchical relationship between the genders.

Though other figures like James Dobson typically receive more attention,[83] Bill Gothard was an important figure in the 1970s and 80s because he was one of the first evangelical figures to link hierarchical gender norms with homeschooling. During Gothard's heyday, his

---

82. The narrative I have provided thus far, focused as it is upon conservative evangelicals, presents a more-or-less monolithic approach to marriage and gender roles among evangelicals. John Bartkowski warns in *Remaking the Christian Marriage* not to assume that evangelical elites, let alone evangelical laypeople, are entirely united on their approach to manhood and womanhood. In fact, Bartkowski goes so far as to argue that "no consensus about gender and family relations" exists among evangelical elites (163). While I concede the point that evangelical feminists and more egalitarian conservatives have always contested hierarchical approaches to gender norms post-1970, I think a case can still be made for a shared construction of gender roles that is historically rooted in the Victorian bourgeois ideal. Even if the rhetoric is varied, the fundamental structure of the marriage and family, I would argue, remains the same.

83. For example, Gallagher relegates Gothard to one footnote in *Evangelical Identity and Gendered Family Life*, 212n10. Gothard does not feature at all in John Bartkowski's *Remaking the Godly Marriage*.

conferences and seminars drew tens of thousands of people at a time, with three hundred thousand people attending his conferences every year.[84] Gothard offered his conference attendees "universal principles of life" that he promised would lead to success if followed correctly. In Gothard's words, "Every problem in life can be traced to seven non-optional principles found in the Bible. Every person, regardless of culture, background, religion, education, or social status, must follow these principles or experience the consequences of violating them."[85]

Gothard placed heavy emphasis on the "chain of command" in the family: children submitting to parents and wives submitting to husbands. His workbooks came with official-looking diagrams and charts, backed up by the claim that every principle is divinely ordained.[86] Gothard taught that women must be homemakers, focused on supporting their husbands and caring for their children, while fathers should be the breadwinners and spiritual heads of their families. Furthermore, God entrusts children to their parents for education, therefore homeschooling is the only real option for Christians. Gothard also warned against the evils of family planning and instructed married couples to welcome all children as divine gifts.[87] Though his influence has faded considerably since the 1980s, Gothard's interpretation and application of scripture has proved immensely influential in Christian homeschooling circles. As Gaither says, "If the public stereotype of the homeschooling family is that of the firm but gentle patriarch, the Titus 2 mom shrouded in a loose fitting jumper and headcovering, the quiver-full of obedient stairstep children dressed in matching homespun, we have Bill Gothard to thank as much as anyone."[88]

Now, how did evangelical homeschooling come about in the first place? As evangelicals interacted with the American counterculture of the 1960s, they developed what might be called their own "counter-

84. Figure provided by Wilfred Bockelman, *Gothard: The Man and His Ministry* (Santa Barbara, CA: Quill, 1976). See also, Institute in Basic Life Principles, "About IBLP," http://tinyurl.com/yd8q5d95.
85. Gothard, quoted by Gaither, *Homeschool*, 151.
86. Bockelman, *Gothard*, 44.
87. This emphasis on inviolate principles for the family "erased all shades of gray." Under Gothard's teaching, one admirer quipped, "I'm convinced that God did not make gray. When it comes to moral issues, things are black or white" (Bockelman, *Gothard*, 117). And, in the words of one observer, "In an era when general morality is at a low ebb he is providing clues for establishing a clear biblical base for Christian thought and action. What's more, people are convinced it will work" (Bockelman, *Gothard*, 49).
88. Gaither, *Homeschool*, 152.

cultural right."[89] Evangelical churches found cultural unity through alternative institutions that simultaneously mimicked and criticized mainstream culture. These included Christian bookstores, radio and television stations, concerts and festivals, music awards, amusement parks, and summer camps. This parallel Christian culture was separatist even as it was accommodating to American cultural mores, and out of it came the politically active Christian Right. Of course, impulses toward political activism had been present in evangelicalism from early on. But, in those days government was generally perceived to be on their side. Now, as Gaither says, "The enemy had suddenly become their own government."[90]

When the Christian Right got organized, they did so in large part through the home-based activism of evangelical women. While employing antifeminist rhetoric, the homemakers of the Christian Right drew on the strides made in women's liberation to forward their causes through reading groups, women's clubs, voter registration drives, and campaign volunteering. Like their Victorian foremothers, conservative women in the 1970s and 80s sought to preserve the safety and purity of the domestic sphere by acting in the public sphere. Issues like abortion, the Equal Rights Amendment (which was perceived as a threat to the wages of male breadwinners), and education especially motivated evangelical women. As public schools were racially integrated and prayer and Bible reading were outlawed, activist evangelical women also joined together in support of private Christian schools. Such schools proliferated in the 1980s and 90s, with conservative estimates ranging from six to fifteen thousand schools in operation.[91] Though the majority of evangelicals kept their children in public schools (and do so to this day), as a group they no longer took for granted the friendliness of "government schools" to their way of life.

Out of this milieu, homeschooling emerged as a viable option. Though previously associated with leftist liberals, conservatives turned to homeschooling as they encountered a variety of challenges posed by private Christian schools, including high tuition, poor organization, theological differences, and dissatisfaction with meeting individual student needs.[92] By the late 1970s, many evangelicals lived

---

89. See also Schäfer, *Countercultural Conservatives*.
90. Schäfer, *Countercultural Conservatives*, 103.
91. Schäfer, *Countercultural Conservatives*, 109.
92. Schäfer, *Countercultural Conservatives*, 110.

in suburban homes presided over by well-educated stay-at-home moms. Why couldn't these accomplished women who had successfully organized against the Equal Rights Amendment also educate their own children? Many decided they could. And as more and more families chose homeschooling, they began putting their administrative skills to work building networks, cooperatives, and other organizations to support families like them. Out of these efforts, evangelicals birthed a movement.[93]

A few leaders distinguished themselves in the blossoming Christian homeschooling movement. Raymond and Dorothy Moore had a handful of education degrees between them, a lifetime of participation in education reform, and the experience of raising nine children. They were also allies of the liberal-minded homeschooling pioneer, John Holt.[94] Despite the growing conviction among many experts that children should start school at earlier ages, the Moores were convinced that "whenever feasible children should remain longer in the home."[95] Their publications elicited a strong reaction from all sectors, some wholeheartedly agreeing and some denouncing the Moores' research as selective and un-nuanced. Their first book, *Better Late Than Early* (1975), led them to take speaking tours across the country, eventually becoming regular guests on Dr. James Dobson's radio show *Focus on the Family*.[96] Their third book, *Home Grown Kids* (1981), was widely influential in the homeschooling movement because it was a comprehensive childrearing manual that spoke the language of evangelicalism. By 1982, Raymond Moore was the most sought-after homeschooling leader in the country, providing expert testimony on behalf of homeschooling families, speaking before legislatures, and appearing on mainstream TV talk shows like *Oprah* and *Donahue*.[97]

---

93. Schäfer, *Countercultural Conservatives*, 110.

94. John Holt was the earliest proponent of homeschooling whose books *How Children Fail* (New York: Pitman, 1964) and *How Children Learn* (New York: Pitman, 1964) argue that formal, compulsory schooling destroys children's curiosity and prohibits learning. Holt devoted his life to helping underground families who were educating their children at home. The tangible result was a newsletter, *Growing Without Schooling*, which served as the beginning of the first homeschool network. Holt became the de facto leader of the homeschool movement, and he spent a lot of his own money traveling the country speaking, witnessing in court, and demonstrating on behalf of homeschooling families. Eventually he became an ally of Raymond and Dorothy Moore (Gaither, *Homeschool*, 123; Stevens, *Kingdom of Children*, 35).

95. Raymond Moore, quoted by Gaither, *Homeschool*, 130.

96. Gaither, *Homeschool*, 132.

97. Gaither, *Homeschool*, 133. See another summation of the roots of the homeschooling movement in Murphy, *Homeschooling in America*, 30–37.

At first the homeschooling movement featured warm cooperation between leftists and conservatives, but that faded away as conservative Christian homeschoolers began to dominate both local networks and national organizations.[98] This dominance was fueled, in part, by the ideological influence of R. J. Rushdoony. Rushdoony was a conservative minister in the Orthodox Presbyterian Church. Drawing on the work of Dutch Calvinist philosopher Cornelius Van Til, Rushdoony was convinced that the presupposition that the Bible is the inspired word of God forms the basis for all rational thinking. The Bible, therefore, should be the basis for all of human life—the divine template for government, schooling, family, agriculture, and more. Rushdoony founded a theological think tank, the Chalcedon Foundation, in 1965, and published his magnum opus, *The Institutes of Biblical Law*, in 1973. *The Institutes* promoted a whole-cloth vision for Christian reconstructionism: a plan for reconstructing society and culture in light of Christian presuppositions drawn directly from scripture.[99] And in *The Messianic Character of American Education* (1963), he asserted the biblical rationale for home education in uncompromising terms. For this reason, Rushdoony was regularly called upon by homeschoolers as an expert witness, conference speaker, and educational advisor. Rushdoony also promoted what he called a *providentialist* interpretation of history, which sees history "not as a narrative of human actions but as a revelation of God's sovereign will."[100] Within this framework, Rushdoony was one of the best promoters of the idea that America was a Christian nation until its recent descent into secularism.

Though Rushdoony's full-scale Christian reconstructionism never gained a large following among evangelicals (most evangelicals do not even know his name), his impact on the conservative wing of the homeschooling movement cannot be exaggerated. His writings gave the evangelical homeschooling movement "both a strong sense of opposition between God's law and human laws and a tendency to

---

98. For more about the ideological differences between left-leaning liberals and right-leaning evangelicals, see Stevens, *Kingdom of Children*, 34–41.

99. Worthen, *Apostles of Reason*, 226. Reconstructionism is also known as *theonomy*, which emphasizes the rule of God's law, drawn from scripture, in all areas of human life. For a thorough discussion of reconstructionism in America, especially the theology of R. J. Rushdoony, see Julie Ingersoll, *Building God's Kingdom: Inside the World of Christian Reconstruction* (Oxford: Oxford University Press, 2015). See also Michael J. McVicar, *Christian Reconstruction: R.J. Rushdoony and American Religious Conservatism* (Chapel Hill: University of North Carolina Press, 2015).

100. Gaither, *Homeschool*, 135.

think of itself as a divinely guided instrument in restoring a Christian America."[101] In other words, if the Moores provided evangelicals with a rationale for homeschooling, then Rushdoony provided evangelicals with a metanarrative and *telos*—a motivating vision of what their work in the home could accomplish on a grand scale. As a result, by the 1990s, American homeschooling was starkly divided between what Mitchell Stevens calls "inclusives" (inclusive homeschoolers from all religious and political perspectives) and "believers" (separatist evangelical Christians).[102] Today anywhere from 65 to 90 percent of homeschooling families are Christian.[103]

While leaders like the Moores and Rushdoony have been important, the evangelical homeschooling movement is sustained by people, organizations, networks, publishers, and merchants, all of which provide a shared culture and sense of identity. At the ground level, homeschooling happens through the work of women who have "jumped headfirst into an elaborate domesticity."[104] Homeschooling mothers often cooperate with a variety of local and regional networks, which pool resources and students for shared classes, social activities, field trips, sports, and more. Mothers also make use of a dizzying range of homeschooling curricula offered by both mainstream and Christian publishers. These mothers often pay for "legal insurance" through the Home School Legal Defense Association (HSLDA), an organization that led the way in getting homeschooling legalized in the United States and, through its aggressive lobbying efforts, has been key in liberalizing homeschooling laws ever since. Moreover, homeschooling mothers often participate in regional and national conferences, which feature notable speakers, offer an array of products and services, and provide the chance to visit with other homeschooling families. Finally, homeschooling mothers often interact with other mothers on the internet through blogs and other online forums, from which they glean ideas, help, encouragement, and support for their work. In all these ways, homeschooling as a religious practice, both now and in its beginnings, is shaped and supported in evangelical Christian homes under the leadership of mothers. Through homeschooling, the evangelical Christian mother could fully embody the Beecher sisters' vision, creating "a small

101. Gaither, *Homeschool*, 137.
102. Stevens, *Kingdom of Children*, 18–19.
103. Murphy, *Homeschooling*, 23.
104. Stevens, *Kingdom of Children*, 16.

church, a school-house, and a comfortable family dwelling" all in one private home.

EVANGELICALS, CONTRACEPTION, AND THE EMERGENCE OF QUIVERFULL

In the midst of the Christian homeschooling movement, some were also rethinking evangelical support for birth control.[105] Prior to the twentieth century, Protestants expressed a variety of views on the subject of fertility regulation. But most leaders agreed with the Catholic Church that artificial birth control was forbidden. Then, in 1930, Anglican clergy decided at their Lambeth Conference to affirm the use of artificial birth control within the confines of marriage. Shortly thereafter many other Protestant denominations followed suit.[106] Even the most conservative groups, such as the Lutheran Church Missouri Synod, underwent a shift in perspective leading to a near-universal acceptance of family planning among Protestants by the mid-1960s.[107]

Still, a few evangelicals took anti-contraception stances between 1965 and 1980. R. J. Rushdoony and Gary North wrote in favor of pronatalism in 1974 and 1982, respectively.[108] Later, anti-contraception and pronatalist ideology was given wider support through the work of Mary Pride in *The Way Home* (1985), Charles Provan in *The Bible and Birth Control* (1989), and Rick and Jan Hess in *A Full*

---

105. Other scholars have told the story of American Protestants and contraception in a detailed way, and I will not seek to replicate their efforts here. See, for example, Michael Koon Hung Cheuk, "Contraception within Marriage: Modernity and the Development of American Protestant Thought, 1930-1969" (PhD diss., University of Virginia, 2004). Also, Norman St. John-Stevas, *The Agonising Choice: Birth Control, Religion and the Law* (Bloomington: Indiana University Press, 1971).

106. Others included the UK Methodists in 1939, the US Methodists in 1956, the Church of Scotland in 1944, and the Dutch Reformed Church in 1952 (McKeown, "U.S. Protestant Reception," 34).

107. This shift is documented by Alan Graebner, "Birth Control and the Lutherans: The Missouri Synod as a Case Study," *Journal of Social History* 2, no. 4 (Summer 1969): 303–32. A good indication of the new consensus was a 1965 symposium sponsored by *Christianity Today* and the Christian Medical Society that produced a "Protestant Affirmation on the Control of Human Reproduction" offering evangelical support for family planning. See Walter O. Spitzer and Carlyle L. Saylor, eds., *Birth Control and the Christian: A Protestant Symposium on the Control of Human Reproduction* (Wheaton, IL: Tyndale House, 1968); McKeown, "U.S. Protestant Reception," 34.

108. Rushdoony and North were more pronatalist than anti-contraception. See, for example, R. J. Rushdoony, *The Myth of Over-Population* (Fairfax, VA: Thornburn, 1974); and Gary North, *The Dominion Covenant: Genesis* (Tyler, TX: Institute for Christian Economics, 1987).

Quiver (1996).[109] Then, *Christianity Today*, which just twenty-three years earlier had published a consensus statement in favor of birth control, offered a cover story in 1991 framing birth control as a matter of serious debate.[110] In the years that followed the *CT* cover story, Christian publishers offered numerous books questioning or denying outright the ethical legitimacy of family planning.[111]

There were significant cultural factors that precipitated this shift. As stated above, American evangelicals had participated in the countercultural movements of the 1960s. Interestingly, both feminists and cultural conservatives called into question the safety and efficacy of the Pill.[112] Then, *Roe v. Wade* was decided in 1973, determining that the right to privacy under the Fourteenth Amendment extends to a woman's choice to have an abortion. Though not immediately a lightning rod among religious conservatives, eventually the Religious Right used abortion as a wedge issue to rally support for the Republican Party. Most evangelical writers who have opposed contraceptives since *Roe v. Wade* intentionally link the practice of contraception and abortion, describing the difference between them as one of degree only.

---

109. See also Joe Morecraft III, who drew on Rushdoony to promote pronatalism among Reformed, homeschooling evangelicals in the late-1980s. Joseph Morecraft, III, "The Bible on Large Families," *The Counsel of Chalcedon* 11, no. 8 (October 1989): 9–10.

110. Patricia Goodson, "Protestants and Family Planning," *Journal of Religion and Health* 36, no. 4 (Winter 1997): 357.

111. See, for example, Samuel A. Owen, *Letting God Plan Your Family* (Wheaton, IL: Crossway, 1990); Randy Alcorn, *Does the Birth Control Pill Cause Abortions?* (Sandy, OR: Eternal Perspective Ministries, 1997); Sam and Bethany Torode, *Open Embrace: A Protestant Couple Rethinks Contraception* (Grand Rapids: Eerdmans, 2002); and Steve and Candice Watters, *Start Your Family: Inspiration for Having Babies* (Chicago: Moody, 2009). Certainly, an anti-contraception ideology does not necessarily lead to pronatalism. Some Catholic families eschew artificial birth control while still choosing to space and limit the number of children they have using other methods. For his part, John McKeown distinguishes between pronatalism (which he defines as the pursuit of an unlimited number of children) and natalism (which he defines as pursuing a more-than-average number of children but still limited). See John McKeown, "U.S. Protestant Natalist Reception of Old Testament Fruitful Verses" (PhD diss., University of Liverpool, 2011), 16. McKeown is building upon the categorization offered by Daniel Doriani, "Birth Dearth or Bring on the Babies? Biblical Perspectives on Family Planning," *Journal of Biblical Counseling* 12, no. 1 (Fall 1993): 24–35.

112. Elaine Tyler May, *America and the Pill: A History of Promise, Peril, and Liberation* (New York: Basic Books, 2011). For example, the Boston Women's Health Book Collective, which published the groundbreaking book *Our Body, Ourselves* (OBOS), offered a very skeptical perspective on the Pill in its 1973 edition due to concerns about side effects and risks of use. The 1984 edition was openly critical of the Pill for the same reasons. By 1998, OBOS no longer supported use of the Pill. But, in the 2005 edition, OBOS reverted back to a full support of the Pill due to the resolution of their concerns about its safety for women (May, *America and the Pill*, 134–36).

One such evangelical writer was Mary Pride, an early leader of the Christian homeschooling movement. "Family planning is the mother of abortion," Pride says:

> A generation had to be indoctrinated in the ideal of planning children around personal convenience before abortion could become popular. We Christians raise an outcry against abortion today, and rightly so. But the *reason we have to fight those battles today is because we lost them thirty years ago*. Once couples began to look upon children as creatures of their own making, whom they could plan into their lives as they chose or not, all reverence for human life was lost.[113]

Mary Pride's anti-contraception, pronatalist message was so important in the late 1980s and early 1990s that she is often called the mother of the Quiverfull movement.[114] Many in the Quiverfull movement speak of Pride's first book, *The Way Home: Beyond Feminism, Back to Reality*, as the catalyst for their way of life. Though over twenty-five years old, the book continues to inspire and motivate women today.[115]

In *The Way Home*, Pride describes feminism as a selfish, power-hungry, man-hating, baby-killing, child-resenting, androgyny-promoting, monolithic, and totalitarian movement that Christians must oppose at all costs.[116] What she offers instead is what she calls a "whole cloth alternative" to feminism: a life characterized by wifely submission, prolific childbearing, homeschooling, and homeworking. In response to the vast numbers of evangelical women who chose employment beyond the home in the 1960s, 70s, and 80s, Pride

---

113. Pride, *The Way Home*, 77 (emphasis in original).

114. It is somewhat anachronistic to call *Quiverfull* what Pride advocates in *The Way Home*, because the movement did not yet have any perceivable unity or bear any particular name when she was writing in the 1980s. But, Pride became the symbolic standard bearer for most Quiverfull adherents in the years to follow.

115. Pride's name still shows up regularly on social networking websites and blogs as an influential exemplar and motherhood "guru" of sorts. A selection of her other books includes the following: *The Way Home* (Wheaton, IL: Crossway, 1985), *The Big Book of Home Learning* (Wheaton, IL: Crossway, 1986), *The Next Big Book of Home Learning* (Wheaton, IL: Crossway, 1987), *The New Big Book of Home Learning* (Wheaton, IL: Crossway, 1988), *All the Way Home* (Wheaton, IL: Crossway, 1989), *Schoolproof* (Wheaton, IL: Crossway, 1988), *The Big Book of Home Learning: Getting Started, Preschool & Elementary, Junior High Through College*, vol. 1–3 (Chandler, AZ: Alpha Omega, 1999); *Mary Pride's Complete Guide to Getting Started in Homeschooling* (Eugene, OR: Harvest House, 2004). *Practical Homeschooling* can be found at http://www.practicalhomeschooling.com.

116. Pride says flatly, "Feminism is a totally self-consistent system aimed at rejecting God's role for women" (*The Way Home*, xii).

calls women back to the domestic sphere in an entirely home-centered lifestyle. And, in contrast to the therapeutic language of self-fulfillment that had proliferated in evangelical marriage manuals to that point, Pride offers a vision of marriage focused primarily on the production of godly offspring.

Pride's vision of home life, however, goes beyond a throwback to Victorian-era ideals discussed above. Instead, she seems to be trying to resurrect the pre-industrial home of the Jeffersonian yeoman farmer, where the wife's work in the home entails both reproduction and production—making babies and making goods. Long before the rise of Etsy and crafty mommy blogs, Pride's book was a DIY manifesto for the Christian woman that offered an inspiring picture of creative housewifery that defied the portraits of bored 1950s suburban housewives.[117] A good Christian woman, she argued, has as many babies as God gives her, educates all of them herself, and works in the home to benefit her husband and family.[118]

In 1985, Pride's aggressive promotion of wifely submission and "homeworking" (which includes homeschooling) was familiar to her evangelical audience. What made Pride's message revolutionary was her denunciation of all forms of family planning. If every child is a blessing, why would Christian couples seek to stop or limit such blessings?[119] "Childbearing sums up all our special biological and domestic functions," Pride says. "Having babies and raising them is our role, and we show we belong to God by persevering in it."[120]

The Christian homeschooling movement was an ideal network for spreading this anti-contraception, pronatalist message. At once countercultural and anti-establishment, many in the homeschooling movement were able to combine their political opposition to abortion rights and fierce sense of familial independence with the practice

---

117. There's an interesting parallel between some of Pride's ideas about domesticity and the so-called "new domesticity" movement. Emily Matchar, among others, thinks there has been a resurgence of the so-called domestic arts in American culture over the past few decades. Under the label *new domesticity*, Matchar includes gardening, the production of homemade goods, attachment parenting and extended breastfeeding, mommy-blogging, and the attempt to make money for the household based upon the mother's productive work in the home. The new domesticity phenomenon is fueled primarily by the internet, both through websites like Etsy, where women can sell their products, and through domesticity blogs, which are overwhelmingly frequented by women. Many women committed to the Quiverfull way of life also participate in this revival of domestic practices. See further, Emily Matchar, *Homeward Bound: Why Women Are Embracing the New Domesticity* (New York: Simon & Schuster, 2013).

118. Pride, *The Way Home*, xiii.
119. Pride, *The Way Home*, 57.
120. Pride, *The Way Home*, 43.

of pronatalism. In a world they perceived to be under attack by feminists and secular humanists, what better form of countercultural rebellion than militant fecundity? While the Religious Right was mobilizing voters to win the "culture war" at the ballot box, pronatalist homeschoolers were committing themselves to a strategy of long-term, family-driven demographic triumph. Eventually, families who eschewed family planning and practiced gender hierarchy and homeschooling would come to be called "Quiverfull," based upon their obedience to the "principle" of Psalm 127:4–5. It is to a more intensive consideration of Quiverfull discourse and subculture that we now turn.

QUIVERFULL IN CULTURAL PERSPECTIVE

There are many lenses through which one might examine the Quiverfull movement, but I find two especially helpful. In what follows I analyze Quiverfull as a three-part discourse and a subculture of evangelicalism.

QUIVERFULL AS A THREE-PART DISCOURSE

The first conceptual lens through which to view the Quiverfull movement is to see it as a discourse with three key practices: homeschooling, gender hierarchy, and pronatalism.[121] In this context, discourse means "systems of thought composed of ideas, attitudes, courses of action, beliefs and practices that systematically construct the subjects and the worlds of which they speak."[122] In this sense, discourse means more than simply written and spoken communication or a way of thinking, but also includes bodily activities, rituals, materials, and places where these things come together, all of

---

121. There is some overlap between discourse and the concept of lived religion. I could just as easily say that the term *Quiverfull* refers to families whose lived religion takes on a particular shape. The term *lived religion* refers to the way a particular people practices their religion in everyday life. Like discourse, lived religion entails not just beliefs and texts, but also the rituals, experiences, relationships, and things that make up a people's religious life. (See Robert Orsi, *The Madonna of 115th Street* [New Haven: Yale University Press, 2002], xxxvii.) For more on the study of American religion in terms of practices, see David D. Hall, ed., *Lived Religion in America: Toward a History of Practice* (Princeton: Princeton University Press, 1997).

122. Michel Foucault, *The Archeology of Knowledge*, trans. A. M. Sheridan Smith (New York: Pantheon, 1982); and Iara Lessa, "Discursive Struggles within Social Welfare: Restaging Teen Motherhood," *British Journal of Social Work* 36, no. 2 (2006): 283–98.

which contribute toward a particular construction of subjects and the world of which they speak and in which they act. Thus, the Quiverfull discourse constitutes not only the content of their published materials and sermons but also the institutions, actions, practices, and objects of material culture that make up their day-to-day life. As Mary McClintock Fulkerson says, "Discourse encompasses any signifying or meaning-making element," and must take into consideration both the signs of language and the "situations of utterance."[123]

Moreover, discourse is not something static and monolithic. Because discourse is more than ideas and beliefs located in the mind, but also daily practices and materials—including "small details" and "subtle arrangements"—Quiverfull discourse must be thought of as constantly emerging through a process of negotiation and conflict.[124] Though I am seeking to make the Quiverfull discourse intelligible to outsiders, which implies the expectation of overall coherence, we must be careful not to assume that there *must* be some internal logic. Furthermore, for Foucault, discourses are "marked by ruptures, lacunae, and incoherences."[125] This means not only can we expect discourses to be contested and internally inconsistent but also that beliefs and practices often work themselves out in unpredictable ways.

For example, Quiverfull families subscribe to male headship (based upon their interpretation of Eph 5:23) such that men are the "spiritual leaders" of their homes. For most families in practice, however, the husband's job requires them to work outside the home for the majority of every weekday (and sometimes on weekends). Due to the husband's physical absence from the home, much of the domestic administration and decision-making is entrusted to the wife. And, within the practice of homeschooling, the daily education of the children is entrusted to the mother. While rhetorically subscribing to

---

123. Mary McClintock Fulkerson, *Changing the Subject: Women's Discourses and Feminist Theology* (Minneapolis: Fortress Press, 1994), 77. Thus Fulkerson is right to say, "The turn to discourse is not idealist in the sense of denying the existence of reality outside of minds; it is, in fact, materialist. The differences that construct signification are widened to include the discourses of a mode of production, the processes of the democratic state and the 'ideological' discursive processes of the culture" (93). Fulkerson is speaking of the construction of woman as a subject, but I think her point applies to my project as well. While I will not be able to be as thorough in my analysis of the women and families of Quiverfull, I hope to be mindful of the wider discourses Fulkerson mentions that come to bear in real ways upon the Quiverfull discourse.

124. Julie Ingersoll, *Evangelical Christian Women: War Stories in the Gender Battle*, Qualitative Studies in Religion Series (New York: New York University Press, 2003), 109–25.

125. Vincent J. Miller, "History or Geography? Gadamer, Foucault, and Theologies of Tradition," in *Theology and the New Histories*, ed. Gary Macy (Maryknoll, NY: Orbis, 1998), 69.

male headship, much of the administration in the home is carried out by the wife and mother. In many cases, therefore, the discourse of gender hierarchy is "ruptured" and works itself out in the home in a way that is unpredictable and incoherent.[126]

All this is to say, Quiverfull discourse must not be assumed to be a consistent whole. Even in the appearance of widespread agreement among practitioners, there will exist shades of conflicting meaning that challenge prevailing ideas and practices. As theologian Kathryn Tanner has pointed out, unity will be found not in widespread agreement, but common engagement with particular practices as reference points for making sense of their way of life. That is, while Quiverfull adherents may use a shared idea to support their practice (i.e., all children are gifts from God), they do not necessarily agree as to the exact meaning and implications of the idea to which they appeal.[127] To miss these shades of difference among Quiverfull families is to misunderstand and do violence to the complexity of their way of life.[128]

Quiverfull families, therefore, are participants in an always-contested discourse of three parts: homeschooling, gender hierarchy, and pronatalism. For Quiverfull families on the ground, the practice of homeschooling is the primary practice by which the family's daily life is ordered. And the Quiverfull couple's militant fecundity has a consistent goal: the rearing of godly Christian children who will carry on the faith and transform society in the centuries to come.[129]

---

126. To be fair, Quiverfull families would not agree that the abovementioned scenario constitutes incoherence. Instead, they would most likely assert that the husband delegates to the wife her authority in administrative and educational work. For homeschooling mothers, this often works out in such a way that the wife calls herself the "teacher" while their husband is the "principal" (Monica Smatlak Liao, "Keeping Home: Homeschooling and the Practice of Conservative Protestant Identity" [PhD diss., Vanderbilt University, 2006], 214–20). Deborah Olson calls herself "the captain" of the ship and her husband "the owner" of the ship. This way of accounting for the apparent contradiction between male headship and a female-led home suggests some Quiverfull families are aware of the tensions in their discourse and have come up with conceptual strategies to address them. We will discuss this phenomenon in more detail in chapters 2 and 3.

127. Kathryn Tanner, *Theories of Culture: A New Agenda for Theology*, Guides to Theological Inquiry (Minneapolis: Fortress Press, 1997), 38–58.

128. This draws on Tanner's notion of theology as "a part of some specific, communally shaped way of life" (*Theories of Culture*, 67), as well as Fulkerson's discussion of "place" as a "kind of gathering," where elements "converge to create some kind of unified reality" (*Places of Redemption: Theology for a Worldly Church* [Oxford: Oxford University Press, 2007], 28).

129. I first encountered the phrase *militant fecundity* in David Bentley Hart's essay, "Freedom and Decency" (*First Things*, June 2004), which is quoted by Joyce, *Quiverfull*, 179. Hart speaks of *militant fecundity* as a means of winning cultural battles. As an Orthodox theologian, Hart is not a member of the Quiverfull movement, even if he is promoting pronatalism as a Christian practice.

Christian homeschooling is the primary means by which this training is carried out. So, while there are many homeschooling families that are not Quiverfull, there is no such thing as a Quiverfull family that does not homeschool.[130]

The practices of homeschooling and gender hierarchy are tightly connected within Quiverfull. Stevens has observed that gender dualism is both ubiquitous and central to the Christian homeschooling movement. He contends, "It is conservative Protestants' deep commitment to fulltime motherhood that has made them such a ready audience for home education."[131] Quiverfull gender ideology can be characterized as *patriarchy*, *gender hierarchy*, *gender dualism*, or, simply, *male headship*.[132] All of these phrases assume the biblically rooted belief in male headship (Eph 5:23), which posits a general principle of male rule in all areas of life. The principle of male rule is derived primarily from the second creation narrative (Genesis 2), which is understood to teach both gender-based roles and a dualism of gendered spheres. Within the home, the discourse of gender hierarchy is performed in a variety of ways. For some, the husband/father plans and leads daily "family worship," in which he enacts the role of "spiritual leader" by leading his family in Bible teaching and prayer. For others, male headship is enacted through the husband's control over the family finances (dispensing money to his wife as she needs it) and the planning of major investments and purchases. For others, male head-

---

130. Blogger and adult Quiverfull daughter Libby Anne, of *Love, Joy, Feminism*, confirms my interpretation in her post "Christian Patriarchy/Quiverfull": "Christian Patriarchy/Quiverfull is made up of a loosely connected group of organizations that promote extremely strict gender differences, submission to the family patriarch, and raising up armies of children for Christ."

131. Stevens, *Kingdom of Children*, 187.

132. The logic of Quiverfull gender hierarchy holds because of its harmony with the gender dualism of the subculture (and the evangelical subculture with which they are intimately related). Gender dualism is distinct from gender hierarchy in that it refers to a fundamental dichotomy between male and female, masculine and feminine. As people, men and women are perceived as fundamentally different in every way: mentally, emotionally, biologically, and spiritually. We can see this sharp divide expressed in the language of some families, as well as the language of their sex and marriage manuals. Gender dualism is supported by the cultural institutions of evangelicalism, everything from the arrangement of evangelical bookstores (with designated men's and women's sections) to the organization of church programs (with sex-specific events, classes, and conferences). These essential differences are also understood to undergird a dualism of spheres. Men and women who transgress these distinct spheres are viewed as anomalous and working against the essential differences between the sexes. Thus, gender dualism is a key part of the "sacred canopy" of the Quiverfull movement. See, for example, the findings of Brenda Brasher in *Godly Women: Fundamentalism and Female Power* (New Brunswick, NJ: Rutgers University Press, 1997). The language of "sacred canopy" originates with Peter Berger, *The Sacred Canopy: Elements of a Sociological Theory of Religion* (New York: Anchor, 1990).

ship is performed as the wife styles her hair, makeup, and clothes in the way that her husband prefers.

Pronatalism describes the Quiverfull rejection of birth control and desire to have as many children as God chooses to give. As I said in the introduction, pronatalism has active and passive aspects. On the one hand, Quiverfull wives reject the Pill, condoms, and other forms of birth control in order to, in their terms, leave control of their fertility to God. In this sense, pronatalism is about what a couple is *not* doing. On the other hand, the choice to have sex during the fertile times in a woman's cycle might be called active pronatalism because it moves beyond merely not preventing pregnancy to actively pursuing it. The active and passive aspects of Quiverfull pronatalism will vary depending on the couple and fluctuate based upon a variety of circumstances in the family's life. No matter how the practice takes shape, however, two convictions are constant: (1) the belief that God is in direct control of conception; and (2) the belief that all children are an unqualified blessing or gift from God.

Some, though not all, families have as the goal of their pronatalism the production of "arrows for the war" over American culture.[133] Among many Quiverfull couples, the activist impulse inherent to evangelical Christianity works itself out in a transformative goal for their pronatalist practice. For these couples, it's not simply about having many children for their own sake, but also for the sake of spurring a massive demographic shift over the next few hundred years. The reasoning is, if the average American family has two children while Quiverfull families have six, and this discrepancy continues for another couple of centuries, then a substantial demographic transformation will occur, thereby "Christianizing" American culture.

As I have said, these three practices—homeschooling, gender hierarchy, and pronatalism—can be conceived as circles in a Venn diagram, so that it is at the center where the circles converge that the Quiverfull discourse is located.[134] This is keeping in mind, however,

---

133. Kathryn Joyce, "The Quiverfull Conviction: Christian Mothers Breed 'Arrows for the War,'" *The Nation*, November 27, 2006, 11–18. Although it draws on biblical themes, the phrase "arrows for the war" seems to have originated with Nancy Campbell in her book *Be Fruitful and Multiply: What the Bible Says about Having Children* (San Antonio, TX: Vision Forum, 2003).

134. I acknowledge that this conception remains dialogic: something that is always emerging and a matter of debate. Nowhere is the dialogic nature of Quiverfull discourse more readily apparent than in Quiverfull online forums, where the question of who is and is not properly called *Quiverfull* is always being debated.

that Quiverfull discourse refers not only to these practices but also to bodily activities, rituals, material things, and the places where the discourse is performed. Because Quiverfull discourse is performed and constantly emerging through negotiation and conflict, I do not assume there will be some inner logic, but expect things to shake out in unexpected ways.[135]

Supporting and informing the three-part discourse of the Quiverfull movement is a particular practice of Bible reading. The vast majority of Quiverfull families persist in their practice of "family unplanning" because they are convinced that the Bible speaks clearly on the matter of children and forbids any attempt to control conception.[136] When one desperate mother of six wrote into the *Quiverfull Digest* online forum looking for a reason besides the Bible why one should "be Quiverfull," one couple responded: "If you don't invoke God's word, there's really no reason. Kids are great and all that, but in reality, it's all about the Bible."[137] Though there are a number of ways one could characterize the Quiverfull approach to scripture, *biblical literalism* seems best for our purposes. Put simply, Quiverfull teachers believe the Bible is literally God's word to humankind and, as a divine document, contains a straightforward, propositional account of God's will for all areas of life. Thus, the precepts found in the Bible are literally true for all people in all times and places.[138]

Based upon their view of scripture, the majority of Quiverfull practitioners utilize a way of interpreting the Bible that seeks the "plain meaning" of the text and an immediate, propositional application to the present day. In this method of interpretation, a number of things work together. First, scripture is read as a unified document

---

135. Ingersoll, *Evangelical Christian Women*, 109.
136. This phrase is borrowed from Craig Houghton, *Family UNplanning: A Guide for Christian Couples Seeking God's Truth on Having Children* (Maitland, FL: Xulon, 2007).
137. Quoted by Joyce, *Quiverfull*, 169.
138. The biblical literalism of the Quiverfull subculture is grounded in a theological concept often called "verbal plenary inspiration." This view of biblical inspiration is based upon 2 Tim 3:16–17, which asserts: "All Scripture is God-breathed and is useful for teaching, rebuking, correcting and training in righteousness, so that the servant of God may be thoroughly equipped for every good work." The Greek word in 2 Tim 3:16 that describes "all scripture" is *theopneustos*, often translated "inspired." But, *theopneustos* literally means "God-breathed" and this leads Quiverfull proponents, along with most evangelicals, to assert that God is the author of every single word of scripture. Moreover, the rest of 2 Tim 3:16–17 suggests the "man of God" is fully prepared "for every good work" through the training in scripture alone. In this way, 2 Tim 3:16–17 becomes the source both of the Quiverfull commitment to biblical literalism and their prioritizing of biblical teaching far above that of knowledge acquired through other disciplines.

with God as the author. They would not deny that God used human authors to write scripture, but they so emphasize God's sovereignty in the process of inspiration that the human author is superfluous. Because the Bible is a unified document with a single divine voice, equal weight is given to the Old and New Testaments because the same voice speaks directly in both.[139] Any apparent tension between the testaments, therefore, must be harmonized. Finally, because God is the author of scripture, there is skepticism regarding interpretations that would take into account the social and cultural context of a passage. Such a move implies that God's commands are changeable according to the shifting patterns of culture. Thus in almost all cases, preference is given to the most simplified, applicable interpretation of a given text. And, in cases where the presumed plain meaning of scripture is contradicted by the findings of any other discipline (i.e., science, history, archeology, etc.), the Bible is upheld as true and the outside evidence is downplayed or dismissed.[140]

Now, many evangelicals in the United States could be classified as biblical literalists in the way I have described above.[141] The vast majority of evangelicals hold to some version of biblical inerrancy and would endorse the "plain meaning" of the biblical text as the primary goal of interpretation. Most American evangelicals, therefore, would say with the Quiverfull couple cited above that it's "all about the Bible." Even so, among the majority of evangelicals one will not

---

139. The presupposition that the voice of God is unchangeable in the Old and New Testaments is grounded in the theological presupposition of an immutable or unchangeable God: "Jesus Christ is the same yesterday, today, and forever" (Heb 13:8).

140. The evangelical emphasis on the "plain meaning" of the biblical text is important. George Marsden has shown that since its earliest days, Protestant fundamentalism has emphasized the unified nature of "God's truth" revealed in the Bible and the capability of all persons with "common sense" to know the truth. These emphases had been at work within Protestantism since the time of the Reformation, but it was the philosophers of Scottish Common Sense Realism that expounded the consequences of these presuppositions. Common Sense Realism relies on the inductive scientific method of Francis Bacon to give solid metaphysical content to commonsense premises—those things that are known through careful, objective observation. Thus, the external world is in fact just as it appears to be and there exists an objective, empirical basis for Truth. Very often, the perspicuity of nature was correlated with the perspicuity of the Bible—both were supposed to be approached with scientific objectivity (George Marsden, *Fundamentalism and American Culture*, new ed. [New York: Oxford University Press, 2006], 14–16). By the time Protestant fundamentalism became self-aware in the 1920s, Common Sense Realism had been the predominant American philosophy for over a century. Moreover, the emphasis on careful observation, the classification of facts, and the "common sense of mankind," has led to the dominance of biblical literalism among the descendants of Protestant fundamentalists like the Quiverfull movement.

141. Vincent Crapanzano, *Serving the Word: Literalism in America from the Pulpit to the Bench* (New York: New Press, 2000).

find birth control forbidden. In fact, one will often see contraception defended, even as they oppose abortion with tenacity.[142] Though they share the biblical literalism of Quiverfull, evangelicals generally do not take it as far in the matter of birth control.

Unlike their evangelical neighbors, therefore, Quiverfull practitioners (following R. J. Rushdoony) approach scripture as a unified blueprint for all aspects of life. From the operations of the family, to the education of children, to the machinations of national government, the Bible as a whole is thought to contain God's direct orders for how everything should be carried out. Doug Phillips is probably the most eloquent Quiverfull teacher in this regard, saying,

> Christians are not to look to popular wisdom, the opinions of secular authorities, or personal emotions to resolve ethical issues, because the Bible is a *complete and sufficient guide for all of faith and practice* . . . the Holy Scripture is a unity which reflects the unchanging righteousness of God and communicates His unchanging character and the perfect harmony of those principles which undergird His law as expressed in both the Old and New Testament dispensations.[143]

Thus, the biblical literalism of Quiverfull discourse includes a presupposition that all of scripture, regardless of genre or cultural context, speaks with unified and equally binding authority on all matters of human life.

QUIVERFULL AS A SUBCULTURE

In addition to being a three-part discourse, Quiverfull may also be understood as a subculture of evangelicalism. Scholars of American religion often speak of evangelicalism as a subculture, so it is a small step to envision Quiverfull as a subculture of evangelicalism

---

142. If Quiverfull proponents and evangelical Protestants both believe essentially the same things about the Bible, and often utilize similar methods of biblical interpretation, then where does the divergence in regard to birth control come from? The most direct answer is that both groups share the unacknowledged tendency to pick and choose those aspects of the Bible to interpret and apply literally. Even though Quiverfull families and evangelical Protestants affirm a commitment to biblical inspiration and biblical literalism, both groups are inevitably inconsistent in the way these commitments work out in biblical interpretation. In the matter of contraception and family planning, Quiverfull adherents take literally and apply universally passages of scripture that the wider evangelical population does not.

143. Douglas Phillips, "A Declaration of Life," Vision Forum Ministries, http://tinyurl.com/ycnfw4g9 (emphasis mine).

that has developed within the Christian homeschooling movement.[144] According to Christian Smith, subcultures are social groups with a collective identity maintained through the establishment of symbolic boundaries, which help create a sense of "us" in opposition to a perceived "them." Smith elaborates:

> Identity distinctions are always created through the use of socially constructed symbolic markers that establish group boundaries. It is through languages, rituals, artifacts, creeds, practices, narratives—in short, the stuff of human cultural production—that social groups construct their sense of self and difference from others.[145]

Yet, this collective identity is not static because the boundaries between "us" and "them" also serve as frontiers for activity and engagement.[146] That is to say, the boundaries of a subculture are porous and always serve as sites of negotiation with outsiders. This ongoing give-and-take between the subculture and the surrounding culture(s) also means that subcultural boundaries are not static, but constantly emerging. In Smith's words,

> Every group's sense of self is always the product, not of the essential nature of things, but of active, continuing identity-work. . . . That is, collective identity is always an ongoing *social achievement*, accomplished through processes of social interaction, in which identity-signifying symbols are collectively generated, displayed, recognized, affirmed, and employed to mark differences between insiders and outsiders.[147]

Thus, a subculture is necessarily relational, created through an interdependent relationship with a variety of "others," and always being performed. It is in this sense that Quiverfull families are a subculture of evangelicalism. By engaging in particular practices, both individually and collectively, they draw symbolic boundaries and form distinctions between themselves and other out-groups.

Typically, this boundary drawing is not the focus of Quiverfull cultural action, but it is a consequence of their chosen way of life. As I have shown, Quiverfull families have larger-than-normal families, school their children at home, rely on the father's income alone for

---

144. The body of sociological research concerning the nature, scope, and composition of subcultures is broad and deep and I will not attempt to summarize all of it here.
145. Smith, *American Evangelicalism*, 92.
146. Thanks to Vincent Miller for calling attention to this dynamic.
147. Smith, *American Evangelicalism*, 92.

financial support, and construe gender roles in a hierarchical fashion. They advocate for, defend, and support one another in these practices through social media, blogs, internet forums, books, and magazines. Discussions on Quiverfull blogs, forums, and chat rooms reveal that most of these families consider themselves part of a collective group that is to be differentiated from broader evangelicalism and American society. Any of the above characteristics taken individually would not necessarily entail the creation of a distinct subculture, certainly not one that differs markedly from American evangelicalism.[148] But viewed together, these characteristics make up a readily distinguishable subculture.

Smith's subcultural identity theory of religious strength, referenced briefly above, says, "In a pluralistic society, those religious groups will be relatively stronger which better possess and employ the cultural tools needed to create both clear distinction from and significant engagement and tension with other relevant out-groups, short of becoming genuinely countercultural."[149] By this definition, it is clear that Quiverfull families, like other evangelicals, view themselves as "embattled." There are multiple ways that evangelicals see themselves as "embattled," and all of them apply to Quiverfull: a sense of strong boundaries with the non-evangelical world; a sense of possessing ultimate truth; a sense of moral superiority; a sense of lifestyle and value distinctiveness; a sense of evangelistic and social mission; a sense of displaced heritage; a sense of second-class citizenship; and a sense of menacing external threats.[150] What is less clear, though, is whether we can say Quiverfull subculture is "thriving." That question will have to be postponed for another project.

As described above, following Mary Pride's *The Way Home* in 1985, a discernible subculture began to emerge within the Christian homeschooling movement that embodied the "home-centered" lifestyle Pride presented as the "whole cloth alternative" to feminism. These families were distinguishable from other evangelical homeschooling families chiefly due to their refusal to control their family size, which often led to having larger-than-normal families of six, seven, or more children. Also, they began to produce organizations, networks, websites, and more that could provide advocacy, apolo-

---

148. For example, most evangelicals affirm male headship of one kind or another, while a sizeable minority have been a part of the advancement of the Christian homeschooling movement.

149. Smith, *American Evangelicalism*, 118–19.

150. Smith, *American Evangelicalism*, 123–43.

getics, and mutual support for their chosen way of life. These institutions, along with the preexisting networks and organizations of Christian homeschoolers, were a means for Quiverfull-minded people to connect and promote their practices. And, as I show in the chapters that follow, Quiverfull families "employ the cultural tools needed to create both clear distinction from and significant engagement and tension with other relevant out-groups, short of becoming genuinely countercultural."

AN OVERVIEW OF THE QUIVERFULL MOVEMENT

With historical context and conceptual tools in place, I want to provide an overview of the particulars of the Quiverfull movement. In what follows I describe the Quiverfull movement today, focusing on the key leaders, organizations, books, and internet sources that serve as touch points for creating and maintaining Quiverfull as a discernible subculture.[151]

To begin, I suggest we imagine Quiverfull institutions in two basic levels: elite and lay.[152] By elite level, I mean the Quiverfull teachers, authors, organizations, and publications that operate at a significant distance from the families at the grassroots. The elites have national name recognition (at least among Christian homeschoolers or American evangelicals), a substantial base of financial support, and disproportionate influence over the construction of the Quiverfull subculture. By lay level, I mean the Quiverfull families at the grassroots, as well as their local homeschooling networks, newsletters, and personal blogs. The laity is concerned mainly with the day-to-day activities of living as growing Christian families in contemporary America, so their cultural production is heavily focused on their local context. The cultural production of the elites is targeted to the laity and the laity consumes, employs, and distributes elite products. But the laity also critically interacts with what is produced by elites, and the platform created by the internet allows lay-level Quiverfull members to voice these critiques to a broad audience. Thus, Quiverfull elites are not necessarily representative of the laity. Both their

---

151. Kathryn Joyce has already covered some of this ground and I will not attempt to duplicate her efforts. Even though for the sake of comprehensiveness I will mention figures that show up in her narrative, I will also include persons and organizations that she does not consider in depth.

152. The distinction between elite and lay level of Quiverfull subculture was inspired by the work of Julie Ingersoll in *Evangelical Christian Women*.

discourse and subculture are constantly contested, emerging through internal and external debate.

ELITE PRODUCERS OF QUIVERFULL SUBCULTURE

Any discussion of the elite-level of Quiverfull subculture should begin with Bill Gothard, discussed briefly above. Historically, Gothard's ministry extends from 1961 to the present day, preceding Mary Pride and *The Way Home* by twenty-four years. Through his Institute in Basic Youth Conflicts (later renamed Institute in Basic Life Principles), Gothard held conferences all over the country in the late 1970s and 1980s, drawing tens of thousands of people at a time. His website claims that 2.5 million people have attended his Basic Seminar.[153] Gothard's influence among homeschooling Christians has been maintained primarily through his homeschooling curriculum, Advanced Training Institute (ATI).[154] Gothard's teaching on the family represents an early unification of the three parts of Quiverfull discourse: a strong affirmation of male headship and female submission,[155] an uncompromising affirmation of homeschooling as the only option for Christian families,[156] and a promotion of intentionally large families.[157] And the popularity of his conferences and seminars

153. Institute in Basic Life Principles, "About IBLP" (http://tinyurl.com/yd8q5d95) and "Bill Gothard" (http://tinyurl.com/ycv35xza).
154. Certainly, not all Quiverfull families are ATI families, but all ATI families are Quiverfull families. Anecdotal evidence of this link between Gothard's ATI and Quiverfull is that the blog *A Quiver Full of Information* includes Quiverfull and ATI blogs under the same heading: "Pro-Quiverfull/ATI Blogs and Websites," http://tinyurl.com/yd3yja2v. ATI regularly convenes national and local conferences for their families, which expand upon and reinforce the content of their homeschooling curriculum. ATI also offers internships and various other service opportunities for children.
155. See, for example, Bill Gothard, *Basic Seminar Workbook* (Oakbrook, IL: IBLP Publications, 1993), 16. Gothard's teachings on male headship are the most well known among evangelicals. Many are familiar with his "umbrella diagram," which depicts a series of three umbrellas, one on top of the other. The wife falls under the umbrella of her husband, who is responsible for provision and protection of his family, and the husband falls under the authority of Christ. To step outside one's "umbrella" is to court disaster. For more on "umbrella of protection," including photos of IBLP materials, and the detrimental teachings that arise from it regarding spousal and child abuse, see "There Is No Victim," *Recovering Grace*, April 25, 2014, http://tinyurl.com/y9xzjgop.
156. In all of his material, Gothard teaches that the home should be a "learning center" based upon the idea that God has instructed parents to teach their children. See, for example, his instructions to fathers in Bill Gothard, *Men's Manual*, vol. 2 (Oakbrook, IL: IBLP Publications, 1993), 169–73. See also the IBLP website, "Home: A Learning Center," http://tinyurl.com/ya8tdfzz.
157. In Gothard's list of "Christ's Commands," number 29 is "Despise not little ones." In practice, this means welcoming all children as gifts of God and not seeking to limit God's gifts.

in the 1970s and 1980s mean that his teachings spread across denominations and traditions within the evangelical milieu.

Eventually, Gothard's influence was affected by a number of scandals, first in the 1980s and then again from 2009 to 2014.[158] In 2013, a blog devoted to people who have exited what they call *Gothardism*, reported the stories of thirty-four women who claim to have been sexually harassed by Gothard since his ministry began, four of whom also claim he sexually molested them.[159] Gothard resigned on March 6, 2014. The IBLP board claims an investigation conducted by "outside legal counsel" uncovered no criminal activity. Still, they say Gothard acted in an "inappropriate manner" and is no longer allowed to serve in the ministry in any capacity.[160] Even as Gothard's influence wanes among Quiverfull families, though, his approach to scripture and emphasis on gender hierarchy and submission to authority remain central to Quiverfull.

Mary Pride has also been referenced above. Pride is a homeschooling mother of nine and an enterprising promoter of stay-at-home motherhood, large families, and homeschooling. She authored countless books and published both *HELP for Growing Families* (now defunct) and *Practical Homeschooling* (ongoing). Due to her early influence in the Christian homeschooling movement, Pride eventually became known as the "queen of the homeschooling movement." Her periodicals provided invaluable reviews of homeschooling curriculum, so much so that her stamp of approval was vital for publishers targeting the Christian homeschooling market. Her trustworthiness on homeschooling also provided a platform for her denunciation

---

Gothard's website includes an article by Lance and Cris Riste, "Receiving Precious Gifts: Learning to Rejoice in God's Gift of Children," *IBLP*, http://tinyurl.com/y79jqngb.

158. From a *Religion News Service* article on Gothard's resignation: "The allegations against Gothard dovetail with financial woes. In recent years, IBLP's net revenue has dropped significantly, and the ministry is losing money. Between 2009 and 2012, it lost $8.6 million. Its net assets dropped from $92 million in 2010 to $81 million in 2012. It held 504 seminars in 2010, but that number dropped to fewer than 50 in 2012" (Sarah Pulliam Bailey, "Conservative Leader Bill Gothard Resigns Following Abuse Allegations," *Washington Post*, March 7, 2014, http://tinyurl.com/y9zb5y3w). In 1980 it was made public that Gothard's brother, Steve, had been having sex with female members of the ministry staff, some of whom were under age. Also, the Gothard family had been using ministry resources for their own purposes, including vacations. Although Steve was fired and the internal finances of the ministry revamped, for many observers Gothard remained suspect.

159. The *Recovering Grace* story that broke the accusations of harassment and molestation was written by the editors, "The Gothard Files: A Case for Disqualification," February 3, 2014, http://tinyurl.com/yccrkf5k.

160. Pulliam Bailey, "Conservative Leader Bill Gothard Resigns." Also, Institute in Basic Life Principles, "A Time of Transition," June 17, 2014, http://tinyurl.com/ycafar5w.

of family planning. Pride's influence is waning now, but her leadership and publications were crucial to the beginning of Quiverfull subculture.[161]

Nancy Campbell is a pastor's wife, homeschooling mother of nine, and the founder of Above Rubies, a thirty-five-year-old nonprofit organization. Above Rubies (taken from Prov 31:10) is devoted to "encouraging women in their high calling as wives, mothers, and homemakers." *Above Rubies Magazine* is a free print magazine that reports an international circulation of 160,000 with readership estimated at half a million. Above Rubies also has a well-trafficked website, which hosts numerous online discussion forums, a blog, a daily "devotional" delivered by email, plus articles on countless topics. Above Rubies began in New Zealand and Australia, but has since spread to the United States, Canada, South Africa, and the UK. In addition to speaking at women's events nationwide, Campbell has also authored a number of books, the most popular of which is *Be Fruitful and Multiply: What the Bible Says about Having Children* (Vision Forum Ministries, 2003).[162] Though well into her seventies, Campbell remains an important influence in the Quiverfull subculture.

Doug Phillips is the son of Constitution Party leader Howard Phillips. He is a trained attorney, as well as a pastor, speaker, and writer, deeply influenced by the mentorship of R. J. Rushdoony. Phillips served in the Home School Legal Defense Association (HSLDA) during the early years of the Christian homeschooling movement and went on to found Vision Forum Ministries and Vision Forum, Inc. in 1998. Vision Forum Ministries was a nonprofit organization devoted to promoting Reformed theology, biblical patriarchy, homeschooling, large families, family integrated church, creationism, and dominionism. Vision Forum, Inc. was a for-profit company that offered a variety of products to homeschooling families, including books, films, and toys, through a print catalogue and website. Through both organizations, Phillips became a regular

---

161. Recently, Pride has taken issue with some of the teachings and practices of other Quiverfull teachers. For example, in the afterword of the twenty-fifth-anniversary edition of her book *The Way Home*, Pride denounces the overemphasis on father-daughter relationships in the teachings of Doug Phillips, as well as the idea that one must have as many children as possible. She differentiates herself from these approaches without denying the underlying gender hierarchy and pronatalism.

162. Nancy Campbell, *The Power of Motherhood: What the Bible Says about Motherhood* (Antioch, TN: Above Rubies, 1996) and *The Family Meal Table and Hospitality* (Antioch, TN: Above Rubies, 1999).

speaker at homeschooling conferences, allowing him to exercise significant influence within Christian homeschooling networks and the Quiverfull subculture.[163] Phillips's organizations folded in 2013, however, following the revelation that Phillips had been sexually abusing the family's longtime nanny.[164] Though Phillips has been publicly disgraced and his organizations dissolved, his stamp on the Quiverfull subculture remains.

Scott Brown is a friend of Phillips, with whom he founded the National Center for Family-Integrated Churches (NCFIC). Brown is a minister, father of four children, and the director of NCFIC, an organizational outgrowth of the so-called family-integrated church movement (FIC).[165] Put simply, FIC is a reaction against the practice of age-segregated teaching in Protestant churches and an attempt to reverse trends that show Christian families are increasingly less successful at keeping their children within the faith as they grow up.[166] FIC adherents eschew any kind of special teaching for children and youth and prioritize the parents' role (especially fathers) as the primary teachers of their children. Most Quiverfull families have a natural affinity with the FIC movement and Scott Brown's NCFIC provides supportive resources for families and churches, as well as a growing database of family-integrated churches.[167] Though no longer associated with his discredited friend, Doug Phillips, Brown remains an active producer of Quiverfull subculture through his own speaking, writing, and activism.

Geoffrey Botkin is another friend of Phillips. Until the closure of Vision Forum Ministries, Botkin and his family played a major role in the organization, writing for their website, speaking at their conferences, and overseeing the publication of his daughters' books.[168]

163. Phillips tapped a number of figures to produce books and speak at events sponsored by his ministry, including Nancy Campbell, Geoffrey Botkin, Anna Sofia and Elizabeth Botkin (Geoffrey Botkin's daughters), Jennie Chancey, Stacey MacDonald, and Voddie Baucham.

164. The details of Phillips's abusive behavior will become more relevant in chapter 5, so I postpone further discussion until then.

165. I am skeptical about the accuracy of the term *movement* in regards to FIC. I do think a case could be made, however, that the FIC is an informal, transdenominational special-purpose group such as Robert Wuthnow explores in *The Restructuring of American Religion* (Princeton: Princeton University Press, 1988), 100–132.

166. See, for example, Scott Brown, *A Weed in the Church: How a Culture of Age Segregation Is Destroying the Younger Generation, Fragmenting the Family, and Harming the Church* (Wake Forest, NC: Merchant Adventures, 2010); Voddie Baucham, *Family-Driven Faith: Doing What It Takes to Raise Sons and Daughters Who Walk with God* (Wheaton, IL: Crossway, 2011).

167. See more at the NCFIC website: https://ncfic.org/about.

168. A number of people have spoken of Botkin's appearance in the fold of Vision Forum as mysterious. Botkin's academic training is unknown, and he has revealed very little of his

Now Botkin is the head of the Western Conservatory of Arts and Sciences, a nonprofit organization whose mission is "to provide the resources and tools to help families and individuals gain the skills they need to become the leaders they wished existed in the arts and the sciences, politics, law, economics, local and international missions, and most of all, their own families, communities and churches."[169] The entire Botkin family is involved in this organization and they produce materials for purchase, including DVDs, books, CDs, and more.

Botkin is also important for the intentional way he markets his own family. The Botkins function as an example to emulate, a resource of wisdom for Christian living, and a product to be consumed. His daughters, Anna Sofia and Elizabeth, have had a special role in the creation and maintenance of the "stay-at-home daughter" ideal, which entails that young women remain "under the protection" of their father until given in marriage to husbands. Rather than go to college or start a career, stay-at-home daughters focus on learning the skills of homemaking, motherhood, and home education in preparation for marriage. Anna Sofia and Elizabeth Botkin promoted this idea in their book *So Much More: The Remarkable Influence of Visionary Daughters on the Kingdom of God* (Vision Forum Ministries, 2005) and the documentary film *The Return of the Daughters* (2007).[170] Today, they maintain this point of view on their blog *Botkin Sisters* (formerly *Visionary Daughters*) and promote it through public appearances.[171]

Voddie Baucham was the longtime pastor of Grace Family Baptist

---

background prior to his cooperation with Vision Forum. According to the research of a number of bloggers, Botkin and his wife were members of a cultic group called Great Commission Ministries centered in Norman, OK. They were close to the leadership of the organization and spent some time with them in New Zealand seeking to run a Christian newspaper and television station. When the endeavor failed, the family returned to the United States and took up work with Doug Phillips, Vision Forum Ministries, and Boerne Christian Assembly (Phillips's former church). This is, however, a description of Botkin's background that he has not verified. See "Who Is Geoffrey Botkin?" *Under Much Grace*, February 2, 2013, http://tinyurl.com/yavceqa8.

169. Western Conservatory of Arts and Sciences, "About Western Conservatory," http://westernconservatory.com/about.

170. Sadly, one of the young women featured in "The Return of the Daughters" was also the Phillips family nanny, whom Phillips was accused of abusing.

171. Interestingly, the Botkin sisters wrote their book, *So Much More*, when they were fifteen and seventeen years old. They are now twenty-six and twenty-eight, respectively, and still living at home, working for their father's organization. One wonders why their advocacy of stay-at-home daughterhood as preparation for wifehood and motherhood has not translated into their pursuit of those vocations. The newest iteration of their blog is available at http://botkinsisters.com/.

Church in Houston, Texas, but now serves as dean of the seminary at African Christian University in Lusaka, Zambia.[172] He is also head of Voddie Baucham Ministries, a homeschooling father of nine children, and "one of the architects of the Family Integrated Church movement."[173] Baucham is also author of numerous books, including *Family Driven Faith: Doing What It Takes to Raise Sons and Daughters Who Walk with God* (Crossway, 2007) and *Family Shepherds: Calling and Equipping Men to Lead Their Homes* (Crossway, 2011). Like Gothard, Baucham's publications link gender hierarchy, homeschooling, and pronatalism, while adding his own emphasis on family-integrated church. In his many speaking engagements across the country, he has shared the stage with both Doug Phillips and Scott Brown. Baucham's daughter, Jasmine, has her own book that mirrors the Botkins': *Joyfully at Home: A Book for Young Ladies on Vision and Hope* (Vision Forum Ministries, 2010). Baucham is unique among Quiverfull elites for two reasons: he is African American and he has been active within a denominational structure, the Southern Baptist Convention.

Though they do not claim the label, the Duggar Family, headed by Jim Bob and Michelle Duggar, are certainly members of the Quiverfull elite. The Duggars had a popular television show that aired for fourteen seasons on the TLC network called *19 Kids and Counting* and have done much over the past several years to bring Quiverfull to public awareness. Even people who have never heard the term *Quiverfull* know who the Duggars are. They have produced a number of books on managing large families, sibling relationships, the challenges faced by teenage girls, and more.[174] Jim Bob and Michelle, as well as a few of their older daughters, are often featured as key speakers at church events, homeschooling conventions, and other conferences. Despite being laypeople, the Duggars' fame gives them an important symbolic valence. In their number of children, financial success, frugal homesteading lifestyle, and apparent normalcy, health,

---

172. Baucham explains this transition on his personal website (http://tinyurl.com/y77yewvb) and fundraising website (http://www.launchthemove.com/about).

173. From the back cover of Baucham's book *What He Must Be . . . if He Wants to Marry My Daughter* (Wheaton, IL: Crossway, 2009), which is billed as an "apologetic of biblical manhood."

174. Jim Bob Duggar and Michelle Duggar, *The Duggars: 20 and Counting!* (New York: Howard Books, 2008); Jim Bob Duggar and Michelle Duggar, *A Love That Multiplies: An Up-Close View of How They Make It Work* (New York: Howard Books, 2012); Jana Duggar et al., *Growing Up Duggar: It's All About Relationships* (New York: Howard Books, 2014).

and happiness, the Duggars have come to represent the Quiverfull subcultural ideal.[175]

All of the above figures are elite proponents of Quiverfull subculture.[176] Through their organizations, speaking engagements, publications, and robust internet presence, they have exerted a significant influence over the Christian homeschooling movement, in general, while also helping to foster a distinct Quiverfull subculture within it. As one would expect, the recent downfall of Bill Gothard and Doug Phillips led to countless blog posts from Quiverfull sources. Some debated the merits of the accusations (defending Phillips and Gothard against "gossip"), some quietly distanced themselves from the men, and some forcefully denounced them as morally bankrupt.[177] Though not everyone within the Quiverfull subculture wanted to claim Gothard and Phillips as "one of them," all of them saw the allegations as significant to their way of life and worthy of response.

It is also worth noting that some Quiverfull elites also exercise influence within American evangelicalism at large. Doug Phillips and Voddie Baucham have provoked discussions of Quiverfull practice within denominational institutions. Baucham and others have sought for several years to pass a resolution at the national meeting of the Southern Baptist Convention to condemn public schooling as anti-Christian and exhort Christian parents to remove their children from government schools. Southern Baptist leaders like Albert Mohler and

---

175. The Duggars' reputation has been significantly tarnished in recent years due to a number of scandals involving their oldest son, Josh. I will discuss these events in some detail in chapter 5.

176. I could have included Michael Farris, Douglas Wilson, and R. C. Sproul Jr. Farris is the head of the Home School Legal Defense Association (HSLDA) and, even though he's been associated with Quiverfull, is more accurately considered a homeschooling leader. Wilson and Sproul are very much embedded in the Reformed or Neo-Reformed evangelicalism and do not necessarily have widespread appeal among Quiverfull families. Also, even though Douglas Wilson endorses patriarchy, he approves of the use of birth control in some cases and prefers a classical Christian school to homeschooling. Also, I could have discussed Michael Provan (*The Bible and Birth Control* [Monongahela, PA: Zimmer Printing, 1989]) and Rick and Jan Hess (*A Full Quiver: Family Planning and the Lordship of Christ* [Brentwood, TN: Wolgemuth & Hyatt, 1990]), all of whom contributed to the early spread of Quiverfull pronatalism through their books. While their ideas and arguments are important, they never had the public status possessed by the figures described above. Also, Joyce deals with these figures in detail in *Quiverfull*.

177. Through multiple blog posts, Douglas Wilson debates the merits of the case against Doug Phillips. See, for example, "Vision Forum and Confessing Your Virtues," *Blog & Mablog*, April 17, 2014, http://tinyurl.com/y9sybw8m. Michael Farris, head of the HSLDA and personal friend of Doug Phillips, distances himself from Phillips and Gothard in a post to the HSLDA website titled, "A Line in the Sand," August 2014, http://tinyurl.com/yaymym8f. Heidi St. John denounces Phillips and Gothard in no uncertain terms on her blog, *The Busy Mom*, with her post, "Don't Turn Away: Trouble in the Homeschooling Movement," March 9, 2014, http://tinyurl.com/y9ftgtfu.

Dorothy Patterson have publicly questioned the use of birth control by Christians.[178] The Council on Biblical Manhood and Womanhood, led by Denny Burk, is actively promoting gender hierarchy as central to the Christian gospel. Although Quiverfull remains on the margins of American evangelical culture today, their discourse is similar to that of conservative evangelicalism, which emphasizes stay-at-home motherhood, wifely submission, the importance of children, and the centrality of the family. Moreover, the cultural production of Quiverfull elites has gradually made their discourse more marketable to the evangelical mainstream. Thus, Quiverfull subculture is beginning to "bleed" into the evangelical subculture in America.

LAY PRODUCERS OF QUIVERFULL SUBCULTURE

Alongside the elite level is the lay level of the Quiverfull subculture, made up of families, churches, co-operatives, local networks, newsletters, internet forums, and blogs. There are numerous blogs, networks, and internet forums specifically designated for Quiverfull families.[179] Alongside of these, most elements of the Quiverfull subculture are connected to the Christian homeschooling movement. For example, within local homeschooling co-operatives one might find a number of families who do not limit their family size alongside Christian families who do. Though not explicitly labeled *Quiverfull*, the homeschooling co-op serves as an institution of the Quiverfull subculture for the way that it connects and reproduces their discourse. The same is true of churches in which Quiverfull families are

---

178. R. Albert Mohler Jr., "Can Christians Use Birth Control?" *AlbertMohler.com*, May 8, 2006, http://tinyurl.com/y98r4mds. While the article stating Dorothy Patterson's views on contraception has been removed from her website, the following column quotes her at length: Bob Allen, "Seminary First Lady Compares Pill to Abortion," *Ethics Daily*, February 22, 2007, http://tinyurl.com/ybyzdb4l.

179. These include *The Quiverfull Digest* (in operation since 1995), *Arrow Collectors* (a network for connecting Quiverfull families in operation since 2009), *Christian Moms of Many Blessings* (an online discussion forum for Quiverfull moms), and *A Quiver Full of Information* (a blog devoted to information about the Quiverfull subculture, both for and against). Apart from *A Quiver Full of Information* blog, each of these forums and networks requires an application process through which the administrators can verify the applicant's adherence to Quiverfull principles. (It is for this reason that I did not gain access to any of the top three Quiverfull discussion forums or networks. Only Quiverfull parents can gain access to these sites by submitting detailed information about their families, practices, and beliefs.) Presumably, this process is meant to protect the privacy of Quiverfull families, ensuring that they are interacting with truly sympathetic Quiverfull faithful. The operators of these websites did not respond to my requests for interviews or information regarding their application process.

prevalent. For example, a Baptist church I visited in Cincinnati does not officially advertise itself as Quiverfull, but the church leadership promotes the three-part discourse of Quiverfull subculture through its teaching, radio ministry, events, and the distribution of pro-Quiverfull materials. The church is almost entirely made up of Quiverfull families. While the church may not identify itself as Quiverfull, it functions in practice as a lay-level institution of Quiverfull subculture. It is primarily through sympathetic churches and homeschooling co-operatives that Quiverfull families find and foster relationships of mutual edification and support.

Homeschooling co-operatives are crucial for many Quiverfull families, but the cultivation of Quiverfull as a discernible subculture would not be possible without the internet. Not only do all of the above elites have very popular websites through which they produce and disseminate their teachings, but there are also countless members of Quiverfull laity, especially mothers and daughters, who operate widely read and influential personal blogs.[180] Through blogs, bloggers create a "social world"[181] oriented around and constantly engaged with the Quiverfull discourse.[182] Some Quiverfull "mommy blogs" simply rework and redistribute the rhetoric provided on elite-level websites and blogs, but most are doing the work of interpreting, modifying, and even critiquing the products of Quiverfull elites.[183] In fact, elite producers of Quiverfull subculture have, on occasion, specifically referenced mommy blogs as a threat to the purity of their

---

180. Rebecca Blood defines *blog* loosely as "a frequently updated webpage with dated entries, new ones placed on top" (*We've Got Blog: How Weblogs Are Changing Our Culture*, with John Rodzvilla [New York: Basic Books, 2002], 12).

181. Greg Myers, *The Discourse of Blogs and Wikis*, Continuum Discourse Series (London: Continuum, 2010), 21.

182. Myers suggests that "sphericules" (a word he borrows from Todd Gitlin, "Public Sphere or Public Sphericules," in *Media, Ritual, and Identity*, ed. James Curran and Tamar Liebes [London: Routledge, 1998], 168–74) is a better description of the social worlds created through blogs. He defines "sphericules" as "multiple publics that pursue their own discussions without reference to a single unified national or global 'public.'" Myers explains, "the blogosphere inherently tends to break up this way; while a television news broadcast or newspaper articles seem to address anyone . . . the successful blogger writes, not for the world at large, but for people just like him or her, wherever they may be. There usually turn out to be a lot of those people, however narrow the group may be, and then turn out to be linked in complex ways" (Myers, *The Discourse of Blogs and Wikis*, 24–25).

183. For more on mommy blogs, see Lynne M. Webb and Brittney S. Lee, "Mommy Blogs: The Centrality of Community in the Performance of Online Maternity," in *Motherhood Online*, ed. Michelle Moravec (Newcastle upon Tyne: Cambridge Scholars, 2011). See also *Mothering and Blogging: The Radical Act of the MommyBlog*, ed. May Friedman and Shana L. Calixte (Toronto: Demeter, 2009).

way of life. Doug Phillips, speaking to a "summit" of homeschooling fathers in 2009, said the following:

> We will lose this movement and this work of God, men, if we do not govern our households. And that means lovingly shepherding our wives. The less you love your wife and the less you shepherd your wife, the more you create an open door for the female sin of the Internet. The male sin of the Internet is pornography. The female sin of the Internet is gossip-mongering.... We don't live in the type of communities where our wives tend to go from house to house gossiping. They tend to go from blog to blog gossiping. And they spend their day going from blog to blog gossiping. And some of you are letting them.[184]

Clearly, Phillips is aware of the cultural power present in the Quiverfull blogosphere. He knows blogging women can, through criticism and dissent, change the course of the movement. Phillips's warning now seems prescient as both he and Gothard were brought down due to revelations spread through blogs run by women.

Mommy blogs also allow for an ongoing give-and-take between the elite and lay levels of the subculture. Quiverfull mommy bloggers use their internet platform to express agreement or disagreement with the teachings of elites and challenge particular ways of embodying Quiverfull discourse. One blog, *Visionary Womanhood*, run by Quiverfull mother of nine Natalie Klejwa, has enough readers to finance the production of a self-published book: *Three Decades of Fertility: Ten Ordinary Women Surrender to the Creator and Embrace Life* (Saint Paul, MN: Visionary Womanhood, 2013).[185] *Three Decades of Fertility* promotes the Quiverfull way of life through the testimonies of ten women who have devoted their childbearing years (typically around three decades) to raising as many children as God gives them. The book is by no means a bestseller, but it is available in paperback and on Kindle, promoted on Quiverfull blogs, and currently has fifty-one reviews on Amazon (78 percent of which rate it with five stars).[186] Thus, even as Phillips fears the subversive potential of Quiv-

---

184. Transcript from the 2009 Men's Leadership Summit, provided by R. L. Stollar, "End Child Protection: Doug Phillips, HSLDA, and the 2009 Men's Leadership Summit," *Homeschoolers Anonymous*, May 14, 2013, http://tinyurl.com/y7bewfo8.

185. Natalie Klejwa, *Three Decades of Fertility: Ten Ordinary Women Surrender to the Creator and Embrace Life* (Saint Paul, MN: Visionary Womanhood, 2013). Klejwa's blog, *Visionary Womanhood*, can be found at http://visionarywomanhood.com.

186. Data taken from the product page at Amazon.com as of January 31, 2017: http://a.co/9MtggzO.

erfull mommy blogs, many blogs like Klejwa's are enthusiastic supporters of Quiverfull discourse.

Also important to the construction of Quiverfull subculture on the internet is the presence of a large number of ex-Quiverfull blogs, the most notable being *No Longer Quivering* and *Love, Joy, Feminism*. Ex-Quiverfull blogs provide outlets for the mothers and grown children of Quiverfull who have "exited" the subculture to speak about their experiences. Ex-Quiverfull bloggers often follow and comment upon the ongoing work of Quiverfull elites, too. They offer summaries and evaluations of Quiverfull works, as well as visit and report on the speakers at homeschooling conventions and other events. In this way, ex-Quiverfull blogs function in therapeutic and journalistic ways, serving the needs of the writers, as well as the interests of readers. The cross-communication between pro-Quiverfull and anti-Quiverfull blogs further contributes to Quiverfull subcultural identity. If one can exit Quiverfull and identify as ex-Quiverfull, there must be something discernibly *Quiverfull* to begin with.

Through the content created by elite websites and lay blogs, Quiverfull subculture is constantly emerging. In the blogosphere Quiverfull identity is constructed not through uniform agreement on all matters but through constant engagement with issues and practices key to Quiverfull subculture. While opinions vary from blog to blog, and Quiverfull proponents may address these issues in a variety of ways, their constant engagement with these matters provides a discernible subcultural identity. It is dialogic, it is always in conflict, it is ever emerging, but it has identifiable focal points of engagement around which Quiverfull subculture coalesces.

THE INTERACTION OF ELITE AND LAY LEVELS WITHIN THE QUIVERFULL SUBCULTURE

I have suggested Quiverfull subcultural institutions can be divided into two basic levels, elite and lay. The cultural production of the elite level is targeted to the lay level and the lay level consumes, employs, and distributes elite products. But it is important to recognize that laypersons do not engage with elite cultural producers in an uncritical way. When asked about what kinds of things she reads and distributes, Deborah Olson offers a long explanation that illustrates well the sifting and negotiating taking place at the grassroots:

We've read a lot of John Piper stuff about marriage and family. We've read things from the Family Life people, Dennis and Barbara Rainey. We've read some [James] Dobson, although it's not my favorite. . . . We've read really radical people like the Pearls. I'm not being recorded am I? [Laughter.] We love the Duggars. We've read Chapman. Oh goodness. I feel like I've mentioned Voddie Baucham. Baucham stood out to us because we used his book almost like a manual. [Tedd] Tripp's book [*Shepherding a Child's Heart*]. . . . I just get nervous about some stuff. I would recommend Baucham. I would recommend David Platt's books. But, when it comes to Christian home and parenting, I get so nervous about that stuff because, well, I mean, I get nervous because there are some things that are good and some that aren't. We read the Pearls and we thought, "OK some of this is good and some of this is uhhh . . . not good." . . . I don't follow only one person or one way. I read *Above Rubies* sometimes. But sometimes I'm like, "For the love of God, give me a break!" . . . I don't know. I don't think you can be good at this by just doing what someone else says. It has to be in your heart and you have to discern what's good for your family and what isn't. . . . It's just so easy to get caught up in the way others are doing it. But, I don't think there's just one way.

Deborah engages critically with what is produced by Quiverfull and other evangelical elites. She picks and chooses what corresponds to her own sensibilities and discernment. And, as we shall see in the following chapters, this picking and choosing leads to a laity that, in some cases, subverts or even reverses the ideology found in elite discourse.

CONCLUSION

Now that I have provided a historical and cultural context for understanding the Quiverfull movement, it's time to focus on the women of Quiverfull. Our shift to the stories of Quiverfull women does not leave behind what has been said so far. The Quiverfull mothers featured in chapter 2 did not choose to become Quiverfull out of nowhere, but were working from within a particular historical narrative and with a particular set of cultural "tools" to construct their lives and the lives of their families in contemporary America.[187] This does not mean that we should deny their agency. The following stories make it clear that the women of Quiverfull are intelligent, creative

187. Gallagher uses the idea of a cultural toolbox in *Evangelicals and Gendered Family Life*.

agents, not brainwashed automatons. These women are willing participants in the three-part discourse of Quiverfull, but they also negotiate with, modify, and subvert their subculture's status quo through their way of life. Moreover, the women of Quiverfull are practical theologians, working out their theologies in the daily work of breastfeeding, meal preparation, and kitchen table lessons. By paying close attention to their embodied theology, we can see more clearly the problems inherent in evangelical theology of the family in the American context.

2.

Stories from the Full Quiver

What are Quiverfull mothers really like? What does their daily life look like? And how did they get into the Quiverfull movement in the first place? This chapter introduces three Quiverfull mothers through sustained attention to their stories as told in their own words.[1] Each of them occupies a different position on the spectrums of age and socioeconomic status, offering a slightly different (sometimes very different) perspective on their way of life. These women's stories cannot be assumed to be a representative sample of Quiverfull women as a whole. They do not tell the whole story of Quiverfull families in America. But, I am confident that the major elements of their stories—especially their language, theological and symbolic themes, and personal struggles—are sufficiently widespread in the movement as a whole to be representative enough for my purposes.[2]

The purpose of this chapter is to give the women of the Quiverfull movement the opening word on the subject of their families and chosen way of life, albeit in a limited and necessarily mediated way. I seek to be as faithful as possible to each woman's own words and phrasing, altering only in the case of grammatical errors (which were few in number). In some cases, I quote at length from

---

1. All of the names of my informants and some of the details of their biographies have been changed to protect their anonymity. These are not the only members of the movement I interviewed, but they are the ones with whom I had the most sustained interaction over the course of two years.

2. This is especially the case given the challenges involved with studying families who value their privacy and tend to be suspicious of academics. It is difficult to find Quiverfull families with both the time and inclination to speak to outsiders about their lives, so finding voices that are "representative enough" may be the best that any researcher can do.

our conversations in order to allow the woman's testimony to speak for itself. All of the following information was gathered in one of the following ways: (1) recorded during an in-person interview on a digital recorder and later transcribed by hand, or (2) transcribed by hand during an interview over the phone. After each story, I present a brief analysis, which gestures toward the themes of motherhood, children, and the nuclear family as these matters will be raised in subsequent chapters.

RENEE'S STORY

When Mary Pride called women to abandon feminism and head "back home," she offered a vision of homemaking that included more than pot roasts and pristine floors by treating motherhood as a divinely ordained profession invested with eschatological meaning. The hand that rocks the cradle would enable Jesus to rule the world. Just as Sheryl Sandberg urged working women to "lean in" to their careers in 2013, Mary Pride was urging Christian moms in the 1980s to "lean in" to stay-at-home motherhood—not just for their own happiness but also for the advancement of the kingdom of God. In the first generation of the homeschooling movement, Renee Tanner was one of many women who embraced this home-centered, "full quiver" vision for Christian motherhood.

Renee and her husband Gary are in their mid-fifties and live in a mid-sized town in the Southwest. Renee is tall with long brown hair. She comes across as confident, outgoing, and smart, with a quick wit and easy laugh. But, she also speaks with care about things that she knows are controversial, demonstrating genuine sensitivity to the feelings of others. Renee married young and from early on was captivated by Pride's vision for motherhood. She describes her acceptance of this way of life in the following way:

> I did not expect to marry young and have lots children. I wanted to do something amazing and exciting. I met Gary at seventeen and married him at eighteen. . . . I wasn't completely living righteously, but as soon as I was married and in a more structured life I began to do everything 100 percent. I'm a very literal person and I listened in church and believed we should do exactly what the Bible said. . . . [The Quiverfull way of life] gave me something big and exciting and a purpose and something to do. It gave a purpose to the male-female roles. It gave me something to do with my brains and talent. Mary Pride writes about that

and her story of journeying from feminism to a Christian, and she made a really good case for the traditional [1950s homemaker] role being wimpy. But if women would really do what they can do for the kingdom it wouldn't be wimpy but necessary and powerful.

Over time, the "big and exciting" vision of motherhood that Renee and other women like her embraced came to be called "Quiverfull" because of the women's willingness to give birth to a "full quiver" of children. And the practices involved in Quiverfull discourse lead to a performance of motherhood that is extraordinary in its scope. Renee welcomed the pronatalist approach to pregnancy as a way of ensuring that their family was within the will of God and working for God's glory:

> It seems that since we can't cause conception, that if it was consistent with God's character, word, and will that children were a blessing directly from him, then this is one area that, if left to [God], would go according to his perfect plan. Everything after that would be us living out what he directly gave us to do. I hoped to gain his will for my life and be a part of transforming a generation for his glory and building up the church with disciples.

Over the course of twenty years, Renee gave birth to eleven children. Today, they range in age from five to twenty-five. In her words, "Having many children means that you never really stop having babies and it's just a way of life. It was just normal to me to have a baby on my hip or in my arms." She admits that this task was incredibly difficult, particularly "the physical labor involved when no one in the family or church or the culture agrees with you or helps you." Still, Renee has no regrets. When asked about the rewards that come from her way of life, she said: "The great thing [God] has done—it is so much more than I ever could have imagined my life to be. There is an unparalleled richness to being surrounded and loved by your own flesh and blood and to see them walking in the truth."

This does not mean, however, that Renee has not developed some perspective on her pronatalism over the past twenty years. For example, she offered the following observation about the fundamentalist roots of her pronatalist commitment:

> I'm not saying that I haven't developed my own ideas about the choices that God gives us because we all keep changing and modifying and learning. I was raised very fundamentalist in terms of theological views.

Inerrancy of scripture, literal interpretation. . . . So that was very easy for me to turn to. A black-and-white view that if God is in control and he's sovereign, then a pregnancy is only going to happen if God wants it to. God literally opens and closes the womb. I don't know that I have changed my mind about that. I haven't thought about it anymore because I didn't have to. I certainly don't go around thinking that if you disagree you're wrong. I don't think everyone else is wrong. It's not black and white for every person.

In addition to welcoming all pregnancies as a gift of God, Renee also embraced the work of homeschooling all of her children from preschool through high school. In the process, she had to make many adjustments for special needs, developmental disabilities, sicknesses, and the births of each new child. Their initial reasons for homeschooling were as follows:

We wanted to avoid the adverse exposure to worldliness in small children and the fact that they would not spend much time with us from age five. We decided homeschooling was cheaper than private education and learned over time that kids in private school usually have the same peer-related character issues as those in public school, as do homeschooled children who are allowed to spend a lot of unsupervised time with other homeschooled children.

Renee had several goals in her work of homeschooling: "[For my children] to know God and his word. To have a strong foundation in reading, writing, and math. To have the freedom to learn about other things they were interested in throughout childhood. To understand history and philosophical ideas. To pursue higher education." She lists the most important priority first: "To know God and his word." It's no exaggeration to say that her daily life was consumed with the task of giving her children a Christian education. In her words, "You live and breathe discipling your kids." "Discipling" is her way of describing an education that not only imparts information but also helps to train and form the child into a follower of Christ. When I ask Renee about the relationship between her work as a homeschooling mother and the culture wars, she responds curtly: "We aren't called to fight culture wars. We were called to make disciples. Raising children in the Lord is making disciples."

Now that she has some perspective on her many years as a homeschooling mom, Renee recognizes that the amount of work expected of her was extraordinary, particularly for the women in the first generation:

> What I've come to see with first-generation homeschoolers is that you're expecting one woman to do the work of two or three fulltime jobs. If you have your little kids and they went to school and you kept your house and cooked and all that—that's a fulltime job. Then you add in that you're responsible for their education. If you're a teacher for one grade level and then you're continuing adding more and more [every year]. We do 4-H and club management and college applications and all that. . . . I mean, we took it all in stride. We said, "We're pioneers. We're figuring it out and covering new ground."

Despite the fact that Gary owns his own business, which allows some flexibility in his work schedule, almost all of the responsibility for the education of the children fell upon Renee, even when she had eleven young ones in the home. In her words:

> Most all of it fell on my shoulders. Yes, all of it. . . . A lot of men take on teaching responsibilities with their kids, but most of the men in my generation didn't do anything. In our situation and with our personalities, I'm the one who does all of it. I was the only one thinking about it and working on it.

Renee coped with this in a number of ways, but the most important were learning to delegate responsibilities to the older children (e.g., meal preparation and chores) and limiting the family's activities beyond the home. Despite these attempts to limit her burden, Renee says that when her children were young she often felt overwhelmed by her responsibilities:

> I didn't have a life. But, that was my fault. I thought that was the way I was supposed to do it. I don't regret that. I don't know if I could've done it differently. I could look back at my marriage and say if he were different, if he weren't passive . . . I wasn't doing so much because I was made to do those things but because that was the level of requirement for myself. I burdened myself. I said to myself, "No, I want to do it perfect." I felt pretty overwhelmed most of the time. I didn't act like it but mentally I was exhausted. . . . All of my standards are just too high. I mean I had eleven kids and somehow they're all spoiled in some way. [Laughter.] I was so determined to treat them as individuals and pay them each attention. Not that I succeeded at that. There were plenty of

times when I failed, but I always expected too much of myself and of them.

A recurring theme in Renee's story is the constant need for friendship and support. Early on, the Tanners' Quiverfull commitment was the cause of conflict in their church. When they asked permission to start an age-integrated Sunday school class with another family, the pastors and other church leaders were skeptical of what they might teach about birth control. They "wanted to be sure that [the teachers] wouldn't push their way of life on the church." The Tanners were taken aback by the suspicion and feeling of persecution. Eventually, the insult was too much to bear and they left. For a time the Tanners held church services in their home with a couple of other likeminded families but later found a small church where they felt welcomed and appreciated. Although they have since been able to return to their home church, Renee notes that the early experience of rejection "was a deep hurt" in her husband's "spiritual development."

But, Renee also suffered from the lack of community and scarcity of likeminded friends. She remembers the times when other Quiverfull moms lived close as times of strength and encouragement. Two mothers in particular were of help to her in the early years as a homeschooling mom. Renee relates that when she and one of those friends would struggle, they would remind themselves of their priorities: "One of our self-talks was that the first reason we homeschool is to teach them to follow God. If we accomplish discipling them, then that's more important than any schoolwork. That was our coping mechanism because you can't do it all, all the time." Now that she is helping younger mothers who are homeschooling their children, she warns them against the hazard of "doing it all" and advises them to get as much support as they can. In her words:

> You need to get others to help so you have a break. Whether it's hiring older kids or grandkids. I think it's very overwhelming and exhausting. I've done all of it. I don't mean that pridefully. I mean, I got help right after a birth or when I really needed it. But, [Gary] doesn't even help like a normal dad would for a kid in public school. It's not like that for all moms, but for me, I did it all.

As she coped with the challenges of homeschooling many children, Renee kept before her the belief that her mothering work carries great eschatological weight:

From the basic biological creation of my body by God, to the physical, spiritual, and intellectual influence and mentoring of the lives I'm blessed to give birth to, I have the greatest possible chance to raise "world changers" and contributors to society. I am only one person ... but my ability to multiply my faith directly in partnership with God himself (he creates and gives grace to the offspring to believe and obey) is exponential. I also believe that the children raised up in the homes of faith, covenant homes, kingdom homes (whatever your focus is) who continue in the faith are miles ahead of their converted counterparts in applied theology and discipline. I think these are possibly those that were destined to be spiritual leaders and teachers in the church. I think of it kind of as the Classical education method: you memorize first in the early years when your brain is a sponge and your heart is soft, then it is gradually explained to you to full understanding as you mature and master more difficult information. If our kids continue in faith and humility, they begin to quickly understand in young adulthood all the things we taught them and understand the principles behind the obedience more fully as they experience life. I think having this increased access to their hearts and minds from homeschooling and being committed to their development above all else helps us raise people who have an easier time disassociating with worldliness and materialism to focus on relationships, love, and the kingdom. And the hand that rocks the cradle rules the world. Hopefully.

In addition to pronatalism and homeschooling, Renee, like other Quiverfull mothers, subscribes to a doctrine of biblical patriarchy—or, at least she used to. As she tells it, Renee embraced patriarchy early on in her marriage, but discovered through time and experience that it simply didn't work in her situation. The ideal did not work itself out in practice. Renee says,

> I started out thinking that patriarchy was the way to go. You know the verse about turning the hearts of children to their fathers and fathers to their children [Mal 4:6]. But, the men I see in my age group in the homeschooling movement aren't involved and aren't close to their children.... My husband didn't want to be that leader. "Why should I do that? Why is all that my responsibility?" I probably would have been into patriarchy, but my husband wasn't one of those men. He just didn't do any of those things that patriarchs were supposed to do.... I mean, what woman doesn't want an amazing man who is godly, kind, strong, has all the answers, and leads the family? Anybody could stay pregnant and serve at home, heck, even serve him, willingly. But, that didn't work out for me so well.... Men that I know [who are] roughly over forty

just understand the authority part of patriarchy, not the service and leadership required.

When pressed further for how her views on gender have changed over the years, she offers the following observations:

> I don't agree with the patriarchal assumption that men are given more wisdom from God about the family leadership or have the deciding "vote" or in any way are above the women in authority. I believe the kingdom teaching that we are all to submit to one another, that there is neither male or female (just like neither slave nor free), that we are each to try to please the other (Paul writes about being bound in marriage, meaning a man has to be concerned about how he should please his wife as well as the woman concerned about how she can please her husband), and that the passages about complete submission and obedience of women were as pertinent to the Jewish and Greek culture at the time as the passages about slavery, and as unnecessary to ours. (I say all this cautiously, as I was raised with the view that this kind of talk is watering down the Bible, and saying it was for them and not us is heresy.) I believe the spirit of all those instructions was humility and deference, and we should all have that attitude toward one another, which kind of makes patriarchy obsolete.

It is at the point of gender hierarchy that Renee recognizes her divergence from the Quiverfull norm, led by her personal experience and supported by a new understanding of scripture. There is no doubt that the literature of the Quiverfull elites has no room for "passive" fathers like Renee's husband. They speak with great emphasis upon the leadership of fathers (the "family shepherd") and the significance of the father's God-fearing instruction of children. But, according to her testimony, Renee's situation isn't unique within the homeschooling movement as a whole. She observes: "From the reading I've done, I don't think it's uncommon nationwide for women to be more passionate and the men to just go along with it." In Renee's experience, the women were the active, passionate leaders of the first generation of the Quiverfull movement, while the men were more or less along for the ride.

Now that the majority of Renee's children have grown and moved away from home, she has begun to work on her bachelor's degree at a local community college. She does so in-between her youngest children's homeschool lessons and extracurricular activities, which are more extensive now that she doesn't have eleven children at home.

Just this year, Renee's oldest son and his wife welcomed their first child and Renee has enjoyed being able to offer help and support. Although time, experience, and study have caused Renee to rethink some of the things that she endorsed so stridently when she was young, she has no substantive regrets. She believes it was all part of God's plan for her life, and she feels immensely blessed by her children and experience as their mom.

ANALYSIS OF RENEE'S STORY

Above all, Renee's story brings into sharp relief the way the discourse of the Quiverfull movement places a heavy burden on the shoulders of its mothers. Although not pursuing careers beyond the home, they take up the task of educating their many children at their schooling levels while also bearing and nursing babies along the way. For Renee, as for all of the women I interviewed, the Quiverfull way of life was something they chose. My research suggests that more often than not it was the wife leading the husband into the Quiverfull discourse, not vice versa.[3] Renee found the prospect of birthing and educating a large family to be a "big and exciting" purpose in life and a task she eagerly imposed upon herself.[4]

Still, the theme of being burdened and overwhelmed looms large. According to her testimony, not only was Renee "overwhelmed most of the time," but also she blames herself and her own high expectations for her exhaustion. She admits that the work she was trying to do was the equivalent of multiple fulltime jobs. Moreover, rearing and homeschooling a large family meant that she experienced many of her struggles in isolation. Not only were likeminded families hard to come by, but she also dealt with alienation from her church community.

Renee shoulders most of the blame for her exhaustion despite the fact that Gary's "passive" approach to fathering left her with most of the household and childrearing responsibility. Although she

---

3. One adult daughter of a Quiverfull family had the following to say: "I've seen a pattern where a husband tends to be more passive, but their wives really like [the Quiverfull] model. I don't really know why. I think maybe they want their husbands to 'man up' or something."

4. Of course, the choice exercised by the daughters of Quiverfull families is another question entirely. It is one thing for a woman not raised within the movement to opt in, so to speak. It is quite another thing for young women, who have never known anything else, to choose to stay. To what extent can we really say these women have "chosen" to be Quiverfull? The subject of choice among second-generation Quiverfull women is fraught with difficulty, but it remains outside the purview of the present project.

"expected too much" of herself and her children, there is no doubt that her husband's lack of involvement played a major role in her fatigue. Unfortunately, the patriarchal ideology of the movement gave her little to work with in this regard. Gary was supposed to be a leading, shepherding, teaching patriarch, but he wasn't: "my husband wasn't one of those men." Thus, Renee made a way on her own with the occasional help of likeminded friends. Although she wishes things had gone differently, her experience has led her to seriously question the strident gender hierarchy of Quiverfull elites and even to reinterpret the Bible in light of her experience.

CARLEY'S STORY

Carley and David Miller are in their mid-thirties, which makes them about twenty years younger than Renee and Gary Tanner. They met at a private Christian college in the Midwest and married before graduation. David finished his degree and went on to a career in pharmaceuticals, but Carley never finished her degree in education. They were both raised within the Baptist tradition, but neither identify as Baptist today. Carley is average height with short brown hair; she dresses stylishly, but simply. She projects a quiet, calm presence—as though she never becomes flustered. In our interviews, Carley moves back and forth between speaking to me and tending to her children in an unselfconscious, unanxious way. Her family had a big influence on her desire to have many children. She says:

> I came from a larger family. There were five biological children and at two different times my parents took in children, too. So, my parents' sacrifice made a big impression on me. Not just taking in other kids but what they did to provide for us. My dad often told us that you don't have to be rich in money, we were rich in family and very blessed. . . . My husband grew up on the opposite end of the spectrum with one brother. David's family was very different. So, I vocalized a lot about that—that was something I would like to continue if we got married. And we prayed a lot about letting the Lord lead our family. So, when we got married we decided we wouldn't use any form of birth control. That's something we felt very convicted about at the beginning. We struggled with a little bit of infertility, too. It was kind of heartbreaking to let the Lord lead our family in that way and have no control over it.

Carley also attributes her pronatalist perspective to the influence of the book *A Full Quiver*, by Rick and Jan Hess, which she read when they were first married. She says that book "maybe hammered in a nail for us." While she was already predisposed to having a large family, the book solidified their commitment. Another factor that contributed toward Carley's commitment to the Quiverfull way of life is that she thinks it was "typical" at one time in America's past:

> I think that back then you didn't have to describe [a big family] at all. That was just a way of life. It wasn't something new or some subculture thing. That was the norm, I guess. If you talk to my grandma, I think there were eleven or twelve children in their family. It was rare that you'd only have one child. I don't feel like when I'd talk to her that she'd call it anything. It's just the norm. It's typical.

After the births of their first two children, the Millers had difficulty conceiving again, so they decided to pursue adoption. Following the adoption of their third child, Carley was able to conceive and eventually gave birth to four more children. Today, her children range in age from two to thirteen years. By her own account, the past couple of pregnancies have been hard on her body and the recovery time has been longer than she would like. She also deals with a chronic condition that requires her to be careful about her diet and need for rest. Despite the challenges—physical, mental, emotional, and financial—of raising seven children, Carley regrets nothing:

> It makes me feel complete. Like I can't even imagine. Just from the short time that I did work with kids, I was never satisfied. But this is what I'm called to do. This is what I'm designed for. I mean, there are days that I could really use a shower! [Laughter.] Like on Saturday morning when I'm in the shower and they're asking me for milk instead of asking dad. [Laughter.] But, there are days when I'm going to bed and I get emotional just thinking about what would have happened if we did choose to use some kind of birth control and wouldn't have had this child or that child and how different our life would have been in a negative way.

Still, Carley shies away from dogmatism regarding their commitment to pronatalism, which is often linked to other elements of the Quiverfull subculture. In her words,

> I wouldn't have any condemnation for anyone who has a small family. "Oh you only have four kids? You can't say you're following the Lord!"

> We kind of get that sense from Vision Forum [and other groups]. . . . We probably aren't as conservative on the modesty thing as others. We think modesty is important but not like others. I wear jeans and I have short hair. I don't have a head covering and I listen to secular music. [Laughter.] . . . When I read some of these [Quiverfull books] it makes me want to vomit because they're creating a routine to follow rather than a relationship to follow. I think large-family materials often err on the side of religion. And I think large families get a bad rap because of that.

Carley sees the Christian faith as a relationship in contrast to a religion. In this point of view, "religion" is necessarily negative because it entails a set of rules to follow without reference to one's "personal relationship with Jesus." When she says "relationship to follow," Carley is condemning the "religion" approach to Christian life as lifeless and rigid, without proper emphasis on God's grace, personal emotions, and the leading of the Holy Spirit. So, when she accuses some Quiverfull books and families of "creating a routine to follow rather than a relationship," she is denouncing their rigidity as counter to the genuineness of a vibrant "relationship" with Christ.

Even so, despite their large family and pronatalist convictions, Carley and David have not fulfilled the Quiverfull "ideal" of never using birth control. At different times throughout their marriage they have used various forms of contraception primarily in order to space their children. And, following a particularly difficult birth experience that threatened Carley's life, they briefly considered David getting a vasectomy. But, in the end they couldn't bring themselves to rule out completely any possibility of life. Thankfully, the pregnancies that followed went smoothly and the labors proved uncomplicated. Although Carley thinks that they may be reaching the end of her fertility, Carley and David remain open to more children.

The Millers enrolled their oldest children in public school when they first reached the proper age. But, that "experiment," as she calls it, lasted less than a semester before Carley pulled them out and began schooling them at home. She was especially concerned about how one of her children with learning disabilities was being treated. Although she acknowledges that it is difficult to teach many kids at many different developmental stages, she expresses joy and contentment about their choice:

I really enjoy teaching my kids and seeing the cracks that I'm filling that were there from brick and mortar schools. We probably do more Waldorf or unschooling or Montessori-type education. Charlotte Mason is probably [a better way to describe it]. We do a lot of free play, eclectic stuff. . . . That is important to me and I see the benefits in general and with my kids in particular.

Another important factor in the Millers' choice for homeschooling was Voddie Baucham's book *Family-Driven Faith*. Baucham is a Reformed Baptist pastor who advocates homeschooling and a family-centered lifestyle as the best means for "raising sons and daughters who walk with God." (I discuss Baucham's writings in more detail in subsequent chapters.) The Millers found this vision compelling, and Carley is convinced that schooling their children at home provides the best opportunity for inculcating their children with a love for God and God's word.

Carley's husband, David, has a corporate job that requires a long commute every day. Despite his willingness to help out with what's needed around the house, he is often physically absent from the home for twelve hours at a time. Carley says that he would prefer to work from home, but his employer won't allow it. David's absence from the home means that all of the children's schooling, along with most of the housework, falls on Carley's shoulders. Although she finds the combination of homeschooling and homemaking difficult, Carley keeps her expectations low:

> We haven't put a whole lot of expectations on life, I guess. The way we do things. It's just nice to have a bunch of little kids at home. I know that things are going to hit chaos in a couple years. We'll have several teenagers. And I've always thought it's not going to get easier, but harder. There's a lot of stuff that goes on, but for now I enjoy it.

Carley describes herself as "very laidback" and speaks with amusement of her struggles to keep a neat house: "I don't know how to run a house that great. There are loads and loads of laundry on the couch right now. I'm not the greatest at planning ahead. . . . I mean it's like five p.m. and I'm like, 'Oh no what are we going to have for dinner?' This isn't good! [Laughter.]" Although she admits that a firmer schedule would probably help with all of the tasks she juggles daily, Carley doesn't think that works for her: "I've tried to schedule but it doesn't work. I don't know. I just like letting God lead our day."

In her mind, "You don't have to micromanage every single detail of motherhood."

Regarding the struggles she faces as a homeschooling mom, Carley points to the tendency to compare her life to the lives of other mothers as a major problem and source of heartache:

> The comparison thing is huge. For me, that's such a horrible thing. That's the big one. Such a horrible sin and [long pause] it can rob so much. You just see the surface level of everyone, you know? I should be grateful and content with where I am. To covet what someone else has without knowing what they've gone through. It's silly to want what someone else has.

When asked if this is something she deals with every day, Carley says,

> Yes, I think that's because of technology with social media. It's even more in your face what others have. Sometimes I have to take a step back and pull away from that. And it simmers things down a bit because I don't have to see it. I still want some of those things, though. I still want a bathroom break to myself. But, I don't need someone's new Jetta when I'm driving a passenger van! [Laughter.] It's funny that these are my struggles.

The temptation to compare her life to that of others is closely connected to her concerns about finances. Money is always "the biggest thing" that Carley worries about. Even though she confesses that "God has proven himself over and over," and she thinks it's wrong that "our society especially puts so much emphasis on that," still she says that money "makes me worry."

Another daily struggle that Carley shares with Renee is what she calls "imbalance." She describes that in the following way:

> This fall we will have five kids in school. My husband hasn't been too involved other than paying for things. So I'm trying to balance how to teach that many kids and nurse a baby and make sure all the needs are taken care of in the home. And I need to be taken care of. What does that mean? I don't know for sure yet. But, it's important not to be lost in the shuffle. And [Mom] is often the first person who is.

When pressed to say more about what it would mean to "be taken care of," Carley points primarily to the need to rest.

I've tried to realize that it's okay to take a nap. I'm up in the night nursing a bazillion times so it's okay to take a nap. This probably comes from growing up in a large family, but it doesn't feel right to me to be alone. I never lived on my own by choice because I didn't like that feeling of being alone. There's always been someone there. So, I'm learning the importance of time alone. It's healthy to be able to sit in silence for a while, I think. And I think it's really challenging to do that.

Now that she has five children in school, Carley's daily responsibilities can be quite heavy. But, she has two remedies for the really tough days: junk food and prayer. She explains:

> I usually make Colby walk to the gas station to get me a Coke and a Milky Way. [Laughter.] I really do and it really does help! [Laughter.] Also, my prayer pattern. Where other people may talk to themselves, I pray constantly throughout the day. I'm totally dependent upon [God], and his mercies really are new every morning. Tomorrow is another day and we can try better tomorrow. No matter what it is. Whether it's me dealing with my selfishness or theirs. But, Coke really does help, too. [Laughter.]

Unlike Renee, Carley is a firm believer in gender hierarchy. She describes her point of view in the following way:

> I think [men and women] are the same in that God created both of us after his image. But, I definitely would say that he has put man in a leadership role to be head over his wife. I think that men process things differently than women. Not all, but I think as a general, overall rule. Sometimes men are a little bit... They don't get hints. Communication can be a bit off. [Laughter.] I would say women tend to be more tenderhearted versus men.

She points to the Bible and her experience with her peers as the evidence for these gender differences, along with what she saw in her family growing up. She describes male headship as follows: "Like a shepherd. That they lead gently. I wouldn't really put controlling in there at all. Like a gentle shepherd that follows the Lord but knows when there's danger, to be aware of things before they're happening." Despite her sense of gender essentialism, Carley describes her marriage as a partnership that, at times, defies the traditional prescribed gender roles:

[David] does lead our house. We try really hard to bounce ideas off [of each other]. I don't feel like he's the only one who makes the decisions, but I think we know that there's an underlying [expectation] that if he needed to put his foot down, I respect that. I think with the number of children we have, some of the things that some people say men can't do—like do dishes and wash clothes and wash hair—those go by the wayside. We need both of us to make our house function. I've had a bout recently with a [chronic condition], and in survival mode David has done way more dishes than I have over the past year. And we know several families and it's not just a special case for us. We have good friends who when you walk in the house you know that he is pulling as much weight as she is and vice versa. It looks more like a . . . It's unspoken. There is no, "Honey, can you help me?" It just gets done.

Carley seems to balance her sense of gender hierarchy with a pragmatic approach to work in the home, particularly because a large family requires so much housework. What matters is that things get done, not so much who is the one to do them. Carley also moderates male headship with the concept of mutual accountability to Christ: "I think if a woman is married that the husband should be the head and the wife should be submissive, but I also think that each of us is an individual and accountable to Christ." Rather than find male headship problematic, Carley thinks that it makes her and David more unified as a couple. "I really think that we are happier. I know that probably sounds silly, but I think we're more of a team because we know our roles and how to work together instead of working against each other."

Even so, Carley and David have run into conflict about gender roles with fellow church members in the past. In Carley's words,

We had a situation when we were in a house church and we were getting ready to multiply. . . . My husband and another member were going to lead one and we were with an organization that had lots of house churches that met for corporate worship together. I had posted on Facebook and I was inviting people to come to our house church on Sunday. And one of the original leaders invited my husband to a coffee shop to correct him for what I did. I felt like I didn't need to be corrected. And if he had a problem with me and something I did, that he should come to me. I would have felt very comfortable if he had invited both of us, but the fact that he invited my husband only—that bothered me. He ended up telling some people that my husband couldn't control me.

The original house church leader thought that it was inappropriate for Carley, a woman, to be seen as taking the initiative to invite people to their house church. The concern was that Carley would be viewed as exercising leadership in a way that was improper for a woman. Eventually, the Millers left the church in question and their house church folded. Although the conflict over gender roles wasn't the primary impetus for this change, it certainly contributed something to the breach. Carley calls this kind of hard approach to male headship "legalism" and cautions that it must not become "a religion."

Another example of Carley negotiating with gender-role ideology is in the matter of clothing. While it is common for those in the Quiverfull movement to promote feminine, modest clothing, typified by long skirts and high collars, Carley takes issue with that approach. Speaking of the wise woman who appears in Proverbs 31, she says,

> I think when it says that she was clothed in nice things, it means she obviously took care of herself. She wasn't frumpy. I mean I sometimes think that this modesty movement puts this picture in your head that you need floral puffy sleeves and a lace collar. And I don't think that's what it means. I think we can be *in* the world—and look like we're *in* the world—and not be *of* it.

Despite the fact that the Millers are committed to gender hierarchy, their interpretation of that doctrine is not always in line with that of their peers. They feel the freedom to negotiate with the concept of male headship and put it into practice in their daily lives in a way that works for them. The gender hierarchy of the Millers is more about pragmatism than attaining a theological ideal for marriage. With the principle of male headship in place, they are free to work out the particulars in daily life as they see fit.

We have seen that Carley is a little different from her Quiverfull peers in her education methodology and goals, her appearance, and her interpretation of gender hierarchy, but she is also different in her preference for organic food, natural or holistic medicine, and natural birth. According to Carley, their family seeks to "let our food be our medicine," eating healthy so that "we don't have to use anything other than food" for healing. All members of the family regularly receive care from a chiropractor and, she says, "When one of the kids is sick we go to the chiropractor first." She sees the use of essential oils and natural remedies as something the Bible supports, questioning why someone would use "synthetic medicine" when "God gave us [remedies found in nature] to nourish our bodies and help us." This doubt about the necessity of "synthetic medicine," along with the writings of Dr. Robert Sears and others, has led her to choose not to vaccinate their children either.[5] Carley is also an advocate for natural birth. All of this is part of one aspect of Carley's life in which she doesn't compare herself to others. She confesses, "It just makes the most sense to me. Why would we do it any different?"

ANALYSIS OF CARLEY'S STORY

Although she identifies with the Quiverfull movement, Carley makes it clear that she does so rather loosely. Part of this looseness may be the result of generational difference. Unlike Renee, Carley is a second-generation Quiverfull and homeschooling mother. By the time Carley began to take part in the Quiverfull subculture, it was developed enough to allow participants to identify with it while also negotiating and debating it. The experience with her house church brings this fact into sharp relief, showing that the outworking of the doctrine of male headship remains a contested matter within these circles. She also distinguishes herself from other Quiverfull families in the way she dresses, wears her hair, and what kind of music she listens to. And she is a proponent of natural birth and natural medicine. Rather than seeing Quiverfull as a strict system of rules and patterns of behavior, Carley focuses on the disposition of the heart: "the direction of the Lord or the conviction that he's placed on our hearts." In her words, "I've always kind of gone against the grain."

Although she is very much committed to homeschooling, Carley does not speak of separation from worldliness as a primary concern. Instead, she is concerned about each of her children receiving the education that is best suited to their needs and a family life that is focused on learning to love God. The educational philosophies she draws upon—Montessori, Waldorf, unschooling, Charlotte Mason—are typically associated with more left-leaning families, which sets her apart from mainstream Quiverfull families who rely

---

5. See, for example, Robert Sears, *The Vaccine Book: Making the Right Decision for Your Child*, rev. ed., Sears Parenting Library (New York: Little, Brown, 2011). Though he denies being "anti-vaccine," Sears is known for promoting delayed vaccinations and, in some cases, total exemption from vaccination. He is now the subject of a complaint by the Medical Board of California, charged with "gross negligence, repeated negligent acts and failure to maintain adequate and accurate records" (Tara Haelle, "Dr. Bob Could Lose License for Medical Negligence," *Forbes*, September 11, 2016, http://tinyurl.com/y7vyhl3v).

on more structured, explicitly Christian curricula. These methods seem well suited to Carley's laidback personality and preference for unscheduled days. In this way, she seems like something of a contrast to Renee, who found structure and scheduling a key part of maintaining her sanity. But what Carley and Renee share is a genuine love for being with and around their children. There are times when Carley expresses frustration with their dependence, but on the whole she sincerely enjoys her children and their domestic orientation. Among the three women described in this chapter, Carley seems the least stressed and overwhelmed by her daily responsibilities.

Another way in which Carley is a contrast to Renee is how she envisions and experiences the gender roles in her marriage. While Renee started out committed to male headship, she felt compelled to give up the doctrine after many years with a husband she describes as "passive" and disconnected. Carley, on the other hand, is very much committed to the doctrine of male headship, believing it to be an important contributor to their happy marriage. Interestingly, though, Carley describes a performance of male headship that prioritizes service, sacrifice, and love. She describes a marriage where domestic chores are shared without acrimony and both spouses pitch in to help out around the house as a matter of course. (Renee did not benefit from that kind of support.) The only mention of leadership in a traditional sense is in the matter of family worship: David leads the family in prayer and Bible study. Thus, the doctrine of male headship in the Miller household is rhetorically emphasized but performatively understated. In Carley's words, "There's that underlying notion that he's the head of the house without anyone having to say it or forcefully make it happen."

By far, Carley was the most surprising informant that I interviewed. More than any other mother in my research, Carley defies the Quiverfull stereotype, which is perhaps best illustrated by Michelle Duggar's long hair, long skirts, minimal makeup, and quiet demeanor. In fact, Carley seems to relish being a bit of a rebel who pushes the boundaries and defies stereotypes. Whether it's her penchant for secular music or her preference for natural remedies, Carley is a woman who goes her own way. A few days after our second interview, she sent me a message that said: "I forgot to tell you two things: (1) I am about halfway done with my birth doula certification. (2) I got my nose pierced." When I responded positively to both pieces of news, she replied, "Thanks and thanks. The nose ring was actually a barter for doula services. The dad is a body piercer. Life may get a little more exciting. ;)"

DEBORAH'S STORY

As explained in chapter 1, Deborah and Dan Olson are in their mid-thirties and have six children, ranging in age from two to eleven years. They live in the suburbs of a mid-sized Midwestern town where Dan works for the city government. While Deborah has a degree in education, she only used it for three years before leaving the teaching profession to stay at home with their children. Deborah is tall with long brown hair and almost always wears long skirts. She is very friendly and talkative, always willing to offer a story from her personal experience with no subject off limits. And while she speaks with passion and conviction, she also laughs easily and shares with Renee and Carley a sense of humility about the limits of her knowledge and experience.

Deborah wanted a large family from early on. "I think I've always wanted a large family," she says. "I can remember being pretty young and wanting lots of children." While they used birth control early in their marriage, the Olsons chose to abandon it entirely after having difficulty conceiving. And, by her testimony, their marriage has grown stronger because of that decision. She regrets ever using birth control to begin with:

> I guess I feel like [children] are blessings from God. Dan and I struggled relationship-wise early on before children. We started out knowing that we wanted a large family but we didn't start out not controlling it. We used birth control early on. But, our relationship has flourished since we stopped controlling it. For us, with every child we get closer and stronger. For us, God wants us to have children as blessings, as refinement, as an extension of his love and our love. A house full of siblings communicates more love, acceptance, goodness. And God created that process. So, I would say we kind of happened upon it. We did a five-year thing of birth control and I regret it deeply. I think about it and think that could've been two more babies. For me, I felt like it was somewhat like time wasted. It wouldn't be true for everyone but just for us, I would've rather let the Lord bless us with children from the beginning.

Even though money is always a significant struggle for the Olsons, Deborah would gladly welcome another pregnancy. For her, the monetary and physical burdens of another child are quite small in comparison to the joy of receiving another blessing from God. She calls the prospect of having another child "thrilling."

Although she was once a public school teacher, when it came time for her oldest children to attend school, Deborah couldn't bring herself to send them. While she knew very few people around her who were homeschooling, she began to look into it and prayed that God would show her what to do. She explains the process as follows:

> I remember thinking why in the world would I send my child away right now? I just had no interest in that. Why would I send him away to kindergarten? [The feeling] just grew. I started the same conversation with Dan and he was miraculously on the same page. So then he and I together started to explore and put the word out and then I started seeing homeschoolers everywhere. I saw it in action and that kind of solidified the decision. Once we started homeschooling, it became a serious spiritual issue for us. Nowadays we would say that our choice is first and foremost spiritual, because you're losing your grip on the persons you're trying to train when they are not under your training for seven hours a day. I mean you can't—children need to be close to you in proximity for you to have influence over them. A college-age student you can influence far away because cognitively you can do that, but with younger children you just can't. So now it's first spiritual and second that we want to be with our children. We want to be together while it is still appropriate for us to be together. It seems unnatural to us that there would be such separation between parents and children for such a long period of time every day. I definitely know that homeschooling isn't for everyone, in my brain, but I just can't imagine sending my kids away for seven hours a day.

More than any other factor, Deborah doesn't want to send her children to school because they would be under the training of someone else for several hours a day, five days a week. The implication is that the teachers providing that training might do so in a manner that Deborah and Dan disagree with. Their primary concern in homeschooling is the ability to maintain "influence" over their children, especially while they are young. They assume that they are the best influencers of their children and Deborah their best educator. Even though she acknowledges that not everyone can or should homeschool, she goes so far as to say that sending your children away for a long period every day seems "unnatural" and beyond the bounds of her comprehension.

Deborah has relatively modest goals for her children's education, hoping that each of them will be well prepared for whatever they want to do in life:

> I want them to be independent learners and skilled enough to do whatever it is in life they want to do. I want the boys and the girls to have some way to make a living for their families. Whatever type of education is required for that, I want them to be able to do it well. And that's different for everybody. If somebody wants their doctorate, that's a different level than someone driving a forklift. I want them to make a good contribution to society. I want them to be literate and organized and aware, educated on what's going on around them.

Deborah is clear that higher education isn't a foregone conclusion in their household. She and Dan both regret the debt they carry as a result of their college degrees and that makes her less enthusiastic about higher education:

> My goal isn't that they all attend a prestigious college or that even they all get a college degree. Dan and I won't insist that they all do that. That's partly because we both have college degrees and a lot of debt that we can't figure out how to pay off. Personally, I wish I could take [my degree] back. If they all want to go to college that's fine, but our prayer is that they would stay near home and do that first in a more cost-effective way. I would like for them to have something they can do other than waiting for a degree. I would like for them to learn trades or skills of some sort that they could earn money with.

Deborah is favorably inclined toward trade schools and apprenticeships, which she sees as routes to more stable and less debt-incurring ways of making a living. She also believes that a trade or small business is something that her boys (the expected breadwinners of their future families) could pass along to their children. She relates that Dan wishes he had a home-based business that would allow him to be more physically present, especially for his boys.

When asked about how she copes with the hard days of homeschooling, Deborah was self-deprecating and honest about her failings:

> Sometimes I do a poor job [of coping]. Sometimes I just whine and complain and get self-pitying. I've done that this week actually. "It's just

too hard! I'm all alone! My husband doesn't love me! Wah wah wah wah wah!" [Laughter.] I feel like I'm pretty good at reminding myself that I'm doing what I'm doing to honor the Lord and nobody else. So, if I feel out of check, I need to be in check with him more so than anyone else. My source of joy and strength needs to come from [God] and not from my husband or my friends or clearly not my children. If I feel like I'm spiraling downward, I can't claim that it's my first response because my first response is kind of to cry and whine. But, typically I can pull myself out of it pretty good by focusing on [the Lord]. Sometimes that means less gets done that day. There will be praise and worship music playing or there will be more Bible reading and more praying. I'll ask my husband to pray for me and he will. Obviously in our flesh we just want to "Waaaaaah!" but I try.

Deborah can identify with Carley's tendency to compare her life to that of other mothers and to want what they have:

The other thing that gets hard in homeschooling is just being in the home and not having all the resources we wish we had. All the things, you know? That's probably more of an issue than anything else. We compare ourselves. We compare our husbands, our children, our homeschools. So it's really hard to be content with where we are because of our problem in our society with having too much. So, when I get that way I try to turn inward and focus on what we do have and focus on what we do have compared with what our parents didn't have. And I try to focus on the fact that compared to most of the world I have way more than they do. I try to think about the fact that it's hard for a rich man to really know his need for the Lord. You know? I mean, I hate to make it all about money, but I think sometimes our down-ness stems from things that we see in our culture and our culture is so about things and having things and doing things a certain way and making everything seem like Pinterest.

"Just being in the home" is a major challenge for Deborah, particularly because their financial limitations mean that they do not have access to the educational resources she wishes they had: "All the things, you know?" In this sense, Deborah sees herself at odds with the values of the surrounding culture. The love of "things," "money," and "making everything seem like Pinterest" is always threatening to pull her down. To combat this mindset, she calls to mind what they do have and how fortunate they are in comparison with their parents and the rest of the world. And she devotes more time to worship music, Bible reading, and prayer.

While Renee credits both her own high standards and her lack of time for herself ("I didn't have a life") as the reason for her mental exhaustion, in Deborah's experience, the sense of being overwhelmed comes mostly when she tries to do things outside the home. She described one busy week in the following way:

> This week I got the opportunity do a couple of nice things for people. We went to the nurse practitioner. We went to see her on Tuesday and she just was not her normal perky self and it troubled me deeply. She walked into the appointment thirty-five minutes late and it looked like she had been bawling. And it just bugged me. It was totally out of character. She's the nurse practitioner we've seen since Garrett [their oldest child] was a baby. She's always kind, always perky, and it really bugged me. Anyway, I had left Garrett at home with a couple of the kids. I just took [the two youngest]. So I took the time that day because I wasn't babysitting and they had already started school. I was just free to do something that I'd love to do every day. I went to the florist and picked out a plant, flowers, and a card, and wrote a little note and took it back to the office and dropped it off for her. It took twenty minutes and, you know, I rarely feel like I have twenty minutes. And anyway, it just felt so good. And a few hours later she called me bawling. "You have no idea, you have no idea," she said. I still to this day don't know what was wrong.
>
> And then the next day I got to cook a meal for someone. I love to cook and I love to cook for people. And then the next day I taught Awana [an evangelical children's education program focused on scripture memorization] and I got to do this fun creative lesson. And then this morning I got to teach [an art class]. . . .
>
> So my life this week has just been filled with those things. And I think, "Oh this feels good!" But then [long pause] I am so stressed! [Laughter.] I have not slept! [Laughter.] Of course, I have also felt awful because I'm eating sugar. I have had headaches. I've not slept well. I've felt jittery. But, my point is, to reel myself back into reality. My time really has to be spent—I mean, to be successful at what I've made a commitment to do, my life can't be filled with that kind of stuff every day. It's hard. It's hard. Because I do have passions for things that have to be kind of put off to the side in order to be . . . Every mom is like that. Every mom is like that. But . . .

In contrast to Renee's experience, Deborah has the most trouble when she attempts to "have a life." When she has a week where she serves people outside the home, whether through a gift, a meal, or a lesson taught (things she has "passion" for), she experiences stress, evidenced by poor sleep, jitters, and headaches. She takes this experience as an indication that she needs to be focused on the home and educating her children. In order to "be successful at what [she's] made a commitment to do," her daily life cannot be filled with her passions. They have to be "put off to the side." She acknowledges this but says, "It's hard. It's hard."

Still, Deborah speaks of the multigenerational faithfulness as a comforting source of hope when life is difficult:

> So, what do we do [when we get discouraged]? We say we're just thinking forward. And that's the one thing about Voddie Baucham's book that got me emotionally—that we have stopped in past generations raising multigenerational Christians, multigenerational anything. We can't take back the past, what we did or didn't do, but we can keep looking to the future.

But, multigenerational faithfulness means more than just producing professing and practicing adult Christians. Deborah wants her children to avoid the common "crisis of faith" that she and her siblings went through in the teen and young adult years. In her words, her goal for her children is that "they don't leave my home until they're prepared to fly spiritually." She explains,

> So they aren't grasping for answers—strong in doctrine and strong in faith. Not just good moral kids who go to church but actually know it and strong enough to defend it even if you are surrounded by no one else who does. I think kids who grow up in Christian homes tend to lose it because they haven't been given a strong background to let them defend their faith. So it doesn't mean that I definitely think they have to grow up and have five kids apiece and homeschool. I would love for them to do that, but that may not happen. I just think there's something about being able to verbally defend their faith. And I felt very weak at that as a young adult.

When I asked Deborah what it was like to try to educate her older children while nursing babies, she laughed boisterously.

> Right . . . Right . . . It's pretty awful! [Laughter.] . . . It's a challenge and you worry. Are they getting enough creative fun things? Are they getting enough one on one? Sometimes I think maybe Drew could have read a year sooner if I had been spending less time chasing toddlers. You're always feeling pulled and it's a challenge. It's hard, hard, hard, hard.

Deborah shares Carley's more laidback personality and awareness of her limitations, but she locates most of her shortcomings in her inability to manage herself:

> My discipline—that's where I'm bad. My self-discipline. I feel like if I had more discipline myself I would struggle less. If I could eat right and exercise I would have so much more energy. I know things would be better. I don't know why I don't do it. If I could pray and read my Bible every morning I know that the day would go better. But it's easier to lie in bed for an extra fifteen minutes. So, things that require self-discipline I struggle with.

Like Carley, Deborah is committed to the doctrine of male headship. That works itself out in a firm conception of gender essentialism:

> [Men and women are] the same in the fact that we are made in the image of God. We have a mind, body, soul, and obviously we coexist and do a lot of the same physical things. But, men are different. They're made differently with different thoughts and wants and desires. And women, vice versa. Women do things differently, have different thoughts, wants, and desires. Obviously, there are physical differences between men and women. And I believe their roles are different. What God created them to be is different.

The bodily differences between men and women are a major factor in Deborah's understanding of men and women's roles, but the narratives of Genesis 1–3 are also important. For Deborah, the differences between men and women are so stark that she calls them "very different creatures." She explains:

> Clearly, there's a reason why God made a woman able to carry children and have children. Men desire physical things from women in a different way than women do men. That's just normal, common, for everyone. The story of creation is obviously important to reflect on. God made Adam to do all these things. Adam was given the responsibility to take care of the earth, naming the animals, all this stuff. But, he felt like he needed a helper. The story of creation makes it clear that the Lord expected woman to be an aid to the husband. I read this book, *Captivating*, that talks about this notion of the man's desire for a woman—clearly God created it. Women can use it manipulatively or the way God designed it, as a motivator to the man. There's something about that as something that draws man to woman. But that's not the same way women are drawn to men. They're drawn to men for the leadership or

emotional support or spiritual support, you know. So, it seems pretty clear to me that God made [men and women] a puzzle to fit together. Of course, that makes it challenging to deal with. We're very different creatures.

Deborah thinks that it is key to the stability and unity of families for the husband to be the provider for and leader of his family. She explains that conviction in the following way:

I do believe it is the man's responsibility or heart or central push to be the provider for the family financially and spiritually. Because of the struggles we've experienced, I feel like I would guide my children in that direction, but I would never want my daughters to think it's atrocious for them to have a job. There are times I wish I could go get a job to help out. . . . But, it's ultimately the husband's role to do that. Spiritually they are focused on the family's worship and discipling the children. I feel like if the father isn't leading in devotions and spiritual training, it sends a focus to people that it's just a woman thing to be spiritual. I believe that when the man's role in the spiritual training of the family becomes stagnant, that's the major source of disintegration of families. I believe that man is placed as leader of the home whether we want him to be or not. He's still the leader and the family will fall short regardless. Dan and I have struggled in the past and I have said that to him, "You're the leader whether you want to be or not." God has placed me in [the role of mother]. It's not up to me to decide that. It's not that the man should be in charge of all of it. I'm the teacher in my home. I'm just naturally gifted and it's easier for me to communicate and teach. I think a lot of women are gifted that way and we're emotionally connected in ways that men aren't. When I say, "Men should take the lead," I mean they're ultimately responsible for it all happening and encouraging the wife where necessary.

Because of her view of gender hierarchy, Deborah thinks that teaching for boys and girls will necessarily have different goals. Although she wants all of her children to read and write proficiently, she expects them to be moving toward different ends in life. In her words,

I have the same goals for them to an extent. I can't expect these girls to live in this house and see these roles of doing life and not think they're going to have babies and be stay-at-home moms. Obviously, I would love to see my girls be stay-at-home moms and homeschool their kids. I would also love for one of them to be a missionary. But, at the end of the day if we're parents for life and love our kids unconditionally, then what happens if one of my children decides to have two kids and put them in daycare and become a hairdresser? I hope I'm spunky enough to be their babysitter! I don't want to quench their spirit either. So, if there's something they can do that would also let them have a family then I would encourage that. And if you look at the boys, I can't help but think that they'll have the pressure of being the sole provider for their family. Ultimately, for the roles in our family, we want the women to be skilled in homemaking and the men to be very driven in being providers for the home. I would encourage any of my kids to do anything that allows more family time and more flexibility in their profession. Because that's definitely what's best for the family, in our opinion. . . .

I think that as they grow the girls need to narrow in on training from older women and the boys need to narrow in on training from older men. I think it gives them opportunities to see God at work in older men and gives them the opportunity to build strong relationships with their fathers and lots of opportunities for conversations and spiritual discipleship from the father instead of the mom. Because I think there comes a point when that's desperately needed for teenage boys. And that gets lost a lot. Public school kids, obviously, there's no time for dads to spend with them. But, it happens for homeschooling families too because dads are working and moms do the majority of hands-on training. So, somehow we make the conscious effort to channel that into the father becoming the mentor in life—spiritually, specifically, but also how to be a husband and be a man and all the things you're supposed to do.

Deborah notes that while she thinks it is vital for men to train boys and women to train girls, within the homeschooling family that is difficult to work out in practice because "moms do the majority of hands-on training." Thus, even though she sees the boys and girls headed in different vocational directions (ideally, boys toward being breadwinning fathers and girls toward being stay-at-home mothers), Deborah is the one on whom the majority of the day-to-day responsibility rests to prepare them for those different roles.

Although she has firm convictions about gender roles and male headship when speaking in theory, when Deborah describes the inner workings of her marriage, the clear gender divisions become muddled. For example, Dan has struggled throughout their marriage to control his temper. His anger is often expressed in loud outbursts and yelling, something he learned from his family. She confesses that "it was very hurtful for me and I was crushed at first." They tried a few forms of counseling to work on it, but eventually she made it clear to him that such behavior was simply "unacceptable." She relates that turning point in the following way:

> At the end of the day I was just kind of snide about it because my Bible says the fruit of the Spirit is self-control. "Sink yourself deeper into his word and into his Spirit and if you are there then there is no way you'll be screaming at your wife and children." I think he was like, "Oh goodness, I've got a hard one now." [Laughter.] And I wasn't willing to make excuses for him. But now I think he's thankful that I was persistent in that mindset.

When I suggest to Deborah that her account of that struggle seems at odds with the doctrine of wifely submission, she laughs knowingly and replies:

> Submission is such a hard subject because you know everything you know about me. I'm passionate and intense and very opinionated and very bold and very wordy. My husband is not. He's a quiet guy. . . . [E]arly in marriage, submission was very difficult for me because I felt like I had a husband who hadn't arrived yet at adulthood. I felt like he hadn't even arrived yet as a Christian. I really wanted a God-centered marriage and he just wanted me. [Laughter.] We just had to grow into a pattern that ultimately became more pleasing to the Lord. Me learning where and when to tone it down and praying that the Lord would convict his heart because I could not be his Holy Spirit. Even though I wanted to be his Holy Spirit. [Laughter.] It's amazing the interaction between him and me now compared to then. It will be fifteen years this August. There are a lot of areas where I don't say anything and he just chooses and does it. It took a lot of pruning on my part and growing on his part.

It's clear that Deborah sees gender roles as fixed patterns of behavior and activities that are the same for all people regardless of personality. So, even though she is "passionate and intense and very opinionated and very bold and very wordy," she had to go through "a lot of pruning" in order to tone that down and learn to defer to Dan's leadership. Their growth in their prescribed roles allowed their marriage to become "more pleasing to the Lord." But, if Deborah's forceful handling of Dan's anger problem doesn't seem like submission, she disagrees.

> In no way would I define submission as a person without an opinion or a person led by a leash. I believe it has to do with me respecting the

authority that the Lord gave Dan as the head of our home. He's the head of our home whether he realizes it or does the right thing. Which is why when he's doing the wrong thing we will suffer for it. If you're not doing the things the Lord wants you to do, then we'll be suffering because of it. There was a time in our marriage that he never would have gotten up on his own on Saturday morning for Bible study. But, he's up at seven a.m. to go to Bible study even though I want to stay in bed. And he takes initiative in church that he never would have done fifteen years ago. It's been a learning process of figuring out our roles. I think a lot of women think they need to not have opinions or be outspoken to be submissive. I think a lot of people can't be vulnerable about that because in Christian circles people might think [the wives] aren't in their place. There's definitely an issue in our culture of men becoming more passive and women becoming more assertive. There have been changes in our culture that aren't good. But, I don't think the Lord would have given Adam a helpmeet that couldn't help him.

Deborah is very much still "in the thick of it" as a Quiverfull mom. She is still in her fertile years and has multiple school-age children at home. She has faced numerous challenges with a special-needs child whose chronic illness requires numerous doctor visits and a special diet. Still, Deborah presses on with their way of life, confident that she is doing what God wants her to do. In fact, just as I was putting the finishing touches on this book, Deborah gave birth to another child.

ANALYSIS OF DEBORAH'S STORY

Like Renee, Deborah's story reveals a Quiverfull mother shouldering a seemingly endless list of responsibilities. But, unlike Renee, Deborah is still in the midst of the hardest years, with six small children still at home. She is often overwhelmed by the challenges that surround her: caring for a child with a recurring illness, juggling the bills and debts their family has incurred, carrying out the daily work of running a home, and educating her school-age children. She speaks of her way of life as a "privilege" and couldn't imagine living any other way, but the weight of the burden remains.

Also, one gets the sense from Deborah's testimony that their family is one disaster away from financial ruin. And, despite a few friends and a church they regularly attend, it seems that they remain largely isolated, lacking a social safety net to help catch them if such an event were to occur. The economic and social vulnerability of the Olsons is clear.

We also see in Deborah's story the common perception among Quiverfull women that they are incrementally less capable as mothers the more they have going on outside the home. On a week when she gets to pursue her "passions," which she speaks about in exhilarated and joyful terms, she still perceives herself as stressed and neglecting her number one priority: the home. Of course, fathers do not face the same expectations because they are tasked with the responsibility of being the breadwinners. While Quiverfull literature, particularly the materials written by men, often emphasize the father's duty to lead and "shepherd" his family, the ideal can look very different in daily practice. Often, what the fathers do by financing the work of the home is enough, while the rest falls on the mothers' shoulders. Deborah describes it this way: "The mom (or whoever is overseeing the children) tends to be the dominant one in the way the house flows. So, [Dan] respects the fact that it's my ship. He owns the ship but I'm the chief operator. The um . . . Director of Operations." This illustration is telling. The owner can live at a considerable distance from the day-to-day activities of the ship. His name is on the deed and he can have as much or as little to do with the ship's operation as he wants. But, if Deborah is the "Director of Operations," then she really does "do it all."

Deborah's story also reveals again the tensions within the Quiverfull discourse of gender hierarchy. Among the three women in this chapter, she is the most verbal and passionate about proper gender roles. And yet, Deborah also seems to exercise significant leadership within her family, particularly in the area of setting expectations for behavior and correcting offenses. She frames it in terms of being a good "helpmeet": "I don't think the Lord would have given Adam a helpmeet that couldn't help him." Her counsel to Dan reveals her leadership: "He's the head of our home whether he realizes it or does the right thing. Which is why when he's doing the wrong thing we will suffer for it. If you're not doing the things the Lord wants you to do, then we'll be suffering because of it." This puts the onus to do "the things the Lord wants you to do" squarely on the man's shoulders through the threat that his family will suffer if he is disobedient. While Deborah takes this approach because she believes it conforms to God's will for the Christian marriage, there is no doubt that she also abides by it because she thinks it works for her. By her testimony, Dan has grown a lot in their many years of marriage, which is evidenced by his participation in church activities and treating her and the children with greater care. She admits that he still fails, but when he does he apologizes to her and the children and seeks to make it right. Thus in the case of the Olsons, rather than resulting in a more authoritarian husband, the doctrine of male headship has led to a more humble and loving husband.

Still, transformation came at a price. As Deborah says above: "It took a lot of pruning on my part and growing on his part." Deborah's boisterous, opinionated personality had to be "pruned"—literally trimmed and cut back—while Dan had to grow. Dan's growth was facilitated by Deborah's diminishment.

CONCLUSION

This chapter has provided a glimpse inside the Quiverfull movement through the stories of three Quiverfull mothers. Although these accounts are by no means exhaustive (there is much that I had to leave out), they provide a sufficient introduction to the complexities and tensions of Quiverfull lived religion as expressed by three different women in three different contexts. As I said at the beginning of this chapter, we cannot assume that these women are representative of the movement as a whole. The "sample" is too small and my time with them too limited to make any substantive generalizations. Just by virtue of being willing to talk to me, the women I have encountered may occupy a more moderate position (if that characterization is even appropriate) within the movement.

Still, their stories and the themes they raise are representative enough for a first-time in-depth study of the movement. The remaining chapters will take up themes raised by Renee, Carley, and Deborah, including the challenges of Quiverfull's construction of motherhood, their vision of children and childhood, and their private construction of the nuclear family. In pursuit of each topic, I will draw upon both Quiverfull elite materials and the stories of Quiverfull mothers in order to show the differences of opinion and approach between the two. Along the way, we will learn more about the lives of Deborah, Carley, and Renee and consider in more detail what they might reveal about the way evangelical Americans imagine and practice family.

3.

Motherhood in the Full Quiver

Deborah Olson has six children, ages two to ten years.[1] One child has severe allergies and a disease that calls for major dietary restrictions, frequent doctor visits, and lots of worry. Deborah freely admits that she and Dan struggle financially, calling it a constant problem. Occasional car or house repairs are serious hurdles for the Olsons, who are already struggling to pay off student loans. Yet, Deborah says, "I would welcome another baby." In fact, she finds the prospect "thrilling." She is not worried about handling the change to the household, or the financial strain, or whether her marriage can withstand the stress. And, she's not worried about the care that a baby requires: "I would not dread getting up with a baby again or nursing a baby again." When I ask what, if anything, scares her about having another baby, she responds:

> That I would have some sort of complication. That I wouldn't be here for my children. That I would be forced to have some kind of major surgery when I'm not in control of scheduling it. Or that, you know, mostly something that would compromise my ability to keep taking care of everybody. That's it.

Despite the family's financial burdens, Deborah Olson doesn't fear the added responsibilities of another child—in fact, she welcomes them. But, her pregnancies and births have gotten increasingly complicated

---

1. A portion of this chapter appeared as "Praying for More: Mothers and Motherhood in the American Quiverfull Movement," in *Angels on Earth: Mothering, Religion, and Spirituality*, ed. Vanessa Reimer (Bradford, ON: Demeter, 2016), 73–90.

over the years. So, her major concern is that her body might fail her. Interestingly, though, it is not because she is afraid of pain or possible surgery, but because she doesn't want to go through something "that would compromise [her] ability to keep taking care of everybody." Even though it is her body that would be compromised, she is thinking mostly of her ability to care for everyone else.

Deborah Olson is pushed to her limit, concerned about the consequences of another pregnancy, yet desirous of more children. And she's not alone. In her book *Quiverfull*, Kathryn Joyce describes the screen names of Quiverfull mothers in the internet chat rooms she explores for her research. Many call themselves "Praying for More" or something similar.[2] This moniker is illuminating, not just because it describes well the Quiverfull mother's constant openness to more children, but also because it accurately describes the Quiverfull approach to motherhood in general. When I see "Praying for More," I think of Deborah, not just her willingness to embrace another life as an unqualified blessing, but also because she wants, above all, to be able to carry on with the gargantuan task she simply calls "my job."

The work of motherhood is challenging, to say the least. Whatever the context or form it takes, motherhood in America is filled with significant emotional and symbolic weight, along with a seemingly never-ending list of daily care-related tasks. But the threefold discourse of the Quiverfull movement means that their mothers bear and nurse children well into their forties, all the while serving as their children's primary educator from preschool through high school (and sometimes beyond). As a result, the Quiverfull mother serves as a nurse, caregiver, administrator, cook, maid, and teacher for longer than even the average stay-at-home mom. Thus, the Quiverfull mother is, in a sense, always "praying for more"—not only praying for more children, if that is God's will, but also more responsibilities. They know that every child they birth will be under their primary tutelage, schooled at home until they enter adulthood. And they are in charge of managing the household while teaching multiple children of various ages, while also nursing a baby or chasing a toddler (or both). Yet, Quiverfull mothers willingly pray for more and, in their words, rely on the grace of God for survival. Deborah says,

---

2. Kathryn Joyce, *Quiverfull: Inside the Christian Patriarchy Movement* (Boston: Beacon, 2009), 161.

[Having more children than most] has humbled me to rely on the strength of God to do my job as a mother rather than relying on myself to keep everything in perfect order. . . . And when I am weak he is strong. I need to be in a position of weakness in order for him to be strong. When I get a compliment about my mothering I say, "Well, the Lord is doing it." I mean my husband has seen me broken many times. It is definitely the Lord doing it.

In chapter 2, I presented the stories of three Quiverfull mothers and analyzed how they embody the Quiverfull discourse. In this chapter, I reflect theologically about motherhood in America alongside the mothers of the Quiverfull movement.[3] This theological endeavor begins with a description of what Quiverfull motherhood looks like on the ground. Then, I offer some theological reflection in two major movements: (1) an examination of Quiverfull practice of motherhood in relation to their rhetoric of gender hierarchy; (2) an examination of the Quiverfull ideal of maternal omnipotence in relation to the experience of maternal vulnerability.

SIX CHARACTERISTICS OF QUIVERFULL MOTHERHOOD

What does it look like to be a Quiverfull mother? First, Quiverfull mothers are pregnant or nursing or both for up to three decades. Because they choose to forgo any kind of birth control to limit or space their children, Quiverfull mothers who are healthy and fertile can have children from their early twenties (when most of them are married) into their late forties. There is even a book titled *Three Decades of Fertility*.[4] In this way of envisioning motherhood, women's bodies are devoted to reproduction and infant care for up to thirty years. In the words of Renee Tanner: "Having many children means

---

3. It is important to keep in mind that experiences of motherhood are always-already interpreted by social, cultural, and symbolic conceptions of motherhood. One cannot separate one's experience of birth, on the one hand, and the cultural ideals associated with birth, on the other. When a mother is experiencing birth, her experience is always-already shaped by her social, cultural, and symbolic imagination about birth. There is no "universal experience" of motherhood to which all women can relate that floats above the concrete experiences of particular women within particular times and places. Adrienne Rich makes a distinction between motherhood as an experience and motherhood as an institution (social, cultural, and symbolic) in her classic work, *Of Woman Born: Motherhood as Experience and Institution* (New York: W. W. Norton, 1986).

4. Natalie Klejwa, *Three Decades of Fertility: Ten Ordinary Women Surrender to the Creator and Embrace Life* (Saint Paul, MN: Visionary Womanhood, 2013).

that you never really stop having babies and it's just a way of life. It was just normal to me to have a baby on my hip or in my arms." Of course, in the days before birth control and in parts of the world where birth control is unavailable, women would not call this way of life *Quiverfull*. It's simply life—and a life that many would change if given the option. But, in the American context, where birth control is relatively easy to obtain and family size is generally small, it can seem like a radical thing to forgo family planning entirely. In fact, in a society where birth control is the norm, one's surrender of fertility to God can be seen as a kind of asceticism, making oneself especially holy and set apart.

The consequences of the pronatalist commitment for women's bodies are significant. The stories of the mothers in *Three Decades of Fertility* contain lengthy explanations of the detrimental physical consequences that come with repeated childbearing: debilitating back pain, sciatica nerve pain, varicose veins, pubis-symphysis dysfunction (the movement or misalignment of the pelvis that can cause moderate to severe pain), hernias, adrenal fatigue, hormone imbalances, multiple miscarriages, depression, anxiety, and more. In these stories, it is clear that the bodily work of repeated pregnancies can exact a heavy toll, even if it is freely chosen and accepted in faith.

The second characteristic of Quiverfull motherhood is due, at least in part, to their devotion to reproduction: Quiverfull mothers see their expansive practice of motherhood as their only vocation. Motherhood is not something to which they are called alongside some other form of work. Due to the financial strain of supporting a large family on the father's salary, some mothers take on occasional jobs. One of the mothers I interviewed cleans a home every week and another teaches piano lessons on the side. But even in these cases, motherhood is viewed as a fulltime job requiring all of one's attention and resources. When they are forced to work for pay in some other fashion, there is a general understanding that the more work they do, the less adequate they are as mothers. (The unstated implication, of course, is that fatherhood is not a fulltime job in the same way. Fathers can work beyond the home and it does not affect their ability to be a father.) For Quiverfull mothers, the care and education of children is their primary work for the majority of their adult lives.

The third characteristic is that motherhood is, to some extent, professionalized due to the practice of homeschooling.[5] Most of the

---

5. This point is also made by Colleen McDannell in "Creating the Christian Home," in

women I interviewed do not see themselves as "just" stay-at-home moms, but *homeschooling* moms, which is motherhood of a different sort. On the one hand, all mothers teach their children things like how to feed themselves, use the bathroom, tie their shoes, and use good manners at the table. On the other hand, homeschooling mothers are the primary educators of their children from preschool through high school. This entails a great deal: reading, writing, literature, mathematics (from long division to calculus), history (state, American, European, and world), geography, science (biology, anatomy and physiology, chemistry, physics), government and economics, art and music. In addition to the many subjects of study, there are also innumerable educational philosophies and pedagogies: progressivist, Montessori, Waldorf, classical education, unschooling, and more. Not all homeschooling mothers undertake all of these subjects, nor do all mothers bother investigating philosophies of education. But, these suggest the potential scope of the homeschooling mother's work. And much like a one-room schoolhouse, they are teaching multiple ages at once. The kindergartner learning to read is working alongside the middle schooler doing geometry. Mothers who approach this work with seriousness (and that's most of them) undertake homeschooling as a kind of professional vocation.

The fourth characteristic of Quiverfull motherhood is that, due to all of the above, the mother's body and work are the de facto center of the household. This is not uncommon in American life, but in the Quiverfull family the mother's centrality increases in intensity. The mother is pregnant and nursing most of the time, requiring regular assistance from her husband and older children. Also, she is responsible for everyone's education. She orders their days, determines their workload, delegates their assignments, and dispenses grades. She is the one to administer housework, plan voluntary work, and order all other activities beyond the home. And even though Quiverfull families strongly endorse the father as the "spiritual head of the family," it is usually the mother who provides regular religious education through Bible reading, prayers, and discipline of various kinds throughout the day. Due to pronatalism and homeschooling, the Quiverfull home is functionally mother-centered.

The fifth characteristic of Quiverfull motherhood is that because of the mother-centered nature of the household, the older children and

American Sacred Space, ed. David Chidester and Edward T. Linenthal (Bloomington: Indiana University Press, 1995).

father are regularly called upon to assist in teaching and household responsibilities. This is particularly true of families with six or more children. In these situations, children are required to learn a degree of self-sufficiency from early on. Older children learn to cook, clean, and help care for their younger siblings. Younger children learn to respect older siblings as authority figures, for good or ill. Also, fathers are often (though not always) required to do more than they would normally do in either a two-income household or a "typical" stay-at-home mom situation. With the mother occupied with the education of children for most of the day, the household work becomes something that requires sharing to get done.

The final characteristic of Quiverfull motherhood is that it is, to a significant degree, a private endeavor. Quiverfull mothers typically lack an extended community of support and lead somewhat isolated lives, especially while their children are young. Sometimes this isolation is purposeful: an attempt to separate themselves from people they consider to be a negative influence. Sometimes this isolation is the result of their family's unusual way of life: they simply can't find other families nearby that share their commitments, and "normal" families are skeptical of their religious devotion. And sometimes this isolation is experienced even while involved in a church or homeschool cooperative. The sheer number of their children and the extent of their daily responsibilities means Quiverfull mothers are sometimes prevented from cultivating friendships and participating in communities that could provide them with support.

QUIVERFULL MOTHERHOOD AND GENDER HIERARCHY

With this overview of the practice of Quiverfull motherhood in mind, I turn now to the theological concerns of this project. Quiverfull discourse centralizes and prioritizes women's bodily work as a mother in significant ways. And yet this practice of motherhood—centered on pronatalism and homeschooling—also seriously complicates the Quiverfull practice of gender hierarchy. To explain this phenomenon, the following section begins with an overview of what Quiverfull materials say about womanhood and motherhood. Put simply, Quiverfull discourse at the elite level is stridently antifeminist and collapses womanhood into motherhood.⁶ But, when this version of womanhood is compared with the real lives of Quiverfull mothers, two things become clear. First, the lives of lay-level Quiverfull practitioners differ significantly from the rhetoric of the elites. Second, the Quiverfull practice of motherhood often conflicts with their purported ideal of gender hierarchy. That is to say, the practice of Quiverfull motherhood can, in some cases, overwhelm and subvert their commitment to gender hierarchy. Where it doesn't break down entirely, male headship is redefined in such a way as to conform to a mother-centered family structure. Thus, the performance of Quiverfull motherhood occurring in the daily lives of many families is far more complicated than the picture painted by Quiverfull elites and cultural commentators observing from a distance.

QUIVERFULL MOTHERHOOD AT THE ELITE LEVEL

As stated in chapter 2, the seminal work to which most Quiverfull families point to as the catalyst for the emergence of Quiverfull is Mary Pride's *The Way Home: Beyond Feminism, Back to Reality*. Despite the fact that *The Way Home* is almost thirty years old, the vision of womanhood Pride sets forth continues to be foundational for Quiverfull today. Pride points to feminism (as she understands it) as the single culprit for widespread ignorance and rejection of biblical teaching on womanhood. She says, *"Feminism is a totally self-consistent system aimed at rejecting God's role for women."*⁷ Jennie Chancey and Stacy McDonald echo Pride in even more pointed terms in their 2007 book *Passionate Housewives Desperate for God*: "Quite simply, there is no such thing as 'Christian feminism.' We either embrace the biblical model and call it 'very good' . . . or we reject it and plummet

---

6. For the purposes of this chapter I am speaking primarily of biological motherhood. There are other forms of motherhood, of course, such as adoptive motherhood and foster motherhood, and these forms have much overlap with the experience of biological motherhood. But, the pronatalist practice of the Quiverfull movement leads them to an almost exclusive focus on biological motherhood. Motherhood is a broad concept that is deeply rooted in pregnancy and birth. While one does not need to become pregnant and give birth in order to mother, no one can mother a child unless that child has been conceived and birthed by someone. Moreover, the experience of motherhood for Quiverfull women is very much rooted in pregnancy and birth, which they undergo repeatedly, often in close intervals. Apart from this biological given, however, conceptions of motherhood vary widely across space and time. That is why this chapter specifically refers to the Quiverfull *construction* or *practice* of motherhood.

7. Pride, *The Way Home*, xi–xii (emphasis in original). Throughout her book, Pride makes a number of connections between feminism and a variety of -isms, including socialism, fascism, Marxism, and liberalism. I am not going to address these ideological claims.

over the cliff with the rest of the passengers on the runaway railcar."[8] The Botkin sisters also see feminism as fundamentally incapable of producing anything positive for women: "A bad tree cannot produce good fruit. And no true good fruit can, or ever has, come from feminism."[9]

An entire book could be written on the way Quiverfull proponents characterize feminism, but their basic perspective can be summed up in three phrases: gender-role obliteration, excessive individualism (or selfishness), and contraception and abortion. *Gender-role obliteration* refers to the perceived feminist attempt to eliminate the eternal differences between the sexes.[10] They claim feminists want to turn women into men by stepping outside their God-given roles and modifying the body to suppress their God-given female-ness.[11] *Excessive individualism* is found in the feminist emphasis on female autonomy.[12] Quiverfull writers see feminists trying to free women from the bondage of husband, home, and children for the sake of individual self-fulfillment. They reject this and point to so-called working moms as a major contributor to the decline of American culture.[13] In the words of the Botkin sisters, "The idea of women going out into the sphere of public industry to compete with men for jobs in the pursuit of 'their true potential' . . . was pushed by God-hating Marxists who wanted to keep woman out of her natural element, tear apart the family, and destroy Christianity."[14] Finally, Quiverfull adherents find the pursuit of autonomy vividly illustrated in *contraception and abortion*. As Pride says, "the quest for autonomous female freedom leads to fear of babies."[15] And "contraception is the mother of abortion," because contraception, which seeks to limit children for the sake of "individualist" interests, provides the rationale and moral justification for abor-

---

8. Jennie Chancey and Stacy McDonald, *Passionate Housewives Desperate for God* (San Antonio, TX: Vision Forum, 2007), 145.

9. Anna Sofia Botkin and Elizabeth Botkin, *So Much More: The Remarkable Influence of Visionary Daughters on the Kingdom of God* (San Antonio, TX: Vision Forum, 2005), 72.

10. See, for example, Botkin and Botkin, *So Much More*, 19–22; Chancey and McDonald, *Passionate Housewives*, 31–36; and Nancy Leigh DeMoss, *Lies Women Believe and the Truth That Sets Them Free* (Chicago: Moody, 2001), 142–45.

11. Pride, *The Way Home*, 31.

12. Pride, *The Way Home*, 57.

13. DeMoss, *Lies Women Believe*, 144, 124.

14. Botkin and Botkin, *So Much More*, 118–19. The Botkin sisters find Marxism as much to blame for contemporary views on womanhood as feminism. They share this emphasis with Pride, who accuses feminism of being inseparable from Marxist socialism.

15. Pride, *The Way Home*, 49.

tion.¹⁶ Indeed, contraception and abortion are linked in the writings of every Quiverfull teacher. The feminist desire for control of one's body, especially one's fertility, is considered fundamentally evil.¹⁷

It's worth noting that Quiverfull proponents are so against feminism, they go so far as to read feminism into the doctrine of original sin. The Botkins claim, "We are all sinners. We all tend to rebel. . . . We rebel because it is our deep-rooted sin nature. We direct our rebellion at God through our rebellion to men. This means that *all women are rebellious feminists at heart.*"¹⁸ Chancey and McDonald agree: "As much as we hate to admit it, as women, we all have feministic tendencies. It is part of our sin nature—the flesh we battle on a daily basis. . . . Feminism is as old as the Garden of Eden."¹⁹ For Quiverfull, feminism is not simply a dangerous ideology or even an attack on marriage and family. Feminism is the unique original sin for womankind.

In contrast to the God-rejecting system of feminism, Quiverfull proponents offer prolific childbirth and "homeworking" to Christian wives as the only whole-scale alternative. Pride's claims on this point are potent and far-reaching:

> Homeworking is the exact opposite of the modern careerist/institutional/Socialist [read: feminist] movement. It is a way to take back control of education, health care, agriculture, social welfare, business, housing, morality, and evangelism from the faceless institutions to which we have surrendered them. . . . *Homeworking, like feminism, is a total lifestyle.*

---

16. Pride explains: "Family planning is the mother of abortion. A generation had to be indoctrinated in the ideal of planning children around personal convenience before abortion could become so popular. . . . Once couples began to look upon children as creatures of their own making, who they could plan into their lives as they chose or not, all reverence for human life was lost" (*The Way Home*, 77, 75).

17. Pride also understands feminism to be naturally wedded to what she considers socialist governmental practices, including public schooling. The second half of *The Way Home* contains a robust (and conspiracy theory prone) deconstruction of American public education, along with advocacy for Christian homeschooling as the proper responsibility of Christian mothers.

At this point, I am forgoing discussion of the accuracy of the Quiverfull portrayal of feminism because I am chiefly concerned with their *construction* of feminism. In Quiverfull literature there is little to no acknowledgment of the varieties of feminism that have developed since the 1980s and the corresponding changes to the ideological tenets within these differing feminisms. In the rare instances when varieties of feminism are acknowledged, they are painted with the same brush: all feminism destroys God's design for the sexes. Even contemporary pro-life feminists are dismissed. For Quiverfull proponents, feminism is an ideology poisoned at its source, and no amount of reformulation can change that. This sets them apart from evangelicalism as a whole, in which even strident defenders of conservative family values are able to acknowledge some benefit arising from feminist activism.

18. Botkin and Botkin, *So Much More*, 31 (emphasis in original).

19. Chancey and McDonald, *Passionate Housewives*, 132, 148.

The difference is that homeworking produces stable homes, growing churches, and children who are Christian leaders.[20]

If feminism is about limiting or eliminating births depending upon personal choice, then Quiverfull is about putting absolutely no limit on pregnancies or births.[21] In place of "gender-role obliteration," Quiverfull asserts gender dualism in the strongest possible terms. And in place of autonomous individualism, Quiverfull offers total self-emptying as the means by which women fulfill their divinely ordained role as helpers to men. Quiverfull teachers promise this "biblical lifestyle" of Christian women will be the means by which families, churches, and society are changed for God's kingdom. Not only is Quiverfull the only consistent Christian choice against feminism, but it is also the method through which the world will be transformed. Thus motherhood is, above everything else, the Christian woman's "battle station" in the war against Satan and a debased American culture.[22] Even the descriptor *Quiverfull* comes from a biblical military metaphor in which children are conceived as "arrows" in the hand of a warrior.[23] Mothers give birth to, shape, and sharpen these "arrows" for spiritual combat.[24] Writing for Quiverfull daughters, the Botkin sisters conclude their book with a dramatic call to motherhood:

> Woman's hope and future is fulfilled through *motherhood*.... Too many women forget that the hand that rocks the cradle really does rule the world. As Christian women, we should pray to have several children

---

20. Pride, *The Way Home*, xiii (emphasis mine).
21. Most Quiverfull teachers even denounce Natural Family Planning (NFP), a method of family planning supported by the Roman Catholic Church, which involves planning children without the use of contraception. For Quiverfull adherents, any attempt to control conception is a violation of God's sovereignty over the womb.
22. The term *battle station* is taken from a letter by Cathi Warren written to David Brooks in response to his *New York Times* piece that concluded that Quiverfull mothers were too busy parenting to wage a culture war. She argued that raising a large Christian family was itself her "battle station," as part of the culture war for Christianity (quoted in Joyce, *Quiverfull*, 137).
23. The original Hebrew for Ps 127:4–5 is actually speaking of *sons* as the "arrows" in the hands of a warrior. It is only contemporary translations of the Bible that render the word as the gender-neutral term *children*. In ancient Israelite culture sons were the "arrows" that gave a man security in his old age, for they could defend the family interests at the city gate, where the legal and economic issues of the community were settled. As biblical literalists on so many issues, it is curious that Quiverfull adherents have not been more attentive to this detail.
24. Campbell says it best: "Arrows do not just happen. It takes hours and hours of patience to straighten and sharpen an arrow that can effectively hit the mark.... We are 'arrow sharpeners,' preparing arrows for God's army. The more 'straight arrows' we prepare, the more we help God fulfill His plans on earth" (*Be Fruitful and Multiply*, 81).

and not limit God in how he wants to bless. We should study and prepare to raise them to be exemplary, effective Christian warriors. We should think ahead, not only to our children but to our grandchildren and great-grandchildren, aspiring to be a mother of thousands of millions, and aspiring to see our children possess the gates of their enemies for the glory of God.[25]

In opposition to the teachings of feminism, therefore, Quiverfull teachers assert the dual role of wife and mother as the fundamental definition of what it means to be a woman. A woman is not understood apart from her biological capacity for reproduction and her natural function as helper of men and nurturer of children. Pride says it simply: "Childbearing sums up all our special biological and domestic functions. . . . Childbearing *is* woman's 'peculiar function.'"[26] Motherhood is wholly constitutive of womanhood. God designed women to be mothers and then commanded them to "be fruitful and multiply" (Gen 1:28), birthing as many children as God sees fit to give.[27] Though the physical inability to conceive is acknowledged as a reality for some, the state of "barrenness" is unambiguously considered a "curse" in Quiverfull literature.[28] Even the salvation of women is tied directly to motherhood. Nancy Campbell says, "Women will be saved from getting into deception and from being lured away from their divine destiny, if they continue to walk in the role of motherhood which God planned for them."[29] Pride says something similar:

25. Botkin and Botkin, *So Much More*, 292–93 (emphasis in original).
26. Pride, *The Way Home*, 41, 42 (emphasis in original). She goes on to say, "Having babies is a Christian wife's calling. . . . Rejecting babies is rejecting ourselves" (43, 45). The Vision Forum statement "The Tenets of Biblical Patriarchy" says, "Since the woman was created as a helper to her husband, as the bearer of children, and as a 'keeper at home,' the God-ordained and proper sphere of dominion for a wife is the household and that which is connected with the home."
27. From the Botkins: "One of the ways God bestows blessings on women is through children. And not just 2.2 or 2.5 children, but many children. . . . As Christian women, we should pray to have several children and not limit God in how He wants to bless" (*So Much More*, 292). This is derived from the belief that God has complete control over the reproductive process. See, for example, Rick and Jan Hess say in their book *A Full Quiver*: "The joyous fact is that God opens and closes the womb! He alone decides when and if anyone will have any (more) children. And not only does He decide, He then makes it happen" (*A Full Quiver: Family Planning and the Lordship of Christ* [Brentwood, TN: Wolgemuth & Hyatt, 1990], 23).
28. For example, Nancy Campbell says in her book *Be Fruitful and Multiply*, "In the Word of God, fruitfulness of the womb is always considered a blessing. Barrenness was considered a curse, a shame, and a disgrace" (*Be Fruitful and Multiply: What the Bible Says about Having Children* [San Antonio, TX: Vision Forum, 2003], 45). For potential situations in which a woman is too physically ill to endure a pregnancy, the Hesses say simply, "If you're too sick to have babies, you're too sick to have sex" (*A Full Quiver*, 102).
29. Campbell, *Be Fruitful and Multiply*, 109.

"Paul says that by persevering in our God-given role—childbearing—with a godly attitude, we will be saved. . . . Having babies and raising them is our role, and we show we belong to God by persevering in it."[30] Quiverfull cannot conceive of a Christian woman who does not fulfill the command to "be fruitful and multiply." A woman who will not or cannot be a mother is something less than a woman.

Of course, Quiverfull elites acknowledge that not all women will be married and not all women will exercise their biological capacity to bear children. But, these are considered rare exceptions and "the exceptional circumstance (singleness) ought not to redefine the ordinary, God-ordained social roles of men and women as created."[31] Moreover, women for whom wifehood and motherhood do not take place are expected to remain under the authority of their fathers, assist their mothers, and serve their families at home.[32] In this way, single women also manifest womanhood in terms of motherhood, even without the biological experience.[33]

While Quiverfull proponents do not deny that women are fully human and God's image-bearers, they quickly move from this kind of affirmation to the explanation that women were created by God primarily to be helpers of men.[34] It is important to realize that they are not simply saying wives are to be helpers to their husbands, but that all women were created to help all men. Thus, women do not have

---

30. Pride, *The Way Home*, 41, 42. DeMoss echoes both Campbell and Pride: "[A] woman's willingness to embrace, rather than shun, her God-given role and calling ('childbearing') is a necessary fruit that will accompany genuine salvation—it is proof that she belongs to Him and follows His ways." She tries to soften the force of this affirmation later, clarifying, "This is not to say that all women are called by God to marry and bear children, but simply that, generally speaking, this is the central role God has established for women" (*Lies Women Believe*, 171).

31. Douglas Phillips, R. C. Sproul Jr., and Philip Lancaster, "The Tenets of Biblical Patriarchy," Vision Forum Ministries, http://tinyurl.com/y8763jme.

32. Again, from "The Tenets of Biblical Patriarchy": "Until she is given in marriage, a daughter continues under her father's authority and protection."

33. The Botkin sisters do not know what to do with single women either, saying only, "Marriage is and always has been the norm, though there are the exceptional few who are given the gift of singleness. Marriage is central to the first part of the Dominion Mandate: to be fruitful and multiply. We do not mean to undervalue the gift of singleness to those young women who have truly been blessed with it, but we do want to emphasize that we young women should not 'choose' to take a gift which has not been offered." Interestingly (and inconsistently), the Botkins dismiss Paul's admonition in 1 Cor 7:26–35, that Christians remain single as a culturally specific instruction due to persecution in the Roman Empire (*So Much More*, 219–20).

34. In the "Tenets of Biblical Patriarchy," tenet number two says, "Both man and woman are made in God's image . . . and they are both called to exercise dominion over the earth. They share an equal worth as persons before God in creation and redemption. The man is also the image and glory of God in terms of authority, while the woman is the glory of man." Thus, even though both men and women are *imago Dei*, only the man images God in terms of God's authority, while the woman is "the glory of man"—his subordinate helper.

selves apart from their relationship to men. McDonald and Chancey write,

> God could have simply raised up a woman from the dust of the earth—an independent creature who could keep Adam company and even partner with him in subduing the earth by pursuing equal and separate ventures. Yet He instead caused Adam to fall into a deep sleep, and from man's own rib God fashioned his glorious completer—woman.... Eve was Adam's perfect complement, his crowning glory.[35]

This reading of Genesis is not altogether unique, as affirmations of male-female complementarity abound in Protestant, Catholic, and Orthodox theology. But, the conclusions Quiverfull teachers draw from male-female complementarity are very different. McDonald and Chancey write: "In all of her tasks, [a woman] seeks to further [her husband] as a man. His work of dominion is her work; she embraces his vision as her own as she promotes and enhances his life pursuits."[36] The Botkin sisters make the same point even more forcefully: "[A] woman's life will always be tied into a man's life, whether she is married or not. This is a basic feature of womanhood, and women are to be dependent upon men's protection and leadership."[37] It seems not only are women inherently complementary to men, but also lacking a complete and independent self. It is within the God-ordained nature of women to enhance, strengthen, and help men, whether their husbands, fathers, brothers, or sons.

Because of the inherent nature of woman as man's complement, Quiverfull elites conclude that women are not allowed to exercise authority over men.[38] "Adam's headship over Eve was established at the beginning, before sin entered the world," so also male leadership is understood to apply in the home, the church, and society.[39] Regarding single women working beyond the home, they clarify: "It

---

35. Chancey and McDonald, *Passionate Housewives*, 32.
36. Chancey and McDonald, *Passionate Housewives*, 32.
37. Botkin and Botkin, *So Much More*, 34.
38. This is another assertion that distinguishes Quiverfull from that of their evangelical neighbors who, for the most part, would not apply the belief in male headship beyond the home and church. Indeed, Quiverfull teachers have repeatedly criticized conservative evangelicals for their perceived unwillingness to carry the doctrine of male headship to its logical conclusion. For example, William Einwechter criticizes evangelicals for supporting the vice-presidential candidacy of Christian wife and mother, Gov. Sarah Palin in his article, "Men and Women and the Creation Order," published on Vision Forum's website: http://tinyurl.com/y9af66ej. Einwechter dismisses the possibility of a woman in this role because it violates God's creation order, which places women in a subordinate position to men in all "spheres of dominion."
39. "A God-honoring society will," Vision Forum declares, "prefer male leadership in civil

is not the ordinary and fitting role of women to work alongside men as their functional equals in public spheres of dominion (industry, commerce, civil government, the military, etc.)." Thus a necessary outworking of the assertion that women are, by nature, dependent upon and completed by men, is that women are barred from participation in public domains. Because women were "created with a domestic calling," all women everywhere are designed by God to work within the home.[40]

Finally, while Quiverfull proponents would not deny that women have agency, they contest the integrity of that agency when it comes to the roles of wife, mother, and homemaker. While women have agency in theory, in practice their biological design and corresponding calling to motherhood is not a matter of choice. In the Quiverfull ideal, women remain under the authority of their fathers until such a time as their father sees fit to give them away in marriage. Then, their authority becomes their husband, to whom they are to look for their goals, aspirations, and vision for life.[41] Regarding a daughter's submission to her father, the Botkin sisters declare, "You will love what he loves, you will hate what he hates, and you will even think his thoughts after him. This will help you know how to be his glory."[42] Although the Quiverfull vision of homeworking includes being the ruler of the home, that reign is subject to the husband who sets the agenda and priorities for his wife. The words of Chancey and McDonald are unambiguous: "In all of her tasks, she seeks to further

---

and other spheres as an application of and support for God's order in the formative institutions of family and church" (Phillips, Sproul Jr., and Lancaster, "The Tenets of Biblical Patriarchy").

40. Phillips, Sproul Jr., and Lancaster, "The Tenets of Biblical Patriarchy." Pride makes a similar argument: "We in the church are confusing the issue by debating whether wives should work.... Scripture draws the line not at *whether* wives work, but *where* we work. The Bible says young wives should be trained to 'love their husbands and children, to be self-controlled and pure, to be *busy at home*, to be kind, and to be subject to their husbands'" (*The Way Home*, 136; emphasis in original).

41. For example, the Botkins speak of submission to their father's authority as preparation for submission to their husbands: "*It's folly to think it will be easier to respect and submit to a husband than a father.* We're not ready to consider ourselves eligible for marriage until we've learned to trust an imperfect individual with our lives.... To submit to an imperfect man's 'whims' as well as his heavy requirements. To order our lives around another person. To accept the burdens a man places on us cheerfully. To esteem and reverence and adore a man whose faults we can see clearly every day" (Botkin and Botkin, "Authoritative Parents, Adult Daughters, and Power Struggles," *Visionary Daughters*, May 14, 2007, http://tinyurl.com/y8zeqr99 [emphasis in original]).

42. Kathryn Joyce recorded these words while attending a Vision Forum Father and Daughter Retreat (*Quiverfull*, 226).

him as a man. His work of dominion is her work; she embraces his vision as her own as she promotes and enhances his life pursuits."[43]

While Quiverfull proponents dismiss the ideas of women's autonomy, choice, and self-fulfillment, they simultaneously offer women the Quiverfull practice of womanhood as truly liberating and fulfilling. Pride rejects the "selfish" idea of self-fulfillment, but offers motherhood and homeworking as the way to receive *true* fulfillment from God.[44] Chancey and McDonald mock the idea of women pursuing their "precious personhood" into the workplace, but offer *real* freedom in the "good life" through wifely submission and motherhood: "Freedom doesn't come from being enlightened. One doesn't shake loose the chains of bondage by 'finding' one's self.... Real life comes when we learn to lose ours—for [God's] sake."[45] In this way, Quiverfull elites trade in the rhetoric of choice and fulfillment even as they denounce it.

Going further, it must be acknowledged that without the perceived enemies of feminism, contraception, and abortion, Quiverfull would not be able to posit their lifestyle as a "choice" at all. It is, in fact, the rise of feminism and the women's liberation movement, along with the proliferation of artificial forms of birth control, that provided the cultural scenario from which the Quiverfull movement could emerge as a "countercultural" alternative. Doug Phillips and his coauthors affirm this symbiosis in the editorial notes to "The Tenets of Biblical Patriarchy": "We emphasize the importance of biblical patriarchy, not because it is greater than other doctrines, but because it is being actively attacked by unbeliever and professing Christians alike.... In conscious opposition to feminism, egalitarianism, and the humanistic philosophies of the present time, the church should proclaim the Gospel centered doctrine of biblical patriarchy as an essential element of God's ordained pattern for human relationships and institutions."[46] Indeed, the specter of feminism provides the existential impetus needed for the spread of Quiverfull.

The Quiverfull construction of motherhood, therefore, is not simply about interpreting and obeying the plain teaching of the Bible, but also the construction of a thoroughly antifeminist way of life. Quiverfull elites posit a construction of motherhood that is both

---

43. Chancey and McDonald, *Passionate Housewives*, 32.
44. Pride, *The Way Home*, 139.
45. Chancey and McDonald, *Passionate Housewives*, 134.
46. Phillips, Sproul Jr., and Lancaster, "The Tenets of Biblical Patriarchy."

antifeminist and dependent upon feminism for its dynamism and appeal. And this way of life is envisioned as the primary means by which the world will be transformed into the coming kingdom of God. Within Quiverfull literature, there is no tension between motherhood as a sacred calling invested with eschatological significance and the idealized rule of men over women. Their gender roles constitute a harmonious antifeminist vision for men and women, with godly women seeing motherhood as the highest good to which they can attain.

QUIVERFULL MOTHERHOOD AT THE LAY LEVEL

Now that it's clear what Quiverfull elites say about motherhood, it's time to consider how the Quiverfull construction of motherhood works in daily life. It's one thing to idealize motherhood in theory, but it's another thing to see it worked out on the ground. First, the Quiverfull practice of motherhood acknowledges and underscores the labor of mothering such that traditional "women's work" is invested with significant power and cultural capital within the movement. Many have noted the ways in which the labor of mothering is overlooked in American society. Even though liberal feminism has expanded the cultural expectations for women such that women are expected to be educated, independent, and have a career, they still maintain disproportionate responsibility for childcare and housekeeping.[47] In addition, standards for the "good mother" have expanded. Today, the good mother provides individualized care for each child's personality and gifts, along with sustained attention to their development, even to the neglect of all other priorities. A mother is expected to "be her own person," while also sacrificing heroically for her children. And in the midst of this no-win scenario, the extent of and consequences for women's expanded responsibilities have been largely ignored.

Why is women's work in mothering so often overlooked? One important reason is that motherhood is considered "natural" for women. It is only when women don't mother, or make mistakes while mothering, that motherhood is recognized for what it is: work. Men are applauded when they take up the work of fatherhood because it is so unexpected for them to do so. The idea that moth-

47. See, for example, Arlie Hochschild and Anne Machung, *The Second Shift: Working Families and the Revolution at Home*, rev. ed. (London: Penguin, 2012).

erhood is "natural" and not "real" labor leads to a disregard of the work mothers do, even in supposedly more enlightened circles. Yet, the Quiverfull movement, at both the lay and elite levels, spends a significant amount of time and energy providing recognition, support, and praise for their mothers. One of the benefits of Quiverfull motherhood, therefore, is that it brings to the foreground the substantial work involved in mothering. Quiverfull invests work that is often unacknowledged with spiritual power and import, thereby giving Quiverfull mothers significant symbolic strength.[48]

This cultural valuation of motherhood is a fact not lost on those who have studied the Christian homeschooling movement. In his book *Kingdom of Children*, Mitchell Stevens notes the way a robust ideology of motherhood fuels Christian homeschooling. He observes that the nonreligious wing of the homeschooling movement often fails to acknowledge the fact that mothers perform the majority of the work of home education. While talking a lot about children's needs, nonreligious homeschooling mothers often have little by way of explanation for why they (and not their husbands) are shouldering the burden of their children's education. In contrast, Stevens observes that the Christian wing of the homeschooling movement regularly recognizes and affirms the maternal labor involved in home education. The gender ideology of Christian homeschooling families gives them tools to explain and support the disproportionate labor of homeschooling moms and endow it with cultural significance. He observes, "If on the [nonreligious] side of the movement mothers are marginal or invisible, among the believers they are often at center stage."[49] Not only do homeschooling families make motherhood central, but they also invest motherhood with eschatological import.

---

48. Even so, the Quiverfull discourse accomplishes this largely by claiming motherhood as every woman's highest calling (both natural and spiritual), which is problematic in its own way. To claim motherhood as woman's highest natural and spiritual calling, they reinscribe cultural limitations on women and cut women off from other forms of work and support beyond the family. If motherhood is "natural" for women, then why would they need a social safety net? If motherhood is "natural" for women, then why would they require equal pay for equal work? If motherhood is "natural" for women, then why would they need improved childcare and childcare regulations? Conceiving of motherhood as the natural and spiritual height of womanhood leads to consequences that undercut women's work as mothers in a variety of ways. Only the mothers of means, who have husbands who can readily support them in their work as stay-at-home moms, can thrive in an environment where women do not have a social safety net, equal pay, or affordable, quality childcare. Mothers who are not financially stable suffer the consequences. And mothers who cannot live up to the ideal ultimately lose out.

49. Mitchell Stevens, *Kingdom of Children: Culture and Controversy in the Homeschooling Movement* (Princeton: Princeton University Press, 2001), 96.

Stevens says, "Godly womanhood and the home work for which it is designed are framed as components of a broader social and moral project for godly women."[50]

Stevens's conclusions regarding the Christian homeschooling movement apply equally well to the Quiverfull movement. Indeed, the narratives of Quiverfull mothers heard in chapter 2 reveal that their practice of motherhood does two things simultaneously: (1) it renders visible the hard work of mothering that is often overlooked in other households, and (2) it invests the work of mothering with eschatological meaning. The explanations given by Quiverfull mothers for their laborious investment in birthing, nursing, and educating a large number of children are deep and complex. All testify to motherhood as a specific calling of God as well as something for which they are "naturally" equipped as women via divine design.[51] Also, they are motivated in their practice of motherhood by Jesus's command to "make disciples of all nations" (Matt 28:19), which begins for them in their own homes. They view the investment of their time and talents in childrearing as a strategy for changing the world. If they are faithful in properly raising their children, they believe there is a better chance that the subsequent generations will be faithful practitioners of the Christian faith.

The commitment to homeschooling as the primary way to make disciples of their children has led many Quiverfull women to view their home as a workplace too. In the words of Colleen McDannell:

> Being the sole provider for their children's education not only increases a mother's responsibility, it gives her a respectable career. . . . Teaching becomes their profession. They no longer see themselves as simply housewives or mothers. They have found an occupation that is fully acceptable within their religious and cultural milieu. . . . Through homeschooling the home becomes a workplace; a "school" where a "teacher" performs her professional duties.[52]

---

50. Stevens, *Kingdom of Children*, 98.
51. As referenced in note 48 above, the claim that motherhood is "natural" for women has its own problems and consequences—and not only for Quiverfull mothers. If motherhood is "natural," then mothers who find their work grueling and overwhelming are assumed to be unnatural or broken in some respect. The assumed naturalness of motherhood is a double-edged sword.
52. McDannell, "Creating the Christian Home," 210–11.

Thus, Quiverfull mothers have both a thick explanation for their laborious work in the home, as well as a firm defense for the eternal significance of their work.[53]

At the same time, though, the experiences of Quiverfull mothers also reveal tensions between their practice of motherhood and ideals of gender hierarchy. More often than not, the practice of male headship has to be modified in a home where the mother plays such a powerful central role.[54] For some, like Deborah Olson, the tension goes unrecognized. She sees no contradiction between the affirmation of male headship and the largely mother-directed nature of their lives. Nor does she think correcting her husband's moral failures as something unbecoming of a "submissive" wife. For others like Carley Miller, the tension is felt mostly in interaction with the expectations of those beyond their home, like the leaders of their former church. Although she affirms male headship, she frames it in terms of service and sacrifice. Within Carley's marriage, an interpretation of gender roles has developed that is pragmatic but still coherent.

But for some, like Renee Tanner, the tension between the ideal of gender hierarchy and the reality of Quiverfull motherhood is too much to bear. Faced with the passivity and inactivity of her husband in the midst of her overwhelming burden of responsibility, Renee felt compelled to abandon entirely any notion of male headship or gender hierarchy. Though desirous of a patriarchal marriage, Renee found the practical matriarchy of her daily life too much at odds with the patriarchal ideal.[55] Though she still maintains the prona-

---

53. The significance of the theological narrative for Quiverfull motherhood is highlighted by the publication of *Three Decades of Fertility: Ten Women Surrender to Their Creator and Embrace Life*, edited by prominent Quiverfull blogger Natalie Klejwa. This book contains the stories of ten women who embraced the Quiverfull way of life, detailing their "conversion" to Quiverfull, as well as triumphs and heartbreaks along the way.

54. Stevens makes a similar observation in his book about the homeschooling movement: "Despite some poignant affinities between the words of ideologues like [Mary] Pride and [Michael] Farris and what many believers say and do, I did not find the kind of strident scripting of motherhood and fatherhood outlined in books like *The Way Home* and *The Homeschooling Father*. True enough, several believer women talked about God's will in their decisions to stay home. . . . I found that there was considerable distance between how the advocates talk about men and women and how the believers' rank and file talk about themselves. Not contradiction, but distance—partial employment of language (God's will) or practice (men leading devotions or playing administrative roles)—rather than wholesale embrace or dismissal of what the advocates have to say. . . . In the end, I concluded that what is most remarkable about the believers' talk about gender and family is not the degree of fit between talk and practice, but rather the sheer amount of talk." See Stevens, *Kingdom of Children*, 101–2.

55. My former colleague Adam Sheridan once suggested that Quiverfull adherents are part of an "androcentric matriarchy." There may be something to this characterization.

talist and homeschooling practices of the movement, Renee's abandonment of gender hierarchy has impacted her so deeply that she now reinterprets the Bible in light of her experience (something she acknowledges is tantamount to "heresy" according to her fundamentalist upbringing). In this way, the Quiverfull practice of motherhood fundamentally undermined the gender hierarchy of the Tanner family.

Recent sociological studies of evangelicals and gender roles show that the tension in Quiverfull homes is not unique. Scholars have found that most evangelicals hold fast to the concept of male headship and view it as an important marker of cultural distinctiveness even while it is modified and reformed in practice. The male headship of my informants is practiced mainly through the father's leadership of family worship (regular times of scripture reading and prayer) and disciplinary "backup" of the mother's role as teacher. Also, the doctrine of male headship provides a protective measure for the instances in which the husband needs to assert himself in marital negotiations. It is common for Quiverfull mothers to speak of their husbands as the "tie-breaker" and "deciding vote." In instances where the couple is unable to reach consensus, male headship means the wife will acquiesce to the will of the husband. While the mother is the primary administrator in the home, even exercising a quasi-professional role in the education of her children, the husband still maintains his symbolic leadership of the family through the rhetoric of male spiritual leadership.[56] This dynamic is very similar to that observed by Christian Smith and his colleagues:

> Many of the evangelicals we interviewed construed "headship" in ways that explicitly undermined male domination and privilege. In fact, of the variety of positions evangelicals took on the meaning of headship, the most common interpretation emphasized not male authority and leadership, but the burdens of responsibility for, accountability to, and sacrifice on behalf of others that headship places on husbands. In this view, headship appears to function not so much to privilege husbands, but to

---

56. This is a dynamic noted by a number of authors, including Judith Stacey, *Brave New Families: Stories of Domestic Upheaval in Late-Twentieth Century America* (Berkeley: University of California Press, 1990); Brenda Brasher, *Godly Women: Fundamentalism and Female Power* (New Brunswick, NJ: Rutgers University Press, 1998); and R. Marie Griffiths, *God's Daughters: Evangelical Women and the Power of Submission* (Berkeley: University of California Press, 1997).

domesticate and regulate them and to extract energy from them for the sake of their wives and children.[57]

This regulation of husbands is most clearly seen in Deborah's story, where she unselfconsciously uses the doctrine of male headship to persuade Dan to do what she thinks is right (e.g., attend Bible study, lead their family in prayer, etc.). This domestication is evident in a less overt way in the home of the Millers, where gender-role distinction has not led to a sharp division of domestic labor; rather, Carley and David carry out household tasks as needed. David's commitment to domestic work is couched in the language of shepherding and service, which are traits associated with Christ. Thus, the Millers' is a pragmatic, service-oriented approach to male headship that retains the spiritual symbolism, while eschewing authoritarianism.

As Smith and his colleagues seek to make sense of the surprising ways evangelicals modify and negotiate with the idea of male headship, they come to the following conclusion:

> [Evangelicals] have largely integrated an older ideology of headship into newer egalitarian languages and practices. In sometimes amazing rhetorical couplings of gender equality and male headship, evangelicals manage to salvage the symbolic image of the husband as head, while simultaneously embracing and expressing the more egalitarian values and practices of their own tradition and the broader culture—and all of this in the context of lived relationships that appear much more equal in practice than evangelical headship rhetoric would suggest.[58]

Of course, Smith's analysis is sociological and Quiverfull notions of male headship are theological. Nevertheless, Smith's findings are illuminating because they show that the gender negotiations taking place in Quiverfull homes are also taking place in the homes of their evangelical neighbors. Even in a movement that promotes a very dualist and hierarchical vision of gender, it seems that the daily requirements of those same gender roles can sometimes serve to undermine hierarchy. In many cases, therefore, the Quiverfull experience of motherhood, particularly as they lead their families in the daily work of homeschooling, stands in tension with and even outright contradiction of, their gender ideology.

Now, it is important to say not every Quiverfull family evidences

---

57. Christian Smith, *Christian America? What Evangelicals Really Want* (Los Angeles: University of California Press, 2000), 175.
58. Smith, *Christian America?*, 190.

the tension laid out above. Many women experience the Quiverfull construction of motherhood as thoroughly oppressive, with detrimental consequences for themselves and their children. The negotiated gender dynamics on display in the lives of Renee Tanner, Carley Miller, and Deborah Olson occur within marriages that do not include patterns of manipulation, exploitation, or abuse, and neither partner suffers from mental illness. There are a growing number of women, mostly in online communities and blogs, who are speaking out about their oppressive experiences in Quiverfull marriages.[59] While none of the women who participated in my research share this perspective, each of them could think of one or more families they know who have unhealthy or abusive home environments. It is vital, therefore, not to gloss over the fact that while some Quiverfull marriages defy the rigid gender roles prescribed at the elite level, there are others that seek after strict conformity—and the results can be treacherous.

OMNIPOTENT MOTHERHOOD, VULNERABLE MOTHERHOOD

The conflict described above between the Quiverfull practice of motherhood and their conception of gender hierarchy is something particular to the movement. But, Quiverfull mothers also raise another matter that is shared with American mothers in general: they are idealized as omnipotent even as their experience is one of acute vulnerability. Quiverfull mothers are considered omnipotent both in what they can accomplish and what influence they can exercise over their children in the long term. They are seeking to "do it all" for their families, especially their children, and expected to be extraordinary mothers as a matter of course. But Quiverfull mothers also embody a life of vulnerability. Due to a number of factors, Quiverfull mothers are deeply vulnerable in their bodies, minds, and emotions, as well as finances and communities. It is at the point of their vulnerability that the Quiverfull practice of motherhood opens women to exploitation and abuse. While they represent an extreme instance of idealized maternal omnipotence and experienced maternal vulner-

---

59. Chief among them is Vyckie Garrison who writes at *No Longer Quivering* (http://tinyurl.com/y7xyvg5j), a blog established primarily for supporting women who have left the Quiverfull movement and educating the public about its teachings.

ability, the tension between the two is something they share with American mothers in general.

OMNIPOTENT MOTHERHOOD

In Stephanie Coontz's book *The Way We Never Were*, she tries to dismantle what she calls "the myth of parental omnipotence."[60] Coontz is referring to the way American parents tend to overestimate both what they are able to do for their children and the long-term effects their parenting will have on their children.[61] The result is an inordinate amount of anxiety and guilt about parenting, particularly the perils of "bad" parenting. Quiverfull mothers also participate in this myth and apply it almost unilaterally to motherhood. As much as any woman in America, the Quiverfull mother is confronted with omnipotence as an internal and external ideal. It is something she puts upon herself and something put upon her by others.

Quiverfull mothers are perceived as omnipotent first in what they can accomplish within their homes. When one considers the daily schedule of a Quiverfull family, the amount of work to be done on any given day is overwhelming. Not only do mothers shoulder the physical labor of bearing and nursing children, sometimes in rapid succession, but they also carry out the work of maintaining a home, including the domestic chores of cooking and cleaning, all while providing an education for each child. And we cannot forget participating in their local church or homeschool co-operative (if they have them), as well as serving as romantic companion to their husbands. As Renee Tanner points out, while they are not employed in paid work beyond the home, Quiverfull mothers are doing the equivalent of two or three fulltime jobs. Indeed, Quiverfull mothers are trying to "do it all," sometimes with little tangible support from their spouses.

Still, the maternal omnipotence of Quiverfull isn't just about the number of children they have and the number of tasks they juggle on any given day. Quiverfull mothers also put significant emphasis on the effect they will have on their children in the future. Most of the women I spoke to describe their mothering aspirations in terms

---

60. Stephanie Coontz, *The Way We Never Were: American Families and the Nostalgia Trap* (New York: Basic Books, 1993), 225.

61. Coontz writes, "As a historian, I suspect that the truly dysfunctional things about American parenting is that it is made out to be such a frighteningly pivotal, private, and exclusive job" (*The Way We Never Were*, 210).

of *multigenerational faithfulness*. Multigenerational faithfulness refers to the focus of Quiverfull parents on raising children who will continue in Christian faith and emulate the lives of their parents in the years to come. As one mother writes,

> We are praying and endeavoring to raise children who will raise children who will raise children who will stand for Christ in their generation. By God's grace, we trust that our fruitfulness will continue in the coming generations through the multi-generational faithfulness of our family.... It is our greatest hope and most fervent prayer that our children—who have been given many spiritual advantages which we did not have—will grow up to exceed us in both love for Christ and godliness.[62]

Homeschooling is central to this plan, and the mother shoulders most of the responsibility to pursue this purpose. The point is for Christian mothers to cease thinking of their daily work in terms of one lifetime, and instead think in terms of several lifetimes. Focused on the goal of producing multiple generations of Christians, Quiverfull mothers can come to view every day as the crux on which the future hangs. And while they will inevitably claim that it is God's grace that keeps their children Christians, the majority of the daily responsibility for passing on the faith falls on the mothers' shoulders.

The warnings of Quiverfull teachers on this subject can be breathtakingly harsh. Pride reads the words of Proverbs 22:6 as a promise to righteous parents who parent correctly: "Train a child in the way he should go, and when he is old he will not depart from it." On this Pride comments, "As for Christian couples you might know whose children have turned out badly, let me ask you this. If the parents are not to blame, *who is?* Society? God? Does God say children are a blessing and then give us children who are fuel for hell?"[63] Though she addresses the generic "parents" in this passage, *The Way Home* is written to mothers, and her vision for "homeworking" is for mothers. The implication is clear: "Mom, if you don't train your children properly, they will end up as 'fuel for hell' and you'll have no one to blame but yourself." Motherly omnipotence includes the present and extends into eternity.

What becomes apparent in talking to Quiverfull mothers and reviewing Quiverfull resources is that they have tremendous confi-

---

62. Molly Evert, "God Changed My Heart," in *Three Decades of Fertility*, 142.
63. Pride, *The Way Home*, 103.

dence in the abilities of Christian mothers. One reason for this confidence is the theological conviction that they are carrying out God's ordained purpose for women. A common factor for all the mothers I interviewed is the belief that God is the one who has called them to their work. Their commitment to homeschooling, pronatalism, and gender hierarchy is the result of their trust that scripture teaches and therefore God commands these things. They have extraordinarily high expectations for mothers because they believe God has the same expectations. By fulfilling the tasks of the Quiverfull discourse, Quiverfull mothers are fulfilling God's highest calling for women. Moreover, faithfully carrying out the tasks of motherhood is part of their service to God and, for some, proof of their salvation.[64]

Quiverfull mothers do not arrive at these conclusions independently, however. Their way of imagining and practicing the institution of motherhood is informed by evangelical Protestant readings of scripture. Though a number of texts are important, two emerge repeatedly in Quiverfull literature: Titus 2:3–5 and Proverbs 31:10–31. Titus is a Pauline Epistle that contains, among other things, instructions regarding the expected behavior for various segments of the church. Verses 3–5 read as follows:

> Likewise, teach the older women to be reverent in the way they live, not to be slanderers or addicted to much wine, but to teach what is good. Then they can urge the younger women to love their husbands and children, to be self-controlled and pure, to be busy at home, to be kind, and to be subject to their husbands, so that no one will malign the word of God.

Many Quiverfull mothers see this passage as a kind of job description, particularly in the admonition to "love their husbands and children . . . to be busy at home, to be kind, and to be subject to their husbands." Also, they understand the last phrase of the passage, "so that no one will malign the word of God," as a warning that if they do not faithfully carry out their work as a homemaker, they will be responsible for the word of God being slandered in society. That is to say,

---

64. Pride argues, "'Childbearing' sums up all our special biological and domestic functions." Arguing from a peculiar verse in 1 Tim 2:15 that says "women will be saved through childbearing," Pride says, "Timothy's particular path to heavenly glory was his preaching and example. Ours is homeworking, all revolving around our role of childbearing. . . . Childbearing is woman's 'peculiar function.' It symbolizes our roles just as preaching symbolized Timothy's role. Preaching was Timothy's role, and persevering in his calling he would be saved. In just the same way, having babies and raising them is our role, and we show we belong to God by persevering in it" (*The Way Home*, 42).

the receptivity of the surrounding culture to Christianity is dependent upon their faithfulness as homemaking mothers. Thus, the conformity of women to prescribed gender roles is seen as a vital aspect of Christian evangelization.

The so-called "Proverbs 31 woman" functions in a similar way for Quiverfull mothers, though the passage contains more than simple instructions. The Hebrew acrostic poem offers a vivid description of the ideal wife in ancient near eastern terms. Proverbs 31 describes a woman who works from dawn till dusk and then long into the night ("her lamp does not go out"). She is a flurry of constant activity, "bringing food from afar," weaving and sewing garments, buying a field, planting a vineyard, speaking wisdom and godly instruction, and still managing to give generously to the poor and needy. As a result of her industriousness, "Her husband is respected at the city gate, where he takes his seat among the elders of the land" (v. 23). Though Proverbs 31 describes a wife from a very different time and place, Quiverfull women, along with most evangelicals, view the Proverbs 31 woman as the paradigm of wifely faithfulness. She makes the home the center of her concern and all she does is for the purpose of blessing her husband and children.

An underlying assumption to the motherhood ideal of Titus 2 and Proverbs 31 is that motherhood is a fulltime job, an all-consuming enterprise (while fatherhood is not). In *Three Decades of Fertility*, one mother describes her conversion to "fulltime" motherhood in the following way:

> During this "unplanned" pregnancy the Lord began a transformational work in both our hearts, giving us a vision for our young family, solidifying our commitment to home schooling, and changing our views regarding gender roles and marriage and a host of other issues. For the first time, I began to catch a vision for serving Christ through my family. I quit the church ministries I had been in charge of which so often took me away from my children, and I intentionally turned my heart toward home.[65]

Deborah expresses the same sentiment when she confesses that the more she works outside the home, the less capable she feels to perform her work within the home. To be a good mother, therefore, means to be exclusively focused on the domestic sphere—anything else is falling short of the ideal. This zero-sum approach to mother-

---

65. Molly Evert, "God Changed My Heart," in *Three Decades of Fertility*, 132–33.

hood is something they share with American culture, which has only increased the expectations of the good mother since the second wave of feminism in the 1960s. This is something a number of authors have chronicled in the past couple of decades.[66]

Still, a thick theological account of motherhood as sacred calling isn't the only reason Quiverfull mothers are imagined as omnipotent. It is important to recognize that Quiverfull mothers are able to aspire to omnipotent motherhood because they possess a modicum of financial stability. Each of the women I interviewed has made significant financial sacrifices in order to live on a single income. Yet, in an era of recession, stagnant wages, a housing crisis, and expanding household debt, the fact that they are able to live on one income without relying on government assistance means they occupy a privileged socioeconomic category. Many lower- and middle-class families cannot sustain themselves on one spouse's wages. Some Quiverfull families get occasional help from Mom doing odd jobs like childcare, house cleaning, tutoring, or music lessons. And some Quiverfull leaders encourage women to turn their homes into sites of production through at-home businesses.[67] But, the majority of Quiverfull family income still comes from the father. So, the omnipotent vision of motherhood in the Quiverfull movement is dependent upon the financial support of the father, who possesses a salary sufficient to support a large family. Without this increasingly less common economic arrangement, the Quiverfull conception of motherhood would be impossible to approach.

The ideals of motherhood culled from scripture combined with widespread cultural expectations mean that the Quiverfull subculture constructs the mother as omnipotent, both in terms of her present abilities and future effects. Of course, none of the Quiverfull mothers I interviewed would call themselves omnipotent, nor would they claim to be grasping for such a standard. Indeed, they would say the reverse. These women repeatedly speak of their daily struggle to keep up with their responsibilities and their desperation for God's help. While they take their duties very seriously, they also bring a lot of self-deprecating humor to their work, which arises from a

---

66. See, for example, Judith Warner, *Perfect Madness: Motherhood in the Age of Anxiety* (New York: Riverhead, 2005), and Sharon Hays, *The Cultural Contradictions of Motherhood* (New Haven: Yale University Press, 1998).

67. Pride asserts, "Homeworking means *working* at home. We are not supposed to be the breadwinners—that's the man's job. But we are supposed to make an economic contribution" (Pride, *The Way Home*, 165 [emphasis in original]).

keen awareness of their weaknesses. But, even as these mothers are aware of the extraordinary endeavor they have undertaken, they do not shrink back from claiming they are their children's best educator and caretaker. They know they have filled the role of "stay-at-home mom" with many more responsibilities than most, but they undertake the task with confidence that God has set them apart for this purpose. Nevertheless, Quiverfull mothers claim for themselves capabilities that most American women do not: to birth and nurse many children in rapid succession, to educate their children from preschool through high school, and to cook, clean, and manage a large family. At the same time they are asserting their weakness, Quiverfull mothers are also claiming for themselves extraordinary strength, ability, and influence.

In this ideal of maternal omnipotence, Quiverfull mothers demonstrate an intensification of broader American tendencies. The work of motherhood in America entails an endless list of demands. Its work is ever expanding and evolving, throughout the growth of one's children from infancy into adulthood. Mothers really are expected to do it all—or at least be *willing* to do it all. Mothers must be teachers, caretakers, disciplinarians, nurses, nutritionists, cooks, maids, household managers, therapists, and more. And the more "natural" they go in these tasks, the more Mom is expected to know and do: extended breastfeeding, so-called "baby-wearing," homegrown vegetables, essential oils, homeopathy, DIY clothing, crafts, décor, and the list goes on. If a mother chooses to educate her children at home, she is expected to be a skillful teacher as well. The more specialized instruction is required, the more a mother has to learn and achieve, particularly if she is helping a child with developmental or learning disabilities. All of these tasks a mother is expected to accept with loving acquiescence, always patient, always joyful, and always willing to sacrifice herself for her children.

There is no one factor to blame for these extraordinarily high expectations for mothers, but our cultural romanticization of motherhood is a powerful contributor to it. The roots of this idealization are many—too many to explore in detail. Simply by virtue of having a child, American mothers are expected to become morally virtuous, self-sacrificing, and extraordinary. In short, mothers qua mothers are required to be superhuman. As Paula Cooey has argued, there is really no such thing as an "ordinary mother" in America because the ordinary mother is supposed to be an extraordinary mother.[68] To be less than extraordinary—whether through character flaws or making mistakes in some respect—is to fail your children and become a "bad mother."[69] And, at the feet of bad mothers is laid the blame for an endless number of things, from the psychological problems of individual grown children to the downfall of entire civilizations. In the words of Adrienne Rich, "Under the institution of motherhood, the mother is the first to blame ... if anything whatsoever goes wrong."[70] Is it any wonder, therefore, that 70 percent of American mothers surveyed in 2000 said that they found motherhood "incredibly stressful"?[71]

The romanticization of mothers as all-powerful, always virtuous, and always capable is the myth of omnipotent motherhood. Despite the fact that each individual mother knows she is incapable of doing it all, most mothers still measure themselves against the standard of nonexistent mothers who can. Of course, the debate about whether women can "do it all" or "have it all" has become something of an American pastime. Every couple of years, it seems, an article is published in a prominent periodical claiming alternately that women *can* or *can't* "have it all."[72] This conversation typically focuses on women who are seeking to have careers outside the home and raise a family simultaneously. The assumption, of course, is that men do not face the tension between the work of fatherhood and employed work in the same way that women do.

But the women under discussion in this project are not facing that conundrum. The Quiverfull movement has made the work of mothers in the home central to their lived religion. Their print and online literature holds up motherhood as a woman's highest calling in life.[73]

---

68. "If being ordinary involves characterological flaws, making serious and sometimes tragic mistakes while bearing or raising children, or leaving one's children while working outside the home, then mothers must be extraordinary. Due to cultural romanticizing of both motherhood and childhood, U.S. society expects nothing less than extraordinary mothers as normative" (Paula M. Cooey, "'Ordinary Mother' as Oxymoron: The Collusion of Theology, Theory, and Politics in the Undermining of Mothers," in *Mother Troubles: Rethinking Contemporary Maternal Dilemmas*, ed. Julia Hanigsberg and Sara Ruddick [Boston: Beacon, 1999], 229).
69. Cooey, "'Ordinary Mother' as Oxymoron," 229.
70. Rich, *Of Woman Born*, 222.
71. Reported by Judith Warner in *Perfect Madness*, 71.
72. The most recent such article from a major news source was Anne-Marie Slaughter's "Why Women Still Can't Have It All," *The Atlantic*, July/August 2012, http://tinyurl.com/y9h4nbpm.
73. Grenholm notes, "Both the glorification and the demonization of motherhood presuppose more maternal responsibilities than there are resources available and a diminishing or clouding of other people's roles. There are biblical parallels here. The Gospel of John

Not only are they physically reproducing and nurturing as many children as the marriage produces, but they are doing the daily work of educating their children and managing the home as well. They have already made the choice to forgo a career outside the home in order to, in a very real way, make the family their career. In the words of Renee Tanner, "I think you can be a stay-at-home mom as fully and professionally and excellently as any career." Yet, Quiverfull mothers remain stuck in the myth of omnipotent motherhood that plagues American society. While Quiverfull mothers are committed to motherhood because they believe it is God's ideal and calling on their lives, their thick theological explanation for their work has left the myth intact. Working mothers might think the choice to focus exclusively on the domestic sphere gives Quiverfull mothers more existential peace and freedom from unreasonable expectations. But for women like Deborah Olson, Carley Miller, and Renee Tanner, the choice to make childrearing their career has led to difficulties and anxieties of another sort. Quiverfull mothers, along with all other mothers in America, are imagined as omnipotent and suffer the consequences of this ideal on a daily basis.

Quiverfull mothers show the myth of omnipotent motherhood as the grotesque setup it is. No mother is all-powerful. Ordinary mothers are not superhuman, no matter how romantic the myth may seem, and it is not a compliment to stereotype mothers qua mothers as invincible. To imagine otherwise is not only a private problem for individual women, but also a communal problem for American society. If mothers as a rule are expected to be omnipotent, then there is no room in our collective imagination for women who can't do it all—who have real weaknesses, who need help. There is no way to take into account the experiences of mothers in poverty, drug- and alcohol-addicted mothers, single mothers, grandmothers who head households, undocumented immigrant mothers, unemployed mothers, and more. Given that ordinary mothers include all of the above, it is important that Christian theologians reject the false doctrine of motherly omnipotence. Quiverfull mothers may come as close as any mothers in America to achieving the omnipotent ideal, but even they struggle under the weight of the expectations put upon them by their lived religion. It is not a slight to the real heroism of these mothers to

---

(7:53–8:11) describes how a woman is caught in the act of committing adultery. She alone is called to account; the man is never mentioned" (*Motherhood and Love*, 47 [see note 74]).

acknowledge their weaknesses and urge others to reckon with them as well.[74]

VULNERABLE MOTHERHOOD

As I have shown, despite the way Quiverfull mothers are glorified rhetorically, and despite the way Quiverfull mothers implicitly claim for themselves extraordinary abilities, they are in fact "ordinary mothers" like all other mothers in America. However, what makes Quiverfull mothers ordinary is not simply their struggle with the myth of maternal omnipotence but also their experience of motherhood as a task of acute vulnerability. Indeed, the omnipotent expectations and the vulnerable experience of Quiverfull motherhood stand in stark contrast to each other.

Theologian Cristina Grenholm reflects upon motherly vulnerability in her book *Motherhood and Love: Beyond the Gendered Stereotypes of Theology*.[75] Though autonomy is an inviolable virtue of modernity, Grenholm says it is not altogether clear how or even if motherhood and autonomy go together. When a mother is pregnant, there is no clear distinction between her and the baby she carries. While the fetus is carried within her womb, the two cannot be completely separated.[76] We may speak of the two as individuals, but the reality is that there is a blending of persons in the experience of the pregnant woman. In the words of Sara Ruddick:

> Birth, more than any other experience except perhaps sexuality, undermines the individuation of bodies. The growing fetus, increasingly visible in the woman's swelling body, an infant emerging from the vagina, a suckling infant feeding off a breast, the mother feeding with and of her body express in dramatic form a fusion of self and other. Any man or

---

74. Judith Warner goes further: "The mess of the Mommy Mystique—the belief that we can and should control every aspect of our children's lives, that our lives are the sum total of our personal choices, that our limitations stem from choosing poorly and that our problems are chiefly private, rather than public in nature—is not an individual problem that individual women should have to scramble to deal with. It is a social malady—a perverse form of individualism, based on self-defeating allegiance to a punitive notion of choice; a way of privatizing problems that are social in scope and rendering them, in the absence of real solutions, amenable to one's private powers of control. It demands a collective coming-into-awareness, at the very least. And, I believe, once that awareness is reached, it cannot be cured without some collective, structural solutions" (*Perfect Madness*, 57).

75. Cristina Grenholm, *Motherhood and Love: Beyond the Gendered Stereotypes of Theology*, trans. Marie Tåqvist (Grand Rapids: Eerdmans, 2011).

76. Grenholm, *Motherhood and Love*, 163.

woman might fear the obliteration of self that such an experience suggests.[77]

Certainly, the experience of pregnancy and birth casts doubt on conventional patterns of thought regarding autonomy. In the modern age, to rule oneself, to be independent, to be in control of one's life, is an important aspect of what constitutes the good life. To be considered a healthy, well-adjusted adult one must be independent, self-supporting, and in control of one's own destiny. The opposite of autonomy, however, is not dependency but *heteronomy*. If autonomy is self-rule, then heteronomy is to be ruled by others. Grenholm explains heteronomy as a reality "in which one lacks control and influence over one's own situation."[78] In the West, this kind of existence is often interpreted as perverse and wrong. Yet, Grenholm points out that what a mother experiences in pregnancy is heteronomy by definition: her body accommodates a creative process over which she does not exercise direct control. In addition, the birth of her child results in the establishment of a relationship that she cannot evade or dictate.[79] In Ruddick's words, "To give birth is to create a life that cannot be kept safe, whose unfolding cannot be controlled, and whose eventual death is certain."[80]

Thus, not only does the experience of motherhood involve the lack of clear distinction between mother and child, but also the acceptance, whether willingly or unwillingly, of a heteronomous life. Grenholm explains:

> Motherhood is necessarily heteronomous in relation to outer circumstances in that the mother cannot protect her child from all danger or control its developmental process. This heteronomy is also the foundation of our respect for the child's autonomy. The child should not be controlled by the mother.[81]

The lives of Quiverfull mothers described thus far offer abundant examples of heteronomy, from the uncontrolled nature of pregnancy and birth to children with chronic illnesses and disabilities. Even the mundane details of our conversations illustrate heteronomy. When

77. Sara Ruddick, *Maternal Thinking: Towards a Politics of Peace* (Aylesbury, UK: Women's Press, 1990), 191.
78. Grenholm, *Motherhood and Love*, 165.
79. Grenholm, *Motherhood and Love*, 165.
80. Ruddick, *Maternal Thinking*, 165.
81. Grenholm, *Motherhood and Love*, 165.

Carley Miller and I met for the first time, she brought her still-nursing baby, whose need for attention and sustenance rightly took priority over our conversation. At that time and on other occasions she has joked that she cannot even get fifteen minutes by herself to take a shower. Later, as she and I continued our discussions over the phone, we were often interrupted by a young child in distress or in need of correction for some infraction. Carley handles these moments with patience and grace, but they are small examples of the fact that she is not in control of her life. The same could be said of Deborah Olson or Renee Tanner, each of whom must schedule time away from their children with great care, being sure to take into consideration everyone's schedule and individual needs. These examples are just a taste of the way the lives of Quiverfull mothers—and all mothers—are directed by the seemingly endless needs of others.

Because the life of a heteronomous person is ordered mainly by the needs of others, they also experience life as one of significant vulnerability. To lack control over one's destiny is to be vulnerable. However, it is important to recognize that vulnerability is not the same as "exposure," the word Grenholm uses to describe a person who has had her vulnerability exploited by another.[82] In her words, "Vulnerability opens up to the possibility of love, whereas exposure is the result of oppression."[83] Also, vulnerability should not be equated with tragedy. Because of what is involved in the process of pregnancy, birth, nursing, and childcare, mothers are necessarily vulnerable, but they are not victims of misfortune (no matter how society may suggest otherwise). The vulnerability of mothers calls for love, which will protect vulnerability rather than exploit it.[84]

Renee Tanner hints at the vulnerability of motherhood and the need for protective love in one of our interviews. Speaking of the "traditional" views on marriage and gender roles in evangelical circles, she makes the following observation:

> I've seen things change from the early years of following the traditional things the books say and then the practical things that change up the rules. I'm not into any certain view on complementarianism except that I can't get away from the practical thing that we're weaker when we're

---

82. Grenholm, *Motherhood and Love*, 120.
83. Grenholm, *Motherhood and Love*, 120. Grenholm references Vincent Brümmer, *The Model of Love: A Study in Philosophical Theology* (Cambridge: Cambridge University Press, 1993), 225.
84. Grenholm, *Motherhood and Love*, 121.

pregnant and nursing, and it helps to have someone look after you and take care of you. You can't get away from the biological thing—that we have to do that part.

The biological given that women give birth and nurse is something that she "can't get away from." And this biological reality puts women in a vulnerable position: "we're weaker when we're pregnant and nursing." For Renee, this weakness means there may be something to "complementarianism," the evangelical doctrine that teaches male headship and wifely submission.[85] But, she interprets this teaching primarily in terms of taking care of the mother in her time of need. The vulnerability of the mother, she says, requires loving, protective care by the father. But, it isn't just the father who should come alongside the vulnerable mother. In the same conversation, Renee went on to say: "It's not where it used to be, where women had communities and relatives to help them and keep them company and help. And then you have eleven kids like me and have no one there to help you." She envisions a time when women had extended family and close-knit communities to help with the burdens of motherhood. Despite her reference to fatherly care, Renee had "no one there to help" her in her time of vulnerability, and she lived under tremendous strain as a result.

Vulnerability that calls for protective love is also a running theme throughout the testimonies in *Three Decades of Fertility*. In each chapter, a woman living out the Quiverfull discourse tells her story of pregnancies, births, and childrearing. While all of them contain sincere testimonies of faith and hope, each story also provides ample evidence of the way repeated pregnancies and births cause real physical, mental, and emotional vulnerability for the mothers involved. Quiverfull mothers testify repeatedly to the need for a husband's support, as well as the help of older children and other family members, as they deal with the consequences of multiple pregnancies and the daily demands of a large homeschooling family.

Historically, heteronomy has been gendered stereotypically as the

85. *Complementarianism* is a term adopted by evangelicals who hold to hierarchy in sex and gender roles. They assert that men and women are equal in worth but different (complementary) in their assigned roles. This is in contrast to what is often called *egalitarianism*, which affirms differences between the sexes but equality in both worth and roles. Complementarianism has been popularized by a number of prominent evangelical pastors and theologians, most notably John Piper, Wayne Grudem, and Albert Mohler. For an overview of the key premises of complementarianism, see the Danvers Statement from the Council on Biblical Manhood and Womanhood, produced in 1988: http://tinyurl.com/ydhuow5m.

lot of women. Mothers in particular have been understood to be naturally heteronomous: always willing and able to relinquish control and sacrifice themselves for their children. The good, saintly mother was understood as the thoroughly self-giving mother. Thus women as mothers were perceived as naturally vulnerable. But, this is not the only way to interpret the heteronomy and vulnerability of motherhood. The truth is, heteronomy is shared by anyone who provides care for children, including fathers, grandparents, nannies, and other caregivers. Anyone who has watched children for any length of time knows that to care for children is to give up a significant degree of control over one's life.[86] And, going even further, lack of control over one's life is a "general life condition and unavoidable phenomenon" of human existence.[87] To be human is to be heteronomous and vulnerable. The poet Mary Oliver expresses this reality well:

> To live in this world
> you must be able
> to do three things:
> to love what is mortal;
> to hold it
> against your bones knowing
> your own life depends on it;
> and, when time comes to let it go,
> to let it go.[88]

Rather than seeing women, and mothers in particular, as the only ones who live in heteronomy, the experience of motherhood brings into sharper relief what is, in fact, a vital aspect of human experience. We should reject the stereotype that women are "naturally" heteronomous and affirm instead the fact that human life is inherently heteronomous. Human beings lack control over their lives, for better or worse. Their days are, to a great extent, determined by the actions

---

86. Like vulnerability, self-sacrifice has traditionally been gendered female and associated with the womanly duties of wife and mother. Despite the problems with this, theologian Bonnie Miller-McLemore is right to point out the need for theologians to reckon with the reality of self-sacrifice in the lived experience of Christian families. The reality is that mothers (and fathers) must regularly experience self-sacrifice in the course of caring for children. See Bonnie Miller-McLemore, "Generativity, Self-Sacrifice, and the Ethics of Family," in *The Equal-Regard Family and Its Friendly Critics*, ed. John Witte Jr., M. Christian Green, and Amy Wheeler (Grand Rapids: Eerdmans, 2007), 17–41.

87. Grenholm, *Motherhood and Love*, 166.

88. Mary Oliver, "In Blackwater Woods," quoted by Bonnie Miller-McLemore, *In the Midst of Chaos: Caring for Children as Spiritual Practice* (San Francisco: Jossey-Bass, 2007), 195.

of others. And to lack control of one's life is to be vulnerable. The only people who are invulnerable have cut themselves off from other human beings. The fact that human beings, male and female, can be exposed and oppressed speaks to the inherent vulnerability of all human life.

To say that all humans are vulnerable and heteronomous, however, does not rule out the particular vulnerability and heteronomy of Quiverfull mothers. Indeed, the vulnerability and heteronomy of motherhood is exacerbated within the Quiverfull family because the family is often so privatized and isolated (a problem I will address in more detail in chapter 5). Quiverfull mothers have a privatized, individualistic vision of motherhood lacking both an ecclesial and social context. All the mothers I spoke to gestured toward this difficulty without naming it as such. Recall Renee Tanner's words referenced above: "It's not where it used to be, where women had communities and relatives to help them and keep them company and help." The mothers of Quiverfull are the sole administrators of their children's nurturance and education. Even in a situation where the father is heavily involved, the majority of the burden for a full quiver of children rests on the narrow shoulders of the mother. While Quiverfull mothers are right in some respect to speak of large families as "normal" in days gone by, they are wrong to think the normal large family was the privatized, isolated nuclear family they currently embody. It is this privatized instantiation of the family that deepens and intensifies the vulnerability of Quiverfull mothers and their children.

Of course, what I have outlined above carries with it the risk of being misunderstood. Generally, feminists have choked on the mother-as-vulnerable or mother-as-sacrificial trope—and, in many cases, rightly so.[89] There is much to be skeptical of. When Christian mothers seek to emulate Jesus, who triumphed through sacrificial death on a cross, the openings for abuse are numerous. But, it doesn't necessarily follow that to take a vulnerable, sacrificial role is to annihilate oneself. There are other ways of envisioning motherhood that correspond with the experience of Quiverfull mothers and do not result in obliteration. Hence, I am not glorifying or romanticizing motherly vulnerability and heteronomy. Instead, I am pointing out the way that the experience of Quiverfull mothers confirms that motherhood is a work of inescapable vulnerability. Mothers expe-

---

89. The choking metaphor comes from Daphne Hampson, ed., *Swallowing a Fishbone? Feminist Theologians Debate Christianity* (London: SPCK, 1996).

rience this vulnerability in different ways at different times in their lives, and it can be mitigated in some respects, but can never be entirely removed. So, the distinction that Grenholm makes between vulnerability and exposure is vitally important. Just because Renee Tanner, Carley Miller, and Deborah Olson are vulnerable in their way of life, that does not mean they are exposed—taken advantage of, mistreated, oppressed. Certainly, we can talk about the ways that their financial dependence on their husbands and isolation in privatized homes, among other things, exacerbates and deepens their vulnerability. And we can talk about how their chosen way of life could unwittingly limit the opportunities available to their daughters. But, at the same time, we must take seriously the fact that the Quiverfull mothers with whom I have spoken find their work enjoyable, fulfilling, and even empowering. These women are vulnerable, stretched, even overwhelmed, but not exploited or defeated. And all mothers could share similar experiences. Whether we like it or not, vulnerability and heteronomy are key aspects of motherhood, both within the Quiverfull movement and beyond.[90]

CONCLUSION

In closing, it must be said that if a number of factors were different, it is likely that the stories of the Quiverfull mothers featured in this book would be different. If the Quiverfull families in question were living below poverty level, or if the mental health of the mothers were to deteriorate, or if the families lived in severe isolation—any of these circumstances could result in radically different experiences for mothers and their children. And as stories in the news media and online support networks have revealed, many of the cases involving

90. Still, doesn't the lack of reproductive choice that my informants face take away most of their power to avoid oppression? It would seem so. But, they have given up the need to choose when and how they become a mother and they do not seem plagued by it. Why not? First, they are mentally and physically healthy and they are more or less financially secure. Even Deborah Olson, who is in the least secure financial situation, does not worry about money with the possibility of another pregnancy, but only her health. She knows they have enough of a social safety net that they will never face homelessness. Also, they are completely focused on the task of raising and educating children. Because that is their focus, there is no career plan with which an additional child would interfere. Their profession *is* their children. Although additional children would disrupt and modify their routine, they are not daunted by the possibility of a new addition. Instead, with each child they grow in their skills for management, delegation, and communication (as Renee's story testifies). On the whole, these are not women who are despairing. They are constantly at the edge of their ability, constantly adding more to their plates. But, they are hopeful, not desperate—challenged, yes, but not exposed.

abuse, neglect, and violence in Quiverfull families have occurred within these very circumstances. Though my ethnographic research has not uncovered firsthand accounts of such toxic family environments, the stories persist and must be acknowledged.

While we have covered much ground and considered Quiverfull motherhood from a few angles, I have also shown that Quiverfull mothers are not as "other" as they may at first appear. They share in many of the challenges and conundrums of contemporary motherhood in America, albeit in a rather intense form. Mothers often find their ideals do not practice as well as they preach. Mothers often try to "do it all." Mothers often try to "do it all" alone. It is at these points where the situation of contemporary American mothers is laid bare and calls for a response far more nuanced than the theologies of motherhood offered to this point. In the next chapter, I turn our attention to the way Quiverfull families construct children and childhood. This analysis will build upon the observations made thus far, particularly the problems raised by vulnerability and privatization.

4.

Children and Childhood in the Full Quiver

Deborah and Dan Olson's oldest child, Garrett, is eleven years old. Almost two years ago, he made a profession of faith in Christ. Although they believe he has had a "personal relationship" with Christ since he was quite young, only recently did he go through the process of confession of personal faith (sometimes called the "sinner's prayer"). As evangelicals, they believe that Garrett should be baptized, but the outworking of that conviction has been difficult for a number of reasons.

First, the Olsons are not comfortable with the baptismal practices of their local church, which closely links baptism and church membership. According to Deborah, immediately following baptism the church takes a congregational vote to include the baptized person in the membership of the church. The Olsons find this problematic. Deborah says baptism should symbolize your union with Christ and the universal body of Christ; the local church or denominational affiliation shouldn't have anything to do with it. The Olsons have long thought Dan would baptize their children. As the family's spiritual leader, it makes sense in their minds that Dan would initiate his children into the life of faith. But, Dan has begun to have doubts. He wonders if baptism is better off performed by a member of the clergy.

In addition to their anxieties about how the baptism will be performed, the Olsons are not sure Garrett is truly ready for it. In Deborah's words, "I made a huge deal about his salvation but wanted baptism to be for a time when he understood it better and really owned it and could publicly share his testimony. The way I view baptism is that it should be a once-in-a-lifetime thing." They are unsure whether Garrett is mature enough—that is, intellectually and emotionally prepared—to make the choice to become a follower of Christ. If baptism should be done only once in a lifetime, then it is crucial that the person knows what he is doing when baptism is performed.

Due to their concern for Garrett's readiness, the Olsons want to provide him with an extended time of personal instruction before they commit to having him baptized. Because of Dan's work responsibilities and the demands of their other children, however, the Olsons have struggled to make this happen. Deborah found a curriculum online she wanted to use, but they have been unable to find the time to teach Garrett one-on-one. As a result, Garrett's baptism has been delayed. As of our last conversation, the Olsons still don't know when he will be baptized and, Deborah says, "We both feel really bad about it."

This story evidences two important themes as we consider the Quiverfull construction of children and childhood. First, the Olsons' reluctance to baptize Garrett demonstrates the Quiverfull tendency to imagine children as potential adults and disciples-in-the-making. Despite emphasizing Christian formation from an early age, they are not sure that a child, due to perceived intellectual and emotional immaturity, is capable of professing faith in Christ. As a result, their children are barred from receiving the sacraments and participating fully in the life of the church until the parents deem them ready. Second, the Olsons' private approach to baptism demonstrates the Quiverfull tendency to view children as the sole responsibility of parents. They determine whether Garrett is ready for baptism and when and how it takes place. Despite recent doubts, their interest in Dan performing the baptism suggests that they think Garrett belongs first to his parents and only secondarily to the church. Also, despite its historic function as an initiation rite of the church, they don't think baptism should be linked to local church membership. In short, the Olsons see baptism as a church practice, but they want complete say-so over how it is carried out. The nuclear family—and the parents' leadership within it—remains primary.

Quiverfull families are devoted to filling their quivers with as many children as God gives them. But, how exactly do they think about children and childhood? This chapter considers the dominant themes through which children and childhood are imagined in Quiverfull discourse. The focus here is not Quiverfull children themselves. Certainly, Quiverfull practitioners do not imagine children in the abstract. Their ways of thinking about children are linked directly to their experiences with real children—usually their own. Still, an ethnographic study of Quiverfull children is beyond the purview of this book. Instead, I am focusing on how adults in the Quiverfull movement construct or imagine children and childhood.[1]

So, this chapter considers four dominant themes and some of their practical consequences: (1) the child as a divine blessing, (2) the child as innocent and sinful, (3) the child as a potential disciple, and (4) the child as the sole responsibility of parents. First, I describe each of these themes as they appear in Quiverfull discourse, along with some important context for these perspectives from Christian scripture. Then, I offer theological reflection on the ethnographic data gathered on the given theme. It will become clear that Quiverfull practitioners are grappling with theological problems shared by other Christians in America. Moreover, Quiverfull families and their stated aim of "multigenerational faithfulness" are not well served by their theology of children. Recognizing some of the weaknesses in Quiverfull culture points Christians toward more fruitful ways of imagining children and childhood.

THE CHILD AS DIVINE BLESSING

Quiverfull practitioners agree that all children are unqualified blessings or gifts from God. This theme is dominant in Quiverfull literature and everyday conversation. They base this conviction on scripture, especially Psalm 127:3–5: "Children are a heritage from the Lord; offspring a reward from him. Like arrows in the hands of a warrior, are children born in one's youth. Blessed is the man whose

---

1. I agree with Joyce Ann Mercer when she says, "The terms *child*, *childhood*, and *children* must be problematized." In truth, there is no universal, natural identity of "the child" that exists across all times and places. Due to the focus of this project, I am primarily concerned with American children, but even in the American context there exist a number of ways of constructing *child* and *childhood*. Children and childhood take a variety of forms based upon their particular historical, social, and cultural contexts. Still, it doesn't help matters simply to do away with all general uses of these terms and declare that there's no such thing as children or childhood. So, with Mercer, I draw upon what Serene Jones has called "strategic essentialism" in the matter of children. In short, this means assuming a general, natural basis for *child* and *childhood*, while also being aware of the need to make decisions about the usefulness of such terminology in particular contexts (*Welcoming Children: A Practical Theology of Childhood* [St. Louis: Chalice, 2005], 18–19).

quiver is full of them; they will not be put to shame when they contend with their opponents in court."[2] For Quiverfull discourse, the gift quality of children is something intrinsic. Children do not have to accomplish anything in order to be gifts to their parents, the church, and the world. For Quiverfull practitioners, a child is a blessing fundamentally, regardless of their perceived worth or the circumstances into which they are born. In the words of Rachel Scott, "The Lord says that *every child is a gift*.... In God's eyes there is no such thing as an unwanted child because to God *each child is sent to be a blessing*."[3] Charles Provan says it most concisely: "Children are a blessing from God: the more the better!"[4] Quiverfull families believe their insistence on this point stands in opposition to the dominant narrative of American culture, which sees children either as expensive burdens or optional accessories.[5]

The Quiverfull conviction that every child is a divine gift rests on two assumptions.[6] First, God has a direct hand in the creation of every

2. There is a curiosity in the Quiverfull interpretation of Psalm 127. The Hebrew text of the psalm clearly indicates not the gender-neutral *children* that are a "heritage from the Lord" (Ps 127:3) but the gender-specific *sons*. Quiverfull writers are not particularly interested in gender inclusivity because they are convinced that men are the God-ordained leaders of the human race and that God is ontologically masculine. In every other instance, Quiverfull hermeneutics is fiercely literal, but in this case, they are content to allow the gender-inclusive English word *children* to substitute for *sons*. This is not only a methodological inconsistency but also a convenient oversight to maintain the plausibility of their argument. If they were to interpret this passage literally, the way it reads in the Hebrew, Quiverfull teachers would be forced to argue that *sons* are a heritage from the Lord and that the more *sons* one has the more blessed one will be. But, this literal reading of the text does not support their universal claim that all *children* are always a blessing. Moreover, it would put them in the uncomfortable position of arguing that daughters are less valuable than sons, something they are always seeking vehemently to deny due to their stridently hierarchical gender ideology.

Also, if they were to deal with the literal meaning of the Hebrew in Psalm 127, Quiverfull leaders would have to acknowledge the socioeconomic and cultural circumstances of the psalmist, ones that would lead him to affirm a multitude of sons as a divine blessing. For Quiverfull teachers to attend closely to the socioeconomic and cultural context would, in their minds, lessen the perceived force of the text. Quiverfull teachers often speak of those who reference the Bible's cultural context as people looking for a way out of obedience, people who want to relativize the Bible in favor of contemporary cultural trends. I suspect that this is why the Hebrew of Psalm 127 remains unexplored in Quiverfull writings thus far.

3. Rachel Giove Scott, *Birthing God's Mighty Warriors* (Maitland, FL: Xulon, 2004), 120.

4. Charles Provan, *The Bible and Birth Control* (Monongahela, PA: Zimmer, 1989), 7.

5. Mary Pride says it most memorably: "All those cute T-shirts for pregnant women with 'Mommy' stenciled on them, all those cute coordinated quilts for baby's room, are not proof that our culture overflows with love for children. They prove, rather, that children have been resurrected as pets" (*The Way Home: Beyond Feminism, Back to Reality* [Wheaton, IL: Crossway, 1985], 38).

6. The argument of Craig Houghton in *Family UNplanning* is a bit different. He starts with the words of Jesus about children (Matt 18:1–5) and extrapolates their gift nature from there (*Family UNplanning* [Maitland, FL: Xulon, 2007], 20).

human life. In Renee Tanner's words, "You see all the passages in the Bible about God opening and closing the womb.... Whether [you interpret that] literally or scientifically, the message is that God is very active in the process in a personal way."[7] If God "open[s] and clos[es] the womb," then every pregnancy is, in some sense, the result of God's creative work.[8] Rick and Jan Hess say it this way: "God sees to it that His blessings are ... not happenstance births, but planned incidents of goodness."[9] Nancy Campbell is even more straightforward: "When you conceive a baby ... God Almighty visits you!"[10]

The second assumption is that every child is a divine gift regardless of the circumstances into which they are born. As Deborah Olson says simply, "They're a blessing because the Lord says they are." Not even poverty changes the gift nature of children. As Doug Phillips says, "God declares children to be a blessing and a source of true wealth and happiness."[11] Thus, the gift nature of children means that Quiverfull families are truly wealthy and happy.

Of course, not everyone is capable of receiving children as a divine gift. Carley Miller says, "It's very clear [from scripture] that children are a blessing. Whether we interpret it that way is a different story." Renee Tanner agrees: "If they're not a blessing, it's circumstantial and not intrinsic to the child. I think the child as a person is a blessing to the world no matter who has to raise them or where they go." Within Quiverfull discourse, therefore, all children are blessings from God, regardless of the circumstances of their conception, birth, or upbringing.

Quiverfull families enact this view of children by refusing to prevent conception. All pregnancies are celebrated as direct gifts from God. As I explained in chapter 1, not all Quiverfull families totally

---

7. I am not going to explore all of the biblical passages that support this contention. Two Quiverfull books provide an exhaustive survey of the relevant literature: Rick Hess and Jan Hess, *A Full Quiver: Family Planning and the Lordship of Christ* (Brentwood, TN: Wolgemuth & Hyatt, 1990), and Nancy Campbell, *Be Fruitful and Multiply: What the Bible Says About Having Children* (San Antonio, TX: Vision Forum, 2003).

8. Mary Pride concurs: "The Bible makes it clear that a baby is a human being made in the image of God from the moment of conception.... From the moment of conception ... a baby has been given life by God" (*The Way Home*, 71). Rachel Scott says something similar: "Each time that a woman gives birth to a child, *she loans herself, her womb, and her body to God* so that He can send His special creation to earth" (*Birthing God's Mighty Warriors*, 41; emphasis in original).

9. Hess and Hess, *A Full Quiver*, 34.

10. Campbell, *Be Fruitful and Multiply*, 68.

11. Doug Phillips, "A Declaration of Life," Vision Forum Ministries, http://tinyurl.com/ycnfw4g9.

refrain from using artificial methods to control conception. But, all Quiverfull families view the total surrender of a woman's fertility as the ideal. When they do use methods of birth control, they see it as a failure of faith on their part, often brought about through fear of the physical or financial consequences of another pregnancy. Nevertheless, every pregnancy is interpreted as a direct work of God's creative hand. Quiverfull families affirm each pregnancy as specifically willed by God and, therefore, worthy of thanksgiving and joy.

Quiverfull mothers speak of this conviction as a matter of faith because they are very familiar with the ambivalence that can surround the news of pregnancy. They do not always feel as though another child is a blessing. During the course of my research, Deborah Olson was surprised to discover that she was expecting another child. With six children already and the physical difficulties she faces with each pregnancy, the Olsons had begun to think that their time for having biological children was over. Though she stubbornly affirms the gift nature of children, Deborah found her feelings mixed. More than anything else, she is fearful for her health and ability to care for her children if her health is compromised. "I'm trying not to be scared about the way I feel," she says. Her answer to this anxiety is to remind herself what she knows to be true:

> Sometimes you have to just go back to the basics. [Children] are a blessing because the Lord says they are. The Bible says that they are a blessing and that having them is a gift from the Lord and an inheritance from him. You know, rain is a blessing, too. But sometimes it's really annoying. [Laughter.] So, I just, I just, yeah. They just are. That's the truth. But, to feel that every day? No, that's not reality.

In their insistence on the gift nature of children, Quiverfull practitioners are well supported by scripture. Throughout the Old Testament, "multiplication" and "fruitfulness" are considered a sign of God's blessing (Exod 1:7, 20). The Pentateuch and historical books present stories continually focused on the propagation of children, most famously in the narratives of Sarah, Rachel, Leah, and Hannah. In these stories, the formula is quite simple: to receive a child from God is to be blessed; to be childless is to be cursed. The Psalms also speak of children as a blessing. God's kindness is illustrated in making the "childless woman" into the "happy mother of children" (Ps 113:9) and, as we have already seen, the man with a "quiver full" of children is blessed with a "reward" and "heritage" from God (Ps 127:3–5).[12]

While the New Testament is not as concerned with reproduction per se, it remains positive about children. Within the ministry of Jesus, children take on a central theological and ethical place in the kingdom of God. Jesus welcomes and blesses children in opposition to the behavior of the disciples who seek to keep them away (Mark 10:16; Matt 19:13). Children are regularly the recipients of Christ's healing, and the daughter of Jairus is raised from the dead (Mark 5:21–23). Jesus teaches "the Kingdom of Heaven belongs to such as these" (Matt 19:14; Mark 10:13–14) and that becoming "like little children" is a prerequisite for entering the kingdom (Matt 18:3). And in a statement reminiscent of Matthew 25:40, Jesus states, "Whoever welcomes one of these little children in my name welcomes me; and whoever welcomes me does not welcome me but the one who sent me" (Mark 9:37). Thus, children are to be welcomed as the mediated presence of Christ and the God who sent him, a perspective that intensifies the perspective of children as a blessing found in the Old Testament.[13]

Yet, when Quiverfull practitioners say all children are blessings, do they really mean *all*? According to my informants, the answer is yes. Even in cases of children born into poverty, disease, or dysfunction, all children are unqualified gifts of God. The problem in such cases is the scenario they are born into and not the children themselves. In Carley Miller's words, "God is the creator and author of life. All life." Moreover, neither their ethnicity nor religion matters because God says all children are blessings without any qualifications. Even the children of non-Christians are blessings because, as Deborah Olson says, "Nonbelievers have many gifts from God. They can enjoy all of creation without ever acknowledging him."

Still, the print materials of the Quiverfull subculture make the gift

---

12. Of course, there are important socioeconomic reasons for this perspective on reproduction. In a patrilineal and patrilocal society the production of male heirs is important for family inheritance and social stability. And, in the agrarian economy of ancient Israel, more children means more hands to help with daily labor. For further discussion, see Leo G. Perdue, Joseph Blenkinsopp, John J. Collins, and Carol L. Meyers, eds., *Families in Ancient Israel*, Family Religion and Culture Series (Louisville: Westminster John Knox, 1997).

13. The Christian tradition offers extensive support for the intrinsic gift nature of children. Indeed, the majority of theologians uphold the Quiverfull conviction that children are a divine blessing. For more information on children in the Christian tradition, see Marcia J. Bunge, ed., *The Child in Christian Thought* (Grand Rapids: Eerdmans, 2001); Patrick McKinley Brennan, ed., *The Vocation of the Child* (Grand Rapids: Eerdmans, 2008); and Jerome Berryman, *Children and the Theologians: Clearing the Way for Grace* (Harrisburg, PA: Morehouse, 2009).

nature of all children a more ambiguous matter. Some writers fail to extend the gift nature of children to those abandoned, non-Christian, or otherwise outside the white Protestant norm. For these writers, the passion for birthing children arises directly from a place of antipathy toward the children of others. For example, when Mary Pride is encouraging her readers to have many children, she offers the following argument:

> Scripture draws a fundamental distinction between the children of the righteous (of whom there are never enough) and the children of the wicked (of whom there are always too many). The children of the righteous are blessings (Psa. 37:26). The man who fears the Lord and delights in his commands will have children who are "mighty in the land" (Psa. 112:2). . . . On the other hand, curses are on the children of the wicked (Psa. 109:10-13; 37:28).[14]

Pride asserts that "the children of the wicked"—presumably non-Christians—are far too numerous and cursed by God. Of course, to state that there are too many of them is to imply that they are less valuable than the children of Christians. The children of "the righteous" are a blessing, but the children of "the wicked" are not. Rachel Scott, who writes from a more apocalyptic perspective, shares Pride's view. She says,

> The enemy is preparing his army for battle. . . . I believe that there are children being born right now who already desire to promote the enemy's agenda. Some are chosen in the womb through satanic rituals or other forms of evil. The only hope these children have is to find Christ, but until they do, they will be increasingly susceptible to the deeds and plans of the enemy.[15]

For Scott, non-Christian children are pawns in "the enemy's agenda" and members of Satan's "army." Her encouragement to Christian families to have more children is, in part, for the purpose of providing soldiers for "God's army" to fight against the "Anti-Christ" in the last days. And, perhaps most alarmingly, Scott sees some children as "chosen in the womb" by Satan. Within this dualistic vision, such children cannot credibly be called a gift of God.

Craig Houghton displays similar contradictions in his book *Family UNplanning*. Houghton points to the demographic rise of American

---

14. Pride, *The Way Home*, 63.
15. Scott, *Birthing God's Mighty Warriors*, vii–viii.

Muslims as one reason for Christians to have many children. "At the present rate," he says, "Satan will win the war against Christians through attrition—and we are cooperating with him, rather than trying to defeat his lies." He goes on to conclude: "We can forecast that with the growth rate of Muslims far exceeding that of Christians, that by the end of this century, Muslims will be the majority in the USA."[16] Houghton does not say so explicitly, but when he follows up a warning about Satan's "war against Christians" with statistics about the natural growth rate of Muslims, it is hard not to conclude he associates the rise of the Muslim population with Satan's triumph. The children of Muslim parents are not blessings to be welcomed or gifts given by God; they are a sign of Satan's victory, and perhaps a tool of Satan himself.[17]

The problem of seeing the children of others as unworthy of love and protection is not new. The Old Testament, which offers strong affirmations of children as divine gifts, also shows some ambiguity about the children of other nations. The stories of the Canaanite conquest involve the apparently divinely directed massacre of conquered children (Josh 6:21; 8:24; 10:28–38), as does the book of Judges (Judg 21:10).[18] In the Law, the children of conquered and surrounding peoples can be taken as slaves (Lev 25:44–46), even though Israelites are instructed not to force each other into slavery (Lev 25:39, 42). Also, the Psalms contain repeated requests for God to curse and bring harm on the children of enemies (Ps 17:14; 109:9–12; 137:9).[19]

Still, inconsistency on the gift nature of children appears primarily in the rhetoric of Quiverfull elites. My informants are united in their refusal to view any children as beyond the pale. For many—perhaps most—women at the grassroots, who do the daily work of raising a quiver full of children, all really means *all*, and this conviction is borne out in practice. Early in their marriage, the Millers adopted a baby whose mother could not care for her. Carley took on extra

---

16. Houghton, *Family UNplanning*, 77.

17. Houghton isn't the only author to specifically mention Muslims. Campbell bemoans the proliferation of Muslim and Catholic children in the United States, while the number of Protestant children dwindles in comparison (Joyce, *Quiverfull*, 182–83).

18. I say "apparently divinely directed massacre" because not all scholars agree that these atrocities were indeed directed by God. See further, Douglas S. Earl, *The Joshua Delusion? Rethinking Genocide in the Bible* (Eugene, OR: Wipf & Stock, 2011); Eric A. Seibert, *The Violence of Scripture: Overcoming the Old Testament's Troubling Legacy* (Minneapolis: Fortress Press, 2012); and Gregory Boyd, *The Crucifixion of the Warrior God* (Minneapolis: Fortress Press, 2017).

19. These are not the only instances of ambiguity about the children of others in the Bible, but they are prominent examples.

work outside the home to raise money for the adoption. The Millers still maintain a relationship with their daughter's birth mother, offering encouragement and assistance as she pursues an independent life. The Olsons have opened their home to a young adult who is without immediate family and in desperate need of a place to stay. They are acting as his parents, providing for his physical, material, and emotional needs, even as they care for their own six children. Renee Tanner has made it a point to make her home welcoming to all of her children's friends, coworkers, and neighbors. They regularly host "extra kids" for extended periods of time because Renee sees the home as her primary site of ministry. Her practice demonstrates her conviction that all children are a gift of God, not just the children she has conceived and birthed.

Within Christian theology, Quiverfull proponents are certainly right to see children as gifts of God. In the Christian tradition, God-with-us arrived in the form of an infant, conceived by an unwed mother and born into Roman-occupied Palestine. Since God the Son became a particular Child, Christians are compelled to view the worth and status of all children differently. As Robin Maas suggests, "From the very moment the Word takes flesh and comes to dwell among us, even in embryo, all reality is altered at its root, that is, in its significance." The fact that Jesus was the revelation of God even as a child tells us there is nothing imperfect or incomplete about children.[20] Indeed, the "human child, vulnerable, utterly dependent and trusting, now becomes the real presence of Christ—a living sacrament of the kingdom of heaven."[21] It is, therefore, incumbent upon Christian theologians to affirm the intrinsic gift nature of children, regardless of the circumstances of their birth or upbringing.

Children are gifts not only to their parents but also to the church and society at large. In the words of Adrian Thatcher, "A child is not bought, not possessed, is not an object, does not exist for another's end. Of all the gifts that the Giving God gives, surely the gift of a child is supremely the greatest, next to the gift of one's life partner, and of life itself."[22] The Triune God revealed in Jesus Christ is also the Gifting God. Thatcher explains: "Parents who receive the gift of a child joyfully are, by that very experience, better able to understand

---

20. Adrian Thatcher, *Theology and Families*, Challenges in Contemporary Theology Series (Oxford: Wiley-Blackwell, 2007), 102.

21. Robin Maas, "Christ as the Logos of Childhood: Reflections on the Meaning and Mission of the Child," *Theology Today* 56, no. 4 (January 2000): 457, 458.

22. Thatcher, *Theology and Families*, 99.

the central claim of the Christian faith. For God the Son is also a gift. God the Son is God the Given. The gift of a child to parents calls forth an endless response of freely-given love."[23] A strong stance for the gift nature of children is an important point of witness in a society that views children either as valuable commodities or economic hardships.

But the conviction of child-as-gift also shoulders the mothers of the Quiverfull movement with enormous responsibility. Given the scope of their daily tasks and often challenging life circumstances, the steadfast openness of Quiverfull mothers to more children is extraordinary. Fathers also affirm the blessing of children and have a hand in the consequences of their choice not to limit fertility. But Quiverfull mothers physically embody this conviction over and over again for up to thirty years. Despite the fact that American society has fetishized pregnancy and babies, it remains generally indifferent and even hostile to children and the demands they make of their caregivers. Quiverfull mothers continue to affirm that children are gifts even as they are giving of themselves repeatedly throughout the long months of pregnancy and nursing, not to mention the many years of schooling and daily care that come with each additional child. In the face of widespread cultural antipathy, the Quiverfull insistence on the child-as-gift functions as a kind of ascetic witness. Yes, children require sacrifice, but it is a sacrifice they are willing to make—over and over and over again.

Still, it is a big step from affirming that all children are an unqualified gift of God to arguing that Christians should never seek to limit or space their children or that Christians should seek to have as many children as possible. Quiverfull teachers usually justify this move from theological description (all children are blessings) to moral prescription (one must not put a limit on children) with the argument that no one wants to limit other kinds of divine blessings, such as money, possessions, power, or influence. Therefore, they say, the same unlimited openness must apply to the gift of children. Yet, it is by no means certain that Christians would not want to limit things like money, possessions, power, or influence. The teachings of Jesus, especially, warn against the dangers of wealth and power, and urge those who would enter the kingdom of God toward a life of simplicity and self-denial. Also, as one evangelical critic of Quiverfull has

---

23. Thatcher, *Theology and Families*, 100. For his part, Thatcher is drawing upon the theology of Jean-Luc Marion and Stephen Webb.

pointed out: the Bible says a wife is a gift from God (Prov 18:22), but that does not mean it is wrong not to marry (see 1 Cor 7:8) or that one should therefore acquire many wives.[24] It simply does not follow that because the Christian tradition affirms that children are divine gifts, then taking steps to regulate, time, or limit these gifts is necessarily wrong.[25]

Furthermore, even as Christian theologians affirm children as good gifts from God, it is important to reckon with the experiences of families for whom the gift of children can also be a burden. This is something Quiverfull mothers understand. Just because something is a gift does not mean one always receives it as a gift. Creation, too, is a gift of God yet humans routinely mistreat and exploit creation without much thought. Perhaps the simplest way to name the discrepancy between conviction and experience is sin.[26] As Deborah Olson, Renee Tanner, and Carley Miller have indicated, children are a mixed blessing to families living in a world marred by sin and suffering. The news of a new life can be greeted with equal parts fear and joy, anxiety and hope. In this respect, Thatcher offers an important caveat: "While the notion of 'planning' a family may seem to be at variance with receiving children as divine gifts, the gift of too many children is also at variance with the 'giftedness' of children. The Catechism [of the Catholic Church] still regards large families as 'a sign of God's blessing and the parents' generosity.' Parents suffering poverty or in poor health regard them differently."[27]

The problem of parental ambivalence toward children is more than simply a personal, private problem of the heart. It is inappropriate, therefore, as Quiverfull teachers are prone to do, to dismiss parents who worry about providing and caring for children as faithless, materialistic, or disobedient. Rather, their concerns must be viewed in light of larger cultural, socioeconomic, political, and environmental factors. There are important socioeconomic reasons so many parents view their children as both profound gifts and heavy burdens. Only when viewed in this larger context can American Christians begin to imagine alternative ways of life that might mitigate these fears, and

---

24. John Piper, "Does the Bible Permit Birth Control?" Desiring God Foundation, January 23, 2006, http://tinyurl.com/yc3oujnw.

25. I say limiting or spacing births is not *necessarily* wrong because this topic is worth a deeper discussion than the present context allows. The ethics of family planning is something that remains a debated issue among Protestants and Catholic theologians alike. The specific subject of family planning (and contraception) will not be treated in depth at this point.

26. Thanks to Jana Bennett for this observation.

27. Thatcher, *Theology and Families*, 228.

provide a more hospitable environment for receiving children as the gifts they are.[28] If children are understood merely as a personal choice, then there's little motivation to enact social and economic policies that make parenting easier and receiving children as blessings more likely.

Moreover, Christians must strongly reject the promotion of Christian reproduction through the demonization of non-Christian children. If all children are divine gifts, then that includes the children of social, cultural, and religious "others." More specifically, the teachings of Jesus do not allow Christians to limit love and care for children to the biological offspring of a Christian marriage. The Christian commitment to the gift nature of children and love of God for all children has serious social and political implications. As Julie Hanlon Rubio says, "Christians love children not because children belong to them, but because children belong to God. Their commitment to their children is rooted primarily in love, not biology."[29] Moreover, all children, not just one's own children, are among "the least of these" that Jesus exhorts his followers to receive and care for as we would for his own person.[30] Thus the commitment to the wellbeing of one's own children should lead to the commitment to the wellbeing of all children.

THE CHILD AS INNOCENT AND SINNER

In Quiverfull materials, the theme of children as divine gifts looms large. The reasoning is simple: if every child is a blessing, then the more children you have, the more blessings you have. But, just because children are gifts from God does not mean that they always behave as such. In works devoted to childrearing, another important theme emerges: children are imagined both as innocent, vulnerable persons in need of protection, as well as sinful offenders in need of restraint and training.[31] These two ways of imagining the child create

28. David Matzko McCarthy has tried to do some of this reimagining regarding the family in America. See *Sex and Love in the Home*, New Edition (London: SCM, 2004).

29. Julie Hanlon Rubio, *A Christian Theology of Marriage and Family* (Mahwah, NJ: Paulist, 2003), 149.

30. Rubio, *A Christian Theology of Marriage and Family*, 151.

31. John P. Bartkowski and Christopher G. Ellison posit a tension in evangelical parenting manuals that mirrors what is being described here. They report that evangelical parents are enjoined both to discipline their children (often with firm defenses of corporal punishment) and to cherish their children (with strong endorsements of loving nurturance and quality time). Evangelical enthusiasm for upholding a hierarchy in the home is matched by a commitment

a subtle tension in Quiverfull discourse. They also lead to a view of childhood in which the child grows in knowledge and capability and thereby becomes less innocent and (potentially) more sinful.

Quiverfull practitioners view children as innocent because they start out ignorant of evil and totally dependent upon their families for care and guidance. As my informants describe it, the innocence of little ones slowly fades as they become more knowledgeable and develop their own will. Renee Tanner says, "You're innocent until you learn things." The perceived innocence of children is employed as the primary reason for familial protection, evidenced especially in the practice of homeschooling. Because children are impressionable and vulnerable, especially early on, it is vitally important that parents, siblings, and other trusted family members be the primary influences in their lives. The "wrong" kind of people can have a profoundly negative impact on children, so it is best that the parents take responsibility for children's education and development in the safety of their own home. Here, the innocence of children refers both to their ignorant, unformed state and their vulnerability to harm. In this twofold sense, the innocence of children calls for protection, and Quiverfull parents do not apologize for "sheltering" their children from harmful "worldly" influences.

Still, the goal isn't constant, unending protection. Renee Tanner describes it in the following way: "I would think your overall goal would be that it's a process of walking them through becoming aware—becoming not naïve anymore. So, you protect their innocence as long as it's necessary, as long as it's a good thing." To illustrate, she offers a recent interaction with her eleven-year-old son, Michael. He had written a short paper in which he misspelled the word *where* as *whore* throughout the document. (She laughed as she related this mistake.) When Renee asked him if he knew what the word *whore* referred to, he said he did not. So, Renee took that opportunity to call over another older child (who is fourteen) and explain to both of them what *whore* means and how it is used. Renee's commentary on this incident is as follows:

---

to "expressive caregiving" with fathers who are more involved with children compared to their peers in other faith traditions. Bartkowski and Ellison conclude, "Evangelical child-rearing practices, then, seem to confound long-standing sociological typologies that aim to fit parents neatly into 'authoritarian,' 'authoritative,' and 'permissive' categories." See John P. Bartkowski and Christopher G. Ellison, "Conservative Protestants on Children and Parenting," in *Children and Childhood in American Religions*, ed. Don S. Browning and Bonnie J. Miller-McLemore (New Brunswick, NJ: Rutgers University Press, 2009), 42–55.

So, you can tell I've obviously protected the innocence in them. I'm not like a huge shield over them, but there are areas that I protect them. . . . I'm not against telling them things. . . . I wait to tell them some things out of social behavior expectations. I don't want them shouting out socially inappropriate things because they don't know any better. But, I do see it as my job to walk them through it and tell them what they need to know.

Thus, while childhood innocence is perceived as something they will lose over time, Quiverfull parents see it as their duty to control both when and how that innocence is lost.[32] Children are unfamiliar with the sinful, dangerous adult world and, as such, are innocent in their ignorance. This state will change, however, as children grow and are led by their parents through the acquisition of knowledge and experience.[33]

Although viewed as a temporary reality, Quiverfull proponents routinely employ the image of innocent children in order to glorify the goods of motherhood and prolific childbirth. Carley Miller and Deborah Olson both speak of the way the unrestrained affection of children blesses parents and how the addition of another child naturally brings additional joy to the family. Also, Quiverfull writers tend to emphasize the innocence of children as they are seeking to convince the reader of the desirability of pronatalism. Rachel Scott says, "God intended for children to always be in people's lives from the beginning of their marriages until their final days on earth. His desire was for people to be surrounded by the innocence, tenderness, and

---

[32.] Quiverfull practitioners are not the only ones to imagine children as innocent. Perhaps the most optimistic view of children came from the Romantic Movement, of which the thinking of Jean-Jacques Rousseau is an important example. Pushing back against longstanding Augustinian anthropology that viewed humanity as born in sin and guilt, Rousseau posits that everything in its "natural" state is inherently good (Rousseau, *Émile*, 24, quoted by David H. Jensen, *Graced Vulnerability: A Theology of Childhood* [Cleveland: Pilgrim, 2005], 6). Later, Horace Bushnell echoed Rousseau's optimism about children in his influential book, *Christian Nurture*. Bushnell never explicitly denied the sinfulness of children, but he thought there was no good reason that a child had to resort to sin and wickedness provided the child has been lovingly guided toward loving God. Through careful nurturance, Bushnell says, the child of a Christian family will find it "all but impossible" to forsake the Christian faith (Horace Bushnell, *Christian Nurture* [New York: Charles Scribner, 1861; reprint, Cleveland: Pilgrim, 1994], 10). For more, see Margaret Bendroth, "Horace Bushnell's Christian Nurture," in *The Child in Christian Thought*, 350–64.

[33.] For some on the progressive side, the child is naturally "enchanted," and the parents' role is to protect and cultivate this enchantment. See, for example, Rebecca A. Allahyari, "Homeschooling the Enchanted Child: Ambivalent Attachments in the Domestic Southwest," in *What Matters? Ethnographies of Value in a Not So Secular Age*, ed. Courtney Bender and Ann Taves (New York: Columbia University Press, 2012), 179–214.

love that only a child can bring."[34] Mary Pride emphasizes the innocence of children to convince mothers of the desirability of stay-at-home motherhood: "Is the old nine-to-five grind, or rat race as it is commonly called, really more wonderful than dandling your very own baby on your knee or teaching her to play 'peek-a-boo' while she squeals with delight?"[35] Quiverfull sources frequently employ pictures of cherubic, docile white children as they extol the goodness of children. On the cover of Nancy Campbell's book *Be Fruitful and Multiply*, a well-dressed, porcelain-skinned Victorian couple leans over the bassinet of a rosy-cheeked infant dressed in white lace.[36] Even though the innocence of children is provisional, it remains an important part of the way children are imagined in Quiverfull discourse.

At the same time, Quiverfull practitioners also imagine children as sinners because they were born with the sinful nature that all human beings since Adam and Even are thought to possess. While the innocence of children is a temporary reality, Quiverfull proponents believe the sinfulness of children is something that endures. Because "all have sinned and fallen short of the glory of God" (Rom 3:23), they believe all humans are born sinful. Lacking proper training and instruction, children will persist in their sinfulness and choose a life of wickedness. This emphasis is evidenced in both the testimony of Quiverfull mothers and the written materials of the subculture. In the following excerpt, Renee Tanner employs the language of innocence and sinfulness simultaneously:

> We're born fallen, not sinners. And that's going to come out in one way or another without any encouragement. But, there's also a personality that's innocent. . . . Some children learn early by picking up things around them, by picking up what appeals to that sin nature. . . . We just have a tendency to sin and always will without guidance not to. I think there's a whole lot of goodness and innocence [in people] and if it's taken care of, it can draw people more toward the good than bad.

Despite the fact that she opts for the descriptor *fallen* over *sinner*, the tension between childhood innocence and sinfulness is evident here.[37]

34. Scott, *Birthing God's Mighty Warriors*, 84.
35. Pride, *The Way Home*, 51.
36. Campbell, *Be Fruitful and Multiply*.
37. Renee Tanner is the only one of my informants to make this distinction between "fallen" and "sinner," and to my knowledge it is not a common distinction made within evangelical culture in general.

Renee affirms simultaneously that children are "innocent until [they] learn things" and that they have a "sin nature" and "tendency to sin." The idea of innocence until the acquisition of knowledge implies that children are a moral blank slate that needs only to be written upon rightly. But, the idea of a fixed sin nature and inherent tendency to sin implies that there's a moral defect in children from the very beginning.

The same tension is present in the way Deborah Olson describes children:

> A baby is the most innocent thing possible. And there are so many things about young children that are innocent—meaning they have not been exposed to the world, the things that make us grow in bad ways. So, in that way, yes, they're innocent. But, I mean, they are *sinners*. They are born sinners and as they grow and develop that becomes way more apparent and obvious. . . . The innocence is going to diminish and their sinful nature is going to increase as they grow up and are controlled by their own flesh. Babies don't do that yet. But, once that starts, they are more and more controlled by their flesh. Because every child will lie. Every child will do things like that. That proves we all sin.

Deborah is using "flesh" in the tradition of the apostle Paul, who imagined the "flesh" constantly at odds with the Spirit in the Christian life: "So I say, walk by the Spirit, and you will not gratify the desires of the flesh. For the flesh desires what is contrary to the Spirit, and the Spirit what is contrary to the flesh" (Gal 5:16, 17). So, the innocence of children is lost as they age, while the "flesh" (or sinful nature) grows in its degree of control over the child. Children grow out of their innocence and grow into their sinfulness. It is of paramount importance, therefore, to begin their training from a young age.

This point of view is in line with what Michael and Debi Pearl say about the moral development of children in their book *To Train Up a Child*.[38] Although considered marginal figures in the homeschooling movement, the Pearls have exercised considerable influence among

---

38. There is a significant amount of controversy surrounding *To Train Up a Child* (Pleasantville, TN: No Greater Joy Ministries, 1994), both inside and outside the Christian homeschooling movement. The book has played a part in a few well-publicized stories of child abuse and neglect, three of which resulted in death. (I will discuss these cases in more detail in chapter 5.) The Pearls flatly deny that their book leads to abuse if parents follow their instructions. See Michael Pearl, "Hana Williams' Death—Official Statement," No Greater Joy Ministries, http://tinyurl.com/ybag553t.

Quiverfull families, especially in the area of childrearing.[39] Deborah Olson and Renee Tanner both draw on some of the Pearls' teachings in their childrearing practices. A central premise for how the Pearls imagine children is, "[Children] begin life in innocent self-centeredness. God does not impute it to them as sin, but it is the foundation of sin."[40] Parents need to be aware that the small child's "selfishness" is not itself sin, but it will "soon move in that direction." They warn, "Drives which are not in themselves evil, nonetheless, form the seedbed on which sin will assuredly grow. As parents train the young child, they must take into consideration the evil that a self-willed spirit will eventually bring."[41] The Pearls argue that the training of children in obedience must begin in infancy. Because the development of the child will mean an increase in the "self-willed spirit," it is vital to bring the will of the child into "complete subjection" from early on.[42] A child who learns to resist selfishness and "voluntarily surrender to the rule of law" early on will be less likely to fall into grave error when he is finally a "responsible, moral soul" (which they imagine takes place sometime between twelve and twenty years old).[43]

Voddie Baucham goes even further than the Pearls in his characterization of children. He says flatly, "All children are shaped in iniquity and conceived in sin." In his sermons, he calls the child "a viper in a diaper."[44] For this reason, children must be trained "from the time they can crawl" to obey their parents immediately and without question, something he calls "first-time obedience."[45] For Baucham, learning to obey parents immediately is the first step in ridding the child's heart of sin and foolishness and teaching them to obey God.

---

39. For example, despite the controversy surrounding it, their book *To Train Up a Child* has sold over 660,000 copies. Voddie Baucham confirms the influence of the Pearls by devoting an entire chapter in his book, *Family Shepherds*, to engaging their view of children as sinners. He says, "The influence of Pearl's work in certain circles cannot be overstated. This is especially true in homeschooling families" (*Family Shepherds: Calling and Equipping Men to Lead Their Homes* [Wheaton, IL: Crossway, 2011], 118).

40. Renee Tanner speaks approvingly of the Pearls on the matter of child training. It may be that her idea that children are born fallen but later grow into sinfulness (note 37 above) is informed by the Pearls' teaching.

41. Pearl and Pearl, *To Train Up a Child*, 19.

42. Pearl and Pearl, *To Train Up a Child*, 21.

43. Pearl and Pearl, *To Train Up a Child*, 21.

44. I was first made aware of Baucham's use of this phrase, *viper in a diaper*, through an article by R. L. Stollar, "The Child as Viper: How Voddie Baucham's Theology of Children Promotes Child Abuse" (2015), which was made available on the *Homeschoolers Anonymous* website: http://tinyurl.com/ybw36hdt.

45. Voddie Baucham Jr., *Family Driven Faith: Doing What It Takes to Raise Sons and Daughters Who Walk with God* (Wheaton, IL: Crossway, 2007), 105.

Without proper training, children inevitably will become unruly and ungodly. So, Baucham says, "Our children must learn that they're sinners. They didn't simply 'pick up bad habits'; they *sin*. . . . Johnny doesn't disobey because he's cranky, tired, or hungry. . . . He does it because he's a descendant of Adam."[46] Child training, therefore, is for the purpose of restraining evil in children. Indeed, for Baucham not only is evil *in* children but also children themselves are evil:

> These small little cherubs—these so-called "innocent ones"—the reason that they do what they do is because they are every bit of Romans, chapter 3, verses 9-18. They come into the world like this. One of the reasons that God makes human babies small is so they won't kill their parents in their sleep. They're evil. . . . "None is righteous; no, not one. None understands. No one seeks God. No one does good." Yes, that little, precious one—you better believe it. If you don't, you miss the big picture and you don't realize your desperate need to get the gospel to your child again and again and again and again.[47]

Because of this view of children's total depravity, for parents to neglect the task of child training and restraining sin is, in a real way, to abandon the child to destruction.[48]

As they imagine children as sinners, Quiverfull practitioners draw heavily on scripture.[49] The psalmist, for example, speaks of being conceived in iniquity and being a sinner from the womb (Ps 51:5). The apostle Paul claims, "all have sinned and fallen short of the glory of God" (Rom 3:23). Many quote from the book of Proverbs to

---

46. Baucham, *Family Shepherds*, 119, 125.

47. Voddie Baucham, "The Doctrine of Total Depravity," sermon delivered on May 2, 2010 at Grace Family Baptist Church, http://tinyurl.com/ybgxtuaf. Transcript by R. L. Stollar available at *Homeschoolers Anonymous*, January 13, 2015, http://tinyurl.com/y8lj2okh.

48. The Pearls say as much: "Anticipating the child's development, and knowing that evil will come to be a part of his moral being, places an urgent sense of responsibility upon parents. The world is a powerful, unrelenting undertow, pulling children to destruction. . . . [T]he probability is overwhelmingly against their moral survival" (*To Train Up a Child*, 19). Both the Pearls and Baucham promote the use of corporeal punishment in infants, toddlers, and young children in order to teach obedience and "restrain evil" (Baucham's phrase). Yet, while the Pearls are most associated with physical punishment, Baucham's instructions are even more extreme. In Stollar's words, "Whereas Pearl believes parents should be more like 'the Holy Spirit' in their children's lives, Baucham believes parents should be 'like that of policemen.' Baucham's system thus ends up being *more authoritarian* than Pearl's, and that is caused by the fact that Baucham not only believes in original sin (as does Pearl), but *also* total depravity" (Stollar, "The Child as Viper").

49. Baucham says, "I have . . . discovered that there is a home training manual. It is called the Holy Bible. Anyone who has read the book of Proverbs knows that the Bible is filled with valuable child-training information. God has not left us in the dark on this issue" (*Family Driven Faith*, 96).

support the use of physical discipline in childrearing, which is considered vital due to the natural sinfulness of children. According to Proverbs 22:15, "Foolishness is bound up in the heart of a child; the rod of discipline will remove it far from him." Also, "Whoever spares the rod hates his son, but he who loves him is diligent to discipline him" (Prov 13:24). The exhortation of Proverbs 23:13-14 is particularly severe: "Do not withhold discipline from your children; if you beat them with a rod, they will not die. If you beat them with the rod, you will save their lives from Sheol."[50]

All of the above are thought to lend support to the Quiverfull commitment to careful religious discipline throughout childhood in order to combat their natural sinfulness. In practice, this vital task is accomplished with a combination of daily prayer and scripture reading, regular instruction and admonition, weekly family worship, and, sometimes, physical punishment. In contemporary conversations about children, the harm and danger of physical punishment is a critical concern. Many scholars have argued that a robust view of children as sinners is directly linked to physical, mental, and emotional abuse of children by parents and other caregivers.[51] Within Quiverfull, too, the child-as-sinner theme is routinely linked to the use of physical chastisement. Though by no means the only, or even most important, practice in Quiverfull childrearing, the promotion and practice of spanking remains commonplace throughout the subculture. And, more often than not, the use of spanking is linked directly to the sin nature of children, which is in urgent need of restraint and correction.

When Quiverfull practitioners imagine children as both innocents and sinners, they are not exceptional. Despite the tension between these two ways of thinking, both strands of thought have a long history in Christian theology. But both tendencies have some inherent

---

50. Through the ages, the view of children as sinners has been widespread among Christian theologians. When Quiverfull parents speak of the need to restrain the natural depravity of children, they do so in agreement with the likes of Augustine, Martin Luther, John Calvin, Menno Simons, John Wesley, Jonathan Edwards, and more. For more discussion on this subject, see Bunge, *The Child in Christian Thought*.

51. See, for example, Alice Miller, *For Your Own Good: Hidden Cruelty in Child-Rearing and the Roots of Violence*, trans. Hildegarde Hannum and Hunter Hannum (New York: Farrar, Straus & Giroux, 1983); Philip Greven, *Spare the Child: The Religious Roots of Punishment and the Psychological Impact of Physical Abuse* (New York: Vintage, 1990); Donald Capps, *The Child's Song: The Religious Abuse of Children* (Louisville: Westminster John Knox, 1995); and Stephen Pattison, "'Suffer Little Children': The Challenge of Child Abuse and Neglect to Theology," *Theology and Sexuality* 9 (1998): 36–58.

problems. On the one hand, those who insist on the inherent sinfulness of children overlook the way that children are mediators of truth, beauty, and goodness to those around them. Jesus holds out the vulnerable child as an example of those who will surely enter into the kingdom of God (Matt 19:13–15; Mark 10:13–15; Luke 18:15–17). He quotes approvingly of the psalmist: "Out of the mouths of infants and nursing babies you have prepared praise" (Matt 21:16; quoting Ps 8:2). Also, he asserts that welcoming children is a means by which disciples welcome Jesus himself (Matt 18:1–6). Thus hard-and-fast notions of childhood iniquity and corruption cannot stand in Christian theology without serious nuance. On the other hand, those who insist on the innocence of children sometimes overlook the way that children are implicated in and influenced by, the vulnerability of human life and the brokenness of their surroundings. Human interdependence means that all human beings are capable of harming and being harmed—including children. Of all people, parents and caregivers know the many ways in which, knowingly or unknowingly, children are capable of harming others. Within a Christian theology of children and childhood, romanticizing the child as a blameless cherub will not stand either.[52]

Thus a Christian imagination about children must recognize that they, like all human beings, are capable of both goodness and wickedness, charity and depravity, selfishness and selflessness—not one or the other but a mixture of both. Moreover, like all human beings, they exist within a web of relationships, in which they can both endure and inflict harm. Bonnie Miller-McLemore argues that children offer as much "difficulty, trouble, and tension" as they do "celebration, admiration, and passionate attachment."[53] She insists we must distinguish between adults and children in a way that does not "rob children of sexual, moral, and spiritual knowledge and agency." Children are not as innocent and carefree as adults imagine, nor are adults as "sophisticated or superior" as they like to think.[54]

Being prone to selfishness, therefore, is not simply the purview of the child, but a problem that afflicts human beings in general. Certainly, children can sin against their parents and others in their

---

52. Mercer agrees with the inadequacy of both the child-as-sinner and child-as-innocent perspectives. See Mercer, *Welcoming Children*, 11.
53. Anne Higonnet, *Pictures of Innocence: The History and Crisis of Ideal Childhood* (New York: Thames & Hudson, 1998), quoted by Bonnie Miller-McLemore, *Let the Children Come: Reimagining Childhood from a Christian Perspective* (San Francisco: Jossey-Bass, 2003), 20.
54. Miller-McLemore, *Let the Children Come*, 22.

sphere of influence, but parents and adult caregivers are just as capable of sinning against those under their care. Most of such violations are minor and easily remedied, such as incidences of unkindness and impatience, unloving looks and words, or unjustified anger. But, parents can also sin against their children in grievous ways, including the neglect of their physical, emotional, and educational needs, physical assault, and verbal abuse. The fact that parents are capable of harming the vulnerable children in their care is a point that must be kept front-and-center in any discussion of "child training" or parental authority. This is especially true of the Quiverfull movement where families are often isolated within the single-family home.

Quiverfull children are not served well by theologies that overemphasize their sinfulness and downplay the sinfulness of parents. Though charged with the important task of raising children, parents and other caregivers are no less in need of training than the children in their midst. This is something Carley Miller especially recognizes:

> Clearly, Jesus loves children. He says that we are to have faith like a child. So, I think that we can learn so much from them. . . . They can teach us so much about life. We get in that mundane routine and forget things that they don't. Maybe they're more free-spirited? They definitely don't worry like we do. . . . I think adults benefit from children. But, also I think that children are learning from adults through their instruction and authority. Maybe there's a pull back and forth. . . . They test our patience, they test our patience, they test our patience. That's just what they do. They humble me, you know? You think you have it figured out and then they shed some new light on it. Sanctify would be a good word.

Certainly, as she acknowledges, parents have a special duty to the instruction of their children that children do not have for their parents. But, Carley also recognizes that there is a kind of sanctification taking place as parents and children relate to each other. Within the church and the Christian family, both parents and children are members of the new covenant in Christ. As both seek to follow Christ, both are in constant need of repentance, forgiveness, and reconciliation. This means the careful examination of family practices, especially those pertaining to training and discipline, is vitally important. And it makes the family's rootedness in the church and its communal practices even more imperative.

In the matter of children and childhood, Christian theologians must move beyond the innocent-sinful dichotomy to include a sense of moral agency and spiritual knowledge, including the capability for good and evil. Moreover, Christian imaginings about children must be closely tied to Christian anthropology as a whole, which envisions adults as well as children as perpetually in need of grace, repentance, forgiveness, and reconciliation. Within the Christian family, the capacity for sin within the heart of the child is found also within the heart of the parent.[55] (Indeed, it is a curious inconsistency that Baucham is not as insistent on the matter of total depravity with parents as he is with children.) Therefore, adults, as much as children, are in need of training and discipline as they learn to resist evil and choose the good. A theology that overly emphasizes the sinfulness of children over against the adults who care for them obscures the fact that adults, who are also spiritual "works in progress," have much to learn from the children in their midst.

THE CHILD AS POTENTIAL DISCIPLE

Thus far, we have seen that the Quiverfull movement imagines children as divine gifts, innocents in need of protection, and sinners in need of training. In this section, we turn to the third theme present in Quiverfull discourse about children: childhood is a period of preparation for adulthood and children are disciples-in-the-making. Although there are some variations within the movement on this subject, the general picture is the same. Quiverfull childhood is understood to be a temporary stage of life that serves as preparation for adulthood. This period of time is for the purpose of learning how to be a responsible, contributing member of the family, church, and society. Most importantly, childhood is the time to prepare to become an adult Christian—a fully functioning and independent disciple of Jesus Christ. So, the primary goal of Christian childhood is Christian adulthood. In addition, childhood is supposed to be a relatively short period of time, ending around adolescence or sexual maturity.

Quiverfull mothers speak of childhood as a temporary period

---

55. It is telling, for example, that Baucham uses the term *viper* to refer to children when, in the gospels, Jesus exclusively applies that term to adults—adult religious leaders, for that matter. A vision of total depravity that applies to all human beings—children and parents alike—would seem to point toward restraint and nonviolence in respect to disciplinary methods. If all humans are totally depraved, then how can parents trust that they will rightly and fairly administer physical discipline with their children?

meant to be spent in preparation for adulthood. In Deborah Olson's words, "It is [about] training and development. Developing into a man or woman. It's [about] growing. The purpose of childhood is growing and training. It is a time to be trained because the Bible says to train them." Because the Bible speaks of the vital importance of "training" children, childhood is viewed as a time of learning with an eye toward their growth into adulthood. Renee Tanner expands on this idea:

> [A child is] moving from awareness to learn[ing] about life—to learn how everything works. To learn about people and learn information. To learn languages and music and all that stuff. To learn kindness and to be trained. From the parent's perspective, childhood is for them to learn that they're loved unconditionally and positively and gently trained toward goodness. That was my goal of parenting: to make goodness normal. . . . So that when they left they did not have bad habits like angry outbursts and bad mouths or temper fits. I've trained them in daily life not to have that. They all had their periods, right? They pushed boundaries and such where they behaved in a lot of ways that I didn't teach them. But, it wasn't their habit. . . . So, my idea would be childhood would be that period to enjoy and be happy and feel loved and secure and trained toward goodness.

In Renee's imagination, children are adults-in-the-making who need unconditional love, security, and "gentle train[ing]" to help them grow "toward goodness." If a parent is responsible and careful with the period of childhood, the child will grow up without "bad habits," viewing goodness, kindness, happiness, love, and "good language" as normal patterns of behavior. Of course, the practice of homeschooling is thought to be crucial to imparting these good patterns of behavior.

The Pearls, referenced above, see children and childhood in the same way. They use the metaphor of a potter and clay (coming from Jer 18:4): "If God is the potter and your child is the clay, you are the wheel on which the clay is to be turned." Then, they switch metaphors and liken children to Adam and Eve:

> There will come a time when your child must stand alone before "the tree of the knowledge of good and evil." As the purpose of God has permitted, he will inevitably partake of the forbidden fruit. Now, in the developing years, you can make a difference in how he will respond after he has "eaten." . . . Will he hide his sin, or repent? Everything a

child experiences, either by way of indulgence or the self-restraint you impose, is preparing him for the day when he will mature into a responsible, moral soul.[56]

The Pearls' language makes explicit that they view children as potential disciples. During childhood, a child is like clay on a potter's wheel, being formed by God through the work of Christian parents. Eventually, children will "mature into a responsible, moral soul," but for now, children must be instructed in "self-restraint" so that when that day comes, they are ready to "repent" and choose the good. Childhood, therefore, is for the purpose of moral training.

Not only is childhood a time of training in morality, but also a time for learning how to be a quasi-independent, contributing member of the family, church, and society. I say "quasi-independent" because my informants do not envision children ceasing to be part of the family once they reach maturity. Indeed, it is an important Quiverfull family goal that close relationships exist among siblings and that parents are trustworthy advisors into adulthood. Moreover, they want their children to feel obligated to contribute positively to church and society through their work. Though moral development takes primacy in Quiverfull families, there always remains an eye toward preparation for work, whether in the home or the marketplace. Renee Tanner saw to it that her teenage children had jobs beyond the home to prepare them for adult work. Deborah and Dan Olson lament that his job doesn't allow him to apprentice his children in some kind of craft or trade. They wish they had a family-based business they could pass on to their children. But the overall point is that Quiverfull families assume the primary posture of a child should be that of student or apprentice, preparing for "real life" in adulthood.

If Quiverfull childhood is a time of training for adulthood, then it is also considered a relatively short time period. Renee Tanner views childhood in the most limited terms. She says society has been "sold a bill of goods" in the idea of adolescence because, in her mind, childhood ends at around twelve years old. There are no "teen years" in this view, just childhood and adulthood. Renee says, "Our culture has it wrong in what we expect of our teens. I think the way Jewish families do it is right. Around twelve or thirteen you're expected to act like an adult and live in light of the Law." Renee is invoking a way of envisioning children that is common within the Christian

---

56. Pearl and Pearl, *To Train Up a Child*, 21.

homeschooling movement as a whole. Arguably, the most important source of this idea is David Alan Black's book *The Myth of Adolescence: Raising Responsible Children in an Irresponsible Society*.[57] Black argues that Jesus should be the model for human development. Since Jesus became an adult at twelve years, so should Christian children today. Moreover, Black argues that scripture as a whole sees human life in only three stages: childhood, young adulthood, and mature adulthood. If Christians are to live in light of scripture, they must abandon modern notions of adolescence and adopt the Bible's view of childhood. (In this assertion, Black is ignoring scientific research on human brain development, which suggests the human brain isn't fully developed until at least the mid-twenties.[58]) This means for many Quiverfull families, childhood is a very short period of training that ends at twelve, even if the child continues to live at home.

Although Deborah Olson and Carley Miller agree that childhood is a relatively short period of time that comes to an end when the child becomes an adult, they are less dogmatic about when that transition takes place. When I ask Deborah when childhood ends, she responds, "Phew ... I don't know. It used to end a lot sooner, didn't it? Now, it's a lot later. I think it just depends. . . . [The end of] childhood just depends on the family, culture, and individual. I mean, [an extended family member of ours] is twenty years old and he's still a child. But, I don't see [my oldest daughter] being a child at twenty." Although still a period of training that ends at adulthood, Deborah doesn't see childhood ending at a set time. Instead, the maturation of each child is different, dependent upon outside factors like the family of origin and the surrounding culture. Carley Miller's experience with special needs children also makes her hesitant to assert one specific age for the end of childhood. Speaking of the existence of "gray areas" in child development, she points to an "age of accountability" as key to knowing when a child becomes an adult. Carley defines *age*

---

57. David Alan Black, *The Myth of Adolescence: Raising Responsible Children in an Irresponsible Society* (Yorba Linda, CA: Davidson Press, 1999). Black is quoted in Voddie Baucham, *Family Driven Faith*, 192.

58. See, for example, the following: J. N. Giedd, "Development of the human corpus callosum during childhood and adolescence: A longitudinal MRI study," *Progress in Neuro-Psychopharmacology & Biological Psychiatry* 23 (1999): 571–88; "Structural magnetic resonance imaging of the adolescent brain," *Adolescent Brain Development: Vulnerabilities and Opportunities* (2004): 77–85; and J. N. Giedd, J. Blumenthal, et al., "Brain development during childhood and adolescence: A longitudinal MRI study," *Nature Neuroscience* 2, no. 10 (1999): 861–63. For more information, see the references offered by the Young Adult Development Project at the Massachusetts Institute of Technology (MIT): http://tinyurl.com/ya7ltu95.

of accountability as a time when a child knows right from wrong and has the mental reasoning to choose one or the other.[59]

Another aspect of Quiverfull practice that evidences their view of the child as a disciple-in-the-making is the lack of attention given to the child's participation and spiritual formation in the church. Of course, Quiverfull parents (especially mothers) devote an exceptional amount of time and energy to the education of children so that they will grow up to be faithful Christians. By their own admission, Quiverfull parents value the spiritual formation of souls over the cultivation of intellectual prowess. Their primary concern is that their children will be committed, practicing Christians upon reaching adulthood. Yet, most Quiverfull parents do not treat their children as Christians until they show evidence of a "conversion experience" and make a "public profession of faith," as is standard practice in American evangelical churches. Thus, they do not imagine their unconverted children as a part of the church, the body of Christ. Natalie Klejwa offers an exemplary perspective on this subject:

> Having babies is one thing, but ultimately my deepest desire is to see them all saved by the blood of Jesus Christ. Since that day I found out I was pregnant for the first time, I have prayed almost daily: *"Father in Heaven, SAVE the souls of every single one of my children. Save them for eternity. Make them Yours. May you keep them in the palm of Your hand and never let them be plucked out."*[60]

Until they go through the prescribed process of conversion, which usually includes the recitation of a "sinner's prayer" of repentance and a public confession of faith, children are treated as unbelievers and subsequently barred from receiving baptism and the Lord's Sup-

---

59. When Quiverfull practitioners view children as adults-in-the-making, they do so with support from a number of thinkers in the Christian tradition, most notably Thomas Aquinas. For a discussion of Thomas's view of children, see Jensen, *Graced Vulnerability*, 9. The concept of the child as adult-in-the-making is also in accordance with the way US law imagines children. By and large, American children are perceived as growing into their roles and responsibilities in society. They do not share in adult cognitive abilities, especially the understanding of consequences, so children, in general, are not held to the same standards as adults. Nevertheless, this distinction has become more muddled in recent years, as US courts are increasingly more open to trying children as adults, particularly in the case of violent crimes.

60. Natalie Klejwa, "Eternal Treasure," in *Three Decades of Fertility: Ten Ordinary Women Surrender to Their Creator and Embrace Life* (Saint Paul, MN: Visionary Womanhood, 2013), 87 (emphasis in original). In *Family Driven Faith*, Baucham offers an exhortation for parents to convert their children: "We must do everything in our power to move our children toward faith in God. . . . [W]e must be committed to proclaim the gospel to our children with a view toward their conversion" (143).

per.[61] This perspective on the sacraments is rooted in the Anabaptist tradition, in which inclusion in the church is dependent upon an individual's profession of faith. Therefore, until they reach a stage of mature decision-making, Quiverfull children are potential converts and potential disciples, not full members of the body of Christ. And, as we saw with the Olson family, sometimes even after children go through a conversion experience, parents are still hesitant to baptize them and initiate them fully into the church.

In addition to complicating the vision of children as innocents and sinners, Christian theologians must reckon with the inadequacy of the view that children are disciples-in-the-making and childhood simply a stage on the way to adulthood. As David Jensen has observed, "The tendency . . . is to consider childhood as a state that will be molded into something more mature once the pernicious tendencies of children are stamped out. Childhood, then, serves partly as a foil to a life of mature discipleship, and is not celebrated for its own sake."[62] Certainly, there are developmental distinctions to be made between adults and children, distinctions particularly important in discussions of educational methods and age-appropriate responsibilities and consequences. But the work of a few contemporary theologians points us toward two important realities: (1) there are aspects of childhood ("childness") that remain part of human beings long after they cease to be considered children; (2) childhood is not a period to be passed through on the way to adulthood, but a vital and enduring part of the mature Christian life.

Childness is the term coined by Herbert Anderson and Susan B. W. Johnson in their book *Regarding Children*. They use this word as a way of referring to the abiding nature of childhood. "In becoming adults, we do not lose childhood," they say. "Childhood is an inevitable dimension of being human."[63] Certainly, changes occur in a person as they grow and mature from childhood into adulthood.

---

61. Of course, this is not true of families that participate in churches that extend the sacrament of baptism to infants. A prominent example is author and blogger Stacy McDonald, who is married to a Reformed pastor. Their church, Providence Church of Peoria, Illinois, extends baptism and communion to the children of Christian parents. Still, the families in my ethnography, along with the majority of elite Quiverfull proponents, fall within the free church, evangelical mainstream that sees the "born again" experience and individual choice to follow Christ as a key part of Christian identity and a requirement for inclusion in the sacramental life of the church.

62. Jensen, *Graced Vulnerability*, 6.

63. Herbert Anderson and Susan B. W. Johnson, *Regarding Children: A New Respect for Childhood and Families*, Family Living in Pastoral Perspective Series (Louisville: Westminster John Knox, 1994), 7.

But, there are enduring elements of childness that remain with every human being regardless of their age.

Two aspects of childness are particularly important. First, childness encompasses vulnerability in relationship to others and the world. To be vulnerable is to be open to harm. Children are vulnerable primarily due to their dependence upon others. Infants, especially, demonstrate profound neediness that is born out of a complete reliance upon others for food, safety, and solace. But, if we consider carefully the nature of human existence, we realize that "we never outgrow the vulnerability of childhood, even when we are no longer obviously small, weak, and needful."[64] Indeed, as David Jensen argues, the "vulnerability-in-relationship" we see so obviously in children is an aspect of the "God-given relatedness" that all are born into and no one outgrows.[65] This is not to romanticize vulnerability or the dangers of childhood, but simply to make the point that all people, including children, are vulnerable.[66] This aspect of childness continues throughout human life.[67]

Second, childness includes an "infinite openness" toward God and creation that is "already an expression of mature religious existence."[68] This is a claim that originates with Karl Rahner, who argues counterintuitively that within the Christian tradition being human is about becoming a child in an ever-increasing degree:

> The mature childhood of the adult is the attitude in which we bravely and trustfully maintain an infinite openness in all circumstances and despite the experiences of life which seem to invite us to close ourselves. Such openness, infinite and maintained in all circumstances, yet put into practice in the actual manner in which we live our lives, is the expression of religious existence.[69]

---

64. Anderson and Johnson, *Regarding Children*, 22.
65. Jensen, *Graced Vulnerability*, 49.
66. Anderson and Johnson, *Regarding Children*, 23.
67. According to theologian Arthur C. McGill, human life is a resting-in-neediness. He says, "In the kingdom of Jesus we always begin with neediness, we always live outward toward neediness, and we always end in neediness" (*Death and Life: An American Theology* [Philadelphia: Fortress Press, 1987], 83).
68. Anderson and Johnson, *Regarding Children*, 22.
69. Karl Rahner, *Theological Investigations*, vol. 8, trans. David Bourke (New York: Herder & Herder, 1971), 48–49; quoted by Anderson and Johnson, *Regarding Children*, 24. At the root of Rahner's view of children and childhood is his "transcendental method" in which "human beings experience a fundamental openness (a self-transcendence) toward God in every truly human act" (Hinsdale, "Infinite Openness to the Infinite: Karl Rahner's Contribution to Modern Catholic Thought on Children," in *The Child in Christian Thought*, 419). Of course, Rahner's perspective is not necessarily shared by Protestants, let alone evangelicals.

If childness is "infinite openness in all circumstances," then the mature Christian adult should embody childness in a fuller, more complete way than the child. For adults to attain to the openness of children, they must repent and be converted; but, "this conversion is only to become what we already are—children." Jensen describes this infinite openness in terms of being a "pilgrim, oriented God-ward and toward the present."[70] Through their attentiveness to the present, he says, children call us "to become who we really are: children of God, attentive to the surprise and mystery of creation."[71] No matter how it is described, however, the point is that the child's enthusiasm for God and God's world is not a quality to be shed in adulthood but "always appropriate for the life that is rightly lived."[72] This profoundly positive view of the child is, of course, lacking in Quiverfull discourse despite their insistence that children are gifts.

Childness is a characteristic of human life in general and childhood is a vital and enduring part of the advanced Christian life. Theologians must resist the tendency, therefore, to view children as disciples-in-the-making and childhood as a stage to be passed through as quickly as possible. In the large families of the Quiverfull movement, it is understandable why childhood would be treated as a short period to be dispensed with swiftly. The practice of homeschooling, in particular, may reinforce the sense that children are unformed or incomplete persons in need of diligent instruction to become full persons (that is, adults).[73] But to be a child is to be vulnerable in relationship with others and to be infinitely open and on pilgrimage in God's world. Viewed in this light, it is clear that adults have as much to learn from children as children do from adults. Again, this is not a romanticization of children, but an exhortation to recognize within children a vital key to what it means to be human.[74] Children are more than simply potential adults, but already full human persons and religious pilgrims in their own right.

---

70. Jensen, *Graced Vulnerability*, 44. Jensen is building on the work of Robert Coles, *The Spiritual Life of Children* (Boston: Houghton Mifflin, 1990).

71. Jensen, *Graced Vulnerability*, 53.

72. Anderson and Johnson, *Regarding Children*, 24.

73. Renee Tanner warns against the tendency to view one's children as always wearing "Post-it notes on their foreheads." She explains that homeschooling mothers are prone to seeing their children as projects to be worked on rather than people to be enjoyed in their own right. After over twenty years of homeschooling, Renee tries to avoid this tendency and works instead on forming a strong friendship with her children.

74. One of the implications here is that our theology of adulthood is deficient in many ways as well. Any altered view of childhood necessarily has consequences for adults and adulthood.

The understanding of children as full Christian disciples stands in tension with standard evangelical practice regarding children and the sacraments. As noted above, children are typically barred from receiving baptism until they are considered capable of experiencing conversion and making an independent choice to follow Christ. Because they have not yet been baptized, such children are also excluded from receiving the Lord's Supper or Holy Communion. Yet, these same children are supposed to be raised in such a way that they never know a day apart from Christ, so that loving God and choosing the good are second nature to them. Within the Anabaptist stream of Protestantism, there are important theological reasons for the practice of "believer's baptism" that I will not explore here. I am concerned simply to point out that the exclusion of children from full participation in the worship of the church works against the aim of equipping children with an enduring Christian identity. Children are expected to conform themselves to the ways of the adult church members until they have a conversion experience and can then participate fully within the congregation. This practice works against the Quiverfull goal of forming children into Christian disciples. Children are welcomed in the sense that they are allowed to be born and mothers reorganize their lives in order to attend carefully to their care and education. But, children are not welcomed in the sense of being fully included in the life of the church. They remain outsiders and observers rather than fully integrated disciples.

THE CHILD AS SOLE RESPONSIBILITY OF PARENTS

Quiverfull practitioners imagine children as divine gifts, innocents and sinners, and disciples-in-the-making. But there is one more important way that children are imagined in Quiverfull discourse: children are the exclusive property of their parents. When Quiverfull practitioners imagine children, they do not see them belonging to themselves or to larger communities or institutions, whether neighborhoods, the nation, or the church. Instead, individual children belong to individual parents within individual families. Because children belong only to their parents, parents are solely responsible for their care and spiritual formation. In other words, their vision of children and childhood is thoroughly privatized, limited to the home of the nuclear family. Of course, Quiverfull families are far from unique in this respect, for they share this privatized vision with evangelicals and American culture in general.

Mary Pride has been a key spokesperson against "governmental interference" in childrearing since the earliest days of the Christian homeschooling movement. This stance is rooted in her view that children belong *only* to parents. Her comments in *The Way Home* are illustrative of this mindset: "God gave parents, and parents *only*, the job of shaping their children's values. . . . *Our responsibility to teach our children their moral and spiritual values cannot be delegated.* Both Deuteronomy 6:7 and Deuteronomy 11:19 make it clear that this training must occur at *home*, throughout the course of the family's day together."[75] For Pride, the major appeal of homeschooling is that it allows parents to have total control over their child's instruction.[76]

Though writing many years later, Voddie Baucham echoes Pride's perspective: "God has designed your family—not the youth group, not the children's ministry, not the Christian school, but your family—as the principal discipling agent in your children's lives. The most important job you have as a parent is to train and disciple your children."[77] Even in Christian households, therefore, children are envisioned not primarily as members of the body of Christ but as the (subordinate) members of the nuclear family. It is the parents' job—and no one else's—to train children and lead them into Christian maturity.[78]

Of course, Quiverfull practitioners do affirm the theological principle that children ultimately belong to God. Pride says, "Who owns our kids? God owns our kids." But, in the very next sentence she insists, "And [God] has given parents the responsibility of making sure they turn out to be his kids."[79] Children belong to God, but God has given children to their parents in the context of the private fam-

---

75. Pride, *The Way Home*, 92–93 (emphasis in original).
76. Pride, *The Way Home*, 97.
77. Baucham, *Family Driven Faith*, 118. It is telling that Baucham names programs of the church but not the church itself in his denunciation of other institutions as "discipling agent[s]." It seems that Baucham either sees the church as equivalent to its programs or he doesn't see the church as having any role at all in the Christian formation of children. In either case, he demonstrates a deficit of ecclesiology.
78. This vision of children is often wedded to a vision of parents in which they are representatives of God and God's character to their children. The Pearls offer a good example of this perspective: "In the limited world of the child, parents are representatives of truth and justice, dispensers of punishment and reward. A child's parents are the window through which he develops a view of what God is like and how moral government functions. . . . Your responses to transgressions are stage-playing the responses of God" (*To Train Up a Child*, 53).
79. Pride, *The Way Home*, 99.

ily home to raise them. And children will not "turn out to be [God's] kids" unless parents teach them rightly. Speaking of the birth of his daughter, Baucham says he and his wife are the "only people" responsible for bringing up their daughter in the faith: "This little girl was *our responsibility*," he says.[80] The future success and failure of every child is laid at the feet of the two-parent nuclear family. Communities and institutions beyond the family have no responsibility in the matter.

Renee Tanner shares Pride and Baucham's point of view. When asked about the responsibility of the church for children, she responds, "I feel like the parents should be the spiritual leaders and disciplers of their children. That's not the job of the church. The church is supposed to equip and empower [parents] and teach in order to undergird and reinforce the parents." Deborah Olson says something similar: "I believe that it's the parents' responsibility for caring, training, everything. . . . I think the church's responsibility should be equipping families to do what the Lord has called them to do." Thus, children are the sole custody of the parents in the family home, and it is the church's role to support and encourage the work of parents. Children do not, in any real sense, belong to the church or the wider community apart from their parents. This perception is exacerbated by the fact that most Quiverfull children are not baptized until they have reached a level of reasoning approaching that of an adult.

The central biblical passage for this insistence that children belong to parents is Deuteronomy 6:4–7, which says, "Hear, O Israel: The Lord our God, the Lord is one. You shall love the Lord your God with all your heart and with all your soul and with all your might. And these words that I command you today shall be on your heart. You shall teach them diligently to your children, and shall talk of them when you sit in your house, and when you walk by the way, and when you lie down, and when you rise." Deborah Olson, in particular, repeatedly refers to Deuteronomy to support her contention that it is her job to teach her children—no one else. And, for Quiverfull families, teaching not only refers to religious training, but also general education. Therefore, home education becomes the primary method by which faithful Christian families fulfill the Deuteronomic command.

Also speaking of Deuteronomy 6:4–7, Baucham says, "Moses saw

---

80. Baucham, *Family Driven Faith*, 91.

the home as the principal delivery system for the transmittal of God's truth from generation to generation. There is no hint here—or anywhere else in the Bible—of the multigenerational teaching of the truths of God being abdicated by parents in favor of 'trained professionals.'"[81] Baucham uses Deuteronomy to enshrine "the home"—understood as the nuclear family—as the "principal delivery system" of the gospel in every generation. He places on the two-parent family total responsibility for the education and formation of children. The delegation of these tasks is abdication. And Baucham insists that the survival of the church is dependent upon the work of Christian parents in the home. He says, "God designed the family to disciple children and insure the faithfulness and perpetuation of the community of faith throughout the ages."[82] In this perspective, the care of children within the private family home is the key to the continuation of the church. And yet, there is no role for the church in the lives of the children who are said to be its future.

Baucham, Pride, and others have the same approach toward other institutions beyond the church, especially the state. Suspicion of the state is a common theme in homeschooling circles. More than any other group, the Homeschool Legal Defense Association (HSLDA) has targeted the state as a major threat to parental control of children. In the literature produced by HSLDA leaders, the inviolability of parental rights looms large. For example, HSLDA's Director of Federal Relations, Will Estrada says, "Children are given by God to parents and families to be loved, to be raised and to be prepared to go on to become leaders in their community. It doesn't take a village to raise a child. It takes parents—loving parents in a home—to raise a child."[83] HSLDA founder and Patrick Henry College president, Michael Farris, also targets the "village" mentality, but intentionally invokes the fear of state force:

> Those who believe that "it takes a village to raise a child" are willing to use coercion, threats, raw police power, and intimidation to enforce

---

81. Baucham, *Family Driven Faith*, 89. Later, Baucham targets Hillary Clinton's *It Takes a Village* as illustrative of what's wrong with today's parents. He mocks her point of view: "It takes big, intrusive government programs and bureaucrats to raise a child." For a fuller discussion, see R. L. Stollar, "Children as Divine Rental Property," *Homeschoolers Anonymous*, January 5, 2015, http://tinyurl.com/y857o2xy.

82. Baucham, *Family Driven Faith*, 118.

83. Will Estrada, quoted by *The Daily Caller*, "Homeschool advocates obliterate MSNBC host over 'collective' view of children," April 14, 2013, quoted by R. L. Stollar, "Children as Divine Rental Property."

their agenda. Parents who raise children in a manner that the village doesn't like have learned to fear the knock on the door lest they hear the dreaded words, "I'm from the government and I'm here to help you raise your children."[84]

As a result of this fear of state power, the HSLDA and many of their member families actively oppose any legislation or entity seen as threats to parental rights, including ratifying the UN's child rights treaty,[85] federal regulation of homeschooling,[86] compulsory vaccination,[87] and the work of Child Protective Services.[88]

When Quiverfull families imagine children, they see them only in the context of the nuclear family. This way of understanding children produces a vision of childrearing that is thoroughly privatized. If parents are solely responsible for the care and education of children in the private family home, then childrearing is the couple's primary, all-encompassing work. Quiverfull writers agree that the rearing of godly children is the most important task given to a Christian couple. The married relationship is not primarily about romance or self-fulfillment, but sacrifice and service. Baucham says it straightforwardly:

---

84. Michael Farris, "Remarks to the World Congress of Families II," presented at the 1999 World Congress of Families, the Howard Center for Family, Religion, & Society, http://tinyurl.com/y7voudlh.

85. The HSLDA has plenty of material speaking against the UN Convention on the Rights of the Child. One concise statement with the most alarmist rhetoric is Christopher J. Klicka and William A. Estrada, "The UN Convention on the Rights of the Child: The Most Dangerous Attack on Parental Rights in the History of the United States," HSLDA, updated March 2007, http://tinyurl.com/y7wg6end.

86. The HSLDA actively opposes any federal laws that have the potential to restrict homeschooling rights for American parents. Their analysis of such laws is ongoing. For a current list of laws they oppose or support, see "Federal Legislation," HSLDA, http://tinyurl.com/y8qxuph5.

87. The HSLDA supports personal beliefs exemptions from mandatory immunizations and provides legal information to parents seeking to navigate changing laws on the subject. See "Changes to Personal Beliefs Exemption for School Vaccine Requirements," HSLDA, December 12, 2013, http://tinyurl.com/y9atmk9c.

88. The HSLDA has a large portion of its website devoted to CPS, including guidance for families dealing with CPS and proposed reforms to child welfare laws. See, for example, "Child Protective Services Investigations," HSLDA, http://tinyurl.com/y8lvad2q. While the HSLDA does not officially oppose CPS as a body, past leaders have spoken out against CPS. In 2009, Doug Phillips said in his speech to the Homeschooling Men's Leadership Summit, "The core problem with Child Protective Services is its existence. . . . At the end of the day, the problem isn't simply Child Protective Services to get better [sic]; it is eliminating it altogether." Transcript of Phillips's speech provided by *Homeschoolers Anonymous*, "Doug Phillips, HSLDA, and the 2009 Men's Leadership Summit," May 14, 2013, http://tinyurl.com/y7bewfo8. The founder of HSLDA, Michael Farris, also founded *ParentalRights.Org*, an organization formed to "protect children by empowering parents through adoption of the Parental Rights Amendment to the U.S. Constitution and by preventing ratification of UN Conventions that threaten parental rights."

"The question is whether or not we are willing to adjust our entire lifestyle around the incredible responsibility God has given us to prepare our children to be launched from our homes as arrows (or ballistic missiles) aimed at the kingdom of darkness."[89] For Quiverfull families, nothing less than "adjust[ing] our entire lifestyle" is required for the proper training of Christian children. The significance of children for the defeat of the "kingdom of darkness" and the triumph of the gospel requires total commitment.[90]

Of course, Baucham and others are adamant that both parents have responsibility in this work. But in practice mothers are tasked with the majority of the childrearing work, which is ordered primarily by the practice of homeschooling. Homeschooling is viewed as the only proper Christian option for parents who take seriously their responsibility for raising their children. As a result, Quiverfull families unanimously believe that the work of Christian parenting requires the total devotion of mothers to the educational task. Mitigating factors like the family's socioeconomic status or the mother's education or skills are not even considered. Quiverfull practitioners insist that the task of education and discipleship cannot be delegated to others. It is only through 24-7, mother-led oversight and instruction of children that Christian parenting is rightly and responsibly carried out.

While the practice of homeschooling is central, Quiverfull parents pursue the training of children through a number of other practices. All of my informants use spanking with their young children. They do so, however, with very specific qualifications about its use. All of them agree that spanking is best used on very young children. The hope is that obedience and respect are instilled in one's children from a young age and, therefore, physical chastisement isn't needed when they are older. Moreover, all agree that spanking should never be done in anger or as a way of venting parental frustration. If a parent is angry, it is better to wait a period of time or forgo spanking entirely in order to avoid wronging the child. Also, once children are verbal, spanking should always be accompanied by an explanation of the offense and the reason for punishment. All of my informants suggest that it is necessary to consider the constitution and personality of

---

89. Baucham, *Family Driven Faith*, 172.

90. Chris Klicka says it this way: "God describes our children as arrows in the hands of a warrior! . . . Have we diligently crafted our 'arrows' so they can be trusted to hit their target as we launch them into the world? . . . Have we personally guaranteed our 'arrows' are the most carefully crafted and have the sharpest point?" (Chris Klicka, *Home Schooling: The Right Choice*, 4th ed. [Nashville: Broadman & Holman, 2002], 103).

each child, too. For some children, spanking is ineffective or counterproductive. Carley Miller will not use physical punishment with her special needs child, saying that particular childrearing "tool" is "not allowed in her toolbox."

Arguably, the most vocal proponents of spanking in the Quiverfull movement are Michael and Debi Pearl and Voddie Baucham. The Pearls' book, *To Train Up a Child*, is adamant about the importance of "the rod" in childrearing and provides very specific instructions on its employment. Though they offer explicit warnings against abusive practices and the misapplication of their principles, the Pearls' work has been linked to a number of heinous child abuse cases, three of which resulted in death. For this reason, despite its popularity, the Pearls' book is very controversial in the Quiverfull movement. Less controversial, but no less supportive of spanking, is Voddie Baucham. At his Family Driven Faith conferences, Baucham begs parents to spank their children: "Please, I am begging you: spank early and spank often." Baucham denies the possibility of raising respectful, obedient children without physical punishment: "There's not been a child born since Jesus who doesn't need regular spanking."[91] Although he acknowledges the possibility of abuse, he does not think anyone should abandon a practice the Bible explicitly endorses.[92]

While spanking tends to get the most attention due to stories of abuse and controversy about its use, the families in my ethnography were not as enthusiastic about spanking as Baucham and the Pearls. They affirm the need for spanking sometimes, but consider it only one of many practices in the work of childrearing—and not even the most effective. Instead, the two most-emphasized methods for child training were including them in domestic labor and regular household worship. Because of the number of their children and the amount of work involved in homeschooling, Quiverfull mothers simply cannot do all of the physical labor necessary to keep the household running. So, as children mature, they are given more responsibility for the care and upkeep of the home. Carley Miller says,

---

91. Recorded from a sermon on child training at a Family Driven Faith conference held at a church in Cincinnati, OH, September 14, 2013.
92. This is another place of interpretive inconsistency in Quiverfull Bible reading. If a parent truly wants to take literally the admonition of Prov 23:13–14, which says, "If you beat [your children] with the rod, you will save their lives from Sheol," then they should be beating their children with rods. Of course, for most families, even families that believe in spanking, this is excessively brutal behavior. Most don't, in fact, "beat them with rods," and Quiverfull teachers like Baucham rarely, if ever, use the language of "beat."

"In our house, our children help us run the house.... I can try to do everything but when they step up and help, it makes the workload lighter for everyone." In *Three Decades of Fertility*, the authors regularly speak of the contribution of their older children to the maintenance of the home. Terry Covey offers the following encouragement: "We do our children no favors when we don't delegate the various duties in a home. There is a two-fold benefit: it gives us the rest we need, and it offers them the practice necessary to prepare for the adult world."[93]

In addition to including children in domestic labor, Quiverfull families emphasize the need to include children in regular family worship. Both Carley Miller and Deborah Olson speak of the importance of their children hearing scripture, praying, and worshiping God as a family. Typically, Quiverfull fathers, who are considered the "pastors" of their families, lead family worship. Baucham is one of the most vocal advocates of regular family worship. He advises fathers to begin and end every day with scripture and prayer, modeling for children the centrality of God's word and teaching them how to apply it to the Christian life. Above all else, though, Baucham views family worship as a way to make the home sacred and ensure that one's children are properly initiated into the Christian faith. In *Family Driven Faith*, he says,

> Through engaging in regular family worship, we can turn our homes into sanctuaries for the worship of Almighty God. No longer will our lives be subdivided and compartmentalized with the sacred on Sunday mornings... and the secular dominating every other moment. Our lives can be fully engulfed with the presence and priority of God.[94]

Of course, the reason for these practices is that Quiverfull parents believe it is their job to raise adult Christians who faithfully reproduce the faith of their parents. Deborah explains: "My goal for my children is that they don't leave my home until they're prepared to fly spiritually. So, they aren't grasping for answers—strong in doctrine and strong in faith. Not just good moral kids who go to church but actually know it and are strong enough to defend it even if you are surrounded by no one else who does."[95] One mother in *Three Decades of Fertility* says it this way: "We are praying and endeavoring to raise

---

93. Terry Covey, "The Lord Directs Our Steps," in *Three Decades of Fertility*, 210.
94. Baucham, *Family Driven Faith*, 148.
95. It is significant, I think, that none of my informants insisted their children must follow

children who raise children who will raise children who will stand for Christ in their generation. By God's grace, we trust that our fruitfulness will continue in the coming generations through the multi-generational faithfulness of our family."[96] In this way, Quiverfull families have redirected the evangelical impulse to public activism into the private family home. The mission of God for the conversion of the world is handled primarily through the birth and training of many children. Quiverfull mother Yvonne Harink says it plainly: "There is no greater way we can influence the future than through giving birth to God's children and raising them to reflect his image. . . . [G]iving birth can actually be God's way of growing a nation. Each new child can grow into generations of children who will inherit the earth."[97] And because Quiverfull families envision children as the sole responsibility of parents, the goal of "multigenerational faithfulness" depends solely on the nuclear family.

Certainly, one cannot deny the primary responsibility of parents for the care of their children. It's not necessary to endorse the totally home-centered vision of Voddie Baucham in order to support the prioritization of childrearing by Christian parents. The intentional cultivation of Christian identity is an important—if not the most important—task for Christian families.[98] To that end, the inclusion of children in household chores and regular participation in household worship are important and profitable practices. When done right, both practices can encourage children to see themselves from an early age as an important part of the family, with something to contribute in both a material and spiritual way.[99] Viewed against the modern tendency for families to be fractured and scattered, stretched between competing priorities, the Quiverfull commitment to the cultivation of an integrated, holistic life is commendable. The sacred must not be relegated to the Sunday-morning church service or Wednesday-night Bible study. In a family that makes childrearing the central task, this dualistic vision might be successfully opposed.

in their footsteps. Deborah Olson states her wish that her children would "have five kids apiece and homeschool," but clarifies, "I would love for them to do that, but that may not happen."

96. Molly Evert, "God Changed My Heart," in *Three Decades of Fertility*, 142.

97. Yvonne Harink, "Through Children's Children," in *Three Decades of Fertility*, 283–84.

98. This is something explored at significant depth by Mercer in *Welcoming Children*, 162–207. Mercer assumes that the Christian formation of children is impossible without the church. I agree with her.

99. Miller-McLemore has written about the significance of chores in the life of the child. See "Children, Chores, and Vocation: A Social and Theological Lacuna," in *The Vocation of the Child*, 295–323.

Still, the Quiverfull insistence that children belong only to parents invites us to consider more carefully: to whom do children really belong? When asked whether the church or broader community has any responsibility for the care and nurturance of their children, Quiverfull mothers respond with puzzlement. It simply doesn't occur to them that others would have any claim or interest in the rearing of their children. On the one hand, this is understandable in an American society that has thoroughly privatized the domestic realm. Imagining children any other way is to go against the grain of a culture that sees children only as a private concern. On the other hand, the Christian tradition casts a much more communal vision for human life, particularly in regard to the church, which the New Testament calls the body of Christ. Indeed, the New Testament epistles envision the church as the household of God formed in Christ to be a new humanity where the former divisions of Jew and Gentile, slave and free, male and female are done away with (Eph 2:14-22; Gal 3:28). Within this vision, the nuclear family should be viewed in relation to the household of God—the church. As the new humanity that points the world toward the new creation in Christ, the church (not the family) is "the principal delivery system for the transmittal of God's truth from generation to generation."[100] Thus the nuclear family, which is a form of life Jesus says will pass away in the eschaton (Matt 22:30), finds its true meaning and purpose within the church.

If the nuclear family is situated within the family of God, then autonomy is not, in fact, the virtue we make it out to be. Certainly, it is good and right for families to be able to support themselves financially and provide proper care and security for their members. These things are a matter of human dignity. But, the Christian faith does not allow any family to be entirely self-sufficient or autonomous. As each family member is adopted through the waters of baptism into the household of God, the family voluntarily takes upon itself the vulnerability-in-relationship that comes with being part of God's family. There is, therefore, no parental authority apart from Christ's authority, no discipleship apart from the community of disciples, and no family practice apart from church practice.[101]

Because they seek to inculcate their children with a strong sense

---

100. Baucham, *Family Driven Faith*, 89.

101. I understand this to be the thrust of Jana Bennett's argument in *Water Is Thicker Than Blood*, where she says, "Good marriages and families, but even more so, good households . . . are sacramental and direct all of humanity toward its ultimate end in God. . . . The focus is no longer a tunnel vision on the family but contemplation of Christ and Christ's Body" (155).

of Christian identity, one would expect the sacraments and worship life of the church to be key to the Quiverfull way of life. But, the literature of the Quiverfull movement is remarkably silent on the role of the church in the spiritual formation of children.[102] All of my informants insist that children do not cease to be a part of families when they enter the church, hence their desire for "family integrated" churches. They believe children belong in families, and the integrity of the family—and leadership of the father—should be protected and supported within the church. The church exists to uphold the family, which is doing God's work of evangelization and making disciples. Thus the church should not subvert family bonds through age-divided Sunday school or other such specialized programs.

But attempts at so-called "family integration" do not necessarily mean that children are welcomed and included in the worship and sacramental life of the church. When it comes to the fidgety, unruly bodies of real, flesh-and-blood children, "family integration" often means children are simply integrated into the established patterns and procedures of adults.[103] And it is parents, not churches, who are entrusted with that responsibility. Parents are supposed to train children to resist and overcome their sinful nature within the home. Parents are supposed to guide children out of childhood and into adulthood within the home. And it is only then, after they've been properly trained and guided into adulthood, that the church takes responsibility for them.

While the intention of Quiverfull practitioners is to empower parents in their work of childrearing, their myopia regarding the church's work in children's formation unwittingly exacerbates the privatization and isolation of the family. It's unclear, for example, how the church is supposed to ensure that parents are doing the work

---

102. Evangelical churches, in general, struggle with place of children in the service and worship of the church—a problem they share with mainline Protestants. Mercer addresses this issue straightforwardly in *Welcoming Children*. See also Holly Catterton Allen and Christine Lawton Ross, *Intergenerational Christian Formation: Bringing the Whole Church Together in Ministry, Community, and Worship* (Downers Grove, IL: InterVarsity, 2012); Michelle A. Clifton-Soderstrom and David D. Bjorlin, *Incorporating Children in Worship: Mark of the Kingdom* (Eugene, OR: Cascade, 2014); and Daniel R. Hyde, *The Nursery of the Holy Spirit: Welcoming Children in Worship* (Eugene, OR: Wipf & Stock, 2014).

103. I witnessed this firsthand at one of Voddie Baucham's Family Driven Faith conferences. Although advertised as a "family event" with no childcare available, children were not included in the conference in any way. They were expected to sit quietly next to their parents through the duration of Baucham's lectures. Children who could not or would not conform were removed from the room and chastised. It was clear this was standard practice for the church hosting the conference.

of education and spiritual formation with their children. Without a robust sense of church-family interdependence, any church involvement in the private family home is perceived as unwanted meddling. Moreover, how can churches benefit from the good that children offer them if children are not provided regular, tangible ways to contribute to church worship?

Toward the end of his book *Family Driven Faith*, Baucham addresses the problem of evangelical youth leaving the church upon reaching adulthood. But, as has been the pattern thus far, his answer is entirely family-focused:

> [The lack of young people in church] is a problem that must be addressed one home at a time. The answer to our current crisis is a renewed commitment to biblical evangelism and discipleship in and through our homes. You and I as individual parents must begin to take responsibility for the spiritual well-being and development of our children. We must commit ourselves to family driven faith. More importantly, our churches must facilitate this commitment.[104]

Although Baucham says "churches must facilitate this commitment," what he means is, the church needs to get out of the family's way. Even though training children in the faith is central to Quiverfull lived religion, their limited ecclesiology means that discipleship is a private affair, lacking both a broader community of disciples and access to the sacraments. Mothers, who do most of the work, are often isolated, pursuing the Christian training of their children alone. Certainly, a discussion is needed about the efficacy and consequences of age-divided practices within the church. Many agree that such programs have been detrimental to both children and adults in the church.[105] But, the prioritization of the nuclear family's unity over and against the church (not to mention the broader community) remains a problematic and incomplete way to redress the perceived failures of American church practices.

Another problem with imagining children as the sole responsibility of parents is that it unintentionally intensifies the vulnerability of children. Just as we saw in the lives of Quiverfull mothers, the isolation of Quiverfull children within their families can, in some cases, lead to neglect, exploitation, and abuse. This is a fact demonstrated

---

104. Baucham, *Family Driven Faith*, 189–90.
105. See note 102 above.

in multiple studies.[106] None of the families in my research evidence this kind of destructive isolation. But, they have struggled and continue to struggle with the detrimental effects of isolation just the same. Also, we must be mindful of the increasing number of testimonies from the grown children of Quiverfull families that point out the exploitation of childhood vulnerability within families that succumb to isolation.[107] In a movement where children are not imagined apart from their parents, it is unclear what can be done in the case of parents who cannot or should not be the primary caretakers of their children. Lacking a broader sense of belonging, the Quiverfull movement does not have the resources to reckon with the many ways families can fail children.

CONCLUSION

As a movement singularly focused on the propagation and education of Christian children, it is no small matter how Quiverfull practitioners imagine children and childhood. Indeed, how they imagine children has a profound effect on the way they order their households, communities, and churches. Quiverfull conceptions of children and childhood are problematic in a number of ways, but three matters are of particular concern. First, Quiverfull practitioners require a more nuanced vision of childhood agency to account for the fact that children are neither totally depraved nor cherubic innocents. Children are agents and people in their own right. Second, the Quiverfull movement requires a vision of childhood that understands it not as a stage to be passed through quickly but an enduring part of human life. In this way, children are not simply unformed adults in need of training but beloved and vulnerable people of God who have much to teach us about the Christian life. Finally, Quiverfull practitioners evidence a deficiency in ecclesiology regarding the way they approach the task of childrearing. It is inadequate from a Christian perspective to view

---

106. See, for example, Kristin A. Kelly, *Domestic Violence and the Politics of Privacy* (Ithaca, NY: Cornell University Press, 2002) and Annemie Dillen, ed., *When 'Love' Strikes: Social Sciences, Ethics, and Theology on Family Violence* (Leuven: Peeters, 2009).

107. So-called Quiverfull "survivor blogs" contain plenty of first-person testimony about childhood abuse and neglect. See, for example, the following: Profligate Truth, "Child Abuse Awareness Month," April 14, 2015, http://tinyurl.com/y92v9wo4; and Permission to Live, "I Am Not My Parents," October 24, 2014, http://tinyurl.com/yala9z47. In addition, Homeschooling's Invisible Children (HIC), which operates under the oversight of the Coalition for Responsible Home Education (CRHE), works to catalogue cases of abuse and neglect and raise awareness on this issue.

children as the sole responsibility of parents. Indeed, participation in a community of practice is essential to the formation of Christian identity.

Just as many of the deficits in the Quiverfull practice of motherhood are shared by American society, so also in their conception of children and childhood. While Quiverfull practice stands out from that of their neighbors, they remain prone to the same privatized vision of childrearing. Within this vision, children are the sole responsibility of the nuclear family, and other institutions have little role to play in their formation. Thus, despite their aim to initiate and witness to a countercultural way of life, Quiverfull families end up replicating the pitfalls of the surrounding culture. Most concerning is the way their vision isolates children within the nuclear family, exacerbating their natural vulnerability, and isolates families from their communities. The next chapter will take up the subject of how the Quiverfull movement imagines and practices "the family," with a continued focus on these concerns.

5.

The Family in the Full Quiver

When Carley and David Miller's oldest daughter, Caroline, was ready to be baptized based upon her confession of faith in Christ, they were not members of a traditional church.[1] For a couple of years, they had been participating in a "house church" made up of a few other families with young children. Though they were convinced David should be the one to baptize her, the lack of church facilities, particularly a baptistery, presented a problem. In the end, they found a friend willing to loan them their swimming pool for an afternoon. There, in their friend's backyard, David baptized Caroline surrounded by the rest of the Millers, their extended families, and a few close friends. Carley knows this scenario is unusual, but she is unapologetic. "We just believe that we all are ministers," she says. "David's plan is to continue baptizing our children, but we aren't picky about where we do it. [Laughter.]"

While the performance of baptism by a layperson in a private swimming pool might be surprising to some, the Millers' actions make sense within their practice of church. At the time, their weekly worship involved informal meetings in private homes. Their time together included singing songs, listening to scripture lessons taught by one of the fathers, and celebrating communion. For the Millers, a few families reading scripture and breaking bread in a private home constitutes a church. And Carley characterizes their family as a "mini-

---

1. Some portions of this chapter appear in "Every Wife Has a Church in Her Home: The Family and the Church in the American Quiverfull Movement," *Ecclesial Practices* 4, no. 1 (April 2017): 133–57.

church" that is seeking to "to serve the Lord as a family." So, why not baptize their children at the time and in a place of their choosing?

This story foregrounds some of the issues at work in the Quiverfull way of imagining and practicing the family. I have argued thus far that the Quiverfull movement's way of life is an intensification of broader American and evangelical tendencies. This has been clear in the Quiverfull performance of motherhood and their construction of children and childhood. The same dynamic is at work in their practice of the family. In the Millers' choice to baptize their daughter outside the confines of an institutional church, there is evidence of the family's privatization and disconnection from broader communities. Also on display is the conviction that the family is itself a kind of church, capable of carrying out the work of discipleship and celebration of the sacraments on its own terms.

This chapter considers the way Quiverfull families imagine the family and seek to practice it in their daily lives. In what follows, I introduce the idealized family according to Quiverfull discourse.[2] This discussion encompasses the family's form (its structure, boundaries, and roles) as well as the family's function (what the family does). After a thorough consideration of the family for Quiverfull practitioners, I offer a theological analysis in two major parts. First, I explain the problem with theological blueprints for the Christian family. Second, I consider in detail three problems with the blueprint provided by the Quiverfull movement.[3]

---

2. Many academic treatments of the family begin by discussing whether there is such a thing as "the family" at all. In contemporary America, family forms are in flux to such an extent that some are inclined to discard the abstract concept of "the family" as an outdated relic. John Drane and Olive Fleming Drane suggest that there are at least seven "distinct types of family structure and domestic arrangements," in *Family Fortunes: Faith-full Caring for Today's Families* (London: Darton, Longman & Todd, 2004), 22–41. Fiona Williams prefers to focus on "family practices: what we do rather than what we are," in *Rethinking Families*, ESRC CAVA Research Group (London: Calouste Gulbenkian Foundation, 2004), 16–17.

3. For more comprehensive approaches to questions concerning Christianity and the family in the United States, the reader is referred to the Religion, Culture, and Family Project, a cooperative research and writing group directed by Don Browning. The group published eleven monographs and books on the family in North America. A full list of the publications can be found in Lisa Sowle Cahill, *Family: A Christian Social Perspective* (Minneapolis: Fortress Press, 2000), 138–39, n. 5.

THE QUIVERFULL FAMILY: GOD-GIVEN FORM AND FUNCTIONS

In any discussion of the family as it is embodied in daily life, one must deal with both ideals and realities. Oftentimes, the two are difficult to disentangle. This is especially true of the Quiverfull movement, which possesses very particular standards for the Christian family. In what follows, I speak in terms of family form and function. *Form* refers to the structure of the family, its boundaries, and the roles family members occupy within it. The Quiverfull sense of form is their answer to the question, "What is the family?" *Function* refers to what the family does, its practices and the impact of those practices. The Quiverfull sense of function is their answer to the question, "What does the family do?" For Quiverfull practitioners, the family's form and function are designed by God and spelled out in scripture. Moreover, Quiverfull family members are always negotiating between the ideal and the actual. The ideal is something toward which they continually strive even as they seek to accept the limitations of their daily lives.

THE FORM OF THE FAMILY

For Quiverfull, the family form is fixed and unchanging, designed by God in the first week of creation. William Einwechter, a pastor and contributor to the now defunct Vision Forum website, summarizes the "traditional family" form in the following way:

> By "traditional family" we mean the family structure that developed in Western society under the direct influence of Christianity and the Bible. In the traditional family, the man is the head of the home and the one responsible for providing those things necessary for the sustenance of life. The woman is a "keeper at home," and the one primarily responsible for the care of the children. The traditional family thus defined is in line with the biblical plan for the home.[4]

This "biblical plan for the home" is a divine blueprint for family life culled from the pages of scripture.[5] Key passages in this regard are

---

4. William Einwechter, "The Feminization of the Family," Vision Forum Ministries, December 8, 2005, http://tinyurl.com/ybw93lmd.

5. I am borrowing the *blueprint* terminology from Nicholas Healy, who speaks of "blueprint

Genesis 1–2; Ephesians 5:21–33; Colossians 3:18–21; 1 Peter 3:1–7; and Titus 2:1–8. As the account of humanity's creation and the first "marriage" between Adam and Eve, Genesis 1–2, is particularly important. Quiverfull reads Genesis 1–2 as a propositional outline of God's intended roles for husbands and wives. Man, the first human created, answers directly to God and is given charge over the world. Woman, the second human, created for the purpose of being the man's "helper," answers to her husband and assists him in his care for the world. She is inherently subordinate and designed to serve him and help with his responsibilities. Together, they are to "be fruitful and multiply; fill the earth and subdue it" (Gen 1:28). For Quiverfull practitioners, this reading of Genesis 1–2 controls the way the rest of scripture is interpreted. And because they believe scripture only speaks with one voice (God's), they find the same family form reinforced in the rest of the Bible.

Within the scripturally sourced blueprint described above, Quiverfull families find a set of divinely ordained roles assigned to the husband, wife, and children. Husbands are the leaders of the family, given "headship" over their wives and children by "God's decree and design."[6] Wives are the equal-but-different "helpmeets" to their husbands, given by God "to complete him, to be suited to his needs" such that her life is centered on his.[7] Together, the married couple is tasked with the job of "populat[ing] the earth with future generations of men and women who would love God and seek to fulfill His purposes in the world."[8] And their children, therefore, are called to faithful obedience to their parents, learning the Christian faith and readying themselves for their own future marriages and children.

Many Quiverfull writers link these family roles to a transcendent reality beyond the earthly family. The proper performance of marriage and family roles is viewed as key both to the revelation of God's character and the realization of God's will in the world. The wife must submit to her husband "as to the Lord" because this is the way that the church submits to Christ, her head (Eph 5:22–24). Husbands

ecclesiologies" in *Church, World, and Christian Life: Practical-Prophetic Ecclesiology* (Cambridge: Cambridge University Press, 2000), 25–51. Baucham uses the term *blueprint* specifically in reference to the husband/father: "Christ's example is the blueprint that shows every family shepherd what his role is in marriage." See Voddie Baucham, *Family Shepherds: Calling and Equipping Men to Lead Their Homes* (Wheaton, IL: Crossway, 2011), 89.

6. Baucham, *Family Shepherds*, 101.

7. Nancy Leigh DeMoss, *Ten Lies Women Believe and the Truth That Sets Them Free*, 2nd ed. (Chicago: Moody, 2006), 126.

8. DeMoss, *Ten Lies Women Believe*, 127.

must lead and love their wives because that is the way Christ behaves toward his church (Eph 5:25–30). As Baucham says, "The headship of the man in marriage is merely an expression of the heavenly reality. . . . [I]t goes to the heart of what we believe about the gospel."[9] Children must submit to their parents because God commands it (Exod 20:12; Eph 6:1–3) and, in so doing, they learn to submit to God. For husbands, wives, and children, each Quiverfull role both reveals and accomplishes something transcendent.

The divinely prescribed family roles in the Quiverfull vision are often juxtaposed with the perceived feminist impulses of other American families, which they assume are the majority. In the most strident rhetoric of the movement, the reconstruction of the "biblical family" is a sacred mission incumbent upon every Christian. Einwechter has the following to say:

> We must take up the task of the de-feminization of the family and the re-Christianization of the family. This task is the work of every individual Christian family; but it is primarily the work of Christian husbands and fathers who have been appointed by God as leaders in the home. Men must lead by precept and example in eradicating all aspects of feminist influence from the life and structure of *their* family and restore it to a *biblical* pattern. Men must prove themselves *men* and shoulder the full load of responsibility given to them by God. Men must stop being intimidated by feminist rhetoric and radicals and fearlessly promote God's order for the family.[10]

Not all Quiverfull practitioners are so vehement in their antifeminism. But, all Quiverfull families speak of the biblical family structure as something opposed to the feminist or liberal family, which they associate with weak-willed men, domineering career women, and disrespectful children. They see this family form as not only anathema to scripture but also a recipe for familial disaster. It is only when each member of the family rightly carries out the role God designed for them that the family will be blessed.

Also key to the Quiverfull form of family is a strong sense of the family as a private institution. As we saw in chapter 4, the Quiverfull movement expressly denies the idea that "it takes a village to raise a child." Instead, they see parents alone possessing inviolable rights over the care and education of their offspring. They root this idea primar-

---

9. Baucham, *Family Shepherds*, 109.
10. Einwechter, "The Feminization of the Family" (emphasis in original).

ily in a particular reading of Genesis 1–2 and Deuteronomy 6:6–9. Genesis 1–2 is thought to provide an account of the private institution of marriage, assumed to be separate from all other institutions within the domestic "garden." Deuteronomy 6:6–9 is thought to give commands to parents on the education of their children. God's commands should be taught "when you sit at home, when you walk along the road, when you lie down and when you get up." Because parents alone are given charge over the care and education of children, the family is viewed as a private sphere, separate from surrounding society. The father governs the private family and is supposed to act as prophet, priest, and king within the home.[11] Thus there are no other institutions to which the family owes allegiance.

Not only is the family imagined in thoroughly private terms, but the family is also viewed as an autonomous entity. Parents are accountable only to God for their success or failure at following God's instructions. Voddie Baucham describes the family's autonomy in his book *Family Shepherds*: "God designed the world with three distinct institutions—the family, the church, and the civil government—each with specific jurisdictions. The church can no more tell the family how to run its affairs than it can tell the state how to run theirs. Certainly, the church has a responsibility to teach, admonish, warn, and guide. However, it may not govern the other jurisdictions."[12] Later, Baucham exhorts "family shepherds" that they are responsible for being a part of a local church that can provide edification and accountability, especially for the father's leadership. But, it is unclear how this accountability is supposed to work if family, church, and state are parallel institutions without the power of overlapping "governance."[13] And Baucham never suggests any accountability of

---

11. The father as prophet, priest, and king of his family is explored in detail by Philip Lancaster in *Family Man, Family Leader: Biblical Fatherhood as the Key to a Thriving Family* (San Antonio, TX: Vision Forum, 2003).

12. Baucham, *Family Shepherds*, 176. The source of Baucham's "three distinct institutions" is unclear. One wonders if there's any room for the community or society beyond the family, church, and government. If these institutions are parallel, autonomous institutions, then there is no sense of a "common good" for society, including local communities and neighborhoods. What about the rest of the world that doesn't fall within these three?

13. Baucham devotes an entire chapter to the church in *Family Shepherds*. He says, "I'm arguing that the most important thing for a family shepherd to do . . . is to ensure that they're healthy members of a healthy church" (147). And later: "I've had conversation after conversation with fathers and mothers who are committed to family discipleship, but who are struggling tremendously as they either attended an unhealthy church or no church at all. These families don't testify of overwhelming joy and fulfillment because 'family is enough.' On the contrary, they testify to struggle, strain, loneliness, fear, isolation, and despair. Family discipleship

the family shepherd to the state, such as in cases of abuse or neglect that exceed the powers of the church to correct.[14]

Deborah Olson suggests that it would be ideal for families to be held accountable to their local church, but she does not see most churches as capable of such oversight. She says most churches neglect God's instructions on marriage and family, making them incapable of helping families in that regard.[15] Renee Tanner touches on the same problem when she says she has found more support from fellow homeschooling families than the churches with which her family worshiped. If the church doesn't do what the family is convinced God commands, then how can the church provide any kind of oversight? And if most churches are not being faithful to God's teachings (as Quiverfull practitioners repeatedly state), then why would Quiverfull families see the need to participate in them at all? This is not to mention their characteristically dismal view of the state. Within Quiverfull, the Christian family is an entirely autonomous entity.

Quiverfull privatization and autonomy of the family affects everything. In *The Way Home*, Mary Pride's "home-centered" vision for life is presented as a way of resisting the perceived threat of outside institutions. She says pointedly, "[Homeworking] is a way to take back control of education, health care, agriculture, social welfare, business, housing, morality, and evangelism from the faceless institutions to which we have surrendered them."[16] Notice that Pride lumps together the state and the church, calling both "faceless institutions," and then places on the shoulders of the nuclear family the responsibility for all of the basic, life-sustaining elements of Western society. She thinks that the family alone should perform these tasks. And because God created the family to be the most important social institution, its right to self-rule must be protected. As a result, Quiverfull families prize self-sufficiency and generally seek to avoid reliance on government assistance.

---

is absolutely crucial, but there's no substitute for healthy membership in a healthy local church" (154). Yet, it is telling that his chapter on church membership is thirteenth out of fifteen.

14. His only consideration of abuse occurs in the following sentence: "A family shepherd would never abuse his children" (Baucham, *Family Shepherds*, 144).

15. Baucham agrees with this evaluation. See *Family Driven Faith: Doing What It Takes to Raise Sons and Daughters Who Walk with God* (Wheaton, IL: Crossway, 2011), 203.

16. Mary Pride, *The Way Home: Beyond Feminism, Back to Reality* (Fenton, MO: Home Life Books, 1985), xiii.

THE FUNCTIONS OF THE FAMILY

In addition to a God-given form with specific roles and boundaries, the Quiverfull blueprint for the family also includes a number of God-given functions. These are the things that a family is supposed to do. Certainly, Quiverfull families believe they are supposed to perform the most basic functions of provision and safety for their members, including food, water, shelter, and bodily safety.[17] But, I want to focus on the functions that have an explicit theological orientation and show up repeatedly in Quiverfull discourse.[18] Beyond basic functions of provision and safety, the functions of the Quiverfull family include the following: (1) to fulfill God's design for the family; (2) to bear, raise, and educate children in the Christian faith; (3) to evangelize others; and (4) to advance the kingdom of God and transform America.

As mentioned above, Quiverfull families are supposed to enact God's design for the family in their daily life. This requires daily dedication to fulfilling the roles delineated in scripture. Quiverfull literature is very much focused on this point, filled with exhortations to wives, husbands, and children regarding the proper performance of their family duties. Though they do not claim gender- and age-based roles are equal in importance with the gospel, they explicitly link the two: to fulfill the former is to properly proclaim the latter. This is an emphasis in broader evangelical culture as well, evidenced by the proliferation of volumes in Christian bookstores devoted to being a godly wife, husband, or child (with considerably more emphasis on wives). Because of their location in evangelicalism, this literature is often a part of Quiverfull homes too, and the language about role fulfillment is a key part of their vocabulary.

Yet, what especially stands out in the Quiverfull family blueprint is their inordinate emphasis on how to be a godly daughter. For Quiverfull elites, Christian girls are called to be obedient to their parents, respectful of and submissive to their fathers, nurturing of their younger siblings, committed to learning the arts of homeworking, and ready to marry, bear children, and homeschool when the time

---

17. Herbert Anderson and Susan B. W. Johnson, *Regarding Children: A New Respect for Children and Families*, Family Living in Pastoral Perspective Series (Louisville: Westminster John Knox, 1994), 49–56.

18. I say *explicit* theological orientation because I think all family functions have theological meaning. But space constraints will not allow thorough consideration of all such practices.

comes.[19] (There is even an internal debate among Quiverfull practitioners regarding the appropriateness of young women attending college. Some teachers think it is folly given God's design for gender roles. They say daughters are better off at home with their family, learning homemaking and childrearing from their mothers until they are married to a man of their father's choosing.[20]) The God-given role for daughters is advocated through websites, magazines, books, DVDs, and merchandise. Among the most ardent proponents, the success of God's kingdom and transformation of American culture is largely dependent upon the Christian daughter's fulfillment of her role.[21]

The second major function of the Quiverfull family is to bear, raise, and educate children in the Christian faith. Certainly, Quiverfull practitioners know that not all married couples will have children, but they do see it as the general norm. And God gives to such couples the task of ensuring that their children grow up to be practicing Christians. In fact, the conversion and Christian education of children is to be the primary focus of the family's life together—everything else is secondary. Baucham calls this family function "multigenerational faithfulness." Indeed, the survival of Christianity is viewed as dependent upon the work of Christian families to rightly form their children in the faith.[22] In movement literature, this familial responsibility for formation of children is often presented in contrast to a view that

---

19. See, for example, the following: Anna Sofia Botkin and Elizabeth Botkin, *So Much More: The Remarkable Influence of Visionary Daughters on the Kingdom of God* (San Antonio, TX: Vision Forum, 2005); Voddie Baucham, *What He Must Be ... If He Wants to Marry My Daughter* (Wheaton, IL: Crossway, 2009); Jasmine Baucham, *Joyfully at Home: A Book for Young Ladies on Vision and Hope* (San Antonio, TX: Vision Forum, 2010); Sarah L. Bryant, *The Family Daughter: Becoming Pillars of Strength in Our Father's House* (Holton, KS: KBR Ministries, 2010). Also, the following websites: King's Blooming Rose Ministries, which is devoted to "encouraging girls to grow in their walk with Christ" (http://kingsbloomingrose.com/); and *Raising Homemakers*, which is devoted to "teaching and preparing our daughters in the art of homemaking" (http://raisinghomemakers.com/).

20. Voddie Baucham, Doug Phillips, and Geoffrey Botkin are among the teachers committed to this point of view. In Baucham's book *What He Must Be*, he discusses the responsibility of fathers for protecting their daughter's virginity and arranging for her marriage to a suitable man. On the other hand, some teachers think that denying women higher education is an overreaction and that treating young women as the property of fathers is dangerous. Mary Pride and Michael Farris are among leaders who articulate this point of view. See Pride, *The Way Home*, 2nd ed., 217–22; and Michael Farris, "A Line in the Sand," HSLDA, August 5, 2014, http://tinyurl.com/yaymym8f.

21. See, for example, Anna Sofia and Elizabeth Botkin's documentary, *The Return of the Daughters* (Vision Forum, 2007).

22. Of course, Reformed-minded leaders like Baucham will deny this dependency because of their view of God's sovereign providence. But, I would argue that regardless of their theologi-

sees the church tasked with this work. Quiverfull practitioners deny that the church is in any way responsible for the formation of children and assign that task to the nuclear family alone.

All Quiverfull proponents view the practices of homeschooling and family worship as key to the work of Christian formation. By spending the majority of every day under the instruction of their mother, children in Quiverfull families are thought to have the best chance of embracing and being formed in the Christian faith. And by being led in worship by their fathers, who are supposed to teach scripture and pray for the family (and in the most devoted homes, teach children with a catechism), children are given an example of faithful discipleship and invited to join in regular devotion to God. Parents are exhorted to ensure they are equipping their children with a "biblical worldview" that prioritizes the truth of the Bible above all and responds to the challenges of life with praise and prayer.[23] Without being "fully engulfed" in God's presence, children are unlikely to embrace and carry on the evangelical faith of their parents. And for Quiverfull children no other goal is more important.

The third function of the Quiverfull family is to do the work of evangelism. Within the evangelical tradition, proselytizing is typically viewed as an individual responsibility that is given direction and organization by the local church. Churches encourage their church members to "witness" to their neighbors individually, which typically means a discussion of the gospel message and an encouragement to repent and be "born again." At the same time, churches will often organize broader, sustained efforts of outreach in an attempt to meet community needs and seek conversions among the church's neighbors. But, in the Quiverfull movement, these tasks are re-centered on the nuclear family. This is not to say that Quiverfull families are not members of churches that participate in personal evangelism and community outreach. But Quiverfull families are content to carry out such work from the "base" of their private family home. This is another instance where what has traditionally been considered the work of the church is turned over to the nuclear family.

How does the Quiverfull family evangelize their neighbors? Elites of the movement have a number of suggestions. Mary Pride advo-

---

cal worldview, in practical instruction they exhort families in such a way that their faithfulness to home education and family worship has eternal consequences.

23. Christian homeschooling researcher Monica Smatlak Liao calls this phenomenon "unification." See Monica Smatlak Liao, "Keeping Home: Homeschooling and the Practice of Conservative Protestant Identity" (PhD diss., Vanderbilt University, 2006), 64.

cates hospitality, pointing to the fabled example of Edith Schaeffer who helped her husband "bring literally thousands to the Lord" through her homeworking and hospitality. "Why did the Schaeffers have such great success?" Pride asks, "For *the same reasons you and I can*. . . . Their two great assets were sound biblical doctrine and a family."[24] James McDonald, a Presbyterian pastor and husband of Quiverfull blogger Stacy McDonald, speaks in a similar way of the home as a site of outreach. He explicitly links the proper fulfillment of God-given family roles as a way to evangelize non-Christians:

> When a husband strives to sacrificially love his wife as Christ loves the church, and when a wife seeks to honor her husband as the church should Jesus, a house becomes a home. There is an aroma of godliness that radiates from such a union, and is attractive to all. First it draws in the children, then extended family and friends take notice and are intrigued. . . . As you commit to glorifying God, the spiritual blessings in your family will naturally shine, and the scent of Heaven drifting through your home will draw even the most stubborn unbeliever.[25]

In Quiverfull subculture, the evangelistic function of the home is also directed in a more specific way toward the conversion and training of young people. Rather than send children or teenagers to church-run programs so that they might be evangelized there, Quiverfull practitioners think it should be the work of the nuclear family to carry out this task. Speaking of the need for American Christians to retain young people in the church, Baucham says the matter must be addressed "one home at a time" with a focus on evangelism and discipleship "in and through our homes."[26] For Baucham, if a Christian family is faithful to train its children, then they will naturally bring others into the faith.

Echoing Baucham, Renee Tanner suggests that non-Christian children should be assigned to Christian families in the church, so that they might form relationships with them, evangelize them, and help with their instruction. She says, "As far as those children that we bring in [to the church] . . . we should win them and take them in as a family and include them because they don't have a Christian family. The

---

24. Pride, *The Way Home*, 202. Pride thinks this is particularly suited for older women: "Perhaps the most exciting ministry the older woman can have is her ministry of evangelism and hospitality" (201).

25. James McDonald, "Like Olive Plants—Watching God Grow a Legacy," *Family Reformation*, June 6, 2010, http://tinyurl.com/y8woms4p.

26. Baucham, *Family Driven Faith*, 189.

kids who get bussed in should be sitting with families in worship and sitting with us when we have meals." Like Baucham, Renee thinks discipleship is best carried out in the context of the nuclear family, even if the family isn't the child's biological family. Deborah Olson has a similar view. Although the responsibility of raising six children under eleven presents many limitations, she wants to host adult Bible studies or "backyard Bible clubs" for children in order to evangelize her neighbors. The evangelical emphasis on evangelism remains, but it is understood to be a function of the nuclear family.

Finally, Quiverfull practitioners see the future of America, in particular, and the kingdom of God, in general, hanging on the obedience of the Christian family to the divine blueprint. All of the family functions described above play a major part in the success of the family in this endeavor. Pride promises her readers that even though her proposal will not "usher in the Millennium" it will certainly "change society." And, she says ominously, "if [Christian] homeworkers don't reconstruct society, the feminists will."[27] More recently, Geoffrey Botkin suggests that "assertive Christian families, even when a small minority, can triumph over conditions of national sin by directing society and culture to greater heights of righteousness. . . . Christian culture can be restored again to the West and it can endure with greater permanence if Christian families refuse to surrender their responsibilities."[28] Baucham says it more succinctly: "The family is the cornerstone of society. . . . [A]s goes the family, so goes the world."[29]

This more far-reaching function of the family does not loom large among Quiverfull families on the ground. My interviews yielded very little reference to national or kingdom-oriented goals for the

27. Pride, *The Way Home*, 181.
28. In the same post, Botkin goes on to say of his own family: "The building of our family legacy continues to be a pioneering effort. At the time of this writing, only a small minority of American families are seeking to recover the foundations of a godly heritage for the purposes of building a civil society according to biblical standards. . . . They know their efforts must begin in the family, and ultimately end with the family. This gives us hope, because we can control the culture of our families, and we know God blesses families that all the ends of the earth may fear him (Psalm 67:7)." Geoffrey Botkin, "A Botkin Family Secret Revealed," *Western Conservatory of Arts and Sciences*, May 14, 2010, http://tinyurl.com/y8xnfsu7.
29. Baucham, *Family Shepherds*, 11. There are two identifiable ways that *world* is regularly used by Quiverfull writers. First, *world* is used in the Johannine sense, where *world* is the realm of darkness, sin, and disbelief. In this understanding, *world* is often placed in juxtaposition to the church, the people of God, and is perceived as a source of defilement. In this sense, God's people are to protect themselves from the world and see to it that they resist the world's influence. At the same time, *world* is also used to refer to creation in a general way, including humanity and human culture within it. In this second sense, the world is not perceived in terms of its sinfulness, but as the location of God's redemptive work.

family other than "multigenerational faithfulness." Renee Tanner says of the conservative Christian "culture wars": "We aren't called to fight culture wars. We were called to make disciples. Raising children in the Lord is making disciples." Deborah Olson distances herself in a similar way from those who would link the Quiverfull family to world transformation: "Never would I have considered myself part of a movement that's conspiring to have more children against the world. . . . We just want to follow God and teach them to follow God." Perhaps the family as catalyst for world transformation and kingdom advancement is a preoccupation of Quiverfull teachers more than the laity.

Elite Quiverfull practitioners imagine the family in such expansive terms because they have been influenced, directly or indirectly, by the work of R. J. Rushdoony, introduced in chapter 1. Rushdoony's writings describe the family as the primary force in God's plan both for human dominion (Gen 1:28) and the spread of the gospel (Matt 28:18–20). In a 1977 article, "The Trustee Family," Rushdoony states:

> In Scripture, *the family is man's basic church, state, school, society, welfare agency, and social power.* Control of the children and their education rests with the family. . . . Inheritance is a family power, in terms of faith. Welfare is a family duty, not only with respect to non-related widows, orphans, and strangers (Deut. 14:28–29), but also and especially with all relatives, for "if any provide not for his own, and specially for those of his own house [or kindred], he hath denied the faith, and is worse than an infidel" (1 Tim. 5:8).[30]

Rushdoony envisions most of the needs of humankind being met by the work of the nuclear family.[31] Some of the most vocal proponents of the Quiverfull movement are intentionally drawing on Rushdoony's expansive vision for the family when they write about the family's divinely ordained functions, but most are simply imbibing his influence from within the Christian homeschooling movement. Whether directly or indirectly coming from Rushdoony, Quiverfull

---

30. R. J. Rushdoony, "The Trustee Family," *Journal of Christian Reconstruction: Symposium on the Family* 4, no. 2 (Winter 1977–78): 12 (emphasis mine).

31. Rushdoony's reconstructionist theology is worthy of more thorough treatment than I can provide here. I recommend Julie Ingersoll's work on the subject: *Building God's Kingdom: Inside the World of Christian Reconstruction* (Oxford: Oxford University Press, 2015). Ingersoll engages deeply with Rushdoony's primary works and later interpreters, including Doug Phillips, and speaks as a former insider to the reconstructionist movement. See also the critical historical perspective offered by Michael J. McVicar in *Christian Reconstruction: R.J. Rushdoony and American Religious Conservatism* (Chapel Hill: University of North Carolina Press, 2015).

elites expect the family to do just about everything. Apart from maintaining a standing military, they believe the family is designed by God to do the rest.

THEOLOGICAL ANALYSIS

Like the Quiverfull conceptions of motherhood and children, there are a variety of ways to go about evaluating the Quiverfull blueprint for the family. The following analysis consists of two major parts. First, drawing on the work of theologian Nicholas Healy, I show that Quiverfull theology of the family represents a *blueprint*. And, despite claims to the contrary, their family blueprint is as much a product of nineteenth- and twentieth-century gender and family constructs as it is a product of the Bible. Yet, whether sourced from scripture or tradition (or both), the construction of family blueprints is wrong-headed in general and ultimately unhelpful for Christian theology. Then, I consider the problems with the particular family blueprint offered by the Quiverfull movement. I suggest the Quiverfull family blueprint results in the following: (1) an excessively privatized vision of the family; (2) a serious deficit in ecclesiology and any sense of the common good; and (3) an imagined sinless space within the home that increases the risk of abuse.

THE PROBLEM WITH FAMILY BLUEPRINTS

Evangelicals, in general, have a penchant for constructing systematic theological models. Twentieth-century evangelical theology is replete with theologians whose primary method is to dissect, extract, collate, and present in systematic fashion the propositional truths of scripture.[32] At least since the Victorian era, evangelicals in America have been applying the same method to define and uphold a particular construction of the family. This has led to a proliferation of evangelical marriage and family manuals, especially since the 1960s, all of which purport to delineate the properly biblical family form and

---

32. Examples of this approach include the systematic theologies of Charles Hodge, Charles Ryrie, Wayne Grudem, Norman Geisler, and Millard Erickson. Hodge famously argues that the task of the Christian theologian is to "ascertain, collect and combine all the facts which God has revealed concerning himself and our relation to Him" (Charles Hodge, *Systematic Theology* [Peabody, MA: Hendrickson, 1999], 11).

function.[33] The Quiverfull theology of the family continues in this tradition. They offer the Christian a very specific, divinely designed model for family life, based upon the purportedly clear commands of scripture. In other words, they offer a family blueprint.

The Quiverfull movement shares with general evangelical literature on the family a number of elements, but the most important is the language of God-given roles and authority. One might argue that the evangelical blueprint for family life is based upon a prior, presupposed gender blueprint that includes both a gender-based hierarchy and dualism of spheres.[34] The result is a pyramid-style distribution of authority, with the father on top, mother below him, and children below both. The father answers to God, the mother answers to the father, and the children answer to mother and father. Thus their conception of gender- and age-based roles arranged into a hierarchical model of authority is the foundation for their family model.[35] On this basis, Quiverfull literature presents readers with a blueprint for family life, an eternal form of the family that must be emulated closely in Christian discipleship.

---

33. See, for example, the following: John R. Rice, *The Home: A Bible Manual of 22 Chapters* (Murfreesboro, TN: Sword of the Lord Publishers, 1964); John R. Rice, *God in Your Family* (Murfreesboro, TN: Sword of the Lord Publishers, 1971); Larry Christenson, *The Christian Family* (Minneapolis: Bethany House, 1970); John Loren and Paula Sandford, *Restoring the Christian Family: A Biblical Guide to Love, Marriage, and Parenting in a Changing World* (Lake Mary, FL: Charisma House, 2009); Andreas Köstenberger, *God, Marriage, and Family: Rebuilding the Biblical Foundation*, 2nd ed. (Wheaton, IL: Crossway, 2010); Martha Peace and Stuart W. Scott, *The Faithful Parent: A Biblical Guide to Raising a Family* (Phillipsburg, NJ: P&R, 2010); Glenn Stanton and Leon Worth, *The Family Project: How God's Design Reveals His Best for You* (Colorado Springs: Focus on the Family, 2014). The description of *The Family Project* is representative of the approach taken by all of the above works: "It provides a solid exploration of God's design and the transformative purpose of biblical families, and also offers down-to-earth helps for living out God's design in your own family."

34. In her book *Godly Women*, Brenda Brasher draws on Peter Berger to argue that a strict sense of gender dualism is a key part of the evangelical or fundamentalist "sacred canopy." See Brenda Brasher, *Godly Women: Fundamentalism and Female Power* (New Brunswick, NJ: Rutgers University Press, 1998).

35. It's possible that other Christian traditions have their own versions of the family blueprint. Don Browning posits the "equal regard family" as the ideal in *Equality and the Family: A Fundamental, Practical Theology of Children, Mothers, and Fathers in Modern Societies* (Grand Rapids: Eerdmans, 2006). Some Catholic theologians present gender complementarity and the family as "domestic church" as the proper model. See Angelo Cardinal Scola, *The Nuptial Mystery*, trans. Michelle K. Borras, Ressourcement (Grand Rapids: Eerdmans, 2005); and Joseph C. Atkinson, *Biblical and Theological Foundations of the Family: The Domestic Church* (Washington, DC: Catholic University of America Press, 2014).

In his book *Church, World, and the Christian Life*, Nicholas Healy offers a trenchant critique of what he calls "blueprint ecclesiologies." While his broader conclusions are beyond the purview of this book, many of the deficits Healy recognizes in blueprint ecclesiologies are also present in family blueprints. According to Healy, blueprints offer systematic and theoretical forms of normative theology; that is, they are abstract systems disconnected from lived experience, yet treated as prescriptive for all times and places. In the case of Quiverfull, practitioners present an imaginary model of the family based upon the supposedly clear commands of scripture. Here is the "biblical model," they suggest, and you are responsible for doing whatever is necessary to emulate this model, regardless of your particular circumstances.

But, as we know, family members and their lives together are, to a great extent, formed by the specifics of their various contexts. One's context comprises, to use Healy's words, "all that bears upon or contributes to the shape of Christian witness and discipleship" within the family. So, the family context includes its generational history (including broader racial and cultural histories), the personal biographies of its members, foundational beliefs and social status, major changes in occupation and lifestyle, experiences of tragedy and strife, individual personalities, styles of communication, and much more.[36] Yet, the systematized family blueprint that Quiverfull offers is, in large part, disconnected from the contexts of particular families. It offers a normative vision for family life against which all families are to measure themselves without reckoning with the real lives of contemporary families.

A clear example of the abovementioned problem is evidenced in the Quiverfull advocacy of "stay-at-home daughters" (SAHD), mentioned above.[37] Because the Quiverfull blueprint presupposes a gender-based dualism of spheres—men in the public sphere and women in the private sphere—daughters are to be brought up differently than sons. Their training and education is to be focused on the domestic sphere. Once they reach adulthood, the ideal situation is that daughters remain at home under the authority of their fathers and tutelage of their mothers until such a time that they are married to a husband

---

36. This is adapted from Healy in *Church, World, and the Christian Life*, 39.

37. For more information about "stay-at-home daughters" (SAHD), see the following articles: Gina McGalliard, "House Proud: The Troubling Rise of Stay-at-Home Daughters," *Bitch Magazine*, November 2010, http://tinyurl.com/y9degtm8; and Karen Swallow Prior, "What Is the Stay-at-Home Daughters Movement?" *Christianity Today*, December 20, 2010, http://tinyurl.com/yamfo5nc.

of the father's choosing.[38] Thus, unmarried daughters are instructed to be happy and productive at home, assisting with housework, the education of siblings, the work of their father's business, and, in some cases, the creation of their own home-based business.[39]

This blueprint for the family assumes a particular socioeconomic situation that not all, or even most, families possess. To fulfill the SAHD ideal, families must be financially secure enough to care for an unemployed adult daughter, the father must have work to which a daughter can contribute, and the family must have enough financial capital to start and maintain a small business. This is not to mention the fact that it assumes that all daughters relish housework and home-schooling their younger siblings. Families who cannot offer their daughters the required financial security or productive at-home occupations have necessarily failed, settling for something less than the divine ideal. And daughters who do not enjoy home-based work or desire higher education or aspire to employment outside the home are understood to be transgressing God's commands.

Elizabeth Harris, an adult daughter of a Quiverfull family, illustrates vividly the problem with the Quiverfull family blueprint. She expresses frustration with the narrow parameters she was offered. The dissonance she encountered between her lived experience (especially her personality, gifts, and passions) and the family blueprint offered by the subculture eventually led her to abandon the movement entirely. Elizabeth's words are worth quoting at length:

---

38. James McDonald's explanation is worth quoting at length: "To be a 'stay-at-home daughter' does not mean that she should lounge about the house waiting for Prince Charming to come along. Our daughters are to be productive and industrious keepers at home. Yes, I said 'keepers at home.' While they are preparing to be keepers of their own homes one day, until our daughters are married, they should serve as keepers at home in the house of their father.... Our daughters are to be busy preparing themselves to be helpers to their own husbands by developing their skills, continuing their education, enhancing their talents, and glorifying God right here where He has them—at home.... Since I am the head of the home, many times the tasks and activities in which our daughters are engaged reflect the occupation that God has given to me. As I am a pastor, many times my daughters (as well as my young son) rise up with my wife in assisting me with pastoral duties.... While the husband and wife are one, and the wife is the suitable helper—the completer of her husband, the entire household should be pointed in the direction of its leader—helping him to fulfill his mission" (James McDonald, "The Blessing of Daughters," *Family Reformation*, October 2, 2007, http://tinyurl.com/y84ncthz).

39. This is a common theme of SAHD literature. Many of the exemplary daughters of the Quiverfull movement operate their own home-based businesses. For example, Sarah Bryant runs a home-based ministry for fellow SAHDs. Her nonprofit, King's Blooming Rose (http://kingsbloomingrose.com), publishes books, calendars, stationary, and hosts annual conferences.

From the age of twelve, I was convinced that I never wanted to get married because I couldn't handle the idea of being a mother and nothing else. My spiritual struggle was trying to accept the idea of female submission and I couldn't do it. . . . Also, I was getting some conflicting messages because my parents didn't really enforce gender stereotypes. My dad would be proud of me when I beat boys at things and I wasn't really raised with seeing those gender stereotypes enforced. It was just a personal struggle that I was raised with all these passions to change the world, but I felt that I couldn't put any of that into action in the way I wanted to or fulfill the kind of mission I wanted to have if I was just a mother. So that was part of it. I was raised with all this passion and I was given only one outlet, and I didn't feel like I could put that into practice with only one outlet. . . .

I think [the Quiverfull] way of life is only possible when you sequester yourself in a tiny community with very little dissent where everyone is the same and believing the same things and no one is disagreeing. Once you leave that community, the entire thing just crumbles. For example, we couldn't implement the model of courtship that we thought we believed in when I lived a thousand miles away [at college]. We tried for a while, but it just didn't work. We just saw that it was impractical for living in modern life.

As I have already suggested, the family blueprint's disconnection from the concrete context of families means that it represents a highly idealized account of the family.[40] Quiverfull practitioners, particularly at the elite level, present a blueprint of what family members are *supposed* to become and what they are *supposed* to do. It is assumed that if only the family blueprint were rightly understood, valued, and implemented, then all of the practical considerations would fall into place.[41] That is, if all members of the Christian family are "doing it right," then there will be no conflict, failure, or harm involved.

---

40. Of course, Quiverfull practitioners are not the only ones to idealize the family. Theological discussions of the family can easily become trapped in abstractions, hovering above the messiness of daily life. Imagining the family as a sacramental expression of the love of the Trinity is well and good, but it doesn't readily connect to discussions about who does the laundry or helps the children with their homework. Speaking of *the family*, with its implied universal ideals, could exacerbate the tendency toward abstraction.

41. To use Healy's words, "The impression is given . . . that theologians believe that it is necessary to get our thinking about the [family] right first, after which we can go on to put our theory into practice" (*Church, World, and the Christian Life*, 36). James Davison Hunter makes a similar criticism of evangelicals, especially in their obsession with "worldview." They emphasize the formation of a Christian worldview in the naïve supposition that if only people could think rightly then they would act rightly and they could thereby transform American culture into something more harmonious with Christianity. See James Davison Hunter, *To Change the World: The Irony, Tragedy, and Possibility of Christianity in the Late Modern World* (Oxford: Oxford University Press, 2010).

In *Family Shepherds*, Voddie Baucham puts forward a hierarchical vision for the family under the rubric of "male headship." He emphasizes the authority of fathers over their children, advocating the frequent use of corporal punishment to "restrain" their wicked hearts.[42] But, of the risk of abuse within this hierarchical model, Baucham states flatly, "A family shepherd would never abuse his children."[43] Never mind that research shows that some Christian men do, in fact, abuse their children and that, in some cases, hierarchical models of the family are a key part of the problem.[44] Rather than reckon with this real contextual factor for American families, Baucham employs the "no true Scotsman" defense: no *real* family shepherd would abuse his children. It is telling that nowhere in his chapters on the training and discipline of children does Baucham explain the difference between spanking and child abuse.

Despite the fact that Quiverfull elites promote a divinely ordained model as the cure-all for familial (and social and cultural) problems, some in the Quiverfull laity are uncomfortable with the blueprint approach to the family. Renee Tanner shares freely the fact that her husband did not live up to the patriarch ideal put forth in Quiverfull literature. She very much wanted a husband who would be the spiritual leader and family shepherd, but found herself addressing the education of her children entirely on her own. While Renee may have struggled in earlier years to make peace with the disparity between her experience and the family blueprint, eventually she let the blueprint slip away. She no longer holds to patriarchy, rejecting it as unnecessary and potentially harmful. The systematized and idealized

42. Baucham, *Family Shepherds*, 113–44.
43. Baucham, *Family Shepherds*, 144.
44. For sources on the relationship of Christianity, patriarchy, and child abuse, see the following: Donald Capps, "Religion and Child Abuse: Perfect Together," *Journal for the Scientific Study of Religion* 31 (1992): 1–14; T. J. Iverson and M. Segal, "Social Behavior of Maltreated Children: Exploring Links to Parent Behavior and Beliefs," in *Parental Belief Systems: The Psychological Consequences for Children*, ed. I. E. Sigel, A. V. McGillicuddy-DeLisi, J. J. Goodnow (Hillsdale, NJ: Laurence Erlbaum, 1992); Philip Greven, *Spare the Child: The Religious Roots of Punishment and the Psychological Impact of Physical Abuse* (New York: Vintage, 1992); Christopher G. Ellison and John P. Bartkowski, "Religion and the Legitimation of Violence: The Case of Conservative Protestantism and Corporal Punishment," in *The Web of Violence: From Interpersonal to Global*, ed. Lester Kurtz and Jennifer Turpin (Urbana: University of Illinois Press, 1996), 45–68; Richard J. Gelles, *Intimate Violence in Families* (Thousand Oaks, CA: Sage, 1997); Stephen Pattison, "'Suffer Little Children': The Challenge of Child Abuse and Neglect to Theology," *Theology and Sexuality* 9, 36–58; Alice Miller, *For Your Own Good: Hidden Cruelty in Child-Rearing and the Roots of Violence*, 3rd ed. (New York: Farrar, Straus & Giroux, 2002); and Janet Heimlich, *Breaking Their Will: Shedding Light on Religious Child Maltreatment* (Amherst, NY: Prometheus, 2011).

family blueprint offered Renee nothing but the recognition that her husband failed to live up to the ideal. And, because he didn't live up to the ideal, neither could she or her children. But, rather than assume failure on her part, Renee traded the Quiverfull blueprint for a more flexible vision based not on form (with clear-cut gender roles) but function: making disciples of her children.

Carley Miller also has an aversion to prescribed family models. When asked whether there is an ideal family, she demurs: "You think about absolute truth and culture, you know? Absolute truth should be firm across any culture, but then you have our cultural differences. So, is [our view of the family] just a cultural thing? Or, is it a biblical model? . . . I don't know if there's something exactly clear like that." Although Carley acknowledges she's associated with a movement that has a very particular vision of the family, she calls herself the "oddball in the group." She firmly believes in "male headship" and that parents are ultimately responsible for instructing their children in the Christian faith, but she's unwilling to spell out in detail what that must look like on the ground. She goes so far as to call it "sin" for her to condemn the practices of another Christian family when she can "see the [spiritual] fruit" of their faithfulness.[45] Carley speaks of the ideal family in terms of practices and virtues, using words like *gathering*, *communication*, *compassion*, *togetherness*, *vulnerability*, and *pitching-in*. Like Renee Tanner, Carley is more focused on the function of the family (what it does) over the form (what it looks like). Ultimately, she says, the family should act like a "mini-church" seeking to "serve the Lord as a family." Role fulfillment takes a backseat to this higher purpose.

Although these stories cannot be said to be representative, they do suggest that some in the Quiverfull laity are dissatisfied with the family blueprint offered by Quiverfull elites. They know from experience that rigid forms and narrowly prescribed roles do not work in organic family life. Also, Renee's story illustrates what Healy says is a problem of theological blueprints in general. Abstract models necessarily float unattainably above the messy settings of contemporary

---

45. When I asked about the instructions of Deuteronomy 6 for parents to teach their children, Carley responded, "I do think that parents are supposed to be the primary teachers [of their children]. Can they send them to school and still be the primary teachers? Absolutely. We have friends that do that. And we see the fruit. I think it would be a sin for me to say that that is wrong. I do. I see families that homeschool that aren't the primary teacher and they're doing their children a disservice. So, I am pretty firm in the belief that we should be our children's primary teacher. Does that mean we have to homeschool? I don't think so."

families. Many families cannot achieve the idealized family form no matter how firmly they believe or how hard they try. Thus the Quiverfull blueprint marginalizes many. This approach may be good for culture war visions of a "faithful remnant" but it is bad for Christian theology as a whole. A tradition whose vision of the family is so impractical and unrealistic cannot hope either to inspire the world through faithful witness or effect transformational change.

Still, both Quiverfull practitioners and evangelicals in general would likely respond to all of the above with a rhetorical shrug. They would say that their "biblical model" for family life is divinely revealed and therefore not dependent on cultural context. The family blueprint does not depend for its veracity on its perceived practicality in contemporary American life. The biblical ideal is to be emulated in faith, whether or not it is perceived as viable. Indeed, some might choose to interpret the impracticality of their family blueprint as an advantage: "Small is the gate and narrow the road that leads to life, and only a few find it" (Matt 7:14).

Yet, the assumption that the Quiverfull family blueprint is a divine design culled straight from the pages of scripture is naïve and simplistic. As we saw in chapter 1, American evangelicals have constructed their model of gender and the family over the past couple of centuries through interaction with a variety of socioeconomic and cultural factors. And, like all theology, the evangelical family blueprint has been conceived within a particular tradition, with a particular understanding of history and God's work in the world. Leaders present the evangelical family blueprint "as if it were a normative and systematic deduction" from scripture, despite the fact that it is dependent upon a host of contextual factors.[46] The nuclear family, for example, is a recent development in human history, born of a number of dynamics including the industrial revolution, urbanization, and consumer capitalism. Moreover, contemporary evangelical writings that put forward the nuclear family led by a male breadwinner as the biblical ideal are not considering the multiplicity of family forms found in scripture, nor are they paying attention to the vast differences between the contexts of the biblical writers and the present day. Even the existence of a stable "traditional" family form has been called into question in recent decades. Stephanie Coontz argues persuasively in *The Way We Never Were* that the "traditional family" of June and Ward Cleaver existed mostly in the imaginative

---

46. Healy, *Church, World, and the Christian Life*, 43.

realm of television. "Like most visions of a 'golden age,'" she says, "the 'traditional family'... is an ahistorical amalgam of structures, values, and behaviors that never co-existed in the same time and place."[47]

The Bible does not, in fact, offer Christians a blueprint for the family. Instead, the Bible provides a collection of texts, within an overarching story, pertinent to theological thinking about the family. In the Old Testament, we see narratives about the lives of some ancient near eastern families, law codes meant to govern patrilinear, patrilocal Israelite families, prophetic denunciations of unjust behavior among families, wisdom literature enjoining the young to reverence their elders, and poetic statements about the blessing of children and virtues of a wise wife. In the New Testament, we hear warnings from Jesus about the trappings of family loyalty, the creation of a new kind of family among Jesus's disciples, and, several decades later, the instructions of Pauline "household codes" promoting both orderly families within the Roman Empire and the participation of all Christians within the "household of God." In these texts, the language of gender roles and the concept of the modern nuclear family (a husband, a wife, and their children) are nowhere to be found.

All this is to say, even by their "biblical" standards, the Quiverfull family blueprint falls short. They claim to possess a biblical, divinely ordained model for family life, but Quiverfull practitioners have no such thing. They are reading a late nineteenth- and early twentieth-century form of white middle-class family life into scripture and extracting from it gender-based roles to circumscribe the behavior of individual family members, especially women and children.[48] Moreover, their systematic and normative vision for family life is problematically detached from the contemporary context. Due to their inattention to the shifting cultural, political, and socioeconomic realities of American families, the evangelical family blueprint constitutes an impractical and unattainable form. Rather than empower the work of faithful discipleship, the blueprint becomes a millstone.[49]

---

47. Stephanie Coontz, *The Way We Never Were: American Families and the Nostalgia Trap* (New York: Basic Books, 1992), 9. See also Coontz, *The Way We Really Are: Coming to Terms with America's Changing Families* (New York: Basic Books, 1998).

48. This is not to mention the fact that many factors go into the particular theologian's reflections on the family. Healy discusses multiple factors that come to bear on a theologian's ecclesiology (*Church, World, and the Christian Life*, 39–43). I could easily put together a similar list of factors that contribute to a theologian's theology of the family.

49. But, one might ask, if the evangelical family blueprint is so problematic for Christian the-

Of course, much of the allure of theological blueprints has to do with the presumption that if one emulates the divinely ordained form, one is guaranteed success. For the Quiverfull movement, *success* takes the form of the blessing of God manifested through godly Christian children, personal satisfaction, and long-term cultural impact. But, the truth is, none of these things are guaranteed, no matter how perfectly a family blueprint is put into practice. In the end, the family is an organism made up of flawed human beings with various strengths, weaknesses, inclinations, habits, and patterns of behavior. The Quiverfull family blueprint cannot and does not guarantee success.

None of the above objections mean we must discard entirely any concept of the family as an ideal. Christian theologians can retain some stable sense of *the family* while also being flexible and nuanced with families. Lisa Sowle Cahill defines the family as "an organized network of socioeconomic and reproductive independence and support grounded in biological kinship and marriage." Yet, Cahill clarifies that while family created by kinship and marriage is "the most basic family form," it is not the only legitimate form of family. She cautions against adopting "punitive attitudes and policies toward nonconforming families."[50] Indeed, it is possible to uphold the basic notion of the family rooted in kinship and marriage without condemning other forms of family as they appear on the American landscape. The key is to focus on what the family does rather than what the family is—its function rather than its appearance. I will say more about this below.

---

ology and practice, then what should take its place? Healy offers a way forward on this subject. He argues that the proper function of ecclesiology is "to aid the concrete church in performing its tasks of witness and pastoral care" within its "ecclesiological context" (*Church, World, and the Christian Life*, 38). I suggest something similar could be said of theologies of the family. The task of family theology is to aid concrete families, regardless of their form, in performing their tasks of witness and discipleship within their multiple contexts. This means that critical analysis of these various contexts and the activities within them should be a central task of family theology, even in an evangelical mode (39). In contrast to the structure of family blueprints, theological reflection on the family must be, from the outset, a matter of practical rather than theoretical reasoning. The practice of family theology should arise out of lived experience and family practices and ordered directly toward them (46).

50. Cahill, *Family*, xi. Cahill goes on to clarify: "Kinship denotes affiliation through reproductive lines. Marriage, in turn, is a consensual and contractual manner of uniting kin groups, especially for the purpose of reproduction, and the perpetuation of kinship structures through which social and economic relations are managed" (xi).

THE PROBLEM WITH THE QUIVERFULL FAMILY BLUEPRINT

There are problems with the use of family blueprints in general, but there are also problems with the Quiverfull family blueprint in particular. A number of issues are worthy of attention, not least of which is their strident gender dualism and patriarchal vision for the home. Yet, critique of their version of Christian patriarchy has been done, both within and beyond American evangelicalism, and some of the issues with Quiverfull gender hierarchy were addressed in chapter 3. In what follows, therefore, I assume the problematic nature of Quiverfull gender hierarchy and consider in more detail three less obvious, but no less important, elements of the Quiverfull family blueprint: (1) the excessive privatization and isolation of the family; (2) the eclipse of ecclesiology and breakdown of social connection; and (3) the construction of the home as a sinless space.

Excessive Privatization and Isolation

The first weakness of the Quiverfull vision of the family has been discussed in a limited way above. Quiverfull elites and laypersons imagine families as private, autonomous entities governed by the father. The family is imagined with well-defined boundaries, wholly distinct from the "parallel institutions" of the church and the nation.[51] Thus the head of the family answers directly to Christ.

While this may sound unusual to some, at this point Quiverfull families are simply doubling-down on broader American tendencies. The family as a private, autonomous institution is essential to our cultural imagination.[52] It is a viewpoint assumed by both the political right and left. For example, most Americans think that what happens "in the bedroom" is a totally private matter. Sexual practices and any resulting pregnancies are the concern of the parties involved and no one else. Likewise, marriage is a matter of romantic love and personal choice with no broader social context or responsibilities. Similarly, most Americans think that caring and providing for children is the private duty of parents, something that should only be

---

51. Philip Lancaster, Doug Phillips, and R. C. Sproul Jr., "The Tenets of Biblical Patriarchy," Vision Forum Ministries, undated, December 12, 2010, http://tinyurl.com/y8763jme.

52. See Coontz, *The Way We Never Were*, and Jean Bethke Elshtain, *Public Man, Private Woman* (Princeton: Princeton University Press, 1993).

supplemented in the most extreme cases. Also, retirement, end-of-life care, and other such matters are the private family's concern. Thus, institutions like universal childcare, universal healthcare, or universal college education are almost unimaginable in the American context. Autonomy and choice reign supreme.

The imagined privatization and autonomy of the American family is made especially plain in the various public conversations about the crisis of the family. Rather than view the nuclear family's decline as a consequence of broader social, economic, and cultural factors, Americans at all levels reverse the correlation and blame most social ills on the dissolution of the family. If only individuals would fix their private families—perhaps by being less selfish, less lazy, or less promiscuous—then American society would be strengthened and stabilized. This perspective is particularly common in discussions of America's "urban poor" (which is almost always coded language for poor people of color), who are offered the institution of marriage as a panacea for persistent poverty, never mind the problems of systemic racism, unemployment, higher-than-average rates of arrest and incarceration, the proliferation of guns exacerbated by loose gun laws, and more. The idea that the nuclear family could be fixed through sheer moral determination persists despite the fact that experts regularly argue there are "multiple realities and therefore multiple responsibilities" at work in the dissolution of the American family. As social systems theorists Jaime Inclan and Ernesto Ferran Jr. explain,

> When families fail in large numbers, their environment contributes to that failure. That is to say, where there is trouble in families, there is likely to be a crisis in the "village" itself. Therefore, we cannot do the urgent work of rehabilitating families without at the same time addressing problems in education, transportation, health care, employment, race and class and sex discrimination, conspicuous consumerism, and the exploitation of the land, all of which contaminate the "village" environment in which families attempt to survive. It is true that a civilization is only as strong as its families because its future lies in the health and welfare of its children. However, the converse is also true: families can only thrive in healthy communities.[53]

There is much more that could be said about the dominant American model of the family, but that is not our focus here. The important

---

53. Jaime Inclan and Ernesto Ferran Jr., "Poverty, Politics, and Family Therapy: A Role for Systems Theory," in *The Social and Political Contexts of Family Therapy*, ed. Marsha Pravder Mirkin (Needham Heights, MA: Allyn & Bacon, 1990), 209.

point is that in their disregard of the importance of the family's environment, Quiverfull proponents perpetuate a longstanding American myopia evidenced across the political spectrum. Because the family is imagined in thoroughly private, autonomous terms, their answers to the dissolution of the family are private, disregarding broader cultural, political, and economic factors. Theirs is a decidedly "pull yourself up by your bootstraps" approach to the family that necessarily fails those who have no boots to begin with.[54]

As a result, the Quiverfull construction of the family is far from innovative. They are simply adding more responsibilities to the dominant American model. Just as the Quiverfull performance of motherhood is like *Lean In* for stay-at-home moms, so also the Quiverfull vision for the family is *Lean In* for the nuclear family.[55] Now, on top of everything else, the nuclear family is tasked with the formal education of children from preschool through high school (and beyond); the spiritual formation and catechesis of children; evangelism, outreach, and discipleship; and the transformation of American society. If American families under the dominant cultural model were weighed down by extensive burdens before, the Quiverfull family blueprint increases the demands tenfold. Mary Pride may be right to claim that government-funded programs for public schools, daycare, healthcare, and more are novel endeavors, but "so too is the idea that a nuclear family can adequately carry all the responsibilities previously carried by the 'village.'"[56]

Some might object that the Quiverfull focus on raising "sons and daughters who walk with God" does indeed stand out from the cultural status quo. This argument has merit insofar as Quiverfull parents prioritize their understanding of spiritual success over the educational or recreational success of their children. Yet, prioritizing the religious formation of children retains the American tendency toward an inward-looking focus on the success of one's own children (however that success is defined). Though they may not understand success as attending an Ivy League school or competing in an elite soccer league, Quiverfull families remain, for the most part, entirely focused upon the protection and formation of their offspring. Certainly, the shift in emphasis to children's spiritual and moral forma-

---

54. Martin Luther King Jr., "Remaining Awake Through a Great Revolution," delivered at the National Cathedral, Washington, D.C., on 31 March 1968: http://tinyurl.com/yae8p7kr.

55. Sheryl Sandberg, *Lean In: Women, Work, and the Will to Lead* (New York: Knopf, 2013).

56. R. L. Stollar, "Children as Divine Rental Property," *Homeschoolers Anonymous*, January 5, 2015, http://tinyurl.com/y857o2xy.

tion is preferable to other, more superficial concerns. But, there is no doubt that the Quiverfull focus on the success of their own children, within the walls of the private family home, perpetuates the prevailing autonomous and self-interested model of the American family.

We see evidence of this privatized self-interest in the testimony of Quiverfull mothers. When I asked Deborah Olson if she felt responsible for the wellbeing of other people's children, she said no: "I feel like I have a responsibility to pray for other people's children. . . . I can't save the world, so I just try to pray for the world. When we [as a family] see those who don't make good choices we just pray for them that the Lord would help them. I think that is our responsibility, but beyond that, I just need to do a good job at the ministry in my home." Carley Miller is more open to the idea that she has a responsibility for the care of others: "I think we should love our neighbors as ourselves—and specifically orphans. I do have a responsibility for that." When I pressed her on the matter of organized care through healthcare, education, and so on, she was hesitant. Eventually she conceded, "I do think it's our responsibility as Christians. And the character of Jesus showed that he cared for people in those kinds of ways. But, to make people do those things as a society is a whole different thing. We should as Christians take care of others in that way, but I don't think we should be forced to." So, Carley acknowledges a personal responsibility to care for others, but rules out the use of broader social or governmental structures to do so. The burden continues to rest squarely on individual families and their choices. Renee Tanner was the most open to organized structures of care for others. She says, "Yes, in the case of poor families or families that neglect their kids, yes, I think as a society, as Americans, we should take care of them." But Renee is still concerned about the family's autonomy: "I think we're still working that out, though, because there's such a fine line on the matter of parental rights, which, of course, people like us want." Familial autonomy remains primary, even when the love of neighbor is acknowledged as a concern.

Of course, the tendency toward inwardly focused self-interest is not surprising given the extensive responsibilities shouldered by Quiverfull mothers and their families. Do Quiverfull mothers really have time to think about the care of others when they have so much to do for themselves? By raising the lack of social vision beyond the nuclear family, I am certainly not seeking to add to the extensive responsibilities already shouldered by Quiverfull families. Rather, I am shedding light on the way the Quiverfull vision for and practice of the family intensifies the general American shortsightedness about anything beyond the walls of the private home. What was already an extant problem in the American cultural imagination is exacerbated within Quiverfull discourse. Because of their unwillingness to address broader social and economic factors, the Quiverfull movement is unable to offer a viable response to the challenges facing American families today.

Due to the fact that they imagine the family in thoroughly private and autonomous terms, Quiverfull families have a tendency to live isolated lives—arguably more isolated than most. There seem to be two interconnected reasons for this. First, the practices of pronatalism and homeschooling inevitably result in an inward-looking focus on the home. And, second, the peculiarity of the Quiverfull way of life works against the formation of friendships and outside systems of support. The majority of homeschooling instruction takes place in the private home, and any schooling beyond the home usually occurs with likeminded families in a voluntary homeschooling co-operative. If the family is involved in a church that is distinct from their homeschooling colleagues, they may interact with others in that environment as well. Still, given their inordinate responsibilities, there is only so much support that fellow Quiverfull mothers can offer each other. When asked if isolation is a problem, Deborah Olson answered in the affirmative. Her response is worth quoting at length:

> Yes, I guess because of our situation. And I think it would be fair to assume that even in a church with a bunch of families that look like us, those families might still feel isolated. Because I don't think you can physically go through what we are going through and not feel isolated. I just don't think you can. We take up an entire pew by ourselves! [Laughter.] When we go to a church meal, we take up a whole table. [Laughter.] I don't have time to do every ladies' coffee that's available. We cannot sign up to volunteer in every single activity that the church decides to serve the community with. . . . There are still ways to have fellowship. When I take my kids to the homeschool co-op, I'm totally happy to have my kids go play and sit and fellowship with the other moms. So, there are ways to not feel so isolated when you're with likeminded people and be encouraged and not discouraged. But any family that chooses to really make family and training their children a priority and chooses to do things like us, I think they often look kind of like hermits. [Laughter.] I have two very dear friends who both have seven children, both homeschool, who I just thought we would be best friends

forever. But, I just went through a really rough time this past year. I was sad and overwhelmed and struggling. And it wasn't my friends who comforted me, but it was random people at our church. . . . So, my friends don't talk to me and I get all worked up about it. "What did I do?" I think, "Why doesn't she talk to me? Why doesn't she call me?" Then I just decided that they could be thinking the same thing about me. We cannot as mothers of seven kids, homeschooling, doing everything we do, still have the time. If you can find the time to [have active friendships] it's like a gem in the rough. But I think it's fine. We do this on purpose. But the enemy can make you feel lonely and down. The enemy can use the isolation to make you feel down and draw your attention away from your home. But, I feel like what we're doing is purposeful and it's okay.

Interestingly, Deborah assumes that "any family" that "chooses to do things like [them]" will face isolation. She links the isolation to their large family size, which causes them to stand out. She also points to the peculiarity of their lifestyle, organized around the priority of "family" and "training their children." So, she assumes that they are unlikely to make connections beyond the bounds of fellow Quiverfull families. And even among those who share their convictions, Deborah acknowledges that friendship and support is hard to come by. Indeed, she sees isolation as a constant avenue for "the enemy" (i.e., Satan) to make her and others like her feel "lonely and down." But, speaking with an air of resignation, there isn't anything Deborah thinks can be done about that. She sees isolation as an inevitable result of their "purposeful" family practices, so she accepts it as a kind of necessary evil.

The same perspective is evident in the story of Renee Tanner. Renee recalls the short periods when she had likeminded friends who lived close by as important times in her life. But, most of the time, she was carrying on her motherly work on her own. She says,

Not having any help or moral support—that was the biggest challenge for me emotionally. Not to get depressed or resentful. Not to have any help built into the culture, whether it's through marriage or extended family. As a big family, no one else understands. They don't know what you need or how to help or even that you need help. And as a person and a woman that was the hardest part. The best years that I did have were when the Smiths lived here and we both had lots of kids and could share and go to each other's houses. That friendship was important but I didn't always have it.[57]

But, it's not just mothers who face isolation; children deal with it as well. Many Quiverfull families intentionally keep their children from socializing with anyone but the likeminded. Depending on where the family lives and their level of involvement in a local church, Quiverfull children may have a very limited number of friends outside their immediate family. Many families are unapologetic about their choice to keep their children from the influence of non-Christian and non-Quiverfull families. Some families are so wedded to the form—focused on getting their performance of the family "just right"—they happily embrace disconnection from church and community. In these cases, the children are expected to socialize with their own family members and the friends of the parents' choosing.

Of course, it is quite common for American families to associate with those within their own religion, race, and socioeconomic status.[58] And certainly Quiverfull parents are not the only ones to exercise control over the friends their children acquire. Unfortunately, the privatized Quiverfull vision for the family, combined with a deep suspicion of government, established churches, and other institutions, does not provide the necessary conceptual tools for a way out of the isolation. Their primary concern for a particular kind of Christian formation for children has trumped all other concerns. Moreover, they think that Christian formation is properly carried out *only* through mother-led schooling in the home. This conviction, combined with pronatalism and gender hierarchy, often results in an isolated mother within an isolated family. Moreover, their theology and practice of the family works against their own aims of Christian formation of children. Their social and ecclesial isolation (to be considered in more detail below) hinders their ability to impart a full Christian identity to the next generation.

---

57. The same is true of Carley. Even though she seems to have the most friends of the three mothers at the center of this project, she conducts the majority of her life on her own within the private family home. Carley's isolation seems more attenuated, however, because of the involvement of her husband. She portrays their work in the home as a partnership and speaks of her husband pitching in when he is home. This more equitable division of the domestic work may lead to a more companionate marriage and less isolation for Carley.

58. For example, on the subject of race, see Andrew Hacker, *Two Nations: Black and White, Separate, Hostile, Unequal*, rev. ed. (New York: Scribner, 2003). See also Michael O. Emerson and Christian Smith, *Divided by Faith: Evangelical Religion and the Problem of Race in America* (New York: Oxford University Press, 2000); and Christena Cleveland, *Disunity in Christ: Uncovering the Hidden Forces That Keep Us Apart* (Downers Grove, IL: InterVarsity, 2013).

There are elements in the Christian tradition that offer a more communally rooted vision for the family. Catholic social teaching, for example, points away from the privatized and autonomous American vision of the family and toward a much more social, others-oriented institution.[59] In his encyclical *Familiaris Consortio*, Pope John Paul II explains the purpose of the family in four parts. He says the family is tasked with the responsibility to guard, reveal, and communicate love, as well as "serve life" by having children, educating them, and forming them in the Christian faith.[60] The family is to participate in the development of society because "far from being closed in on itself, the family is by its nature and vocation open to other families and to society and undertakes its social role."[61] Finally, the family is to be a "domestic church," serving the world as a manifestation of the body of Christ in the community.[62] Building upon John Paul's teaching, Julie Hanlon Rubio writes, "The genius of Catholic teaching on the family is its refusal to limit families by telling them simply to focus on themselves. Christian families, from this perspective, are to grow in self-giving love within and outside the bonds of kinship."[63] Lisa Sowle Cahill says something similar: "In my view, the Christian family is not the nuclear family focused inward on the welfare of its own members but the socially transformative family that seeks to make the Christian moral ideal of love of neighbor part of the common good."[64] Despite their desire to be witnesses and effective agents of change, it is clear that it is the latter point with which Quiverfull families have the most difficulty.

The Family Eclipses the Church

In addition to a general problem with the privatization and isolation of the family, Quiverfull discourse has a tendency to emphasize the family so much that the church is eclipsed.[65] This is somewhat sur-

---

59. Of course, this account of the family is rooted firmly in Catholic social teaching regarding the common good, which evangelicals do not necessarily share.
60. Pope John Paul II, *Familiaris Consortio*, no. 17, 37.
61. Pope John Paul II, *Familiaris Consortio*, no. 42, 44.
62. Pope John Paul II, *Familiaris Consortio*, no. 49–64.
63. Julie Hanlon Rubio, *Family Ethics: Practices for Christians* (Washington, DC: Georgetown University Press, 2010), 30.
64. Cahill, *Family*, xi, xii.
65. I could just as well say that Quiverfull discourse tends to replace the church with the nuclear family; that is, the nuclear family essentially becomes the church. I have chosen not to characterize matters in this way because I do not accept the Quiverfull premise that the family

prising given the fervency with which Quiverfull families are seeking to embody and pass on the Christian faith. One might expect their commitment to Christian formation to translate into faithful church participation, but the opposite is often the case. What I have found is that, more often than not, their commitment to Quiverfull discourse takes precedence over ecclesial loyalty; sometimes their practices bring them into direct conflict with churches.

At base, much of Quiverfull discourse involves the pursuit of purity: purity in theology and practice. Quiverfull families are seeking to be the most committed and most faithful Christians they can be. Their practices of pronatalism, homeschooling, and gender hierarchy are often not shared by other Christians. Although the intensity of the rhetoric varies on this point, most see other American Christians implicated in a pattern of compromise with and capitulation to, the surrounding culture. In this respect, Quiverfull represents a discourse of reform or protest within American Christianity and American culture. They think they are pointing the way to a purer, more focused practice of Christianity, as well as a more faithful, socially beneficial way of life for American society. This perspective has enormous consequences for the way they interact with churches. If the family is the location of God's reforming work in America, then it makes sense that the family would eclipse the church in their theology and practice.

At the level of Quiverfull elites, the nuclear family is consistently prioritized over the church. Quiverfull teachers read the Bible through the lens of the nuclear family, seeing the family—and the godly patriarch at its head—as the key to God's salvation of the world. In Baucham's words, "From Genesis to Revelation, we see a clear picture of the role of the family in redemptive history, and the role of the father in the family."[66] A pastor of a family-integrated church in the Midwest put it this way: "The family is God's plan for revealing himself to the world. He had to create family in order for us to understand God as Father. The married couple is a picture of Christ and the

---

constitutes a church. Certainly, there is a fundamental relationship between the two in Christian theology and practice, but the two are not (indeed, cannot be) equivalent. Rather, I agree with Jana Bennett's contention that Christian families ("households") are completely reconfigured in light of the church ("the Household of God"). For a fuller discussion, see Jana Bennett, *Water Is Thicker Than Blood: An Augustinian Theology of Marriage and Singleness* (Oxford: Oxford University Press, 2008).

66. Baucham, *Family Shepherds*, 25. I contest Baucham's assertion that the family is central in the New Testament. Perhaps the patriarchal family is central from Genesis to Malachi, but certainly not from Matthew to Revelation.

church. The unity of the two becoming one is ultimately a picture of Christ and the church to the world. [What we see in America today is that] one of the most important pictures of God to the world is breaking up."[67] In this perspective, the family is central both to God's revelation and salvation. This is not just the way of God in the past; it is the way God continues to work today.[68]

The prioritization of the family isn't without biblical precedent. The Old Testament, especially the stories of the patriarchs and God's covenant with David, is filled with accounts of God establishing a relationship with patriarchs and using his descendants to bring about God's purposes. The Lord is "the God of Abraham, Isaac, and Jacob." In these stories, little attention is given to "the village" or assembly of God's people apart from the patriarch's or king's family. Still, the New Testament does not maintain this patriarch-driven, family-focused perspective on God's work. In the Gospels, apprenticeship to Jesus takes priority over family ties and, at the very least, relativizes the authority of the patriarch. "Whoever does God's will is my mother and sister and brother," Jesus says in Mark 3:34. Also, "If anyone comes to me and does not hate father and mother, wife and children, brothers and sisters—yes, even their own life—such a person cannot be my disciple" (Luke 14:26). The call to join Jesus in his kingdom is a call that ultimately trumps all other calls.

Later, in the Pauline epistles, the centrality of the church becomes clearer. Ephesians 3:7–11 reads as follow:

> I became a servant of this gospel by the gift of God's grace given me through the working of his power. Although I am less than the least of all the Lord's people, this grace was given me: to preach to the Gentiles the boundless riches of Christ, and to make plain to everyone the administration of this mystery, which for ages past was kept hidden in God, who created all things. His intent was that now, through the church, the manifold wisdom of God should be made known to the rulers and authorities in the heavenly realms, according to his eternal purpose that he accomplished in Christ Jesus our Lord.

The gospel of God's "eternal purpose" and "boundless riches of Christ," the author says, is made manifest through "the church." It is the church through which God is making known "the manifold wis-

---

67. Joshua Lenon, Pastor of Red Door Church, Cincinnati, OH, phone interview, August 28, 2013.
68. Baucham, *Family Driven Faith*, 214.

dom of God." Evidently, the family is no longer the primary locus of God's saving activity in the world. This is not to say that the family does not have a key role in the education and formation of children. Certainly, it does. But, that is a different matter from seeing the family as "God's plan for revealing himself to the world." Whereas the biblical story begins with God's command to humankind to "be fruitful and multiply" and "rule" over the earth (Gen 1:28), the story of Jesus culminates with his proclamation that "all authority" has been given to him; "Therefore go and make disciples of all nations, baptizing them in the name of the Father and of the Son and of the Holy Spirit, and teaching them to obey everything I have commanded you" (Matt 28:18–20). In the kingdom of God, "be fruitful and multiply" has been elevated and fulfilled by "make disciples of all nations." Therefore, theologian Jana Bennett is correct: water—the water of baptism—is thicker than blood.[69] But, this is not the point of view of Quiverfull elites for whom the replication of the family blueprint remains the key to Christian faithfulness and the triumph of God's kingdom.[70]

When Quiverfull elites do talk about church, their message is mixed. In *Family Shepherds*, Voddie Baucham is adamant about the significance of the church, even devoting an entire chapter to it. He says, "The most important thing for a family shepherd to do . . . is to ensure that they're healthy members of a healthy church."[71] Later, he elaborates:

> I've had conversation after conversation with fathers and mothers who are committed to family discipleship, but who are struggling tremendously as they either attended an unhealthy church or no church at all. These families don't testify of overwhelming joy and fulfillment because "family is enough." On the contrary, they testify to struggle, strain, loneliness, fear, isolation, and despair. Family discipleship is absolutely crucial, but there's no substitute for healthy membership in a healthy local church.[72]

---

69. Bennett, *Water Is Thicker Than Blood*.

70. Baucham argues in *Family Shepherds*, "There's nothing in the New Testament to support any approach that would undermine, redefine, or abandon the family discipleship model in the Old Testament" (23). For Baucham, the family remains the central institution in the propagation and preservation of the Christian faith. Even though he says, "The church/family dynamic is not an either/or scenario," he certainly envisions a conflict between the two institutions and makes clear that the family is most important. As he says in *Family Driven Faith*, "the family is the key" (214).

71. Baucham, *Family Shepherds*, 147.

72. Baucham, *Family Shepherds*, 154.

Baucham acknowledges the struggle of isolation, fear, and despair that many Quiverfull families face, and he promotes church involvement as one way of mitigating those challenges. Yet, the phrase "healthy church," which he uses repeatedly throughout the chapter, makes things complicated. What qualifies as a "healthy church"? Later he references "healthy, theologically sound local bodies,"[73] but never explains what this means. Certainly, it is up to the family shepherd to determine the theological fitness of a given church. Moreover, the equation of "healthy" and "theologically sound" raises the problematic issue of purity. Is it better for a family shepherd to avoid church entirely if he can't find one that is healthy and theologically sound? Or, is something better than nothing? Baucham never says. Also, despite his insistence on "church membership," the reasons Baucham gives for it are entirely family-oriented. He offers four—including "identification with Christ and the church," edification, cooperation, and accountability—but each explanation is focused on how church participation benefits the family. There is no sense that the church constitutes a vital, enduring institution in its own right that the Christian family needs in order to understand itself. The relationship between church and family goes no deeper than utility. Within Baucham's vision, the church is a voluntary association the family shepherd can opt in and out of depending upon his biblical convictions.[74] The crucial authority figure remains the patriarch, and the primary locus of God's activity is the family.

In other Quiverfull sources, the family is seen as an institution in opposition to the church. In these instances, the Quiverfull family stands for God's truth in a godless age, while the church is, by and large, a weak, capitulating institution in need of reformation. In these caricatures, it is good and right for Quiverfull families to resist the influence of such misguided, sub-Christian bodies and go it alone. In *Birthing God's Mighty Warriors*, Rachel Scott consistently speaks of the church and church members as antagonistic critics of godly families. She speaks of church members as people who have been tricked by Satan into limiting their family size through birth control and sterilization: "Today, most people in our churches . . . are on the pill, sterilized, or planning to be sterilized, and everybody is justifying their

---

73. Baucham, *Family Shepherds*, 149.
74. Admittedly, the majority of evangelicals share Baucham's view of the church as a voluntary association. More will be said about evangelical ecclesiology below. But, the difference between Baucham and other evangelicals is the disproportionate emphasis he gives to the family over and against the church.

decisions."[75] From Scott's point of view, Quiverfull families represent a very small, faithful remnant that is often, if not always, standing in opposition to the church.

While Scott focuses exclusively on birth control and sterilization, Mary Pride has her sights set on feminism, which she considers an anti-Christian "false religion" that has infiltrated American churches.[76] Speaking of self-described "biblical feminists," Pride claims: "We are being asked to kill our babies, endorse homosexuality . . . nag our husbands to do our job so we can do theirs—under the threat of divorce—and all in the name of *Christ!*"[77] For Pride, the willingness of many Christian women to embrace careers outside the home is a symptom of "a massive loss of Christian perspective" in the American church.[78]

In *Family Driven Faith*, Baucham adopts a similar point of view. Baucham's chief concern is the education and formation of children, which he seeks to "take back" from the state and church, respectively. In his account, most American churches are not teaching the right things about family and not conducting ministry among families correctly. His book is intended to persuade parents into a "complete lifestyle and worldview overhaul" and in the final chapters he calls the church to assist families in this endeavor rather than get in their way.[79] Baucham understands himself to be leading a revival, and he encourages families who read his book to be "a catalyst to wake the sleeping giant and move your church toward family integration."[80] Baucham claims that without a radical change to Christian practice of church and family, "we will not see an end to the decimation of both institutions in our culture."[81] Again, the assumption is that most American churches (and families) are failing miserably and Quiverfull families, through their faithfulness, hold the key to getting everything back on track.

In light of how badly the church is portrayed in the writings of Quiverfull elites, it makes sense that ecclesiology and ecclesial involvement is often lacking (or nonexistent) in the Quiverfull movement. If most American churches are apostate, or nearly so, then

75. Scott, *Birthing God's Mighty Warriors*, 218, 219, 282.
76. Pride, *The Way Home*, 4–13.
77. Pride, *The Way Home*, 11.
78. Pride, *The Way Home*, 12.
79. Baucham, *Family Driven Faith*, 169.
80. Baucham, *Family Driven Faith*, 169, 202.
81. Baucham, *Family Driven Faith*, 213.

what is the point of being concerned with them at all? Elite writings by and large portray Quiverfull families as self-sufficient units, capable on their own to bring about revival and cultural transformation. Who needs the church, anyway?

The eclipse of the church by the family is also evident at the lay level, emerging in different ways among my informants. I detailed the church struggles faced by the Tanners in chapter 2, so I won't revisit their story here. Dave and Carley Miller, whose story of baptism begins this chapter, prefer a home-based church but they have had trouble implementing it in the past. The Millers conducted house church for a few years, supplemented by occasional Sunday attendance at a nearby church. But, after a falling out over Carley's violation of unspoken gender norms (detailed in chapter 2), the Millers' house church was discontinued. For now, the Millers attend a Baptist church within driving distance of their home. They feel that their way of life is respected and that the pastoral staff shares their convictions about children's education and formation. They've been there for over a year and plan to continue.

Deborah and Dan Olson have had a somewhat different experience. Though raised in a charismatic church, the Olsons decided they were no longer at home in their tradition and left to find another church. They attended a house church for a significant period of time, but Deborah never felt like that was sufficient. She protests the lack of "accountability" in that setting and believes "seeking out fellowship with other believers [and] worshiping in public is what the Lord wanted." After several months of exhausting "church shopping," the Olsons decided to take a totally different approach. They settled on three essential factors for a church: (1) they preach Jesus, especially his sacrificial death; (2) their children are safe; and (3) the church is in close proximity to their home. They made a list of five churches within three miles of their home and visited each until they found one that met their three criteria. At present, they have worshiped with the same church for two years.

Even though the Olsons have committed to remain with their church for the foreseeable future, they characterize it as nostalgic, lacking passion, and uninterested in the "newer culture." And, Deborah says, "We are not like the other families there." As the only Quiverfull, homeschooling family in the church, the Olsons often feel isolated and alone. They feel a pull toward "homeschooling churches," which are made up of likeminded families committed to the same way of life. Deborah asks, "Do I just stick to where they aren't teaching false doctrine and contribute to my community where I can best serve? I am really convicted by that. Sometimes that takes precedence over feeling lonely." Even in times when church is "a big challenge," the Olsons continue to try to be faithful in their attendance. Yet, as detailed in chapter 4, the Olsons are unlikely to have their oldest son baptized in their church due to differences on the proper function of baptism. At the same time, Dan is uncomfortable with the thought of baptizing his son on his own terms. For now, the issue remains unresolved.

What I see in my informants is a struggle to reconcile their convictions with existing church structures. Although they affirm the significance of the church in theory, the practice of church presents many complications. What should a family do when the church doesn't support their way of life? If there is no church that embodies a family's views on the sacraments, should they simply administer them privately? Is the purpose of the church to be in community with the likeminded or to be in community with one's Christian neighbors? The church is good if you can find one sufficiently healthy and theologically sound—that is, consonant with Quiverfull convictions. If not, perhaps it's better to retreat to the house church or family worship so as not to risk the sub-Christian influences of less-than-healthy American churches. As the framed verse on the Olsons' wall says defiantly, "As for me and my house, we will serve the Lord" (Josh 24:15).

The tendency to dismiss established churches as flawed and superfluous is not unique to Quiverfull but an impulse inherent within Protestant Christianity. Once sixteenth-century Protestant Reformers accepted the Bible alone, apart from church and tradition, as the authority for Christian faith and practice, they created an inherently unstable movement in which division was an ever-present possibility.[82] The Protestant impulse to divide over biblical truth and purity, combined with a low view of church, is intensified within American evangelicalism.[83] The free-church tradition in the United

---

82. Alister McGrath, *Christianity's Dangerous Idea* (New York: HarperOne, 2007), 2–7.

83. Brad Harper and Paul Louis Metzger speak of evangelicalism's ecclesiology problem in the introduction to their book, *Exploring Ecclesiology: An Evangelical and Ecumenical Perspective* (Grand Rapids: Brazos, 2009). They call evangelical ecclesiology "problematic yet promising" due, in part, to the fact that evangelicalism is not a denomination but "a movement." This has resulted in what they call "a lack of ecclesial distinctives" as well as "a lack of loyalty to any particular ecclesial tradition" (15). Indeed, they assert most evangelicals have a "weak ecclesiology" characterized by a "minimalist view of God's role for the church in his plan of salvation," an emphasis on the individual Christian, a view of the church as a vehicle for nurturing the indi-

States, with its inherent individualism (a decidedly me-and-Jesus approach to spirituality), offers little in terms of theology and practice to help Quiverfull families resist the pull into family-focused isolation. Within the evangelical tradition, church is a voluntary organization not essential to one's personal relationship with Jesus Christ. Like their evangelical neighbors, Quiverfull families imagine that they have direct, unmediated access to Christ and the sacraments of baptism and the Lord's Supper. For some, there is little need for a church because they, as a family, are a church. In this context, it is easy to see why some Quiverfull families come to prioritize their family's pursuit of holiness in the home over the necessity of communion with other Christians. If the church only exists as a conglomeration of individual Christians, then it is an optional aspect of the Christian life.[84]

Another contributing factor to the eclipse of the church in Quiverfull theology and practice can be traced to the "culture war" mentality of American evangelicalism over the past several decades. As evangelicals face the dissolution of their power in the cultural and political centers of American life, many have responded by retreating into the nuclear family. When all institutions, even churches, are viewed as having capitulated to secularism, feminism, and a variety of other -isms, then the private family is all that remains for Christians to control. For many, especially those in the Quiverfull movement, the nuclear family has become the last bastion of resistance against the onslaught of secularism in America. Christian Smith calls this a "lifestyle evangelism" approach. Rather than seek to change culture from the top down through institutions, they look to the witness of the family and face-to-face encounters, trusting in individual Christians to transform America.[85] The Quiverfull movement has solidified such evangelical inclinations in significant ways.[86]

---

vidual, and an emphasis on the "universal" and "invisible" nature of the church to the detriment of the "local" and "visible" church (295n11).

84. For a more detailed discussion of privatization in American religion, especially conservative Protestantism, see Stephen Hart, "Privatization in American Religion," *Sociological Analysis* 47, no. 4 (1987): 319–34. For a consideration of the impact of American consumerism on religious practice, as well as the cultural significance and impact of the single-family home on American religion, see Vincent J. Miller, *Consuming Religion: Christian Faith and Practice in a Consumer Culture* (New York: Bloomsbury Academic, 2005).

85. Christian Smith, *Christian America? What Evangelicals Really Want* (Berkeley: University of California Press, 2000), 92–128.

86. A final factor that might be considered in the Quiverfull eclipse of the church is the practical concern of families that their children be welcome in worship. Many churches unfamiliar with Quiverfull practice have difficulty welcoming their many children. When Quiverfull

Therefore, in place of the church, which is often considered unhealthy or unbiblical, Quiverfull families seek to remake the home into a church. In *The Way Home*, Pride calls women to view the home as their church and primary place of Christian service:

> Christians have a wide-open market for the genuine, unadulterated product of a truly Christian home. Those agitating for ordination for women are throwing away with both hands the biggest ministry we could ever have in favor of a mere second-rate shadow. . . . What a day it will be when all God's women return to homeworking and every wife has a church in her home.[87]

Carley Miller explicitly says that this is her aim: "I think [the purpose of the family] is to model the relationship between Christ and the church and also to be the church. I think we can glorify the Lord together as a family. . . . I guess kind of like a mini-church. We want to serve the Lord as a family." In pursuit of a "mini-church" in the home, Quiverfull families use practices that we have already reviewed in some depth. Homeschooling allows them to pursue their children's education from within an explicitly Christian worldview and incorporate instruction in the Bible and spiritual disciplines into their curriculum. Family worship brings the family together under the father's leadership to sing, pray, read scripture, and receive instruction. Also, the Olsons and Millers often have worship music playing throughout the day. All three families have Christian-themed art hanging in their homes, usually accompanied by Bible verses.

As we saw in chapter 1, this is not the first time in history that evangelicals have sought to create a domestic church. The sacralization of the home and family is an ongoing theme of American evangelical religion. What's different about this instantiation is the central role played by the father (at least symbolically if not in practice). Whereas Victorian-era attempts to create a domestic church were overseen by the virtuous mother, the contemporary Quiverfull movement seeks to create a family church led by the virtuous father. So, at the same time that Quiverfull discourse seeks to make the family home into sacred space, they are also seeking to solidify the authority of the father within a traditionally feminine space.

While the problems of privatization and isolation are evident in

---

families feel that their children aren't included in worship, such families often withdraw from church. This further weakens their ecclesiology and sacramental theology.

87. Pride, *The Way Home*, 202.

the lives of most American families today, the Quiverfull discourse exacerbates this tendency. Most Americans struggle to see beyond the bounds of the family home, but Quiverfull families experience this isolation even more acutely. Very often, this isolation has an impact on their connectedness to the church. Already inclined to a weak ecclesiology because of their evangelical heritage, Quiverfull families often find themselves without good reason for church participation. Theologically and practically, the nuclear family comes to eclipse or even replace the church.

The Home as Sinless Space

Another result of Quiverfull theology and practice is that the home is often imagined as a sinless space. When the family is filled with great theological and eschatological import, idealized beyond the on-the-ground reality, and isolated from surrounding people and institutions, it is difficult to recognize the family as a sinful and even potentially dangerous place.[88] The home is imagined as a holy haven from sin and temptation, both of which are located "out there" in the world. Certainly, Quiverfull families cannot be faulted for seeking personal holiness or an integrated Christian life in the home; but what about sin in the family? What about the ways that spouses sin against each other and parents sin against their children?

On the one hand, there are the daily, ordinary ways that family members sin against each other. Husbands and wives can be insensitive to each other's hurts and neglect each other's needs. Pride and defensiveness can make spouses quick to be offended and slow to apologize. Parents can be impatient, harsh, and unkind to their children, treating them as annoyances to be tolerated rather than gifts to be treasured. Children can speak heartbreaking words to their parents and take advantage of their provision and care. Families as a whole can participate in daily practices that perpetuate patterns of unkindness and disrespect. Indeed, because they are composed of flawed human beings, families are often the places where we are hurt in the deepest and most lasting ways. Even though these kinds of ordinary hurts constitute real violations of human dignity, they would not necessarily be considered abusive. All families experience such regular failures to love.

88. Thanks to Susan Trollinger for helping me think through the Quiverfull construction of the home as a sinless space.

Domestic violence and child abuse, on the other hand, are extreme instances of failure in the family. Domestic violence, also called intimate partner violence (IPV), is "a pattern of assaultive and coercive behaviors including physical, sexual, and psychological attacks, as well as economic coercion used by adults or adolescents against their current or former intimate partners." Sexual abuse includes coerced sex through threats or intimidation or through physical force. Psychological abuse involves isolation from others, excessive jealousy, control of activities, verbal aggression, intimidation through harassment or stalking, threats of violence, and constant belittling and humiliation.[89] Child abuse is "any recent act or failure to act on the part of a parent or caretaker, which results in death, serious physical or emotional harm, sexual abuse, or exploitation, or an act or failure to act which presents an imminent risk of serious harm."[90] The definition of child abuse includes physical abuse (typically defined as "any nonaccidental injury to a child"), neglect,[91] sexual abuse or exploitation, emotional abuse,[92] parental substance abuse, and abandonment.

Neither domestic violence nor child abuse is rare. Nearly one in every four American women between the ages of eighteen and sixty-five has experienced domestic violence.[93] On average, more than three women each day are murdered by their husbands or boyfriends.[94] Up to 10 million children are exposed to domestic violence annually.[95] In 2012, an estimated 686,000 children were victims

---

89. Mary Ellsberg and Lori Heise, *Researching Violence against Women: A Practical Guide for Researchers and Activists* (Washington, DC: World Health Organization, PATH, 2005), quoted in the UNICEF report, "Behind Closed Doors: The Impact of Domestic Violence on Children," 2006, http://tinyurl.com/y9zvhgg4.

90. Definition comes from the Child Abuse Prevention and Treatment Act (CAPTA) of 2010 (P.L. 111–320), § 3.2, http://tinyurl.com/ybtdb4xb.

91. Child neglect is defined as "the failure of a parent or other person with responsibility for the child to provide needed food, clothing, shelter, medical care, or supervision to the degree that the child's health, safety, and well-being are threatened with harm." Twenty-five states also include failure to educate the child as part of child neglect. See the Child Welfare Information Gateway, *Child Maltreatment 2012: Summary of Key Findings* (Washington, DC: US Department of Health and Human Services, Children's Bureau, 2014), http://tinyurl.com/yall7x2z.

92. Most states use the following language to describe emotional abuse of a child: "injury to the psychological capacity or emotional stability of the child as evidenced by an observable or substantial change in behavior, emotional response, or cognition" and injury as evidenced by "anxiety, depression, withdrawal, or aggressive behavior." See the Child Welfare Information Gateway, *Child Maltreatment 2012*.

93. Center for Disease Control and Prevention, "Intimate Partner Violence: Consequences," March 3, 2015, http://tinyurl.com/aebay8t.

94. Callie Marie Rennison, "Intimate Partner Violence, 1993-2001," *Bureau of Justice Statistics Crime Data Brief*, February 2003, http://tinyurl.com/ycsdaw97.

95. Albert R. Roberts, ed., *Battered Women and Their Families* (New York: Springer, 2007).

of abuse and neglect nationwide; an estimated 1,640 children died due to abuse or neglect and more than 80 percent of child abuse perpetrators are parents.[96] These statistics only encompass *reported* cases of abuse. Many more cases go unreported.

From the work of Quiverfull elites, however, you would never know domestic violence or child abuse constitute prevalent problems. In Quiverfull materials, the family is idealized such that if Christian couples would only surrender their fertility to the Lord, their home would immediately become a virtuous refuge from the sinful world. Mother and father are almost always imagined in ideal terms: an always patient, always gentle, educator-mother working in perfect harmony with the always supportive, always godly father-leader. Remember, "A family shepherd would never abuse his children."[97] And children, blessings given directly by God, are never understood to be burdensome. If you're doing family the "right" way, you won't have any serious problems.

But the truth is, mothers and fathers are often deeply flawed, and children, particularly in their more dependent years, are often difficult. The work of organizing and running a household is laborious and demanding, taxing even the most earnest Christians. Altogether, these challenges are hard on any family, but for a large homeschooling family, often living in isolation, the hardship can become unbearable. In their neglect of the real weaknesses within the nuclear family and the threats these weaknesses pose to women and children, Quiverfull elites fail to consider the lived experiences of the families they claim to support.

My informants did not indicate any sign of abuse at the hands of their husbands, nor did I perceive any signs of abuse in their children. (Of course, I cannot be certain that abuse has not occurred. But, after meeting in person multiple times and talking, on average, once a month for two years, I would expect some evidence of abuse to arise, whether mental, emotional, economic, or physical. So far, nothing has materialized.) But it is clear my informants perceive threats to women and children's welfare existing beyond the bounds of the home. That is to say, none of the women in my research were keen to recognize the home as a potentially dangerous place for women and children. The concern for familial autonomy and

---

96. Child Welfare Information Gateway, *Child Maltreatment 2012*.
97. Baucham, *Family Shepherds*, 144.

"parental rights" seems to constrain their ability to imagine families as potentially harmful.

Every person I interviewed from Quiverfull families could point to at least one family where they claim to know abuse is taking place—some more than one. Elizabeth Harris, an adult daughter of a Quiverfull family, shared the following from her experience:

> [The church we attended] got weirder and weirder over the years. It attracted more and more dysfunctional people. At first the families were pretty healthy but the ideas attracted people who were really sick and had sick relationships. I saw that those ideas attracted those kinds of people. And we had a family that looked perfect on the outside but then the wife just disappeared and went into hiding from her husband. And it turns out that the guy all of us thought was mild mannered was actually a verbal and physical abuser. And my church was trying to deal with the problem but it was all very much in the church. But, I felt like that was a pattern: people would look fine on the outside and then everything would fall apart and they'd be nothing like they appeared.

Indeed, over the past several years an increasing number of stories have emerged from journalists and amateur journalist-bloggers, detailing numerous instances of abusive behavior in Quiverfull homes. Many such stories involve spousal abuse of wives by their patriarch husbands.[98] Natalie Klejwa runs the popular blog *Visionary Womanhood* and also edited the book for Quiverfull mothers *Three Decades of Fertility*. On January 1, 2015 she announced on her blog that her husband has been living apart from their family since September 2014. His departure was at Natalie's request following twenty-two years of abusive behavior.[99] Since that announcement, Natalie has offered numerous posts aimed at helping Christian women identify and address various forms of abuse in their relationships. Natalie's story is not an isolated incident, however. Vyckie Garrison's important blog, *No Longer Quivering*, has numerous contributors who tell similar stories.[100] Speaking of Garrison's blog, Natalie Klejwa says frankly, "I'm glad they are raising awareness . . .

---

98. *No Longer Quivering* is a blog on the Patheos Network run by former Quiverfull mother, Vyckie Garrison, who was a victim of abuse. Her blog has numerous ex-Quiverfull contributors with similar stories (http://tinyurl.com/y7xyvg5j).

99. Natalie Klejwa, "What I Didn't Tell You about in 2014," *Visionary Womanhood*, January 1, 2015, http://tinyurl.com/y7kj7c95.

100. See Vyckie Garrison, "Voices," *No Longer Quivering*, http://tinyurl.com/yanbnxft.

of an insidious evil disguised as holiness.... It's disgusting. It should make us all want to vomit. That's the truth. That's reality."[101]

In addition to stories of spousal abuse are cases of child abuse. Because of the lack of formal leadership and organization, there is no way to know in concrete terms the number of child abuse cases within Quiverfull families. The Coalition for Responsible Home Education (CRHE) runs a website, Homeschooling's Invisible Children (HIC), that tracks cases of child abuse and neglect among homeschooling families.[102] The site has reported several hundreds of such cases dating back to 1986. The site is devoted to abuse in all homeschooling families, regardless of their religious or ideological reasons for homeschooling. Certainly not all the cases reported by HIC involve Quiverfull families, but many do.

The most extreme examples of abuse in Quiverfull families have made national news. At least three children have died.[103] Hana Williams, the daughter of Larry and Carri Williams, was adopted from Ethiopia when she was thirteen years old. One of nine children in the Williamses' Quiverfull family, she was homeschooled exclusively. On May 11, 2011, Hana died of hypothermia in the family's backyard after spending several hours in the rain. The coroner determined that because she was regularly denied food as punishment for misbehavior, her abnormally low weight prevented her from retaining heat in the cold. By their own admission, the Williamses were attempting to "train" their adoptive daughter using the book *To Train Up a Child* by Michael and Debi Pearl.[104] Larry Williams was

101. See Klejwa, "Escaping Duggarville with My Faith Intact." She has also written sympathetically of the *No Longer Quivering* blog in her post, "Escaping Duggarville with My Faith Intact," *Visionary Womanhood*, February 2, 2015, http://tinyurl.com/yd9t2p8p.
102. From the website: "Homeschooling's Invisible Children (HIC) operates under the oversight of the Coalition for Responsible Home Education (CRHE). HIC works to catalogue horrific cases of abuse and neglect and raise awareness on this issue while CRHE works to educate and promote the need for adequate safeguards for at-risk children who are homeschooled." See the Coalition for Responsible Homeschooling, http://www.responsiblehomeschooling.org/, and Homeschooling's Invisible Children, http://hsinvisiblechildren.org/.
103. See Kathryn Joyce, "Hana Williams: The Tragic Death of an Ethiopian Adoptee, and How It Could Happen Again," *Slate*, November 9, 2013, http://tinyurl.com/p6kg8ts. So far there are two other cases of child death associated with the Pearls' teachings. Lydia Schatz, the adopted daughter of Kevin and Elizabeth Schatz, died after being spanked for several hours with a quarter-inch diameter plastic tube (Edecio Martinez, "DA: Kevin and Elizabeth Schatz Killed Daughter with 'Religious Whips' for Mispronouncing Word," *CBS News*, February 22, 2010, http://tinyurl.com/ya7vq5s4). Sean Paddock, son of Lynn Paddock, suffocated to death after his mother swaddled him too tightly in a blanket for several hours (Amanda Lamb, "Adoptive Mother Convicted in Boy's Death," *WRAL.com*, June 12, 2008, http://tinyurl.com/y9g4jjqz).
104. In each case of child death referenced above, the parents were using the Pearls' book *To Train Up a Child*. The Pearls, for their part, deny that their teachings lead to child abuse

convicted of manslaughter, with a twenty-eight-year sentence, and Carri Williams of homicide by abuse, with a thirty-seven-year sentence.

In addition to such stories of child abuse, three high-profile Quiverfull leaders have been exposed as abusers in the past few years. Thirty-four women have accused Bill Gothard of habitual harassment and molestation over the forty years of his ministry's operation.[105] While Gothard has resigned and admits to some "wrong" behavior that "crossed the boundaries of discretion," he denies charges of harassment and molestation.[106]

In the fall of 2013, Doug Phillips, head of Vision Forum, Inc. and Vision Forum Ministries, was forced to resign and close his organizations due to what he called a "lengthy, inappropriate relationship" with a young woman who worked for his family.[107] The woman in question, Lourdes Torres, filed a lawsuit against Phillips accusing him of sexual battery, fraud, and sexual exploitation, claiming that he used her as his "personal sex object" from 1999 to 2012.[108] She also claims that Phillips manipulated her and abused his authority over her. In the words of the civil suit:

> Phillips was the dominant authority figure in Ms. Torres's life and family. He made himself her spiritual father. He was her authority figure with regard to where she lived, where she worked, where and how she worshipped, her education, her interpersonal relationships, her time and schedule, and even acted as her counselor. In other words, Phillips was the pastor of her church, her boss, her landlord, and the controller of all aspects of her life—obedience to Phillips was as obedience to God.[109]

and say that the parents in each of these cases were not properly following their instructions. See Michael Pearl, "Hana Williams' Death: Official Statement," No Greater Joy Ministries, http://tinyurl.com/ybag553t.

105. The operators of the website and blog *Recovering Grace* carried out most of the work of exposing Gothard's ongoing abuse. Their files on Gothard, along with the stories of his thirty-four accusers, can be found in "The Gothard Files: A Case for Disqualification," February 3, 2014, http://tinyurl.com/yccrkf5k.

106. Gothard says, "My actions of holding of hands, hugs, and touching of feet or hair with young ladies crossed the boundaries of discretion and were wrong. They demonstrated a double-standard and violated a trust. Because of the claims about me I do want to state that I have never kissed a girl nor have I touched a girl immorally or with sexual intent" (Bill Gothard, "A Statement from Bill Gothard," BillGothard.com, April 17, 2014, http://tinyurl.com/ybp28oy8).

107. Douglas Phillips, "Statement of Resignation," Vision Forum Ministries, October 30, 2013, http://tinyurl.com/y9dp2xff. Although the content of the Vision Forum Ministries (VFM) website has been completely dismantled, Phillips's two public statements remain, along with two statements from the VFM Board.

108. The explicit allegations against Phillips, detailed in the civil suit *Lourdes Torres-Manteufel v. Douglas Phillips et al.* are disturbing. See David C. Gibbs, Esq., "Civil Case Information Sheet," April 15, 2014, http://tinyurl.com/y8luh7sw.

109. "Facts" in the Civil Case Information Sheet for "Lourdes Torres-Manteufel v. Douglas

Then, in 2015 it came to light that Josh Duggar, the oldest child of "Quiverfull royalty" Jim Bob and Michelle Duggar, sexually molested five girls when he was a teenager in 2002 (four sisters and a babysitter). The Duggars attempted to handle the matter within the family and, when that didn't work, went to their church's elders. After a year of multiple incidences, the Duggars consulted a police officer who was also a family friend. Though the police interviewed the victims, they did nothing further with the accusations. Josh was sent to do manual labor for three months with a family associate. When his past crimes came to light, Josh apologized publicly for his wrongdoing and resigned from his post with the Family Research Council. Eventually, it also came out that Josh was simultaneously carrying on extramarital affairs with multiple partners using, among other things, the notorious *Ashley Madison* website.[110]

For their part, Jim Bob and Michelle Duggar have repeatedly downplayed Josh's molestation of their daughters, saying Josh was "just curious about girls."[111] The Duggars treated Josh's actions as personal sins to be corrected rather than crimes against the girls in their care. Thus it took them over a year to act decisively to end the abuse. Then, when they did act, they did not send Josh for professional help because they were too worried the people he would encounter in counseling or therapy for sex offenders would be a detrimental influence.[112] Not only did they focus on Josh's sin rather than the girls' victimization, they also remained convinced that the "real" evil is located "out there," beyond the bounds of the home. Despite the fact that Josh was molesting young girls, his parents were primarily concerned that he not be polluted by the negative influence of outsiders.

Of course, we should not assume that the different cases of abuse detailed above are indicative of the Quiverfull movement as a whole. Certainly not all Quiverfull families are abusive to women and

---

Phillips et al.," 5.18. Phillips denies these allegations, saying that their relationship was mutual and consensual and that she is trying to destroy him and his family.

110. See Josh Duggar's statement on this matter at their family website: http://tinyurl.com/ya99npbo.

111. Abby Olheiser, "Josh Duggar Molested Four of His Sisters and a Babysitter," *Washington Post*, June 4, 2015, http://tinyurl.com/oga4lc7.

112. This is according to the statement given in the police report on the case: "James said that one of the elders was a chaplain at the Piney Ridge program at Vista Hospital. James said that they had concerns about the program at Piney Ridge because they felt [Josh] might be exposed to other offenders and other things that they did not want him exposed to." See the entire police report, dated May 19, 2015, with names of the victims redacted: http://imgur.com/a/zqPMi#14. A timeline of the matter is provided by Mary Bowerman, *USA Today*, "Timeline: Duggar Sex Abuse Scandal," May 25, 2015, http://tinyurl.com/y8lf3n45.

children. I am sure most are not. Domestic abuse in the United States is a problem that crosses the categories of religion, race, and class. Even so, there is no doubt that in all of the above cases both patriarchal ideology and social isolation played a major part in the perpetuation of abuse. Numerous studies show that instances of spousal and child abuse are closely connected to social isolation.[113] The social isolation of a family can be the result of a lack of social skills, poor contact with others, the avoidance of contact, or the lack of transportation or methods of communication (i.e., internet and telephone). And, in Quiverfull families, the isolation of mother and children can be the indirect consequence of pronatalist and homeschooling practices.[114] But, no matter the source, scholars agree: "Social isolation is a risk factor for domestic violence, especially because it entails a lack of social support."[115]

I argue in chapter 3 that the isolation of Quiverfull mothers exacerbates their vulnerability, leaving them open to abuse. The same is true of children. Children need advocates outside the immediate family because, among other things, they can provide protected channels through which children can make complaints and contact the right institutions for intervention if needed.[116] At the very least, children who attend brick and mortar schools or participate in church or other outside activities, come into contact with people not related to them who could serve as advocates. The Quiverfull tendency to encourage strict separation from "the world," resulting in isolation from broader networks of support, thereby becomes deeply problematic. As the theologian Adrian Thatcher warns: "The family . . . cannot be isolated

---

113. See, for example, Kristin A. Kelly, *Domestic Violence and the Politics of Privacy* (Ithaca, NY: Cornell University Press, 2002); Annemie Dillen, ed., *When 'Love' Strikes: Social Sciences, Ethics, and Theology on Family Violence* (Leuven: Peeters, 2009).

114. In a recent report from Homeschooling's Invisible Children (HIC), the following claim is made: "Our preliminary research suggests that homeschooled children are at a greater risk of dying from child abuse than are traditionally schooled children. This preliminary finding is based on an analysis of the cases in our Homeschooling's Invisible Children (HIC) database and on national government reports on child maltreatment. When we compare the rate of child abuse fatalities among homeschooled families to the rate of child abuse fatalities overall, we see a higher rate of death due to abuse or neglect among homeschooled students than we do among children of the same age overall" (HIC, "Some Preliminary Data on Homeschool Child Fatalities," http://tinyurl.com/y9lm283e).

115. Annemie Dillen, "Domestic Violence and an Integral Family Ethic," in *When 'Love' Strikes*, 349.

116. Anderson and Johnson, *Regarding Children*, 59–60.

from wider, caring influences. . . . Families can be pernicious, evil places for children."[117]

Quiverfull elites never entertain the possibility that the privatized nuclear family might be ill equipped to handle the pressures that their religious practice entails in contemporary America. Theologian Don Browning has written at length about the problems that modernization poses for marriage and the nuclear family. He says,

> The forces of modernity themselves may help cause domestic violence. . . . [T]echnical rationality tend[s] to reduce parts of life to efficient means toward short-term satisfactions and function to undermine the cohesion producing interdependence of families, civil societies, and communities of faith. Under the impact of modernization, the regulation of sexual, marital, and family life decreases as communities of tradition deteriorate. Sexual exploitation and violence tend to increase throughout society. . . . But modernity also creates dramatic divisions in society between the rich and poor, between those who are educated to handle the tools of technical reason in an increasingly digital society and those who cannot. Poverty is clearly associated with domestic violence, especially those poor who are also alienated from supportive and culture building communities of tradition.[118]

For all their interest in changing the way American Christians receive the gift of children, Quiverfull teachers ignore the ways that the family as it has been constructed over the past century may not be capable of sustaining their religious practice. Though the nuclear family has been the dominant model within American Christianity since at least the Victorian period, it has proven to be a relatively weak structure.[119] As the United States has undergone a plethora of social, economic, and cultural shifts in the past hundred years, the nuclear family has become less and less stable. This is not due to a lack of principles—most Americans still view the nuclear family as the ideal family form—but because of the dissolution of broader social and institutional structures of support along with declining economic opportunities and stability in the American workforce. And now Quiverfull

---

117. Adrian Thatcher, *Theology and Families*, Challenges in Contemporary Theology (Oxford: Wiley-Blackwell, 2007), 166.

118. Don Browning, "Toward a Family Ethic of Equal-Regard," in *When 'Love' Strikes*, 138.

119. Vincent Miller rightly suggests the weakness of the American nuclear family stands in stark contrast to the strength of the patriarchal family and the rules of kinship that are assumed in Josh 24:15: "as for me and my house, we will serve the Lord." Quiverfull proponents rarely if ever give any attention to the social and cultural differences between the context of such passages of scripture and the context of families in the present day.

elites want to shore it up by making the family numerically larger, giving it more work to do, and investing it with even more theological and eschatological import. This impulse is understandable, perhaps, but ultimately misguided.

A number of factors contribute to Quiverfull's problematic construction of the home as a sinless space. Their idealization of the family—what I have called the "family blueprint"—is a key part of the problem. When abiding by a particular form of the family is understood as the key to holiness and God's blessing, the occlusion of sin is more likely to occur. Ideal appearances too easily become more important than virtuous practices. As I suggested above, instead of prioritizing a particular family form, a better approach is to focus on family functions. The words of Anderson and Johnson are particularly apt at this point:

> The family has endured in part because it has adapted to changing needs and circumstances. Moreover, structures of the family have changed over centuries and will continue to change while its purposes have remained more constant. We assume that a family is what it does. This idea that form follows function is a theological reality as well as an architectural principle. Christian teaching has more to say about what families must do than what they should look like.[120]

But, what is the purpose of the family? And what does the family do for its members? Assuming the presence of children, Anderson and Johnson suggest several things: they feed and protect children; they embody safety as a sign that shelter is possible; they provide attention for children befitting each age group; they offer the enduring involvement of at least one adult in ongoing care; they give developmentally appropriate expectations for behavior; they provide role models for adulthood; and they show respect for personal boundaries.[121] But, there is more to be said from within the Christian tradition. I have already mentioned the writings of John Paul II and his four major tasks for the family, none of which include abiding by a gender- or age-based hierarchy.[122] Christian theologians also have to be attentive to the inevitable sin and failure within families. All families "have problems, face crises, cope with stress, struggle with illness, manage complicated situations. They may even have to endure

---

120. Anderson and Johnson, *Regarding Children*, 48.
121. Anderson and Johnson, *Regarding Children*, 49–56.
122. Pope John Paul II, *Familiaris Consortio*, no. 17, 37, 42, 44, 49–64.

tragedy." But, as Anderson and Johnson explain, "Coping effectively with a crisis, or assisting a family member during a time of upheaval, is, in fact, what it means to be family. Even when outside help is needed, the family may still be a crucible of coping. A family's success or failure is measured by its ability to cope."[123]

Any idealized family form, whether Quiverfull or otherwise, is prone to disruption and failure. Most families do not fail so catastrophically as to produce abuse and neglect, but fail they certainly will. As Rubio reminds us, we must "hold grace and sin together" in any conversation about the family.[124] Indeed, there is an "already-not-yet" dynamic within the Christian family. As John Paul II suggests, the family is *already* a community of love, a location of God's grace simply by virtue of its existence. But, at the same time, the family is a flawed and sinful institution marked by human failings, *not yet* fully what it should be. In the pope's words, "There is no family that does not know how selfishness, discord, tension and conflict violently attack and at times mortally wound its own communion: hence there arise the many and varied forms of division in family life."[125] Or, as Klejwa says simply, "All families sin and they do it every day in numerous ways."[126] Both grace and sin are present, and not always in equal portions.[127] Because of the inevitability of failure and the prevalence of domestic violence and child abuse today, it is vitally important that theologies of the family bear this context in mind.

Some Quiverfull families already know how to do this. Despite the idealized Quiverfull blueprint extant in her subculture, Carley has no delusions of perfection. She describes their life together as a work in progress: "Since we started our family years ago, we've changed. We've stopped doing things that aren't working and started doing things that are working. We don't just do things because we're part of this movement. We grow and change depending on what works." For Carley, the most important thing is learning to love and serve God as a family. And part of pursuing that goal is reckoning with how family members fail each other. When I ask her to describe her

---

123. Anderson and Johnson, *Regarding Children*, 57.
124. Rubio, *Family Ethics*, 73.
125. Pope John Paul II, *Familiaris Consortio*, no. 21.
126. Natalie Klejwa, "Eternal Treasure," in *Three Decades of Fertility* (Saint Paul, MN: Visionary Womanhood, 2013), 88.
127. As Joan Heaney Hunter says, "God builds on the imperfections present in every family life, and makes it holy" (Hunter, "Toward a Eucharistic Spirituality of the Family: Blessed, Broken, and Shared," in *Marriage in the Catholic Tradition*, ed. Todd A. Salzman, Thomas M. Kelly, and John J. O'Keefe [New York: Crossroad, 2004], 132).

family, she says "big" (accompanied by raucous laughter), "young" ("I feel like we're still learning"), and "open" or "vulnerable." She says, "We offer grace and forgiveness because we aren't perfect—none of us. And as much as I forgive my kids, I hope they forgive me, because I'm flawed, too."

CONCLUSION

The Quiverfull movement envisions a divinely ordained form of the family, organized mainly by gender- and age-based roles within the home. The Quiverfull vision of the family also includes a strong sense of familial privacy and autonomy such that the family is disconnected from other communities and institutions. Quiverfull practitioners believe the family has four major functions: (1) to faithfully fulfill God's design for family roles; (2) to bear, raise, and educate Christian children; (3) to evangelize and disciple others through the home; and (4) to transform America and advance the kingdom of God. These are broad brushstrokes, but they make up the major pieces of the Quiverfull construction of the family.

The Quiverfull family form operates as a "blueprint," and theologian Nicholas Healy helps us recognize the problems with such blueprints. Put simply, theological blueprints are systematic and theoretical models, which are disconnected from local environments and the experiences of real people. Despite protestations to the contrary, the Quiverfull family blueprint is a historically and culturally conditioned ideal with roots in the Victorian period and based upon a selective reading of scripture and Christian tradition. Thus, the Quiverfull blueprint shares with all other theological blueprints a deficit of both particularity and practicality.

Moreover, the Quiverfull blueprint itself has some specific problems. First, the excessive privatization of the Quiverfull family often leads to families that are disconnected from broader communities. Isolation is a common problem for Quiverfull mothers and their children. Also, the singular focus on the family often leads to an eclipse of ecclesiology and deficit of ecclesial involvement. For many in the Quiverfull movement, the nuclear family has eclipsed or even replaced the church. Finally, the Quiverfull family blueprint often leads to the construction of the home as a sinless space. In cases where family isolation is acute, the inability to recognize sin in the home can contribute to the suppression of neglect, exploitation, and violence. Quiverfull families want a pure, fully integrated Christian family where everything is holy and Christian formation is central. And they desire an insulated and autonomous family that is yet able to have a broad social, cultural, and even global impact for the kingdom of God. Despite their lofty goals, however, the Quiverfull movement produces an idealization of the family that leads to social isolation, the eclipse of the church, and, in some cases, the cover-up of sin.

Conclusion

It is a maxim of American evangelicalism that Christians must be "in the world but not of the world." Although not a direct quote from scripture, this sentiment is based upon the words of Jesus in John 17:14–19, where he prays the following for his disciples:

> I have given them your word, and the world has hated them because they are not of the world, just as I am not of the world. I do not ask that you take them out of the world, but that you keep them from the evil one. They are not of the world, just as I am not of the world. Sanctify them in the truth; your word is truth. As you sent me into the world, so I have sent them into the world. And for their sake I consecrate myself, that they also may be sanctified in truth.

The biblical source notwithstanding, evangelicals mean many things when they say Christians should be "in the world but not of the world." Some mean that Christians should "fit in" among their non-Christian neighbors in minor matters like appearance and lifestyle, but should stand out in major matters like personal morality, family, and career choices. Carley expresses this perspective when she criticizes Christian women who intentionally wear modest, outdated clothing in order to stand out from the crowd. She thinks that kind of stylistic differentiation is unnecessarily alienating to non-Christians. When she says Christians should be "in the world but not of the world," she means that Christian women should wear fashionable, up-to-date clothing provided it doesn't violate their conscience. At the same time, when someone of a more separatist persuasion says Christians should be "in the world but not of the world," they mean that even though Christians are residents of the world, they should separate themselves from the world's pleasures and any "worldly" people who indulge in them. Renee seems to have had this point of view early on in her life when she chose to keep her children out of their church's youth group so as not to risk their exposure to ungodly, corrupting influences. No matter how stringently or loosely it is interpreted, the "in the world and not of the world" adage expresses well a core tension of American evangelical religion: withdrawal from culture versus engagement with and transformation of culture.

But the claim that Christians must be "in the world but not of the world" is almost always based on the assumption that it is possible to refrain from being "of the world" at all. In truth, no Christian community can escape being "of the world" entirely—that is, a product of their time and place with a way of life constructed in relationship with the surrounding culture. There is no pure, self-contained Christian community that exists autonomously from culture. Christian identity is inherently relational, constantly emerging at the boundaries of the community, drawing on and modifying the cultural materials and practices they share with their non-Christian neighbors.[1] In fact, there's a sense in which Christian communities *need* the surrounding culture from which to construct its alternative way of life, distinct in some ways and similar in other ways. In the words of Kathryn Tanner, "A Christian way of life . . . has to establish relations with other ways of life, it has to take from them in order to be one itself."[2] This observation is no less true of American evangelicals and the Quiverfull subculture within it.

As I have shown, the Quiverfull movement is a form of evangelical lived religion struggling to construct a distinctive practice of the family within the cultural environment of twenty-first-century America. In the end, even though Quiverfull represents in some ways an unconventional evangelical practice of the family, they remain very much embedded in the American culture they purport to challenge. They are, despite protests to the contrary, very much "in the world *and* of the world"—a thoroughly evangelical and thoroughly American phenomenon.

Framed in this way, I suggest there are a few ways to interpret, on a macro level, what is happening in the Quiverfull movement. Each of the following interpretations involves reference to some

---

1. Kathryn Tanner, *Theories of Culture: A New Agenda for Theology* (Minneapolis: Fortress Press, 1997), 115.
2. Tanner, *Theories of Culture*, 113.

major features of evangelical history and the particular details of how Quiverfull discourse functions on the ground. I am not suggesting we must choose only one of these points of view; rather, each of them sheds light on Quiverfull as an instance of evangelical lived religion in America.

One way to understand Quiverfull is as a kind of reforming or purifying movement within American evangelicalism. As Amy DeRogatis suggests in her book *Saving Sex*, there's a sense in which Quiverfull practitioners are attempting a purification of evangelical practice as it pertains to sex and reproduction.[3] Indeed, they take the conservative Christian pro-life commitment and put it into practice in a thoroughgoing way. They are against not only the practice of abortion but also any and all attempts to control reproduction. They see Quiverfull as a truly consistent pro-life practice. In support of this perspective, Quiverfull authors directly challenge mainstream evangelical writings on sex and marriage. As DeRogatis notes, they do so first by disconnecting marriage from romance and sex-for-pleasure and then by insisting on the unqualified sexual submission of wives to husbands.[4] In contrast to their mainstream evangelical peers, Quiverfull practitioners believe that truly pious believers "demonstrate their faith through large families and the knowledge that marriage is about self-sacrifice and not sexual pleasure."[5] I would add that their commitment to gender hierarchy and homeschooling are also part of this purer evangelical piety. While almost all evangelicals espouse what could be called pro-life, pro-family, and antifeminist ideas, Quiverfull families press in to this ideology and seek to embody it in a comprehensive and thoroughgoing way.

Viewed as a purist movement within American evangelicalism, it becomes clear how Quiverfull practitioners set themselves apart from Americans in general and evangelicals in particular. Their practice creates firm boundaries between the (perceived) faithful and unfaithful. Of course, comparatively few families in America identify with their way of life, which leads to the perspective that they represent a divinely ordained faithful remnant. But are they really as different as they appear? The answer, as we have seen, is yes and no. Certainly, they set themselves apart by their focus on "multigenerational faith-

---

3. Amy DeRogatis, *Saving Sex: Sexuality and Salvation in American Evangelicalism* (Oxford: Oxford University Press, 2014), 107.
4. DeRogatis, *Saving Sex*, 107.
5. DeRogatis, *Saving Sex*, 127.

fulness" and willingness to raise a large family toward that end. Most American families do not live on the father's income alone and most American women do not have more than two children. Also, despite its popularity, most American families do not homeschool their children, and the ones who do homeschool only do so for a limited time period. Cultivating a large family, living on one income, and educating all their children at home—in all these ways Quiverfull families are setting themselves apart from American society through a more rigorous form of evangelical piety.

At the same time, there are ways that the Quiverfull discourse is very much in harmony with dominant American social norms. Americans generally value and romanticize pregnancy and motherhood. Media coverage of celebrity mothers has made it somewhat "cool" to be pregnant, breastfeed, and mother children.[6] Parenting, in general, is becoming more important to marriage as a practice of ultimate focus.[7] Americans have also come to accept homeschooling as a legitimate way of educating children such that homeschooling is no longer the strange, countercultural practice it once was. Many Americans now homeschool for a variety of reasons that have nothing to do with religion.[8] Also, even though the Quiverfull focus on children's spiritual formation sets them apart, the inward-looking concern for the success of their own children is by no means countercultural. Indeed, channeling the efforts of the nuclear family for the betterment of kin, even to the detriment of others, is mainstream American practice. Finally, despite the advances made in a variety of sectors, gender dualism persists in American culture. Certainly, it is no longer socially acceptable to say publicly things like, "Women belong in the home," or "Mothers should be in charge of the children." But these ideas persist nonetheless, albeit in less explicit ways. Sexist prejudices rooted in gender dualism are evident in the persistence of unequal pay, the dearth of adequate maternity and paternity

---

6. As long as you are beautiful, well put together, and svelte while doing so. There remains little room in the American cultural imagination for women who carry in their bodies the real physical effects of pregnancy and nursing. But, these expectations are the same in all other areas of activity as well. Certainly, women can do anything—mother children, run for office, head a Fortune 500 company, serve in the armed forces—as long as they are beautiful and sexually appealing. Women who fail to adhere to dominant standards of beauty, however, are unworthy of affirmation.

7. There is even a name for married couples who are totally focused on childrearing: HIP or heavy-investment parenting. See Richard V. Reeves, "How to Save Marriage in America," *The Atlantic*, February 13, 2014, http://tinyurl.com/y7llhm9e.

8. "Homeschooling in the United States: 2003: Statistical Analysis Report," National Center for Education Statistics, February 2006, http://tinyurl.com/y7n2pknb.

leave policies, the disproportionate domestic labor still shouldered by women, and more. Thus Quiverfull gender ideology is an intensification of persistent ideas about gender in America. Accordingly, Quiverfull can be understood as a purifying movement within evangelicalism that, like evangelicalism itself, creates the appearance of clear boundaries from American culture without going so far as to be genuinely countercultural.[9]

Another way to view the Quiverfull movement is as a kind of evangelical monasticism of the family. That is to say, Quiverfull families are attempting to create a lived religion within the home that is unified so that all of life is lived, in their words, "under the lordship of Christ."[10] Within a Protestant religious culture that generally dichotomizes the public and private, home and work, spiritual and secular, Quiverfull families are seeking an integrated Christian existence within the home where every aspect of life is sacred and oriented toward God.[11] Their practice of homeschooling is especially important in this regard. The hope is that all Quiverfull family members, especially those spending the most time in the home, will come to see all areas of life under the reach of Christian faith. Rather than a sacred-secular divide, where the divine is encountered in "religious" spaces but not in others, Quiverfull families try to order all of life under God and God's word. Thus, everything from schoolwork to ballet practice to pulling weeds is portrayed as an arena over which Christ is Lord. Even the homeschooling curriculum used by Quiverfull parents seeks to order academic knowledge under Christ's lordship so that everything from arithmetic to zoology is connected to scripture and Christian teaching. The effect of this unification is that Quiverfull lived religion renders all things potentially sacred.

While they do not have a "rule" like those of monastic orders, the daily lives of Quiverfull families evidence a combination of work and worship, labor and prayer, which are essential to such communities. Also, there are plentiful examples of self-denial and self-discipline as parents and children commit themselves to homeschooling and "homeworking" as the primary tools of their sanctification. Yet, rather than a community of celibates within an ecclesial and social

9. Christian Smith, *American Evangelicalism: Embattled and Thriving* (Chicago: University of Chicago Press, 1998), 119.
10. Monica Smatlak Liao, "Keeping Home: Homeschooling and the Practice of Conservative Protestant Identity" (PhD diss., Vanderbilt University, 2006), 61–116.
11. Thanks to Sandra Yocum for first offering this observation about Quiverfull similarity to monasticism.

context, the nuclear family in the private family home becomes the site of Christian formation and service. Viewed as a holy obligation of Christian parents and the organizing focus of family life, homeschooling inevitably leads to a version of Christianity that is domestically oriented. In this way, the domestic space is the site of religious instruction and the primary location for parents and children to live out their Christian convictions. This is especially true of Quiverfull daughters, most of whom are raised from very young to view the home as their proper sphere of "dominion" and the space in which they express their obedience to Christ. But, all family members are initiated into an instantiation of Christianity that is primarily domestic in orientation. And, as we have seen, this kind of domestic monasticism, focused as it is on the preservation of "multigenerational faithfulness," can have detrimental consequences for their ecclesiology.[12] In some cases, the church is replaced by the nuclear family, while in other cases, the church is simply subordinated to the family. Like some monastic movements of old, many Quiverfull families believe the church is in desperate need of reform, and their lived religion is the primary way to see that reform take place. Of course, just how American churches can be reformed by such family-focused efforts remains to be seen.

Yet, to view Quiverfull as a form of family monasticism may not do justice to the central place antifeminism and "biblical womanhood" occupies in their discourse. Chapter 3 made clear that a particular interpretation of gender is key to the Quiverfull subculture, which has important consequences for women. Quiverfull discourse provides an account of womanhood that is rooted solely in wifehood and motherhood. This mother-oriented account of womanhood is evidenced in their print and internet publications, reinforced in their

12. There is another factor worth mentioning here: selling "biblical family values" can be very profitable. US religious publishing and products is $6 billion industry, and homeschooling curriculum and resources constitute a $1 billion share of that market. As of 2010, there were approximately 2 million homeschoolers in America with an increasing rate of 7–15 percent every year (Brian D. Ray, "Homeschool Population Report 2010," National Home Education Research Institute, January 3, 2011, http://tinyurl.com/yddlfabs). Estimates are that each family spends $500 on curriculum per child (Vicki Bentley, "What Does It Cost to Homeschool?" HSLDA, Fall 2013, http://tinyurl.com/y7cqcaa2). Though not all families homeschool for religious reasons, a 2003 study by the National Center for Education Statistics shows that 30 percent of parents cite "religious or moral instruction" as their primary reason for homeschooling, while 72 percent cite "religious or moral instruction" as one reason for homeschooling ("Homeschooling in the United States: 2003," National Center for Education Statistics). Clearly, there is a lot of money to be made selling curriculum and other resources to such families, especially large families with six or more children. Quiverfull families, especially, see the purchase of such resources as a worthy investment.

cultural institutions (churches, networks, conferences), supported by their material culture (music, art, clothing), and embodied in their daily practice. Women in the "full quiver" perform this account of feminine identity through repeated pregnancies, extended breastfeeding, and a daily life organized around the care and instruction of children. To be sure, the practice of homeschooling allows some women to acquire a more professionalized identity as teacher and administrator of their children's education. But, it is a professionalized vocation that is entirely in keeping with the overarching construction of women as privatized, mothering subjects.[13] Mothers in Quiverfull families often garner significant cultural capital due to their perceived expertise in the care of the home and instruction of children. Even this is a double-edged sword, however. The power and authority given to mothers in the Quiverfull discourse reinforces an already-present American evangelical tendency toward the illusion of maternal omnipotence, an unattainable ideal that is forever beckoning and condemning mothers. Moreover, cultural capital cannot make up for lack of economic power. Were they to suffer the death of a spouse or the breakup of their marriage, Quiverfull mothers do not have the earning potential to be able to support their many children. In this way, despite the variety of ways Quiverfull women negotiate with and receive cultural capital from the notion of womanhood as the teachers and "keepers of the home," they remain limited by the overwhelmingly privatized, maternal character of female identity. Thus as we consider broader perspectives on Quiverfull within American society and evangelical culture, it is possible to understand Quiverfull as an antifeminist movement as well. In this respect, Quiverfull discourse is a forceful rejection of feminism (as they understand it) in both American society and evangelical religion.

A final way to view the Quiverfull movement as both thoroughly American and thoroughly evangelical is to see it as a part of the recent drift of conservative Christians into ever-increasing individualism.[14] Over the past couple of decades, some elements of libertarian political philosophy have begun to gain ground among Americans, especially conservative Protestants. In many ways, the American libertarian impulse to maximize autonomy and freedom of choice and protect the primacy of individual judgment blends well with the individu-

---

13. The practice of homeschooling also reinforces the gender dualism of evangelical Christianity. See Liao, "Keeping Home," 178–224.

14. For a fuller discussion of privatization within conservative Protestant homeschooling families, see Liao, "Keeping Home," 126–77.

alist impulses of evangelical Protestant Christianity. And there are a number of Quiverfull leaders today who are promoting libertarian approaches to American politics, including Voddie Baucham, Doug Phillips, and Geoffrey Botkin. Already skeptical of American government for its perceived secular, anti-Christian posture (a narrative inculcated by the politically conservative Religious Right), the libertarian commitment to individual liberty is magnified so that it applies to all areas of life. Religion, commerce, schooling, healthcare—everything becomes a matter of individual prerogative and choice.

But, what does this have to do with Quiverfull families on the ground? Certainly, the choice to keep one's children out of community schools and provide their education within the home is an individualistic and privatizing exercise. Most homeschooling families only have extended interaction with fellow homeschooling families within the context of co-operative events and gatherings. Put simply, they rarely interact with people not like them. The lack of cooperation with "government schools" reinforces the tendency of these conservative white evangelicals to see themselves as outsiders to American culture and people in desperate need of protecting their individual liberties. In the words of one homeschooling advocate, the rejection of public schools is an exercise of the "individual right to choose how you want to live, how and when you want to participate in 'the mainstream' culture, and especially how you want to raise your children."[15] Within this perspective, the choice to opt out of state schooling is an intentional rejection of social connectedness and obligation. But, as David Sessions has pointed out, this perspective doesn't represent political conservatism, but a new kind of anarchic ultra-individualism. In Sessions's words, "There is no conservatism without community, without traditions, institutions, rites of passage.... You can't magically create those things inside a single household."[16] And yet, many Quiverfull families are trying to do just that. Thus, Quiverfull discourse seems to constitute further isolation of conservative Christian families from American society, retreating from public cooperation into the individual choices of the nuclear family.

As we noted in chapter 5, the ultra-individualist denunciation of social connection and cooperation is matched among many

15. Georgi Boorman, "Americans Think School Is for Socializing," *The Federalist*, June 16, 2014, http://tinyurl.com/y7bxzvqz.

16. David Sessions, "When Reactionary Anarchism Meets Homeschooling," *Patrol Magazine*, June 16, 2014, http://tinyurl.com/y84fhfum.

Quiverfull families by an anemic ecclesiology and lack of ecclesial involvement. This is something that their own leaders acknowledge in explicit and implicit ways.[17] Without a developed ecclesiology or strong ecclesial cooperation, Quiverfull families see themselves as self-sufficient units, with parents (really, fathers) as the solitary figures responsible for the propagation of the faith. This is especially the case in families that view most American churches as beyond the pale in terms of correct theology and practice. If most churches fall short of God's ideal, then why bother participating at all? Thus, the (properly ordered) Christian family becomes the principal locus of religious observance and formation, and the church becomes an optional, voluntary institution that supports the private work of individual family units.

This privatized vision of the family has a number of detrimental outcomes, but the one that is most concerning is how the privatized family names and addresses sin. The practice of Christian homeschooling, which trades in language of "protection" and views parents as the highest God-ordained spiritual authorities, can lead to the obfuscation of sin in the household. Quiverfull families may not be well equipped to address the ways parents sin against their children or the fact that, for many women and children in American society, the family can be a dangerous place. If the family is considered a sacred, autonomous, self-sufficient haven from the sinful world, then it can become nearly impossible to address the breakdowns and failures that take place within it. Moreover, the lack of connection to the outside world leaves families with precious few resources to help when their burdens and conflicts exceed their ability to cope. Though many American families suffer in various ways from the effects of privatization and isolation, Quiverfull families represent an intensification of this larger trend, mostly due to their religious devotion to familial self-sufficiency in every respect.

All of the above interpretive perspectives on the Quiverfull movement help us to see that they are a thoroughly evangelical and American phenomenon. Quiverfull families are indeed "in the world *and* of the world." I hope this book has been sufficiently revelatory as to satisfy the curiosities of outsiders who view these families

17. In his book *Family Shepherds*, Voddie Baucham is compelled to devote an entire chapter to making the case for why church cooperation is even necessary for the biblical shepherd and his family. Meanwhile, Scott Brown and the National Center for Family Integrated Churches (NCFIC) have to devote a bulk of their attention to the conflicts between families and churches and the need for families to participate in church.

as cultural oddities on the American religious landscape. What truly sets them apart within American culture today are their thoroughgoing practices of gender hierarchy, homeschooling, and pronatalism. The women, in particular, with their fierce commitment to male headship and eagerness to bear "as many children as God gives," stand out as peculiarly countercultural. Also remarkable is the Quiverfull reorientation of the family around the Christian education and formation of children. I venture to guess few families today would be willing to sacrifice so much for the sake of passing on their faith to the next generation. In all of these ways and more, Quiverfull families are practicing a distinct lived religion within American evangelicalism today. I hope that this project has sufficiently and fairly rendered these distinctions intelligible to outsiders.

At another level, though, I have tried do more than simply explain an unusual contemporary religious movement. To view Quiverfull families merely as a religious curiosity is to miss something vitally important. In addition to rendering their practice intelligible, a close study of Quiverfull families reveals a way of life that reinforces and intensifies some distinctly American and evangelical habits. In this way, if we look closely into the lives of Quiverfull families many of us will see ourselves staring back. Their weaknesses are our weaknesses. Their blind spots are our blind spots. Their failures in imagination are our failures in imagination. Rather than offer a radical, countercultural vision for the Christian family, the Quiverfull movement presents a slightly modified version of something quite commonplace: a privatized, isolated nuclear family struggling (and often failing) to maintain their bonds to the broader community, the church, and other institutions.

Truth be told, the Quiverfull solution to crises facing American families today is a thoroughly private one that does not take into consideration broader social and economic factors. They, like many of us, remain caught in the same trap that caused the advances of second-wave feminism to flounder at the end of the twentieth century: an eclipse of the social and communal by a focus on the individual and private. Certainly, as a society Americans love to talk about the importance of motherhood, children, and the family. We publicly applaud those who prioritize their family or sacrifice for their children. But, we also remain unwilling to seek solutions to the problems of the family beyond the four walls of the private home. "As long as my family is doing okay," we say, "why should I worry about how the family is doing down the street?" We assume that if other families aren't thriving in the American meritocracy, it must be due to some moral failing on their part. Never mind the problems in our common life that come to bear on individual families: persistent inequality, lack of access to adequate childcare, crippling student loan debts, unemployment and underemployment, disproportionate minority incarceration rates, unaffordable housing, drastic disparities in educational quality, lack of access to healthcare, and more. All of these things play a role in the crisis of the family today, but Quiverfull families, along with the rest of us, ignore them at our collective peril.

Certainly, given their history, it makes sense that evangelicals turn to the private family as the means for social and cultural transformation. We saw in chapter 1 that when the American government ceased to enforce the "traditional family" through government programs and public schools, evangelicals turned inward for protection. They sincerely thought that by preserving some vestige of the traditional family in their homes they could have a transformative effect on society. Quiverfull families remain motivated by this impulse today. But, not only is the bottom-up approach to cultural transformation wrongheaded, what Quiverfull families are offering in the home is far from transformative.[18] Lacking a broader social vision, wider social engagement, or any sense of the church as an alternative society, Quiverfull families simply cannot be radical agents for change. Instead, they reinscribe the norms of American individualism and privatization but with a more thoroughly religious sheen. In the end, the problem is not that the Quiverfull movement is too radical but that it is not radical enough.

---

18. In his book *To Change the World: The Irony, Tragedy, and Possibility of Christianity in the Late Modern World* (Oxford: Oxford University Press, 2010), sociologist James Davison Hunter provides a concise explanation of why the bottom-up approach to cultural change rarely, if ever, works. His discussion is especially helpful because he is in direct conversation with the assumptions of evangelicalism. In his words, "By themselves or even together, evangelism, politics, and social reform, then, will fail to bring about the ends hoped for and intended." Moreover, "change does not always occur in the direction that people propose or with the effects for which people hope. There are almost always unintended consequences to human action, particularly at the macro-historical level and these are, often enough, tragic. . . . Culture is endlessly complex and difficult, and it is highly resistant to our passion to change it, however well intentioned and heroic our efforts may be" (47).

Bibliography

Anderson, Herbert, and Susan B. W. Johnson. *Regarding Children: A New Respect for Childhood and Families*. Family Living in Pastoral Perspective Series. Louisville: Westminster John Knox, 1994.

Atkinson, Joseph C. *Biblical and Theological Foundations of the Family: The Domestic Church*. Washington, DC: Catholic University of America Press, 2014.

Baker, David. "Schooling All the Masses: Reconsidering the Origins of American Schooling in the Postbellum Era." *Sociology of Education* 72, no. 4 (October 1999): 197–215.

Bartkowski, John P. "Changing of the Gods: The Gender and Family Discourse of American Evangelicalism in Historical Perspective." *History of the Family* 3, no. 1 (1998): 95–116.

———. *Remaking the Godly Marriage: Gender Negotiation in Evangelical Families*. New Brunswick, NJ: Rutgers University Press, 2001.

Bartkowski, John P., and Christopher G. Ellison. "Conservative Protestants on Children and Parenting." In *Children and Childhood in American Religions*, edited by Don S. Browning and Bonnie J. Miller-McLemore, 42–55. New Brunswick, NJ: Rutgers University Press, 2009.

Baucham, Jasmine. *Joyfully at Home: A Book for Young Ladies on Vision and Hope*. San Antonio, TX: Vision Forum, 2010.

Baucham, Voddie. *Family Shepherds: Calling and Equipping Men to Lead Their Homes*. Wheaton, IL: Crossway, 2011.

———. *Family-Driven Faith: Doing What It Takes to Raise Sons and Daughters Who Walk with God*. Wheaton, IL: Crossway, 2011.

———. *What He Must Be . . . if He Wants to Marry My Daughter*. Wheaton, IL: Crossway, 2009.

Bebbington, David. *Evangelicalism in Modern Britain: A History from the 1730s to the 1980s*. London: Routledge, 1989.

Bendroth, Margaret Lamberts. *Fundamentalism and Gender, 1875 to the Present*. New Haven: Yale University Press, 1993.

Bennett, Jana Marguerite. *Water Is Thicker Than Blood: An Augustinian Theology of Marriage and Singleness*. Oxford: Oxford University Press, 2008.

Berryman, Jerome. *Children and the Theologians: Clearing the Way for Grace*. Harrisburg, PA: Morehouse, 2009.

Bielo, James. *Emerging Evangelicals: Faith, Modernity, and the Desire for Authenticity*. New York: New York University Press, 2011.

———. *Words Upon the Word: An Ethnography of Evangelical Group Bible Study*. New York: New York University Press, 2009.

Black, David Alan. *The Myth of Adolescence: Raising Responsible Children in an Irresponsible Society*. Yorba Linda, CA: Davidson Press, 1999.

Bloch, Ruth A. *Gender and Morality in Anglo-American Culture, 1650-1800*. Berkeley: University of California Press, 2003.

Bockelman, Wilfred. *Gothard: The Man and His Ministry*. Santa Barbara, CA: Quill, 1976.

Botkin, Anna Sofia, and Elizabeth Botkin. *It's (Not That) Complicated: How to Relate to Guys in a Healthy, Sane, and Biblical Way*. Centerville, TN: Western Conservatory, 2011.

———. *So Much More: The Remarkable Influence of Visionary Daughters on the Kingdom of God*. San Antonio, TX: Vision Forum, 2007.

Brasher, Brenda. *Godly Women: Fundamentalism and Female Power*. New Brunswick, NJ: Rutgers University Press, 1998.

Brekus, Catherine. "Searching for Women in Narratives of American Religious History." In *The Religious History of American Women: Reimagining the Past*, edited by Catherine A. Brekus, 1–34. Chapel Hill: University of North Carolina Press, 2007.

———. *Strangers and Pilgrims: Female Preaching in America, 1740-1845*. Chapel Hill: University of North Carolina Press, 1998.

Brennan, Patrick McKinley, ed. *The Vocation of the Child*. Grand Rapids: Eerdmans, 2008.

Brook, Joanna L. "Reclaiming America for Christian Reconstruction: The Rhetorical Constitution of a 'People.'" PhD dissertation, University of Massachusetts-Amherst, 2011.

Brown, Scott. *A Weed in the Church: How a Culture of Age Segregation Is Harming the Younger Generation, Fragmenting the Family, and Dividing the Church.* Wake Forest, NC: National Center for Family-Integrated Churches, 2010.

Browning, Don S. *A Fundamental Practical Theology.* Minneapolis: Fortress Press, 1996.

———. *Equality and the Family: A Fundamental, Practical Theology of Children, Mothers, and Fathers in Modern Societies.* Grand Rapids: Eerdmans, 2006.

Brusco, Elizabeth. *The Reformation of Machismo: Evangelical Conversion and Gender in Colombia.* Austin: University of Texas Press, 1995.

Bryant, Sarah L. *The Family Daughter: Becoming Pillars of Strength in Our Father's House.* Holton, KS: KBR Ministries, 2010. E-book.

Bunge, Marcia J., ed. *The Child in Christian Thought.* Grand Rapids: Eerdmans, 2001.

Bushnell, Horace. *Christian Nurture.* New York: Charles Scribner, 1861. Reprint. Cleveland: Pilgrim, 1994.

Butler, Judith. *Gender Trouble: Feminism and the Subversion of Identity.* New York: Routledge, 1990.

Cahill, Lisa Sowle. *Family: A Christian Social Perspective.* Minneapolis: Fortress Press, 2000.

Campbell, Nancy. *Be Fruitful and Multiply: What the Bible Says about Having Children.* San Antonio, TX: Vision Forum, 2003.

Capps, Donald. *The Child's Song: The Religious Abuse of Children.* Louisville: Westminster John Knox, 1995.

———. "Religion and Child Abuse: Perfect Together." *Journal for the Scientific Study of Religion* 31 (1992): 1–14.

Carpenter, Joel A. *Revive Us Again: The Reawakening of American Fundamentalism.* New York: Oxford University Press, 1997.

Chancey, Jennie, and Stacy McDonald. *Passionate Housewives Desperate for God: Fresh Vision for the Hopeful Homemaker.* San Antonio, TX: Vision Forum, 2007.

Cheuk, Michael Koon Hung. "Contraception within Marriage: Modernity and the Development of American Protestant Thought, 1930-1969." PhD dissertation, University of Virginia, 2004.

Cittadino, Emily M. "Multiple Birth Families, Religion, and Cultural Hegemony: Patriarchal Constructions in Reality Television." MA Thesis, Florida Atlantic University, 2010.

Clapp, Rodney. *The Reconstructionists.* Downers Grove, IL: InterVarsity, 1987.

Cohen, Lizabeth. *A Consumer's Republic: The Politics of Mass Consumption in Postwar America.* New York: Knopf, 2003.

Coles, Robert. *The Spiritual Life of Children.* Boston: Houghton Mifflin, 1990.

Cooey, Paula M. "'Ordinary Mother' as Oxymoron: The Collusion of Theology, Theory, and Politics in the Undermining of Mothers." In *Mother Troubles: Rethinking Contemporary Maternal Dilemmas,* edited by Julia Hanigsberg and Sara Ruddick, 229–49. Boston: Beacon, 1999.

Coontz, Stephanie. *The Way We Never Were: American Families and the Nostalgia Trap.* 2nd ed. New York: Basic Books, 2000.

———. *The Way We Really Are: Coming to Terms with America's Changing Families.* New York: Basic Books, 1998.

Cott, Nancy F. *The Bonds of Womanhood: Woman's Sphere in New England, 1780-1835.* New Haven: Yale University Press, 1977.

Crespino, Joseph. "Civil Rights and the Religious Right." In *Rightward Bound: Making America Conservative in the 1970s,* edited by Bruce J. Schulman and Julian E. Zelizer, 90–105. Cambridge, MA: Harvard University Press, 2008.

Dayton, Donald W. "Some Doubts about the Usefulness of the Category 'Evangelical.'" In *The Variety of American Evangelicalism,* edited by Donald W. Dayton and Robert K. Johnston, 245–51. Knoxville: University of Tennessee Press, 1991.

DeBerg, Betty. *Ungodly Women: Gender and the First Wave of American Fundamentalism.* Minneapolis: Fortress Press, 1990.

DeMoss, Nancy Leigh. *Lies Women Believe and the Truth That Sets Them Free.* Chicago: Moody, 2001.

DeRogatis, Amy. *Saving Sex: Sexuality and Salvation in American Evangelicalism.* Oxford: Oxford University Press, 2015.

Dillen, Annemie, ed. *When 'Love' Strikes: Social Sciences, Ethics, and Theology on Family Violence.* Leuven: Peeters, 2009.

Doriani, Daniel. "Birth Dearth or Bring on the Babies? Biblical Perspectives on Family Planning." *Journal of Biblical Counseling* 12, no. 1 (Fall 1993): 24–35.

Duggar, Jana, Jill Duggar, Jessa Duggar, and Jinger Duggar. *Growing Up Duggar: It's All About Relationships.* New York: Howard Books, 2014.

Duggar, Jim Bob, and Michelle Duggar. *The Duggars: 20 and Counting.* New York: Howard Books, 2008.

———. *A Love That Multiplies: An Up-Close View of How They Make It Work.* New York: Howard Books, 2012.

Ellison, Christopher G., and John P. Bartkowski. "Religion and the Legitimation of Violence: The Case of Conservative Protestantism and Corporal Punishment." In *The Web of Violence: From Interpersonal to Global*, edited by Lester Kurtz and Jennifer Turpin, 45–68. Urbana: University of Illinois Press, 1996.

Ellsberg, Mary, and Lori Heise. *Researching Violence against Women: A Practical Guide for Researchers and Activists*. Washington, DC: World Health Organization, PATH, 2005.

Elshtain, Jean Bethke. *Public Man, Private Woman*. Princeton: Princeton University Press, 1993.

Finn, Nathan. "Complementarian Caricature." In *The Journal for Biblical Manhood and Womanhood* 15, no. 2 (Fall 2010): 48–49.

Franks, Myfanwy. *Women and Revivalism in the West: Choosing 'Fundamentalism' in a Liberal Democracy*. Women's Studies at York Series. New York: Palgrave Macmillan, 2001.

Friedman, Jean. *The Enclosed Garden: Women and Community in the Evangelical South, 1830-1900*. Chapel Hill: University of North Carolina Press, 1985.

Friedman, May, and Shana L. Calixte, eds. *Mothering and Blogging: The Radical Act of the MommyBlog*. Toronto: Demeter, 2009.

Fulkerson, Mary McClintock. *Changing the Subject: Women's Discourses and Feminist Theology*. Minneapolis: Fortress Press, 1994.

———. *Places of Redemption: Theology for a Worldly Church*. Oxford: Oxford University Press, 2007.

———. "Practice." In *Handbook of Postmodern Biblical Interpretation*, edited by A. K. A. Adam, 189–98. St. Louis: Chalice, 2000.

Gaither, Milton. *Homeschool: An American History*. New York: Palgrave Macmillan, 2008.

Gallagher, Sally. *Evangelical Identity and Gendered Family Life*. New Brunswick, NJ: Rutgers University Press, 2003.

Garriott, William, and Kevin Lewis O'Neill. "Who Is a Christian? Toward a Dialogic Approach to the Anthropology of Christianity." *Anthropological Theory* 8, no. 4 (2008): 381–98.

Gelles, Richard J. *Intimate Violence in Families*. Thousand Oaks, CA: Sage, 1997.

Goodson, Patricia. "Protestants and Family Planning." *Journal of Religion and Health* 36, no. 4 (Winter 1997): 353–66.

Gothard, Bill. *Basic Seminar Workbook*. Oakbrook, IL: IBLP Publications, 1993.

———. *Men's Manual*. Vol. 2. Oakbrook, IL: IBLP Publications, 1993.
Graebner, Alan. "Birth Control and the Lutherans: The Missouri Synod as a Case Study." *Journal of Social History* 2, no. 4 (Summer 1969): 303–32.
Grenholm, Cristina. *Motherhood and Love: Beyond the Gendered Stereotypes of Theology*. Trans. Marie Tåqvist. Grand Rapids: Eerdmans, 2011.
Greven, Philip. *Spare the Child: The Religious Roots of Punishment and the Psychological Impact of Physical Abuse*. New York: Vintage, 1990.
Griffith, R. Marie. *God's Daughters: Evangelical Women and the Power of Submission*. Berkeley: University of California Press, 1997.
Hall, Amy-Laura. *Conceiving Parenthood: American Protestantism and the Spirit of Reproduction*. Grand Rapids: Eerdmans, 2007.
Hall, David D., ed. *Lived Religion in America: Toward a History of Practice*. Princeton: Princeton University Press, 1997.
Harding, Susan. *The Book of Jerry Falwell: Fundamentalist Language and Politics*. Princeton: Princeton University Press, 2000.
———. "Representing Fundamentalism: The Problem of the Repugnant Cultural Other." *Social Research* 58, no. 2 (Summer 1991): 373–93.
Hart, Stephen. "Privatization in American Religion," *Sociological Analysis* 47, no. 4 (1987): 319–34.
Hatch, Nathan. *The Democratization of American Christianity*. New Haven: Yale University Press, 1990.
Hays, Sharon. *The Cultural Contradictions of Motherhood*. New Haven: Yale University Press, 1998.
Healy, Nicholas. *Church, World, and the Christian Life*. Cambridge: Cambridge University Press, 2000.
Heimlich, Janet. *Breaking Their Will: Shedding Light on Religious Child Maltreatment*. Amherst, NY: Prometheus, 2011.
Hess, Rick, and Jan Hess. *A Full Quiver: Family Planning and the Lordship of Christ*. Brentwood, TN: Wolgemuth & Hyatt, 1990.
Hewitt, Nancy A. "Religion, Reform, and Radicalism in the Antebellum Era." In *A Companion to American Women's History*, edited by Nancy A. Hewitt, 117–31. Malden, MA: Blackwell, 2002.
Higonnet, Anne. *Pictures of Innocence: The History and Crisis of Ideal Childhood*. New York: Thames & Hudson, 1998.
Hochschild, Arlie, and Anne Machung. *The Second Shift: Working Families and the Revolution at Home*. 2nd ed. London: Penguin, 2012.
Houghton, Craig. *Family UNplanning: A Guide for Christian Couples Seeking God's Truth on Having Children*. Maitland, FL: Xulon, 2006.

Hughes, Korey. "Mobilization Dilemmas of the Quiverfull." Paper presented at the annual meeting of the Northeastern Political Science Association, November 13–15, 2008.

Hunter, James Davison. *To Change the World: The Irony, Tragedy, and Possibility of Christianity in the Late Modern World*. Oxford: Oxford University Press, 2010.

Hunter, Joan Heaney. "Toward a Eucharistic Spirituality of the Family: Blessed, Broken, and Shared." In *Marriage in the Catholic Tradition*, edited by Todd A. Salzman, Thomas M. Kelly, and John J. O'Keefe. New York: Crossroad, 2004.

Inclan, Jaime, and Ernesto Ferran Jr. "Poverty, Politics, and Family Therapy: A Role for Systems Theory." In *The Social and Political Contexts of Family Therapy*, edited by Marsha Pravder Mirkin, 193–213. Needham Heights, MA: Allyn & Bacon, 1990.

Ingersoll, Julie. *Building God's Kingdom: Inside the World of Christian Reconstruction*. Oxford: Oxford University Press, 2015.

———. *Evangelical Christian Women: War Stories in the Gender Battle*. Qualitative Studies in Religion Series. New York: New York University Press, 2003.

Iverson, Timothy J., and Marilyn Segal. "Social Behavior of Maltreated Children: Exploring Links to Parent Behavior and Beliefs." In *Parental Belief Systems: The Psychological Consequences for Children*, edited by I. E. Sigel, A. V. McGillicuddy-DeLisi, and J. J. Goodnow, 267–89. Hillsdale, NJ: Laurence Erlbaum, 1992.

Jensen, David H. *Graced Vulnerability: A Theology of Childhood*. Cleveland: Pilgrim, 2005.

———. *Parenting: Christian Explorations of Daily Living*. Minneapolis: Fortress Press, 2011.

John Paul II. *Familiaris Consortio*. Washington, DC: United States Catholic Conference, 1981.

Joyce, Kathryn. *Quiverfull: Inside the Christian Patriarchy Movement*. Boston: Beacon, 2009.

———. "The Quiverfull Conviction: Christian Mothers Breed Arrows for the War." *The Nation*, November 27, 2006, 11–18.

Juster, Susan. *Disorderly Women: Sexual Politics and Evangelicalism in Revolutionary New England*. Ithaca, NY: Cornell University Press, 1994.

Kaufmann, Eric. *Shall the Religious Inherit the Earth? Demography and Politics in the Twenty-First Century*. London: Profile Books, 2010.

Kelly, Kristin A. *Domestic Violence and the Politics of Privacy*. Ithaca, NY: Cornell University Press, 2002.

Klejwa, Natalie. *Three Decades of Fertility: Ten Ordinary Women Surrender to the Creator and Embrace Life*. Saint Paul, MN: Visionary Womanhood, 2013.

Klicka, Chris. *Home Schooling: The Right Choice*. 4th ed. Nashville: Broadman & Holman, 2002.

Köstenberger, Andreas. *God, Marriage, and Family: Rebuilding the Biblical Foundation*. 2nd ed. Wheaton, IL: Crossway, 2010.

Kruse, Kevin M. *One Nation Under God: How Corporate America Invented Christian America*. New York: Basic Books, 2015.

Kunzman, Robert. *Write These Laws on Your Children: Inside the World of Conservative Christian Homeschooling*. Boston: Beacon, 2009.

LaHaye, Tim, and Beverly LaHaye. *The Act of Marriage*. 2nd ed. Grand Rapids: Zondervan, 1998.

Lancaster, Philip. *Family Man, Family Leader: Biblical Fatherhood as the Key to a Thriving Family*. San Antonio, TX: Vision Forum, 2003.

Lerner, Gerda. "The Lady and the Mill Girl: Changes in the Status of Women in the Age of Jackson." In *The Majority Finds Its Past: Placing Women in History*, edited by Gerda Lerner, 15–30. Chapel Hill: University of North Carolina Press, 2005.

Liao, Monica Smatlak. "Keeping Home: Homeschooling and the Practice of Conservative Protestant Identity." PhD dissertation, Vanderbilt University, 2006.

Manning, Christel. *Fundamentalism and American Culture*. New Edition. New York: Oxford University Press, 2006.

———. *God Gave Us the Right: Conservative Catholic, Evangelical Protestant, and Orthodox Jewish Women Grapple with Feminism*. New York: Rutgers University Press, 1999.

———. "Quiverfull: Inside the Christian Patriarchy Movement." *Journal for the Scientific Study of Religion* 49, no. 2 (June 2010): 376–77.

Marsden, George M. *Understanding Fundamentalism and Evangelicalism*. Grand Rapids: Eerdmans, 1990.

———. "Review of *Fundamentalism and Gender* by Margaret Lamberts Bendroth." *Journal for the Scientific Study of Religion* 33, no. 3 (Spring 1994): 286.

Matchar, Emily. *Homeward Bound: Why Women Are Embracing the New Domesticity*. New York: Simon & Schuster, 2013.

May, Elaine Tyler. *America and the Pill: A History of Promise, Peril, and Liberation.* New York: Basic Books, 2011.

———. *Homeward Bound: American Families in the Cold War Era.* 2nd ed. New York: Basic Books, 2008.

McCarthy, David Matzko. *Sex and Love in the Home: A Theology of the Household.* 2nd ed. London: SCM, 2010.

McDannell, Colleen. "Creating the Christian Home: Home Schooling in Contemporary America." In *American Sacred Space,* edited by David Chidester and Edward T. Linenthal, 187–219. Bloomington: Indiana University Press, 1995.

McKeown, John. "U.S. Protestant Natalist Reception of Old Testament Fruitful Verses." PhD Dissertation, University of Liverpool, 2011.

McVicar, Michael J. *Christian Reconstruction: R.J. Rushdoony and American Religious Conservatism.* Chapel Hill: University of North Carolina Press, 2015.

Mercer, Joyce Ann. *Welcoming Children: A Practical Theology of Childhood.* St. Louis: Chalice, 2005.

Miller, Alice. *For Your Own Good: Hidden Cruelty in Child-Rearing and the Roots of Violence.* Trans. Hildegarde Hannum and Hunter Hannum. New York: Farrar, Straus & Giroux, 1983.

Miller, Vincent J. *Consuming Religion: Christian Faith and Practice in a Consumer Culture.* New York: Continuum, 2004.

Miller-McLemore, Bonnie. *Also a Mother: Work and Family as Theological Dilemma.* Nashville: Abingdon, 1994.

———. "Children, Chores, and Vocation: A Social and Theological Lacuna." In *The Vocation of the Child,* edited by Patrick McKinley Brennan, 295–323. Grand Rapids: Eerdmans, 2008.

———. *In the Midst of Chaos: Caring for Children as Spiritual Practice.* The Practices of Faith Series. San Francisco: Jossey-Bass, 2006.

Moore, Raymond, and Dorothy Moore. *Home Grown Kids.* Waco, TX: Word, 1984.

Morecraft, Joseph, III. "The Bible on Large Families." *The Counsel of Chalcedon* 11, no. 8 (October 1989): 9–10.

Morgan, Marabel. *The Total Woman.* Old Tappan, NJ: Fleming H. Revell, 1973.

Murphy, Joseph. *Homeschooling in America: Capturing and Assessing the Movement.* Thousand Oaks, CA: Corwin, 2012.

Noll, Mark. *America's God: From Jonathan Edwards to Abraham Lincoln.* Oxford: Oxford University Press, 2002.

———. *The Rise of Evangelicalism*. Downers Grove, IL: InterVarsity, 2003.

North, Gary. *The Dominion Covenant: Genesis*. Tyler, TX: Institute for Christian Economics, 1987.

Orsi, Robert. *The Madonna of 115th Street*. 4th ed. New Haven: Yale University Press, 2002.

Ouellet, Marc Cardinal. *Divine Likeness: Toward a Trinitarian Anthropology of the Family*. Grand Rapids: Eerdmans, 2006.

Owen, Samuel A. *Letting God Plan Your Family*. Wheaton, IL: Crossway, 1990.

Parkerson, Donald H., and Jo Ann Parkerson. "'Fewer Children of Greater Spiritual Quality': Religion and the Decline of Fertility in Nineteenth Century America." *Social Science History* 12 (1988): 49–70.

Pattison, Stephen. "'Suffer Little Children': The Challenge of Child Abuse and Neglect to Theology." *Theology and Sexuality* 9 (1998): 36–58.

Pearl, Michael, and Debi Pearl. *To Train Up a Child*. Pleasantville, TN: No Greater Joy Ministries, 1994.

Perdue, Leo G., Joseph Blenkinsopp, John J. Collins, and Carol Meyers. *Families in Ancient Israel*. Family Religion and Culture Series. Louisville: Westminster John Knox, 1997.

Post, Stephen G. *More Lasting Unions: Christianity, the Family, and Society*. Grand Rapids: Eerdmans, 2000.

Pride, Mary. *The Way Home: Beyond Feminism, Back to Reality*. Westchester, IL: Crossway, 1985.

Provan, Charles D. *The Bible and Birth Control*. Monongahela, PA: Zimmer Printing, 1989.

Rahner, Karl. *Theological Investigations*. Vol. 8. Translated by David Bourke. New York: Herder & Herder, 1971.

Rice, John R. *God in Your Family*. Murfreesboro, TN: Sword of the Lord, 1971.

———. *The Home: Courtship, Marriage, and Children*. Murfreesboro, TN: Sword of the Lord, 1946.

Rich, Adrienne. *Of Woman Born: Motherhood as Experience and Institution*. New York: W. W. Norton, 1986.

Roberts, Albert R., ed. *Battered Women and Their Families*. 3rd ed. New York: Springer, 2007.

Rubio, Julie Hanlon. *A Christian Theology of Marriage and Family*. Mahwah, NJ: Paulist, 2003.

———. *Family Ethics: Practices for Christians*. Washington, DC: Georgetown University Press, 2010.

Ruddick, Sara. *Maternal Thinking: Towards a Politics of Peace.* Aylesbury, UK: Women's Press, 1990.
Rushdoony, R. J. *The Institutes of Biblical Law*, Vols. 1–3. Phillipsburg, NJ: Presbyterian and Reformed, 1973.
———. *The Myth of Over-Population.* Fairfax, VA: Thornburn, 1974.
———. "The Trustee Family." *Journal of Christian Reconstruction: Symposium on the Family* 4, no. 2 (Winter 1977–78): 16–23.
Sandeen, Ernest R. *The Roots of Fundamentalism: British and American Millenarianism, 1800-1930.* Chicago: University of Chicago Press, 1970.
Schäfer, Axel R., ed. *American Evangelicals and the 1960s.* Studies in American Thought and Culture Series. Madison: University of Wisconsin Press, 2013.
———. *Countercultural Conservatives: American Evangelicalism from the Postwar Revival to the New Christian Right.* Madison: University of Wisconsin Press, 2011.
Scharen, Christian, ed. *Explorations in Ecclesiology and Ethnography.* Studies in Ecclesiology and Ethnography. Grand Rapids: Eerdmans, 2012.
Scharen, Christian, and Aana Marie Vigen, eds. *Ethnography as Christian Theology and Ethics.* London: Continuum, 2011.
Scher, Abby. "Biblical Womanhood." *Women's Review of Books* 26, no. 3 (May/June 2009): 5–8.
Scott, Rachel Giove. *Birthing God's Mighty Warriors.* Maitland, FL: Xulon, 2004.
Sherfinski, Melissa Beth. "Blessed Under Pressure: Evangelical Mothers in the Homeschooling Movement." PhD dissertation, University of Wisconsin-Madison, 2011.
Smith, Christian. *American Evangelicalism: Embattled and Thriving.* Chicago: University of Chicago Press, 1998.
———. *Christian America? What Evangelicals Really Want.* Berkeley: University of California Press, 2000.
Smith-Rosenberg, Carroll. *Disorderly Conduct: Visions of Gender in Victorian America.* New York: Oxford University Press, 1985.
Spitzer, Walter O., and Carlyle L. Saylor, eds. *Birth Control and the Christian: A Protestant Symposium on the Control of Human Reproduction.* Wheaton, IL: Tyndale House, 1968.
Spruill, Marjorie J. "Gender and America's Right Turn." In *Rightward Bound: Making America Conservative in the 1970s,* edited by Bruce J. Schulman and Julian E. Zelizer, 71–89. Cambridge, MA: Harvard University Press, 2008.

St. John-Stevas, Norman. *The Agonising Choice: Birth Control, Religion, and the Law*. Bloomington: Indiana University Press, 1971.

Stacey, Judith. *Brave New Families: Stories of Domestic Upheaval in Late Twentieth Century America*. San Francisco: Basic Books, 1990.

Stevens, Mitchell. *Kingdom of Children: Culture and Controversy in the Homeschooling Movement*. Princeton Studies in Cultural Sociology. Princeton: Princeton University Press, 2003.

Sutton, Matthew Avery. *American Apocalypse: A History of Modern Evangelicalism*. Cambridge, MA: Belknap, 2014.

Tanner, Kathryn. *Theories of Culture: A New Agenda for Theology*. Minneapolis: Fortress Press, 1997.

Taylor, Megan. "Quiverfull: Family Reformation and Intentional Community." BA Thesis, Texas Christian University, Fort Worth, 2012.

Thatcher, Adrian. *Theology and Families*. Challenges in Contemporary Theology. Oxford: Wiley-Blackwell, 2007.

Toft, Monica Duffy. "Wombfare: The Religious and Political Dimensions of Fertility and Demographic Change." In *Political Demography: How Population Changes Are Reshaping International Security and National Politics*, edited by Jack A. Goldstone, Eric P. Kauffman, and Monica Duffy Toft, 213–25. Oxford: Oxford University Press, 2011.

Torode, Sam, and Bethany Torode. *Open Embrace: A Protestant Couple Rethinks Contraception*. Grand Rapids: Eerdmans, 2002.

Trachtenberg, Alan. *The Incorporation of America: Culture and Society in the Gilded Age*. New York: Hill & Wang, 2007.

Ward, Pete. *Perspectives on Ecclesiology and Ethnography*. Studies in Ecclesiology and Ethnography. Grand Rapids: Eerdmans, 2012.

Warner, Judith. *Perfect Madness: Motherhood in the Age of Anxiety*. New York: Riverhead Books, 2005.

Watters, Steve, and Candice Watters. *Start Your Family: Inspiration for Having Babies*. Chicago: Moody, 2009.

Webb, Lynne M., and Brittney S. Lee. "Mommy Blogs: The Centrality of Community in the Performance of Online Maternity." In *Motherhood Online*, edited by Michelle Moravec, 242–56. Newcastle upon Tyne: Cambridge Scholars Publishing, 2011.

Welter, Barbara. "The Cult of True Womanhood: 1820-1860." *American Quarterly* 18, no 2.1 (Summer 1966): 151–74.

———. *Dimity Convictions: The American Woman in the Nineteenth Century*. Athens: Ohio University Press, 1976.

Worthen, Molly. *Apostles of Reason: The Crisis of Authority in American Evangelicalism.* Oxford: Oxford University Press, 2013.

Wuthnow, Robert. *The Restructuring of American Religion: Society and Faith Since World War II.* Princeton: Princeton University Press, 1988.

WEBSITES

Above Rubies Ministries. Last updated July 22, 2015. http://aboverubies.org.

Allen, Bob. "Seminary First Lady Compares Pill to Abortion." *Ethics Daily.* February 22, 2007. http://tinyurl.com/ybyzdb4l.

Bailey, Sarah Pulliam. "Conservative Leader Bill Gothard Resigns Following Abuse Allegations." *Washington Post.* March 7, 2014. http://tinyurl.com/y9zb5y3w.

Bentley, Vicki. "What Does It Cost to Homeschool?" Home School Legal Defense Association. Fall 2013. http://tinyurl.com/y7cqcaa2.

Boorman, Georgi. "Americans Think School Is for Socializing." *The Federalist.* June 16, 2014. http://tinyurl.com/y7bxzvqz.

Botkin, Anna Sofia, and Elizabeth Botkin. "Authoritative Parents, Adult Daughters, and Power Struggles," *Visionary Daughters,* May 14, 2007. http://tinyurl.com/y8zeqr99.

Botkin, Geoffrey. "A Botkin Family Secret Revealed." *Western Conservatory of Arts and Sciences Blog,* May 14, 2010. http://tinyurl.com/y8xnfsu7.

Centers for Disease Control and Prevention, Division of Violence Prevention. "Intimate Partner Violence: Consequences." Last updated March 3, 2015. http://tinyurl.com/aebay8t.

Child Welfare Information Gateway. "Child Maltreatment 2012: Summary of Key Findings." Washington, DC: U.S. Department of Health and Human Services: Children's Bureau. http://tinyurl.com/yall7x2z.

Coalition for Responsible Home Education. Last updated April 23, 2015. http://www.responsiblehomeschooling.org/.

Einwechter, William. "The Feminization of the Family." Vision Forum Ministries. December 8, 2005. http://tinyurl.com/ybw93lmd.

———. "Men and Women and the Creation Order." Vision Forum Ministries. April 13, 2009. http://tinyurl.com/y9af66ej.

Farris, Michael. "A Line in the Sand." Homeschool Legal Defense Association Court Report, August 5, 2014. http://tinyurl.com/yaymym8f. http://tinyurl.com/y7voudlh.

———. "Remarks to the World Congress of Families II." Speech at the 1999 World Congress of Families. The Howard Center for Family, Religion, & Society.

Garrison, Vyckie. "Quiverfull Royalty vs. Quiverfull Reality." No Longer Quivering. August 31, 2010. http://tinyurl.com/mpx8ecl.

Gerstein, Ted, and John Berman. "When Having Children Is a Religious Experience." *Nightline*. January 3, 2007. http://tinyurl.com/y8yln7jw.

Gibbs, David C., Esq. "Civil Case Information Sheet." *Lourdes Torres-Manteufel v. Douglas Phillips et al.* April 15, 2014. http://tinyurl.com/y8luh7sw.

Gothard, Bill. "A Statement from Bill Gothard." April 17, 2014. http://tinyurl.com/ybp28oy8.

Hart, David Bentley. "Freedom and Decency." *First Things*, June 2004. http://tinyurl.com/ya8vd4yc.

Homeschooling's Invisible Children. "Some Preliminary Data on Homeschool Child Fatalities." http://tinyurl.com/y9lm283e.

Hopewell, Lisa. *A Quiver Full of Information: The Who, What, Why of the Quiverfull Movement and Lifestyle.* Last updated February 28, 2014. https://quiverfullmyblog.wordpress.com.

Institute in Basic Life Principles. "About IBLP." http://tinyurl.com/yd8q5d95.

———. "Bill Gothard." http://tinyurl.com/ycv35xza.

———. "Home: A Learning Center." http://tinyurl.com/ya8tdfzz.

———. "A Time of Transition." June 17, 2014. http://tinyurl.com/ycafar5w.

Joyce, Kathryn. "All God's Children." *Salon*. March 14, 2009. http://tinyurl.com/lc5zuw6.

———. "Hana Williams: The Tragic Death of an Ethiopian Adoptee, and How It Could Happen Again." *Slate*. November 9, 2013. http://tinyurl.com/p6kg8ts.

———. "Inside the Duggar Family's Conservative Ideology." *Newsweek*. March 16, 2009. http://tinyurl.com/pl86upu.

———. "Missing the 'Right' Babies." *The Nation*. March 3, 2008. http://tinyurl.com/ybgalby9.

———. "My Womb for His Purposes." *Religion Dispatches*. July 12, 2009. http://tinyurl.com/ms6guam.

Klejwa, Natalie. "Escaping Duggarville with My Faith Intact." Visionary Womanhood. February 2, 2015. http://tinyurl.com/yd9t2p8p.

———. "What I Didn't Tell You about in 2014." Visionary Womanhood. January 1, 2015. http://tinyurl.com/y7kj7c95.

Klicka, Christopher J., and William A. Estrada. "The UN Convention on the Rights of the Child: The Most Dangerous Attack on Parental Rights in the History of the United States." Home School Legal Defense Association. November 1999. Updated March 2007. http://tinyurl.com/y7wg6end.

Ladies Against Feminism. Accessed December 4, 2012. http://www.ladiesagainstfeminism.com.

Lamb, Amanda. "Adoptive mother Convicted in Boy's Death." WRAL.com. June 12, 2008. http://tinyurl.com/y9g4jjqz.

Lancaster, Philip. "About." *Patriarch Magazine.* http://tinyurl.com/yafeft9j.

Libby Anne. "Christian Patriarchy/Quiverfull." *Love, Joy, Feminism.* Accessed May 5, 2014. http://tinyurl.com/p6fxhaw.

Martinez, Edecio. "DA: Kevin and Elizabeth Schatz Killed Daughter with 'Religious Whips' for Mispronouncing Word." *CBS News.* February 22, 2010. http://tinyurl.com/ya7vq5s4.

McDonald, James. "The Blessing of Daughters." *Family Reformation.* October 2, 2007. http://tinyurl.com/y84ncthz.

———. "Like Olive Plants—Watching God Grow a Legacy." *Family Reformation.* June 6, 2010. http://tinyurl.com/y8woms4p.

McDonald, Stacy. "Jesus-Full." *Steadfast Daughters in a Quivering World.* December 12, 2010. http://tinyurl.com/ycr4vpyb.

———. *Your Sacred Calling.* http://yoursacredcalling.com/blog.

McGalliard, Gina. "House Proud: The Troubling Rise of Stay-at-Home Daughters." *Bitch Magazine.* November 2010. http://tinyurl.com/y9degtm8.

Mohler, R. Albert, Jr. "Al Mohler Responds: The Evangelical Unease over Contraception." *Washington Post.* January 8, 2014. http://tinyurl.com/yc389vvh.

———. "Can Christians Use Birth Control?" AlbertMohler.com, May 8, 2006. http://tinyurl.com/y98r4mds.

Moore, Ray E. The Exodus Mandate. http://exodusmandate.org.

National Center for Education Statistics. "Homeschooling in the United States: 2003: Statistical Analysis Report." February 2006. http://tinyurl.com/y7n2pknb.

National Center for Family Integrated Churches. "About." https://ncfic.org/about.

———. "Husbands Love Your Wives." Accessed March 17, 2014. http://tinyurl.com/y7qggrsn.

Newsweek Staff. "Making Babies the Quiverfull Way." *Newsweek.* November 12, 2006. http://tinyurl.com/ybqdbwlt.

Olheiser, Abby. "Josh Duggar Molested Four of His Sisters and a Babysitter." *Washington Post.* June 4, 2015. http://tinyurl.com/oga4lc7.

Pearl, Michael. "Hana Williams' Death—Official Statement." No Greater Joy Ministries. http://tinyurl.com/ybag553t.

Phillips, Douglas. "A Declaration of Life." Vision Forum Ministries. March 6, 2002. http://tinyurl.com/ycnfw4g9.

———. "Statement of Resignation." October 30, 2013. http://tinyurl.com/y9dp2xff.

Phillips, Douglas, R. C. Sproul Jr., and Philip Lancaster. "The Tenets of Biblical Patriarchy." Vision Forum Ministries. http://tinyurl.com/y8763jme.

Prior, Karen Swallow. "What Is the Stay-at-Home Daughters Movement?" *Christianity Today.* December 20, 2010. http://tinyurl.com/yamfo5nc.

Quiverfull Digest. http://www.quiverfull.com/digest.php.

Ray, Brian D. "Homeschool Population Report 2010." National Home Education Research Institute. January 3, 2011. http://tinyurl.com/yddlfabs.

Recovering Grace. "The Gothard Files: A Case for Disqualification." February 3, 2014. http://tinyurl.com/yccrkf5k.

———. "There Is No Victim." April 25, 2014. http://tinyurl.com/y9xzjgop.

Rennison, Callie Marie. "Intimate Partner Violence, 1993-2001." Bureau of Justice Statistics Crime Data Brief. February 2003. http://tinyurl.com/ycsdaw97.

Riste, Lance and Cris. "Receiving Precious Gifts: Learning to Rejoice in God's Gift of Children." *Institute in Basic Life Principles.* http://tinyurl.com/y79jqngb.

Sessions, David. "When Reactionary Anarchism Meets Homeschooling." *Patrol Magazine.* June 16, 2014. http://tinyurl.com/y84fhfum.

St. John, Heidi. "Don't Turn Away: Trouble in the Homeschooling Movement." *The Busy Mom,* March 9, 2014. http://tinyurl.com/y9ftgtfu.

Stollar, R. L. "The Child as Viper: How Voddie Baucham's Theology of Children Promotes Child Abuse." Homeschoolers Anonymous. January 16, 2015. http://tinyurl.com/ybw36hdt.

———. "Children as Divine Rental Property." Homeschoolers Anonymous. January 5, 2015. http://tinyurl.com/y857o2xy.

———. "End Child Protection: Doug Phillips, HSLDA, and the 2009 Men's Leadership Summit." Homeschoolers Anonymous. May 14, 2013. http://tinyurl.com/y7bewfo8.

———. "Transcript of Voddie Baucham's 'The Doctrine of Total Depravity.'" Homeschoolers Anonymous. January 13, 2015. http://tinyurl.com/y8lj2okh.

———. "What 'Christian Patriarchy' Is Not." Homeschoolers Anonymous. April 28, 2014. http://tinyurl.com/y8th82fx.

US Department of Health and Human Services. Child Abuse Prevention and Treatment Act (CAPTA) Reauthorization of 2010 (P.L. 111–320), § 3.2. http://tinyurl.com/ybtdb4xb.

Under Much Grace. "Who Is Geoffrey Botkin?" Updated February 22, 2013. http://tinyurl.com/yavceqa8.

UNICEF. "Behind Closed Doors: The Impact of Domestic Violence on Children." Updated 2006. http://tinyurl.com/y9zvhgg4.

Vision Forum Ministries. Last updated April 17, 2014. http://www.visionforumministries.org.

Voddie Baucham, "The Doctrine of Total Depravity." Sermon at Grace Family Baptist Church. May 2, 2010. http://tinyurl.com/ybgxtuaf.

Western Conservatory of Arts and Sciences. "About Western Conservatory." http://westernconservatory.com/about.

Index

19 Kids and Counting, ix, 47

abolitionism, 12
abortion, 20, 23, 28, 29, 30, 94–95, 101, 225
Above Rubies, 44, 53
adoption, 65, 134
Advanced Training Institute (ATI), 42
age of accountability, 150
Anderson, Herbert, 152, 176, 218–19
Arminianism, Arminian, 10, 13

baptism, 125–26, 151–52, 152n61, 155, 157, 164, 169–70, 202, 206–7
barrenness, 97
Bartowski, John P., 7–8, 12, 21n82, 137n31
Baucham, Jasmine, 47, 177n19
Baucham, Voddie: on children and child training, 142–43, 147, 156–58, 159–60, 162, 165n103, 166; on church, 202–3, 204, 230, 231n17; on the family, 172n5, 173, 174, 177, 179, 180, 200; as Quiverfull leader, xxi, 1, 46–47, 48, 53, 67, 79; on spanking, 161, 187
"be fruitful and multiply" (Gen 1:28), 97, 172, 202

Bebbington, David, 5
Beecher, Catharine, 10–11, 26–27
Bendroth, Margaret Lamberts, 5, 13–14, 17–18, 139n32
Bennett, Jana M., 136n26, 164n101, 200n65, 202
Bible: inspiration of, 36n138, 37–38, 38n142; interpretation of, 14n53, 36–38, 58, 62, 128n2; reading (as a practice), 36–37, 73, 77, 80, 91, 208
biblical literalism, 14, 36, 36n138, 37n140, 38, 38n142
Bielo, James, xxii n24, 5n14
birth. *See* childbirth
birth control. *See* contraception
blogs, blogging, xxviii, xxix, 2, 40, 41, 42n154, 48, 49–52, 108, 167n107. *See also* mommy blogs
Botkin, Anna Sofia and Elizabeth, 45n163, 46, 94, 95, 96–97, 98n33, 99, 100, 177
Botkin, Geoffrey, 45–46, 177n20, 180, 230
Brown, Scott, 45, 231n17
Browning, Don S., 170n3, 183n35, 217

Cahill, Lisa Sowle, 170n3, 191, 199

Calvinism, Calvinist, xxiv, 7, 10, 14, 17, 25, 28n109, 44, 48n176, 67

Campbell, Nancy, xx n22, 35n133, 44, 96n24, 97–98, 129, 133n17, 140

"chain of command," 22. *See also* "umbrella of protection"

Chancey, Jennie, 93, 95, 99, 100–101

child, children: as constructed, 10, 127n1; as divine blessing or gift, 127–37; as innocent and sinner, 137–47; as potential adult or disciple, 147–55; as sole responsibility of parents, 155–67

child abuse, child sexual abuse, 42n155, 141n38, 144, 161, 167, 187, 210–17, 219

childbirth, xv, 15n56, 57, 60, 65, 66, 71–72, 84, 87–88, 89n3, 90, 93n6, 96–97, 117–18, 120, 129

childhood: changing conceptions of, 10, 151n59; definition of, 127n1; as enduring part of human life, 152–54; as loss of innocence, 137–39; as short time period, 147–50; and vulnerability, 138–39, 153, 164, 166–67

childness, 152–54

chores, 59, 73, 161–63, 163n99

Christianity Today, 27–28

Christian Right, 20, 22–24

church, 199–209; attendance, 174n13, 202, 205–6; conflict with, 60, 70–71, 200, 202n70, 205, 231n17; in a private home, 60, 70–71, 169–70, 205, 206

Coalition for Responsible Home Education (CRHE), 167n107, 213

complementarianism, complementarity, 19, 21, 99, 199, 120n85, 183n35

contraception, xv, xx, 35, 38, 48n176, 60, 64, 74, 90, 101, 130, 136, 203; changing evangelical views on, xxiv n29, xxiv n30, 18, 27n105, 27–31, 38, 49; linked with abortion, 28, 94–96; use by Quiverfull couples, xxii, 2, 35, 66, 74, 130

corporal punishment. *See* spanking

Council on Biblical Manhood and Womanhood (CBMW), 49, 120n85

Coontz, Stephanie, 9, 10, 109, 189–190,

culture: evangelical, xxii–xxv, 5–6, 18–19, 22–23; study of, xxv–xxvi; transformation of, 25, 35, 57, 96, 180–82, 186n41, 189, 205, 207, 233

culture wars, 31, 58, 96n22, 181, 189, 207

DeBerg, Betty, 11, 12

demography, 3n6, 7, 31, 35, 132–33

DeRogatis, Amy, 18, 225

discipleship (of children), 57–58, 82, 104, 126, 147–55, 155–58

discourse: definition of, 31–32;

and the internet, 50–52; of Quiverfull, xv n9, xvi–xxii, 31–38
dispensationalism, 14
domestic violence, 210–13, 216–17, 219
dominion, xxvii, 17, 97n26, 98n33, 98n34, 99–101, 181, 228
dominionism. *See* reconstructionism
Duggar, Josh, xxiii, 215
Duggar family, Jim Bob and Michelle Duggar, ix, xxiii, 47–48, 53, 215

ecclesiology, 156n77, 166, 191n49, 199–209, 228, 231
ethnographic methodology, xxviii–xxxi, 55–56
ethnography: as a research method, xxv–xxviii; and theology, xxxi–xxxiii
evangelicals, evangelicalism: and the Bible, 5, 12–13, 14n53, 23, 36–38; and birth control, 27–31; definition of, 5–6; and fundamentalism, 6n15, 12–16; and gender, xviii–xx, 6–27, 34–35, 183n34, 229n13; and homeschooling, 6–27; and Quiverfull, xxii–xxv; and the sexual revolution, 16–19; as a subculture, xxiin24, 5–6, 34n132, 48–49
exposure, 119, 123
ex-Quiverfull, xixn18, 52, 212n98

Falwell, Jerry, 20. *See also* Christian Right

family (nuclear), 122, 163, 175, 189, 232–33; and children's formation, 126, 155–58, 159, 163–67, 177–78; and the church, 164–66, 199–209; definition of, 190–91, 199; form of, 171–75; function of, 176–82, 227–28; weakness of, 193–94, 217–18
family blueprint (Quiverfull), 171–75, 176, 180, 220–21; problems with (in general), 182–91; problems with (in Quiverfull), 192–220
family integration (in church), 44, 45, 60, 165, 204
Family Integrated Church movement (FIC), 45, 47, 231n17
family shepherd, 62, 171n5, 174, 175n14, 187, 200, 202, 211, 231n17
family worship, 34, 73, 106, 144, 162–63, 178, 208
Farris, Michael, 48n176, 48n177, 105n54, 158–59, 159n88, 177n20
feminism: anti-, 14, 19, 29–30, 95–102, 173, 228–29; liberal, 102, 113, 232; Quiverfull construction of, 29–30, 93–95, 95n17, 204, 207
feminization (of the church), 13, 171, 173
Foucault, Michel, 31n122, 32
fruitful, fruitfulness, 97, 130, 163, 172, 202
Fulkerson, Mary McClintock, xi, xiii, xxvi–xxvii, 32, 33n128

fundamentalism, xxiii n26, 5n11, 6n15, 7n18, 12–16, 37n140, 57

Gaither, Milton, xviii n15, 15, 16, 22, 23
Garrison, Vyckie, 108n59, 212
gender dualism, xviii, xix, 10, 34, 96, 183n34, 229n13
gender hierarchy, xvi, xviii–xx, 5–6, 8–9, 18, 31, 43, 62, 69–70; and homeschooling, xviii–xix, 32–34; in practice, 32–33, 61–62, 64, 69–71, 80–84, 105–7, 225–27
Gothard, Bill, 21–22, 42–43, 48, 51, 214
Gothardism, 43
government schools. *See* public schools
Grenholm, Cristina, 115n73, 117–19, 121, 123

Healy, Nicholas, 171n5, 182, 184, 186n41, 188–89, 190n49
Hess, Jan and Rick, xiv, 27, 48n176, 65, 97, 129
heteronomy, 118, 120–23
Hewitt, Nancy A., 9
Holt, John, 24
Home School Legal Defense Association (HSLDA), 26, 44, 48n176, 158–59
Homeschoolers Anonymous, xix n18, 51n184, 142n44, 143n47, 158n81, 159n88, 194n56
homeschooling; curriculum, xviii, 42–44, 208, 227, 228n12; definition of, xv, xvii–xviii; as domestic Christianity, 7n18, 33, 178, 208, 227–28; institutions and leaders of, xxviii, 26–27, 42–48, 48n176, 49–52; as mother's profession, 90–91, 102–7, 110–11, 160, 229; origin of, xvii n15, xxiii, 19–20, 22–27, 40–41; reasons for, 58, 61, 66–67, 72, 75–76, 138–39, 148, 156–59, 178, 208; research on, xxx–xxxi, 4n8, 213, 216n114, 226, 228n12
Homeschooling's Invisible Children (HIC), 167n107, 213, 216n114
Houghton, Craig, 36n136, 128n6, 132–33

individualism, xxxiv, 8n24, 229–31, 233; and the family, 17, 206–7; and motherhood, 117n74; Quiverfull perception of (in feminism), 94–95, 96
infertility. *See* barrenness
Ingersoll, Julie, xxvi n37, 25n99, 32n124, 41n152, 181n31
Institute in Basic Life Principles (IBLP), 42
Institutes of Biblical Law, The (book by R. J. Rushdoony), 25
integration (of schools), 20
isolation: of children, 165, 166–67, 198, 210, 216; of the family, 123, 174n13, 192–98, 202, 207–9, 210, 216–17, 230–31; of mothers, 63, 92, 198

Jensen, David H., 152, 153, 154
John Paul II, 199, 218, 219

Johnson, Susan B. W., 152, 176, 218–19
Joyce, Kathryn, xi, xiv, xvii, xxiii, 3n6, 4, 41n151, 48n176, 88, 213n103

Klejwa, Natalie, xxx n40, 51, 89n4, 105n53, 151, 212–13, 219
Klicka, Chris, 159n85, 160n90

Libby Anne (blogger), xvii n11, xviii n14, xx n20, 33n130
Love, Joy, Feminism (blog), 52. *See also* Libby Anne (blogger)

male headship, xvi, xix–xx, 19, 21, 32–35, 42, 69–71, 73, 80, 98–101, 105–7, 120, 172–73, 187, 232
Marsden, George M., 5n11, 37n140
McDannell, Colleen, 7n18, 11, 90n5, 104
Miller, Vincent J., 32n125, 207n84, 217n119
mommy blog, 30n117, 50n183, 51–52
Moore, Dorothy and Raymond, 24, 26
Moral Majority, 20
motherhood; as natural for women, 97–98, 102–4; and omnipotence, 108–17; and pregnancy, 93n6, 97–98, 117–18, 123n90, 130, 135; romanticization of, 10, 114–15, 226–27; and vulnerability, 117–24
multigenerational faithfulness, xvii, xviiin13, 79, 110, 127, 158, 163, 177, 181, 225–26, 228
muscular Christianity, 13–14
Myth of Adolescence, The (book by David Alan Black), 150

National Center for Family Integrated Churches (NCFIC), 45, 231n17
natural birth, 71–72
natural family practices, 71–73, 114
Natural Family Planning (NFP), xx n21, 96n21
neo-evangelicals, 16–17
No Longer Quivering (blog), 52, 108n59, 212
Noll, Mark, 5n12, 7n19, 8n26, 10n37

obedience: of children, 61, 142–43, 160, 172, 228; to God's design, 17, 31, 128n2, 180; of women, 62, 214
omnipotence (maternal), 89, 108–17, 229

patriarch. *See* family shepherd
patriarchy, xii, xv, xvii n11, xix, 34, 44, 61, 101, 187, 192
Pearl, Michael and Debi: and child abuse, 161, 213–14; and child training, 53, 141–44, 148–49, 156n78
Phillips, Douglas, 38, 44–46, 47, 48, 51, 101, 129, 159n88, 177n20, 181n31, 230; and sexual abuse accusations, xxix, 45, 46n170, 48, 214–15

population control, 27n108, 132–33
Pride, Mary, xiv, xxi, xxiii, 27–30, 40, 43–44, 56; on children and childrearing, 128n5, 129n8, 132, 140, 156–57; on the family, 175, 177n20, 178–80, 194, 208; on motherhood, 93–96, 97, 98, 100n40, 101, 105n54, 110, 111n64, 113n67
private Christian schools, 20n81, 23, 58, 156
privatization: of childrearing, 136–37, 155–67, 229n14; of family, 170, 173–75, 178–79, 192–99, 207n84, 208–9, 229n14, 230–31; of motherhood, 92, 109n61, 117n74, 122–23, 229
pronatalism: as an ideology, xv–xvi, xx–xxii, 27–28, 30–31, 35–36, 48n176, 139–40, 200; in practice, 35, 57–58, 66, 90, 196–98, 216, 232
Provan, Charles D., 27, 48n176, 128
"Proverbs 31 woman", 71, 111–12
Psalm 127, xiii, xvii, 31, 96n23, 127, 131, 218n2
public schools: history of, 14–16, 19–20, 23; Quiverfull rejection of, 48, 58, 66, 75, 82, 95n17, 194, 230

Quiverfull: definition of, xiii–xii, 3–4; and evangelicalism, xxii–xxv, 27–31, 48–49; institutions and leaders, 41–49; and the internet, 50–52; as a movement, 3–4; origin of term, xiii–xiv, 29–31; and pop culture, 47–48, 215; as a subculture, 38–41; as a three-part discourse, xv–xxii, 31–38
Quiverfull (book by Kathryn Joyce), xi, xiv, xxiii, 3n6, 4, 36, 48n176, 88, 96n22, 100n42
Quiverfull Digest, xiv, 36, 49n179

race, racism, xxx, 9n32, 15n56, 20, 23, 131–33 140, 193, 198
Rahner, Karl, 153
reconstructionism, 25, 44, 181
Reformed. *See* Calvinism, Calvinist
Religious Right. *See* Christian Right
Roe v. Wade, 28
Rubio, Julie Hanlon, 137, 199, 219
Rushdoony, R. J., 25–26, 27, 38, 44, 181–82

sacraments, 126, 151–52, 155, 165, 166, 170, 207
Self-Made Man, 7–10, 11–13
Sessions, David, 230
sexual abuse. *See* child abuse, child sexual abuse
singleness, 98, 99–100
Smith, Christian, 6, 39–40, 106–7, 207, 227
spanking, 137n31, 144, 160–61, 187; and the Bible, 143–44, 161
spiritual leader, spiritual leadership:

of husbands, 12, 16, 32, 34, 106–7, 125, 187; of parents, 157
spousal abuse. *See* domestic violence
stay-at-home daughters (SAHD), 46, 184–85
Stevens, Mitchell, xviii, xxxi n41, 4n8, 25n98, 26, 34, 103–5
Stowe, Harriet Beecher, 11
subculture (Quiverfull): elite level of, 42–49; lay level of, 49–52; negotiation within, 52–53; Quiverfull as, xvi, xvii n24, xxxiii, 3–4, 6, 34n132, 36n138, 38–41; and Quiverfull discourse, 31–36

Tanner, Kathryn, 33, 224
"The Tenets of Biblical Patriarchy" (Vision Forum), 97n26, 98, 99–100, 101, 192
Thatcher, Adrian, 134–36, 216–17
Three Decades of Fertility (book edited by Natalie Klejwa), 51, 89–90, 105n53, 112, 120, 151, 162, 163, 212, 219
To Train Up a Child (book by Debi and Michael Pearl), 141–43, 148–49, 156n78, 161, 213
True Woman, True Womanhood, 7–10, 12

"umbrella of protection," 42n155

vaccination, 72, 159
Victorian era, xxii n25, 7–14, 19n78, 21n82, 30, 208, 217
Vision Forum, Inc., Vision Forum Ministries, 44, 45, 66, 97n26, 171, 214
vulnerability: and motherhood, 108, 117–23; and children, 216–17

Western Conservatory of Arts and Sciences, 46, 180n28
white, whiteness, xiii, xxx, 2, 9n32, 10, 13, 15, 17, 20n81, 132, 140, 190
Wilson, Douglas, 48n176, 48n177
women's activism, 11–14; in homeschooling movement, xxiii, 23
Worthen, Molly, 5–6, 16n64, 25n99